APPLIED RESEARCH IN FINANCIAL REPORTING

Text and Cases

APPLIED RESEARCH IN FINANCIAL REPORTING
Text and Cases

Mohammad Abdolmohammadi
Ralph J. McQuade

Boston   Burr Ridge, IL   Dubuque, IA   Madison, WI   New York
San Francisco   St. Louis   Bangkok   Bogotá   Caracas   Kuala Lumpur
Lisbon   London   Madrid   Mexico City   Milan   Montreal   New Delhi
Santiago   Seoul   Singapore   Sydney   Taipei   Toronto

McGraw-Hill Higher Education

A Division of The McGraw-Hill Companies

APPLIED RESEARCH IN FINANCIAL REPORTING: TEXT AND CASES
Published by McGraw-Hill, a business unit of The McGraw-Hill Companies, Inc., 1221 Avenue of the Americas, New York, NY 10020. Copyright © 2002 by The McGraw-Hill Companies, Inc. All rights reserved. No part of this publication may be reproduced or distributed in any form or by any means, or stored in a database or retrieval system, without the prior written consent of The McGraw-Hill Companies, Inc., including, but not limited to, in any network or other electronic storage or transmission, or broadcast for distance learning.
Some ancillaries, including electronic and print components, may not be available to customers outside the United States.

This book is printed on acid-free paper.

1 2 3 4 5 6 7 8 9 0 FGR/FGR 0 9 8 7 6 5 4 3 2 1

ISBN 0-07-000480-3

Sponsoring editor: Melody Marcus
Developmental editor: Kelly Odom
Marketing coordinator: Melissa Larmon
Associate project manager: Catherine R. Schultz
Production supervisor: Susanne Riedell
Coordinator freelance design: Artemio Ortiz Jr.
Supplement producer: Betty Hadala
Cover design: Artemio Ortiz Jr.
Interior design: Artemio Ortiz Jr.
Typeface: 10/12 Palatino
Compositor: Lachina Publishing Services
Printer: Quebecor World Fairfield Inc.

Library of Congress Cataloging-in-Publication Data

Abdolmohammadi, Mohammad J. (Mohammad Javad), 1950–
    Applied research in financial reporting : text and cases / Mohammad J.
    Abdolmohammadi, Ralph J. McQuade.
        p. cm.
    Includes index.
    ISBN 0-07-000480-3 (alk. paper)
    1. Accounting—Research—Methodology. 2. Accounting—Case studies. 3. Financial
statements. I. McQuade, Ralph J. II. Title.
HF5626 .A223 2001
657'.3—dc21   2001026618

Copyright © 2002.

www.mhhe.com

This book is dedicated to our families:
Tabi, Yusef, Jacob, Yasi, and Bobby
Jan, Julia, and Bryan
whose understanding and sacrifices have been
instrumental in the successful completion of the book.

BRIEF CONTENTS

CONTENTS

LIST OF CASES:
Illustrative Cases:

Chapter 10 Cases on Financial Accounting and Reporting
Revenue and Expense Recognition

Accounting Policy Issues and Overview Cases

Ethics

LIST OF EXHIBITS:

APPENDICES:

PREFACE

Applied research for solving complex accounting and reporting issues is the focus of this book. Knowledge of applied research is expected of accounting graduates in addition to knowledge of the accounting concepts, methods, and procedures typically covered in intermediate and advanced accounting courses. The AICPA has taken the position that an integration of real world events and ideas and the use of unstructured problems in the curriculum are needed for students to be successful in the profession in today's volatile, global business environment. Using the real world case analysis and issue-based research approaches, this book aims to assist students in learning to learn, critical and creative thinking, and problem solving as a basis for the development of lifelong learning skills.

The book has two sections. Section I provides the foundation of applied professional research where a general accounting model is provided in Chapter 1 followed by an overview of applied accounting research in Chapter 2. The case method of research is discussed in Chapter 3 with two illustrative cases depicting simple and more complex case studies. The authoritative sources of accounting information including databases and search engines for electronic and manual searches are discussed in Chapter 4, with an illustrative case study. Issue-based research is presented in Chapter 5, where a list of issues is also provided for possible course projects. The final chapter in Section I is on the methodology of professional accounting research. Methods of data collection and analysis are briefly discussed in this chapter followed by a discussion of the professional research process from identification of a research issue to the communication of its results. The chapter ends with an appendix in which an example of issue-based research is provided.

Section II covers application issues. Judgment and decision making in accounting are discussed in Chapter 7, followed by critical and creative thinking and problem solving in Chapter 8. Chapter 9 focuses on ethical considerations in judgment and decision making in accounting where a primer is provided on individual ethics, professional ethics, corporate ethics, and ethics audit services. Each of these chapters ends with an illustrative case study.

The final chapter in the book provides 55 cases on financial accounting and reporting. The cases cover revenue and expense recognition, accounting policies, current and noncurrent assets, liabilities, leases and pensions, income taxes, accounting changes, stockholders' equity, business combinations, ethics, and others. The objective of these cases is to have students experience some of the more unique situations that accounting professionals must deal with when a solution is unclear. The cases are intended to stimulate discussion and do not focus on quantitative responses or journal entries. They allow students to be active, creative and critical thinkers, and independent learners and problem solvers rather than passive recipients of knowledge. The cases are designed to enhance the analytical, research, and communicative skills of students as well as increase their overall understanding and appreciation of applying generally accepted accounting principles in the real world.

The cases were developed primarily from interviews, discussions, and correspondence with practicing accountants. Due to the confidential nature of the data, it was necessary to maintain the anonymity of the majority of actual companies and individuals involved. Therefore, certain facts, names, dates, and amounts were changed for all cases as a matter of policy. All company and individual names are fictitious and any association with an actual company or individual name is not intended and purely coincidental. However, the substantive issues and applicable business circumstances remain faithful to the actual case. All cases use data from the 1980s or 1990s, and such data is identified as from 20X1, 20X2, and so on, unless actual dates are necessary. However, the dates are meant to represent current dates, but the most current accounting pronouncements should be applied to any case analysis.

Due to the varying degrees of complexity of the cases, instructors are the best judges for sequencing the case assignments. Particularly complex cases often are most effective as a group assignment, providing an opportunity for students to develop interpersonal skills.

Detailed teaching notes for the chapters (including PowerPoint slides) and cases are available to accompany this book. In order for instructors to adequately evaluate the cases and make appropriate assignments, it is essential that the teaching notes be reviewed. The teaching notes represent an extensive research effort. They include a discussion of the relevant issues, alternative strategies, basis for recommendations, and the technical research of authoritative accounting literature. Comments, suggestions, and contributions of material for future cases from users of this book will be appreciated.

The book has been designed to serve two distinct markets. The first is the capstone course, generally called accounting seminar or methods and practices of professional research in the traditional course sequence at the graduate and undergraduate levels. The second is the intermediate and advanced accounting courses where independent applied research can be introduced to investigate complex accounting issues.

ABOUT THE AUTHORS

Mohammad J. Abdolmohammadi, DBA, CPA, is the John E. Rhodes Professor of Accountancy at Bentley College. He obtained his Doctorate in Business Administration from Indiana University in 1981 and taught at Indiana University, Boston University, and the University of Illinois at Chicago before joining Bentley College in 1988. Having interest primarily in behavioral auditing research, Professor Abdolmohammadi has published in *Accounting and Business Research, The Accounting Review, Auditing: A Journal of Practice and Theory, Behavioral Research in Accounting, Contemporary Accounting Research, Issues in Accounting Education, Journal of Business Ethics, Organizational Behavior and Human Decision Processes, Research in Accounting Regulation,* and *Arthur Andersen's KnowledgeSpace* among others.

Ralph J. McQuade, MBA, MST, CPA, is an Associate Professor of Accountancy at Bentley College. He holds an MBA from Babson College and an MST from Bentley College. He has public accounting experience with Deloitte & Touche (formerly Touche Ross) and is a licensed CPA in the Commonwealth of Massachusetts. He has authored two previous case books: *Cases in Financial Accounting and Reporting,* McGraw-Hill, Inc., and *Cases in Financial Accounting,* Allyn and Bacon, Inc. In addition, he has published in *Management Accounting, Issues in Accounting Education,* and several practice-related journals.

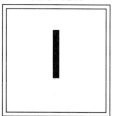

FOUNDATION

This section provides the foundation of applied accounting research. It contains six chapters that cover a general accounting model (Chapter 1), applied accounting research (Chapter 2), the case method of research (Chapter 3), the authoritative sources of accounting information (Chapter 4), issue-based accounting research (Chapter 5), and the methodology of professional accounting research (Chapter 6).

$\boxed{1}$ INTRODUCTION

We cannot expect to breed respect for law and order among people who do not share the fruits of our freedom.

Hubert Humphrey

Objectives

In this chapter we provide an overview of the financial accounting and reporting model. We also discuss the power position of various organizations and corporate groups in establishing accounting standards. Upon completion of the chapter, you will have learned the:

1. Basics of a general model representing the real world.
2. Links between the general model and the accounting model.
3. Concept of the power position in setting accounting standards.
4. Meaning of corporate accounting policy and promulgation and regulation of accounting standards.
5. Securities and Exchange Commission's (SEC) power position.
6. Promulgatory accounting standards-setting organizations in the U.S.
7. Organizations influencing standards setting in the U.S.
8. Financial Accounting Standards Board's (FASB) standards-setting process.
9. Effects of corporate accounting policy on standards setting.
10. International accounting standards-setting organizations.

As a field of inquiry, accounting follows a general model in formulating its goals, definitions, assumptions, principles, measurements, and constraints. We briefly illustrate this general model with a sports analogy in the first section. This is followed by a discussion of the accounting model, which closely follows this general model.

The components of the accounting model must be defined and enforced by credible standards. The question is who should establish and enforce these standards? The proponents of governmental regulation argue that the government should be the ultimate force in setting accounting standards, keeping in mind the interests of the society at large. Others argue that private professional organizations are best at understanding accounting, thus they are in the best position to promulgate and enforce accounting standards. There is a third group that argues that corporate management should be left alone to use accounting standards and methods of its choice following the dynamics of the free market economy. The truth of the matter is that the accounting standards and practices we have today are the product of a long history of debate that has resulted in a mix of these three schools.[1] These issues are discussed in the second section.

A General Model

We engage in many activities every day of our lives. While we perform some of these real world activities almost automatically, we may have difficulty formulating the complex relationships between various aspects of each activity. However, we can simplify this process if we have a model to guide us through various steps of the process. A basic definition of a model is that it is:

> . . . a simplified picture of a part of the real world. It has some of the characteristics of the real world, but not all of them. It is a set of interrelated guesses about the world. Like all pictures, a model is simpler than the phenomena it is supposed to represent or explain.[2]

This definition implies that because models are simplified pictures of the real world, they may have limitations in representing some of the complexities that are observed in the real world activities. However, a simplified model is a good start. The model can be developed further over time to incorporate more of the complexities of the phenomenon it intends to represent. Furthermore, if a model is a picture, its development may be viewed as a kind of [photo] studio activity.[3] We may not stop and explicitly specify the components of a model for every activity that we engage in every day.

---

1. The mix of regulatory, promulgatory, and corporate policy has also been a topic of debate in other countries in search of a balanced approach to standard setting. For a critical debate of the issue in Australia, see R. G. Walker, "A Feeling of Deja vu: Controversies in Accounting and Auditing Regulation in Australia," *Critical Perspectives on Accounting* (1993), pp. 97–109.
2. See C. A. Lave and J. G. March, *An Introduction to Models in the Social Sciences* (New York, NY: Harper and Row, 1975), p. 3.
3. Ibid., p. 4.

However, we may implicitly, if not explicitly, use a general model with six components: goals, definitions, assumptions, rules, exceptions, and measurement. We elaborate on this common sense and intuitive model through a sports analogy.

Consider the case of a marathon runner who uses a model with the following components to guide his or her marathon activities. First, the marathon runner has a goal that may range from physical fitness to gaining commercial endorsements. Second, the marathon runner has certain definitions in mind such as the marathon being defined as a 26-mile race. Third, the marathon runner makes several assumptions regarding the race. For example, an assumption in running the Boston Marathon in April is that the temperature is in the 40° to 60° range and, perhaps, the sky is overcast so that it will not be too hot or too cold nor will there be too much sun for the marathon run.

Fourth, the marathon runner has to adhere to the rules of the race set by appropriate bodies such as the Boston Athletic Association or the general standards set by a national or international body. Such rules or standards promulgated by appropriate bodies are the results of long-term processes and are applied consistently.

Fifth, exceptions may be allowed under certain circumstances. For example, one rule may be that the runner must have successfully completed qualification tests by a certain date, such as completing a marathon in the previous 12 months on a certified course in less than three hours, before being admitted to participate in the actual marathon race. However, the marathon committee may make an exception based on circumstances for certain runners. For example, an exception may be made for an international runner who missed a deadline due to entry visa delays. The runner also applies cost/benefit criteria as a general quantitative and qualitative constraint for participation in the marathon. Do the benefits of participation exceed its costs? The criteria used to answer this question are different from person to person.

Finally, all components of the model require a measurement system. The quantification of the goals, such as endorsements generating $100,000, requires monetary measurement. Definitions such as running a 26-mile course require a distance measurement. An assumption about the climate such as overcast with 45 degree temperature requires a temperature measurement. Rules such as having the application in by a certain date require time measurement. Finally, quantitative or qualitative considerations such as cost and benefit require an appropriate measurement such as measuring health benefits of running in the marathon as compared with the risk of injury. As is evident from these limited examples, measurement is multidimensional and complex.

The general model described above is generic enough to apply to many other activities, including accounting. This model is used to describe a general accounting model in the next section.

The Accounting Model

The intuitive model described on the previous page is useful for the marathon runner in his or her decision to participate in the Boston Marathon. It is applicable to many other activities, such as accounting. The basics of the accounting model with reference to the professional literature are presented in Exhibit 1–1. The model presented in Exhibit 1–1 is based on the conceptual framework constructed in the *Statements of Financial Accounting Concepts (SFAC) Nos. 1–7* and is dubbed the *decision-usefulness* model of accounting. The components of the model are presented in column 1 followed by the meaning of these components in column 2 and the primary authoritative sources in column 3.

Early efforts to create a comprehensive theoretical model for accounting can be traced to 1961 when the Accounting Research Division of the Accounting Principles Board issued *Accounting Research Study No. 1 (ARS*

Exhibit 1–1	A General Accounting Model	
Model Component	*Meaning*	*Primary Source*
1. Goals	Several objectives of accounting, such as provide information useful for economic decisions	*SFAC No. 1*, "The Objectives of Accounting for Business Enterprises," and *SFAC No. 4*, "The Objectives of Accounting for Nonbusiness Enterprises"
2. Definitions	Definitions of accounting and its elements, such as assets and liabilities	*SFAC No. 6*, "Elements of Financial Statements," which superseded *SFAC No. 3*, "Definitions of the Elements of Financial Statements for Business Enterprises"
3. Assumptions	Postulates or axioms of accounting such as going concern or continuity	*ABPB Statement No. 4*, "Basic Concepts and Accounting Principles Underlying Financial Statements of Business Enterprises"
4. Rules and Standards	Generally accepted accounting principles such as the revenue recognition principle	APB opinions, FASB statements and their interpretations, and emerging Issues Task Force interpretations (EITFs)
5. Constraints	Qualitative characteristics such as objectivity	*SFAC No. 2*, "The Qualitative Characteristics of Financial Information"
6. Measurement	Recognition and measurement of accounting elements such as monetary unit	*SFAC No. 5*, "Recognition and Measurement in Financial Statements of Business Enterprises" and *SFAC No. 7*, "Using Cash Flow Information and Present Value in Accounting Measurements"

No. 1) and called for such a model.[4] *ARS No. 3,* issued in 1962, presented a tentative set of broad principles for business enterprises.[5] Although these research studies were not accepted by the APB in their entirety, they did pave the way for the formulation of *APB Statement No. 4* that defined many of the components of the model.[6] The FASB followed up on the process of formulating a framework in the mid-1970s in a project called the Conceptual Framework Project that has led to seven *SFACs* by early 2000. These concept statements provide the foundation on which financial accounting and reporting standards are to be established.

An important aspect of model development in accounting is that it focuses on decision-usefulness as an objective of accounting information. Simply put, decision-usefulness implies that accounting information should have the attributes that are useful in making economic decisions by managers of the firm as well as other stakeholders such as investors and creditors. For example, the American Accounting Association stressed that accounting is a process of "identifying, measuring, and communicating economic information to permit informed judgments and decisions by the users of the information."[7] This theme has been repeated in the professional literature. The decision-usefulness objective is broader in scope than the stewardship objective that was widely used in practice earlier. Stewardship was used to describe the manager's responsibility toward the owners of the firm where the manager was viewed as the owners' agent and, thus, accountable to the owners of the firm. Financial reporting by management was viewed as a means of discharging this accountability.

The accounting model has become increasingly more complex over time in response to the complexity of the business environment. As discussed in the next section, the standards-setting process that addresses various components of the model is a very complex process. Of particular importance in the new millennium is the need for changes to the accounting model to respond to the complexity of the information technology. The measurement component of the model may need to be changed to measure the value of certain assets not prominent in the last century's brick and mortar industries. For example, in the environment of electronic commerce and dot-com companies, an asset of tremendous value is the intellectual capital of these companies' human expertise and unique systems infrastructure. The current accounting model has no method to measure this important asset. However, research studies are under way to develop such a measure.

---

4. Accounting Principles Board, "The Basic Postulates of Accounting," *Accounting Research Study No. 1* (New York, NY: AICPA, 1961).

5. Accounting Principles Board, "A Tentative Set of Broad Accounting Principles for Business Enterprises," *Accounting Research Study No. 3* (New York, NY: AICPA, 1962).

6. Accounting Principles Board, "Basic Concepts and Accounting Principles Underlying Financial Statements of Business Enterprises," *APB Statement No. 4* (New York, NY: AICPA, 1970).

7. American Accounting Association, *A Statement of Basic Accounting Theory* (Sarasota, FL: AAA, 1966), p. 1.

Accounting Policy, Promulgation, and Regulation

To have credibility and acceptance by users, the general accounting model presented in Exhibit 1–1 must be carefully developed through a rigorous standards-setting process. Who should have the authority and responsibility for this standards-setting process? Exhibit 1–2 summarizes the three schools of thought on standards setting and accounting practice that are discussed in the following paragraphs.

Exhibit 1–2	Accounting Policy, Promulgation, and Regulation	
Type	*Description*	*Example*
1. Policy	A body of standards, opinions, interpretations, rules, and regulations used by management in its corporate financial reporting practices	Management can calculate the cost of stock options by selecting a method it deems appropriate.
2. Promulgation	Making standards, opinions, and interpretations by private professional organizations	In *SFAS No. 123*, the FASB requires the disclosure of the cost of stock options in annual reports
3. Regulation	Setting rules and regulations by governmental agencies	Deeming the provisions of *APB Opinion No. 25* inadequate, the SEC pressured the FASB to issue *SFAS No. 123.*

1. *Policy.* Corporate accounting policy is a body of standards, opinions, interpretations, rules, and regulations used by corporate management in its financial reporting practices.[8] At the heart of the issue is whether corporate management should be allowed to develop the standards and methods that it uses in its accounting policy, or should this task be left to a professional private body or a governmental entity? There is an important distinction between promulgation of accounting standards and regulation of accounting.

2. *Promulgation.* Promulgation of accounting standards refers to the power of private professional organizations (e.g., the FASB) to set such standards.

3. *Regulation.* Regulation of accounting, on the other hand, refers to a governmental agency (e.g., the SEC) setting the rules by which accounting is to be practiced.

Currently, the model used in the U.S. is a mix of all three schools of thought. Namely that the financial accounting standards are set by the FASB and its predecessors, the Accounting Principles Board (APB) and Committee on Accounting Procedures (CAP). The SEC rules support the promulga-

---

8. This definition is adapted from E. S. Hendriksen and M. F. Van Breda, *Accounting Theory*, Fifth ed. (Boston, MA: Richard D. Irwin, 1992), p. 235.

tory standards of practice, leaving corporate management with the choice of the alternative method it deems reasonable for use under various circumstances. For example, by issuing *SFAS No. 123*, "Accounting for Stock-Based Compensation," the FASB required the disclosure of the cost of employee stock options in corporate annual reports. The SEC was also involved in the issuance of *SFAS No. 123* because its staff viewed the provisions of *APB Opinion No. 25*, "Accounting for Stock Issued to Employees," inadequate in the early 1980s and pressured the FASB to reconsider these provisions. However, under *SFAS No. 123* the FASB left the method of calculating the cost of stock options up to corporate management. The point is that management is given the opportunity to make a choice from among several stock option pricing methods.

The Theory of Power Position

What determines the influence of each of the three schools of thought on standards setting? According to one theory, it is the power position of each of the bodies that determines its influence. There are five different levels of power in this theory as presented in Exhibit 1–3.[9] The legitimacy of corporate

Exhibit 1–3	Power Position and Its Relationship with Accounting Policy, Promulgation, and Regulation	
Type	*Meaning*	*Argues for*
1. Reward power	Market's power to reward management or withdraw punishment (e.g., through stock price) based on management's accounting policy.	Management has the legitimacy and means of establishing accounting policy
2. Legitimate power	Standards-setting organizations having a sanctioned right (e.g., self-regulation) to prescribe behavior.	Promulgation by private body
3. Referent power	Business community identifies with standards-setting body (e.g., executives identified with high-powered members of the FASB).	Promulgation by private body
4. Expert power	Business community identifies the standards-setting body as possessing specialized knowledge or expertise (e.g., knowledge of accounting and finance matters in addition to business).	Promulgation by private body
5. Coercive power	Business community identifies standards-setting body as able to enact punishment or withhold reward (e.g., the legal power of the SEC).	Regulation by governmental organzations

9. The discussion of power positions is based on J. R. P. French and B. Raven, "The Bases of Social Power," in D. Cartwright and A. Zander (Eds.), *Group Dynamics* (Evanston, IL: Row and Peterson, 1960), pp. 607–23 as discussed by L. Kelly-Newton, *Accounting Policy Formulation: The Role of Corporate Management* (Reading, MA: Addison-Wesley, 1980), pp. 53–62.

management versus a private standard-setting body or a regulatory body is dependent on their power position. Also presented in Exhibit 1–3 is the power position that primarily supports each of the three bodies in a free market economy.

The first power in the theory is the *reward power*. It is based on the ability of the free market to reward reliable financial reporting or punish a company for unreliable financial reporting. It is used to argue for accounting policy at the company level. The ability of the market to grant rewards or punish through stock prices is the main incentive for management to establish reasonable accounting standards and practices. The market rewards a company for the generation and dissemination of reliable information to the public so investors can make informed decisions about the company. In other words, the information will be reflected in the company's stock price upon disclosure to the public. Thus, while reliable information will enhance the company's stock price, misleading or unreliable information will eventually negatively affect the value of the stock.

A case in point is the drug store chain, Rite Aid. *The Wall Street Journal* disclosed on July 12, 2000, that the company had manipulated its earnings by a number of improper accounting tricks over the years. For example, it had capitalized ordinary expenses, such as routine maintenance bills and some interest costs, in order to overstate its net income. As a result of these revelations, the company's stock price plummeted from a high of $26\frac{1}{4}$ on July 7, 1999, to $5\frac{1}{2}$ on July 13, 2000. This is an example of how relentless the stock market is in punishing companies for unreliable information. The opposite is also true where the market rewards perceived reliable information. Cisco Systems is a good example here. Its stock went from $28\frac{5}{64}$ on August 10, 1999, to $65\frac{1}{4}$ on July 13, 2000, due to investors' confidence in the quality of its financial reporting.

The next three power positions argue for the legitimacy of promulgatory standards-setting organizations. *Legitimate power* indicates that the business community perceives the standards-setting body as holding a sanctioned right to prescribe behavior. For example, the legitimacy power of private standard setting in the U.S. has been based on a desire among the business community and professional accountants for self-regulation. *Referent power* refers to the business community identifying with the standards-setting body. This means that business executives arguably identify with the members of the FASB as their peers and representatives. This is because the members of the FASB are selected from a pool of highly qualified academics, CEOs, CFOs, and CPAs. *Expert power* adds another level of power to the members of the private standards-setting body. Here, the business community perceives the standards-setting body as possessing some specialized knowledge or expertise. Stringent qualification requirements are used for the selection of members of accounting standards-setting bodies. Consequently, the members of these bodies are viewed as having the expertise to promulgate accounting standards.

The final power, *coercive power,* is the ultimate power to enact rewards or punishment. The SEC and other governmental regulatory agencies gain their legitimacy from the coercive power granted to them by the law. The law gives these regulatory organizations the power to administer punishment or grant rewards. For example, the SEC has the legal power to require public companies to file certain reports that have very specific requirements (e.g., Form 10-K). Similarly, the Internal Revenue Service (IRS) has the legal power to collect taxes in accordance with the provisions of the tax code. During the Kennedy administration in the 1960s, Congress passed a law that provided a tax reward to companies for new capital investment. Called the *investment tax credit,* a company that invested in capital assets was rewarded with a tax credit equal to 10 percent of the cost of the qualified investment. Just as Congress enacted this reward in the 1960s, it repealed it in the Tax Reform Act of 1986. The point here is that these powerful regulatory organizations can provide rewards for certain activities, or impose penalties on violators of their rules.

Currently there is a mix of all five powers in operation in setting financial accounting standards in the U.S. While the primary standards-setting body is private (the FASB), there is a strong presence of regulatory influence (the SEC). However, the standards provide enough flexibility that corporate management has to make choices in setting its corporate accounting policy.

Promulgation of Financial Accounting Standards in the U.S.

Since 1973 financial accounting standards have been primarily promulgated by the FASB in the United States. Before the FASB, in 1936–1959, the CAP provided a codification of practice in the form of *Accounting Research Bulletins (ARB)*. The APB replaced the CAP in 1959 as the authority for establishing accounting principles. While a limited number of the *ARBs* and *APB opinions* are still essentially in effect and constitute GAAP, others have been amended or superseded by subsequent authoritative FASB pronouncements.

A full-time research and technical staff supports the FASB. In addition, there are some temporary "fellow" positions that bring either a special expertise or differing points of view to the FASB. For example, there are several practice fellows from CPA firms, an occasional fellow from industry, a faculty fellow from academia, and several recent graduates from colleges and universities who are called graduate interns. Altogether, there are over 50 people on the FASB's staff with different areas of specialization.

The FASB goes through an elaborate and lengthy process before it issues a statement, interpretation, or technical bulletin. The process is designed to "permit timely, thorough, and open study of financial accounting and reporting issues and to encourage broad public participation in the process of establishing and improving standards of financial accounting and reporting."[10] The FASB's due process begins with an identification of an important accounting problem worthy of the board's consideration followed by a process to specifically identify the accounting issues related to the problem. The problems and issues may be brought to the attention of the board by its Emerging Issues Task Force (EITF), the SEC, or other constituents. Once the accounting issues are identified, the alternative courses of action are researched and documented and an evaluation of the alternatives is conducted leading to the selection of the preferred alternative.

This process is influenced by many organizations and groups representing various points of views or interests, and varying degrees of power position. These organizations include, but are not limited to, the American Accounting Association (AAA), the American Institute of Certified Public Accountants (AICPA), the Financial Analysts Foundation (FAF), the Financial Executive Institute (FEI), the Institute of Management Accountants (IMA), the Governmental Accounting Standards Board (GASB), the Institute of Internal Auditors (IIA), the Cost Accounting Standards Board (CASB), the National Council on Governmental Accounting (NCGA), as well as international bodies such as the International Accounting Standards Committee (IASC) and the International Federation of Accountants (IFAC). The Department of the Treasury (particularly its Internal Revenue Service), the Department of Energy, and a host of state regulatory commissions also influence accounting standards and practice. However, as discussed below, the most influential organization is the SEC with its coercive power as the protector of creditors and investors. Corporate management groups also mount powerful campaigns to influence the FASB.

Other countries' standards-setting practices vary from complete government control (mostly for tax purposes) to standards setting by private bodies. For example, while private committees such as the Accounting Standards Committees are in charge of setting standards in Canada and England, complete government control is exercised in certain communist or socialist countries.[11] Established in 1973, the International Accounting Standards Committee (IASC) promulgates accounting standards in an attempt to harmonize accounting standards across various countries whose standards-setting bodies have joined the IASC as members.

Accounting Regulation

The beginnings of accounting regulation by federal agencies can be traced to 1913 when the Federal Trade Commission (FTC) was established to oversee

---

10. Financial Accounting Standards Board, *Rules of Procedure, Amended and Restated* (Stamford, CT: FASB, 1978), p. 8.
11. G. G. Mueller, "Accounting Principles Generally Accepted in the United States versus Those Generally Accepted Elsewhere," *International Journal of Accounting Education and Research* 3, no. 2 (1986), pp. 91–103.

the provisions of the antitrust laws. The FTC requested that the American Institute of Accountants (the predecessor of the AICPA) publish a guide on balance sheet audits in 1917. While this request implicitly indicated the legitimacy of the AIA as a promulgatory body in the eyes of the FTC, it also signaled the beginning of the federal agency's influence over this process. Today, several governmental bodies either establish and/or influence standard setting in the United States. For example, the congressional-funded CASB is in charge of setting cost accounting standards to be used by federal contractors.

The SEC is by far the most influential regulatory agency concerning financial accounting and reporting. The SEC was established after the Great Depression caused by the stock market crash of 1929. It was established to enforce the newly enacted securities laws of 1933 (relating to initial public offerings) and 1934 (relating to periodic information filings). Since June 6, 1934, when the SEC was formally established, it has had the authority to set accounting standards. This position has been strengthened by the passage of many other security-related laws such as the Investment Company Act of 1940, the Foreign Corrupt Practices Act of 1977 as amended in 1988, and the Securities Enforcement Remedies and Penny Stock Reform Act of 1990.

Currently, the SEC is an "independent, bipartisan, quasi-judicial agency of the United States government."[12] It regulates companies engaged in the purchase or sale of securities, people who provide investment advice, and investment companies. The Commission reports annually to the Congress of the United States on the administration of the securities laws.

The accounting standards-setting power, however, has been designated to private standards-setting organizations since 1937 when the SEC voted that it would not legislate accounting standards. Simply put, the SEC does not have the funding, expertise, or personnel to develop accounting standards itself, but it has kept its coercive legal power to oversee the standards-setting process. Occasionally, it has developed and enforced rules that have differed from those established by the FASB. An example of this is accounting for oil and gas reserves. Initially, *SFAS No. 19*, "Financial Accounting and Reporting by Oil and Gas Producing Companies," issued in 1977 allowed the use of the so-called *successful efforts* method. However, the SEC ruled in *Accounting Series Release* (*ASR*) *Nos. 253, 257*, and *258* that both *successful efforts* and *full cost* methods are acceptable and also proposed a third method called *reserve recognition accounting*. These *ASRs* forced the FASB to issue *SFAS No. 25*, "Suspension of Certain Accounting Requirements for Oil and Gas Producing Companies (an amendment of FASB Statement No. 19)." *SFAS No. 25* allowed the use of both *successful efforts* and *full cost* methods. The FASB issued *SFAS No. 69*, "Disclosures

---

12. F. K. Skousen, *An Introduction to the SEC* (Cincinnati, OH: South-Western Publishing Co., 1991), p. 1.

about Oil and Gas Producing Activities," later, which requires companies to disclose information on the *reserve recognition accounting* method.

Another example is accounting for inflation, for which the SEC required the disclosure of certain replacement cost data in *ASR No. 190* when the inflation rate reached double-digit levels in the early 1970s. This *ASR* forced the FASB to issue *SFAS No. 33*, "Financial Reporting and Changing Prices," which required supplementary replacement cost disclosure by large companies. However, the SEC requirement was eased later as fears of double-digit inflation vanished. Consequently, the FASB issued *SFAS No. 89*, "Financial Reporting and Changing Prices," by which it withdrew *SFAS No. 33* requirements.

These examples illustrate the coercive power of the SEC to set and enforce accounting standards. While the SEC has delegated the task of standards setting to the FASB, it has kept a veto power for itself.[13] The SEC has used its legal authority to develop many regulations. Major regulatory requirements concerning accounting information are listed below:[14]

1. *Regulation S-X.* This regulation specifies the type of reports and the forms that are to be filed; The SEC publishes *ASRs* that provide amendments, extensions, or additions to Regulation S-X;

2. *Regulation S-K.* This regulation specifies the type of reports and the forms that are to be filed for information that is not covered under Regulation S-X;

3. *Financial Reporting Releases (FRR).* The *FRRs* describe the accounting principles to be used in preparing reports to be filed with the SEC. *FRRs* generally support the APB and FASB pronouncements, but occasionally differ from these pronouncements;

4. *Accounting and Auditing Enforcement Releases (AAER).* The *AAERs* are issued to provide information and requirements for enforcement of the SEC's reporting and disclosure requirements.

The SEC has been issuing *FRRs* and *AAERs* since 1982. In addition, the SEC publishes a series of *Staff Accounting Bulletins (SABs)* that provide answers to accounting questions much like the FASB's *Technical Bulletins.*

Regulations S-X and S-K require that public companies file a number of forms. Form 10-K is filed annually and reports on annual financial information, Form 10-Q is filed quarterly, while Form 8-K is filed whenever a significant accounting matter occurs (e.g., change of the corporate controller or auditors). In recent years, the SEC has taken steps to take

---

13. N. D. Melumad and T. Shibano, "The Securities and Exchange Commission and the Financial Standards Board: Regulation through Veto-Based Delegation," *Journal of Accounting Research* 32, no. 1 (Spring 1994), pp. 1–37.

14. This section is adapted from T. R. Weirich and A. Reinstein, *Accounting & Auditing Research: A Practical Guide,* Fourth Ed. (Cincinnati, OH: South-Western College Publishing, 1996), pp. 24–50.

advantage of the information technology by developing the electronic data gathering, analysis, and retrieval (EDGAR) system. EDGAR allows electronic filing of the forms by companies. Interested users of these forms can retrieve them shortly (currently 24 hours) after companies file them. Its Internet address is http://ww.sec.gov/edgarhp.htm.

These regulations and reporting forms are designed to protect the investing public by ensuring that (a) the securities markets operate fairly and efficiently, and (b) public companies disclose material information on publicly traded securities. This is a very challenging objective for the SEC. As SEC Chairman Arthur Levitt recently testified before the House Committee on Commerce, ". . . evolving uses of technology, increasing globalization, the continuing creation of new financial instruments, and the presence of more inexperienced investors in the market than at any time in history makes the process very complex."[15]

The SEC requirements apply to domestic and foreign registrants although different forms are required. For example, while domestic registrants are required to file Form 10-K for annual reports, foreign registrants use Form 20-F. Quarterly reports required of domestic registrants in Form 10-Q are not required of foreign registrants. Finally, foreign registrants use Form 6-K for reporting material current information instead of Form 8-K used by domestic registrants.

The fact that foreign registrants are not required to file Form 10-Q or its equivalent indicates that the SEC is less stringent about foreign registrants than the domestic registrants. This is designed to attract foreign companies to list their securities on U.S. stock exchanges. In fact, foreign registrants can present their financial statements in accordance with their local GAAP as long as material deviations from U.S. GAAP are explained. According to Regulation S-X Rule 3-20, foreign registrants can even present their financial statements in their local currency although major companies usually present the information in both local currency as well as U.S. dollars. An example is Honda Motor Company, which presents its annual report in both yen and dollar amounts using the year-end currency conversion rate.

The organizational structure of the SEC is quite complex, with over 2,700 employees consisting mostly of lawyers, but also accountants, engineers, and security analysts.[16] These employees work together in four divisions and a large number of offices such as the Office of the Chief Accountant. The divisions are market regulation, investment management, corporate finance, and enforcement. The Division of Corporate Finance and the Office of the Chief Accountant are directly involved with corporate accounting and reporting issues. The Chief Accountant is the

---

15. A. Levitt, "Prepared Testimony," *Federal News Service* (March 1997).
16. Budget of the United States Government, Fiscal Year 1998 indicates that in 1996 the SEC had 2,789 employees.

SEC's link to accounting and auditing promulgatory organizations. The office of the Chief Accountant also drafts rules and regulations for financial statements.

Corporate Accounting Policy

Corporate management has the authority to select accounting principles and methods of applying those principles that are most beneficial to its own interests and the interests of the corporate shareholders. Professional pronouncements recognize the importance of attention to corporate accounting policy and management's role in setting such policy. For example, *APB Opinion No. 22*, "Disclosure of Accounting Policies," defines accounting policy as:

> . . . the specific accounting principles and the methods of applying those principles that are judged by the management of the entity to be the most appropriate in the circumstances to present fairly financial position, changes in financial position, and results of operations in accordance with generally accepted accounting principles and that accordingly have been adopted for preparing the financial statements.[17]

This definition recognizes management's latitude in setting initial accounting policy as it sees fit. A question arises as to whether management can make changes to accounting policy once it is initially established. The answer is that professional standards allow such changes over time to newer or more preferred principles or methods subject to meeting certain conditions. For example, the SEC requires that management file a letter from its independent public accountant stating whether or not the change is to an alternative principle that is preferable under the circumstances.[18] *APB Opinion No. 20*, "Accounting Changes," provides the rules on how such changes are to be reported on the body of the financial statements and the disclosure required for the changes.[19]

Organizations such as the Financial Executive Institute (FEI) and the Institute of Management Accountants (IMA) present the views of corporate management and its accountants. These organizations lobby heavily to influence standards setting by the FASB. Unfortunately for the FASB, the interests of external users and those of corporate management are diametrically different from time to time making it difficult to reach an optimal standard. In trying to be responsive to the interests of all constituents, the

---

17. Accounting Principles Board, *APB Opinion No. 22*, "Disclosure of Accounting Policies" (April 1972), Par. 6.
18. *SEC Accounting Rules: Accounting Series Releases* (Chicago, IL: Commerce ClearingHouse, 1982), *ASR No. 177*, p. 3397.
19. Accounting Principles Board, *APB Opinion No. 20*, "Accounting Changes" (New York, NY: American Institute of Certified Public Accountants, 1971), Par. 20.

FASB generally opts to compromise. For example, the FASB originally proposed that the cost of stock options be expensed, which was a position that the regulatory bodies, investors, and creditors favored, but corporate management vehemently opposed. However, as a compromise, the FASB finally issued *SFAS No. 123*, which requires only the disclosure of these costs (as compared with the recognition of the expense in the body of financial statements). Companies can expense the cost of stock options under the new standard if they elect to do so, and they have the option of choosing the method of calculating the cost under *SFAS No. 123*.

Corporate management reacts negatively to accounting standards and practices that it perceives to adversely affect its financial reports. The mechanism corporate management uses to influence accounting standards-setting is lobbying through its powerful professional organizations. Organizations such as the Business Roundtable and the Financial Executive Institute (FEI) are particularly influential. The Business Roundtable is composed of the chief executive officers of large corporations. It is concerned with a variety of issues of interest to business ranging from accounting standards to minimum wage and price controls. The FEI is a similar organization with a more limited agenda. It is composed of large corporate financial executives and has been very effective in communicating to the FASB and the SEC the position of the corporate management through its powerful Committee on Corporate Reporting.[20]

Auditors are also pressured by their clients' management to support the clients' positions concerning financial reporting issues on the FASB's agenda. For example, the then Big Six accounting firms communicated a single opposing view to the FASB's accounting for stock compensation project first in 1993 and then again in 1994 after meeting with representatives of the Business Round Table.[21] Research shows that while auditors make efforts to reduce audit risk and maximize their own profits, they also engage in lobbying efforts on behalf of their clients' preferences.[22]

Given these pressures, a question arises about the influence of the lobbying efforts mounted by corporate management and its auditors. Empirical evidence shows that these lobbying efforts in fact influence the FASB in a major way. In particular, large corporations and those with diverse businesses have powerful influences over the FASB.[23] *SFAS No. 123's*

---

20. From FEI, "Profile: FEI's Committee on Corporate Reporting," *Financial Executive* (September/October 1992), pp. 68–69.
21. D. J. Kirk, G. D. Anderson, and R. S. Saul, "Big Six Alliance Undermines FASB, Tarnishes Profession," *Accounting Today* 8, no. 22 (November 7, 1994), pp. 12, 14.
22. R. L. Watts and J. L. Zimmerman, *Positive Accounting Theory* (Englewood Cliffs, NJ: Prentice-Hall, 1986) and H. H. Meier; P. Alam and M. A. Pearson, "Auditor Lobbying for Accounting Standards: The Case of Banks and Savings and Loan Associations," *Accounting and Business Research* 22, no. 92 (1993), pp. 477–87.
23. L. D. Brown and E. Feroz, "Does the FASB Listen to Corporations?" *Journal of Business Finance and Accounting* 19, no. 5 (September 1992), pp. 715–31.

disclosure requirement concerning the cost of employee stock options is a good example of this influence. As stated earlier, corporate management and accounting firms forced the FASB to adopt a compromise solution in which it required only a footnote disclosure as compared with the original proposal of recognizing the value of stock option plans as an expense. Critics allege that this type of disclosure "will not quite explain what shareholders need to know."[24]

Corporate management's reactions to standards and methods of accounting are not always coherent or rational.[25] In general, management favors the choice of accounting methods that provide flexibility in reporting earnings. For example, management usually likes to defer the reported earnings when the earnings are strong to the years when the earnings are weak. Called *income smoothing*, this strategy is supposed to influence naive investors into believing that the smoothed income numbers are indicators of substantive economic fundamentals. However, this strategy ignores the fact that security markets are not fooled by income smoothing strategies because they are more interested in the firm's actual cash flows than the reported earnings.[26] Thus, reporting and disclosure standards that do not affect a firm's cash flows should not result in management opposition, but they do because both management and some naive investors are said to be more fixated on certain accounting numbers than the underlying economic fundamentals.

Alternative accounting methods can produce different accounting results providing the management with the opportunity to manipulate accounting numbers for earnings management.[27] This is not to say that management is not sensitive to cash flow effects of new standards. In fact, cash flow effects of factors such as future tax rates, regulatory actions such as rate setting, political costs from antitrust action, as well as the firm's bookkeeping costs are always analyzed by management.[28] It follows that new accounting standards are evaluated not only for their effects on current cash flow, but also for their effects on future cash flows. However, when it comes to reporting, management may focus on selecting methods that result in favorable earnings reports instead of the underlying cash flows.

24. R. Lowenstein, "The Cost of Employee Stock Options, Now Hidden, Might Earn a Footnote," *The Wall Street Journal* (July 6, 1995), p. C1.

25. For a discussion of irrational behavior by management see D. Solomons, "The Politicization of Accounting," *Journal of Accountancy* (November 1978), pp. 65–72.

26. M. Pincus, "Accounting Methods and Differential Stock Market Response to the Announcement of Earnings" (Professional Adaptation), *Journal of Accounting, Auditing and Finance* 8, no. 3 (Summer 1993), pp. 221–48.

27. S. M. Tinic, "A Perspective on the Stock Market's Fixation on Accounting Numbers," *The Accounting Review* (October 1990), pp. 781–96.

28. R. L. Watts and J. L. Zimmerman, "Towards a Positive Theory of the Determination of Accounting Standards," *The Accounting Review* (January 1978), pp. 113–14.

Summary

In this chapter, we presented a general model with six components: goals, definitions, assumptions, rules, exceptions, and measurement. We used this model to describe various components of accounting with an emphasis on the authorities with the power position to establish accounting standards. While the task of standards setting in the U.S. is delegated to the FASB, the SEC has the ultimate regulatory power to require various types of information. Nevertheless, there is enough flexibility in the promulgatory standards of the FASB and the regulatory requirements of the SEC that corporate management has the opportunity to make choices in its corporate accounting policy. The theory of power position provides arguments for the sources of power for the forces influencing standards setting in accounting. While three powers (legitimate, referent, and expert) were presented in support of promulgation of accounting standards by a private body, the coercive power supports regulation by the SEC. Reward power is used to argue for the legitimacy of management to set corporate accounting policy.

The FASB has a relatively small organization with 50 professional staff to promulgate financial accounting standards in the U.S. In contrast, the SEC has developed into a complex organization with over 2,700 employees organized in four divisions as well as several offices. The Division of Corporate Finance and the Office of the Chief Accountant are directly involved with the regulation of accounting standards and reporting. Corporate management lobbies to influence both the FASB and the SEC through its powerful professional associations such as the Financial Executive Institute.

Questions

1. A marathon example was provided to illustrate a general model of activity. Choose another example and discuss its components with reference to this model.

2. How does the model in this chapter help in solving an accounting research problem?

3. What are the qualitative characteristics in the accounting model? List and discuss two of them.

4. Give two examples of assets that companies control but that are not measured by the current accounting model.

5. Define promulgation and regulation of accounting standards and corporate accounting policy.

6. Present a list of power positions and relate them to promulgation and regulation of accounting standards and corporate accounting policy.

7. Provide a brief history of promulgation and regulation of accounting standards in the U.S.

8. What organizations influence the FASB's standards-setting process?

9. List and discuss the major steps in the FASB's due process.

10. Where does the SEC get its power position for regulation of accounting standards?

11. Why has the SEC delegated its legal authority to set accounting standards to private accounting bodies?

12. List and briefly discuss SEC's major regulations affecting accounting.

13. List and briefly discuss SEC's major forms used to collect accounting information from public companies.

14. What are the SEC's major publications that affect accounting?

15. Describe the effects of corporate accounting policy on standards setting.

16. What are the major trade organizations representing the interests of management in the FASB's standards-setting process?

17. Why is corporate management interested in managing earnings by the use of alternative accounting standards or methods? Is the income smoothing strategy effective in gaining a stock price premium?

18. Give three examples of how management can manage earnings.

AN OVERVIEW OF APPLIED ACCOUNTING RESEARCH

What is wanted is not the will to believe but the wish to find out, which is the exact opposite.

Bertrand Russell

Objectives

This chapter is an overview of applied accounting research and professional judgment. Supported by a number of case studies from practice, details of the issues introduced will be provided in future chapters. Upon completion of this chapter, you will have learned the:

1. Meaning of professional accounting research.
2. Factors that necessitate professional research.
3. Organizational units designed to conduct research in large accounting firms.
4. Sources of information for smaller accounting firms.
5. Role of professional judgment in accounting research.
6. Characteristics of quality research.
7. Categories of accounting research.
8. Differences between scientific and professional research.

Professional accountants have specialized knowledge that they use to solve complex problems facing their clients. The nature of the problems that accountants face and the types of professional judgments that they make continually change with changes in the economic, technological, promulgatory, and regulatory environment. For example, consider the immense changes that have occurred in information technology over the past decade. Being in the business of producing accounting information and auditing such information, accountants are directly affected by these changes in the way they produce computerized accounting information and they audit such information (e.g., continuous on-line auditing). In Chapter 4 we introduce some of the information technology sources that are useful for research.

Professional accountants use systematic research to keep up with the changes in it, and to enhance their critical thinking, problem-solving abilities, and professional judgment. Research-based practice focuses on current professional literature as well as current information (such as on-line information and databases) to provide a basis for problem solving and professional judgment. This issue is closely related to the concept of "learning to learn" whereby professional accountants have the education, motivation, and capacity to continue to acquire new knowledge through independent research throughout their professional lives.[1]

In this chapter we provide an overview of research in the context of accounting practice. We first present a definition of accounting research and then discuss the need for professional research. We also provide a set of examples where professional judgment is needed along with research. Also included in this section is the organizational structure used in large accounting firms for professional research, followed by a discussion of sources of information for smaller firms. We then discuss the characteristics of quality research with a focus on those characteristics that make research reliable. Finally, two types of research, scientific and professional, are discussed, along with some of their subcategories. Methods of carrying out the research are also presented.

Definition of Accounting Research

Accounting research is defined broadly as a systematic process of investigating an issue of concern to the accountant. The key word in this definition is *investigating*. This is in contrast to accounting theory, which is a systematic formulation of the relationships between various components of an accounting issue or phenomenon. The key word in accounting theory is *formulation*. Thus, one formulates the relationships in theory and investigates those relationships through research. The concern of this book is applied accounting research, not accounting theory.[2] However, it is important to note that the systematic process in research is designed to

---

1. Accounting Education Change Commission, *Positions Statement No. 1*, "Objectives of Education for Accountants" (Torrance, CA: 1990), p. 6. Also see M. C. Francis, T. C. Mulder, and J. S. Stark, *Intentional Learning: A Process for Learning to Learn in the Accounting Curriculum* (Sarasota, FL: Accounting Education Change Commission and the American Accounting Association, 1995), p. 93.

2. Interested readers are referred to standard accounting theory books such as E. S. Hendriksen and M. F. Van Breda, *Accounting Theory*, Fifth Ed. (Boston, MA: Richard D. Irwin, 1992).

verify or refute established accounting theories or expectations about an issue of interest. If no formal theory exists, the accounting professional will implicitly or explicitly develop a theory to form research expectations. Alternatively, the accountant may simply design research for the purpose of exploring or describing an issue. Either way, professional research relates to what an accountant normally does in everyday practice. Accountants are defined broadly to include those in public or private practice, governmental accountants, and cost and managerial accountants, including auditors.

To illustrate, suppose that an accountant is interested in finding out whether or not companies use a method of immediate recognition of the transition obligation of post-retirement benefits other than pensions or amortize the cost over a period up to 20 years. Since *SFAS No. 106* allows either method, one can theorize that companies would select the amortization method because this method allows them to spread the expense up to 20 years. The lump-sum charge against income in the first year results in an immediate and significant charge against current year's earnings. Systematic research of the practice shows that some companies have elected to use the immediate charge method, while other companies adopted the amortization method.[3]

By issuing *SFAS No. 106* in December 1990, the FASB triggered these practices. Consequently, a researcher might design a longitudinal study (i.e., a study of the changes over a period of time) to investigate the reasons why companies elected the immediate charge method and compare those reasons to the reasons for the amortization method. Called an *event study*, such an investigation might focus on a period of time, say five years, pre- and post-1991 when *SFAS No. 106* became effective. The pre- and post-effective date investigation provides insight into the effects of *SFAS No. 106*. Of course, event studies can be used to investigate the effects of any event on a variable of interest as long as one can establish a reasonable causal relationship between the event (as an independent variable) and the variable of interest (as a dependent variable).

The FASB and other promulgatory organizations carefully investigate issues of accounting and reporting before issuing new statements, interpretations, or positions. Nevertheless, as the *SFAS No. 106* example indicates, the nature of these pronouncements provides room for choice in the amount and timing of expense (or revenue) recognition. Consequently, a major area of applied professional research for accountants is to use various authoritative literature, as well as professional judgment, to provide solutions to

---

3. As P. McConnell, *Accounting Issues* (Bear Sterns & Co., April 1991), pp. 1–8 reported, unlike pensions, other retirement benefits are rarely funded. This forced adopters of *SFAS No. 106* to create a huge unfunded liability with a huge negative impact on income. General Motors, for example, took $20.8 billion as a one-time charge against income in the year of adoption. This figure was $7.5 billion for Ford Motor Company and $2.3 billion for IBM.

revenue or expense recognition or cost capitalization problems. This is why a large number of the cases we have developed for this book cover revenue or expense recognition or cost capitalization.

The Need for Professional Research

Accountants perform research on many aspects of their work. Examples include budgetary processes, inventory systems, transfer pricing, taxation issues, audit processes and procedures, and consulting practices. For example, in a budgetary process, accountants use research-based information on the economic outlook to investigate its effects on sales forecasts, future material costs, labor markets, and the like to establish budgets. Inventory systems require the capture and use of current information on inventory items on a real-time basis so that the information in the inventory system is current and reliable. Transfer pricing between various divisions of a company requires that accountants use current information, regulatory guidelines, and local laws to establish acceptable transfer prices. Suppose that one of the divisions is located in a country whose currency was just devalued. The accountant must consider this information in adjusting the transfer price between the division in that country and the domestic division. Similarly, taxation issues require research for the most current status of various city, state, federal, and foreign tax laws.

Auditing and professional consulting too are dependent on professional research. While knowledge-based professional judgment is the core of these activities, much research is needed to support such judgments. In fact, the promulgatory and regulatory bodies mandate the use of research. These bodies hold the accountant liable if sufficient research is not conducted on a contentious problem. For example, the SEC charged that a public accountant failed to exercise due professional care while performing an audit. The SEC stated that:

> Failure to conduct any research . . . constitutes a failure to act with due professional care.[4]

Research in the contemporary accounting and auditing environment is challenging due to its complexity. Professional standards, regulatory rules, accounting methods and procedures, and the information technology advances are numerous, detailed, and multidimensional. This situation has created a state of information overload for the professional accountant. One way that the professional accountant tries to cope with this situation is to specialize in a particular area of accounting or auditing. However, the complex nature of accounting and auditing, even within areas of specialty,

---

4. Securities and Exchange Commission, *Accounting and Auditing Enforcement Release No. 420* (Washington, DC, September 1992).

may exceed a specialist's knowledge base. Consequently, the need arises frequently for research on various issues. The reasons for research can be summarized as follows:

- *Standards Overload.* It is extremely difficult, if not impossible, for accountants to know everything related to their work. This is due to information overload caused by the continual and rapid nature of environmental changes, accounting standards and regulations, and advances in information technology. The accountant is simply faced with information overload from both the standard-setting process and the information generated by the new technology. Researchers reported in the early 1980s that the volume of pronouncements in accounting had already become too large to be recalled and applied with reliable accuracy.[5] Of course the speed with which standard setters have produced new pronouncements over the past two decades has accelerated, resulting in a more severe standards overload than the one that existed in the early 1980s.

Consequently, researchers have advocated that accounting education should follow the example of law where theoretical courses are supplanted with a series of courses emphasizing legal research skills.[6] The recent changes in the requirements for practice provide an opportunity to follow this recommendation. Since the late 1990s, accountants have been required to complete 150 credit hours of education in order to practice accounting. This requirement has essentially made a graduate degree program a requirement for practice of accounting as compared with an undergraduate or lower degree requirement in the past. However, even with this change, an accountant cannot be completely prepared for all possible issues that will confront him or her in practice. Frequently, new problems and reporting issues arise in practice before academics, promulgators, or regulators can address them.

- *Knowledge Differentials.* One way accountants have responded to the information and standards overload is by specialization. For example, an accountant might specialize in accounting and/or auditing issues for mergers and acquisitions, thus focusing on standards and regulatory requirements of these economic activities. Others might specialize in a functional area of accounting such as managerial or financial accounting, while yet other accountants become information technology specialists. Of course, general practice, which tackles various types of accounting and auditing issues, is now limited to small practices.

Whether a specialist or a generalist, an accountant can have various degrees of expertise based on level of education, training, experience, and a host of other factors such as personality. Thus, while some accountants may

---

5. For example, see S. C. Dlilley, R. B. Hayes, and P. Steinbart, "Development of a Paradigm for Applied Accounting Research: A Way of Coping with Subject-Matter Complexity," *The Accounting Review,* LVIII, no. 2 (April 1983), p. 406.
6. Ibid., p. 406.

be naives in the area of their practice, others may be novices or experts.[7] Naives have only a broad knowledge of the issues and need supervision in their accounting work. Novices have some experience with the work in addition to their knowledge of the basics. Experts, on the other hand, are highly knowledgeable and experienced in their specialty areas. These differences in knowledge and experience make a difference in the need for professional research. For a given area of specialization, a naive needs more research than a novice, who in turn needs more research than an expert in performing an accounting or auditing task.

• *Knowledge as a Moving Target.* The need for professional research has an inverse relationship with levels of knowledge, but even experts need to engage in professional research because knowledge in professional accounting is a moving target. Standard setters and regulators introduce new rules and regulations continually, and the professional accountant must keep abreast of these new rules and regulations.

• *New Problems.* Many socioeconomic factors also make knowledge demands on accountants that traditionally may not have existed. For example, public interest laws such as environmental protection and clean-up laws make demands for accounting for environmental clean-up costs and the recognition of contingent liabilities that are very complex in nature. To address these issues, the accountant needs to perform research in areas not covered well in the professional literature.

• *Litigation.* Accountants are viewed as deep pockets and have been the targets of an increasing number of lawsuits in the past century. For example, many lawsuits have been brought against auditors for violation of Securities and Exchange Acts of 1933 and 1934 by third parties that had relied on the auditors' reports to purchase securities. Under the joint and several liability arrangements that existed for CPAs, plaintiffs could go after the assets of accounting firms and their partners even if only one partner was responsible for the problem. The Private Securities Litigation Reform Act of 1995 brought some relief to accountants because it changed the joint and several liabilities to a proportionate liability for defendants who are found liable, but who have not engaged in intentional violations of the securities laws. The full joint and several liability system is still in force for those who intentionally engage in violating the securities laws. This law cleared the path for accounting firms to change their form of organization from the professional form that was based on joint and several liability to the limited liability partnership form, or LLP, that recognizes proportional liability.

While the Private Securities Litigation Reform Act of 1995 is intended to reduce the number of frivolous lawsuits, it does not limit the number

---

7. For a detailed discussion of this classification and the characteristics of expertise in auditing see M. J. Abdolmohammadi and J. Shanteau, "Personal Attributes of Expert Auditors," *Organizational Behavior and Human Decision Processes* 53 (November 1992), pp. 158–72.

of legitimate litigations against accountants. To defend themselves, accountants must show that they have performed adequate research in forming their professional judgment. As stated earlier, the SEC cited insufficient research as failure to exercise due professional care by an accountant.

Research Units and Systems in Large Accounting Firms

Because of the need for professional research, most large accounting firms now have organizational units of various kinds to provide the research support that their professionals need. Individuals working in these units are selected from knowledgeable practicing accountants who are also talented and trained in the research processes. They are trained and mentored in the effective use of the library, databases, and the Internet for the purpose of answering professional research questions. The objective of such units is to provide research needed to address specific questions. The Internet provides a vehicle to actually go beyond just answering research questions. Accounting firms have begun to use this technology to place the knowledge base of the whole firm at the fingertips of a professional seeking help on a research issue. You will hear terminology such as *knowledge management system* or *knowledge sharing system* used to describe these systems.

A typical research unit in an accounting firm includes a policy committee, an executive research committee, and research units.[8] A policy committee on research typically governs the research unit of accounting firms. This committee is charged with the task of generating and maintaining a firmwide policy on various accounting and auditing issues. Members of this strategic committee are selected from a pool of highly competent partners with expertise in various areas of accounting, auditing, and technology. A lower level, but nevertheless very knowledgeable, group of practitioners is selected to develop operational policy decisions on a daily basis. This group is typically called an *executive research committee*. This committee assigns specific accounting and auditing research projects to be conducted by research units. One or more professionals ranging from senior to higher-level personnel staff research units. These units have access to research resources such as the firm's library, proprietary databases, and websites on an ongoing basis.

Resources for Smaller Accounting Firms

Large accounting firms have the resources to develop sophisticated research resources. For example, the Knowledge Management group that operates out of KPMG's Boston office was given hundreds of millions of dollars to develop its Internet based system. KPMG professionals around the world

---

8. This exhibit is an adaptation from T. R. Weirich and A. Reinstein, *Accounting & Auditing Research*, 4th ed. (Cincinnati, OH: South-Western College Publishing, 1996), p. 9.

have access to this elaborate system. Small accounting firms do not have the resources to develop such sophisticated systems. Instead these firms rely on other resources. For example, the technical services of the AICPA can be accessed via the AICPA website (http://www.AICPA.org). One can also log on to http://raw.rutgers.edu to reach the technical information from the FASB, GASB, AAA, IIA, and other professional associations. We discuss various issues relating to the search of these websites in Chapter 4. For example, to find the information needed, one must have a clear understanding of the issue of research and a clear strategy for the search of these resources. Otherwise, finding relevant information may turn out to be like finding a needle in a haystack.

The Role of Judgment

Accounting and auditing practices are characterized by the frequent need for professional judgment. The research process presented in this chapter focuses on the importance of attention to fact and freedom from bias. However, the professional accountant may be performing advocacy research (e.g., tax research for the benefit of a client) and making repeated judgments at various stages of the engagement. Details of judgment and decision-making issues are discussed in Chapter 7. A brief discussion is provided here supported by a detailed example to show the extent of the role of judgment in the practice of professional accounting. The use of judgment to solve accounting and auditing problems is part of professional practice and its importance has been recognized by professional organizations. For example, the AICPA views judgment as the most important factor in an audit.[9]

Exhibit 2–1 presents an indication of the number of judgments that auditors make in the course of an audit. From the beginning of the audit process, the auditor combines professional judgment with professional research to make significant decisions. The intent is not to discuss auditing tasks in detail here. These issues are covered in standard auditing textbooks. Suffice it to say that each of the judgments listed in Exhibit 2–1 requires a mix of research and judgment. For example, in establishing materiality, the auditor searches the accounting firm's archives as well as the authoritative literature for guidelines about accounting and auditing materiality and business risk. These guidelines are used as decision aids for the auditor who will make materiality and risk judgments based on specific characteristics of the audit client.

Similarly, the auditor uses judgment in performing many other activities. These activities include identifying important objectives, assessing the inherent risk, evaluating internal controls, developing an audit strategy, generating an audit program, selecting and evaluating analytical review

---

9. AICPA, *A Case Study on the Extent of Audit Samples* (New York, NY: American Institute of Certified Public Accountants, 1955).

Exhibit 2–1	Examples of Professional Judgment in an Audit
Activity	*Judgment*
1. Establishing materiality	• Accounting materiality • Audit materiality • Acceptable business risk
2. Identifying important audit objectives	• Important audit areas • Important transaction streams and balances • Important financial statement assertions
3. Assessing the inherent risk environment	• Implications of the client environment for identification of potential audit concerns, focuses of audit attention, and control structure • Inherent risk assessment for financial statement assertions
4. Evaluating internal controls	• Potential for improved audit efficiency or effectiveness based on assessing control risk as less than maximum • Key controls for testing • Control risk for financial statement assertions • Weaknesses in controls (reportable conditions)
5. Developing an audit strategy	• Reliance on tests of controls • Potential for different audit approaches • Emphasis on balances or transaction streams • Identification of strategic assertions
6. Generating the audit program	• Selection of an appropriate combination of specific audit procedures and determination of the scope and timing of application
7. Selecting and evaluating analytical review procedures	• Particular procedures to be applied, data to be used, relevant formulae, and calculations • Development of expectations • Identification of significant fluctuations • Formulation and corroboration of explanations of fluctuations
8. Evaluating the results of audit testing	• Conclusions on the results of specific audit procedures in relation to their objectives and to the results obtained
9. Considering the materiality of unadjusted audit differences	• Consideration of the nature and amount of unadjusted audit differences individually and in aggregate in relation to their potential impact on users of the financial statements • Decision whether to press for adjustment by the audit client or to accept the differences as immaterial
10. Determining the going concern basis	• Whether the client can reasonably be expected to continue in operation for the coming 12 months
11. Applying generally accepted auditing standards and accounting principles	• Identification of relevant accounting and auditing standards • Determination whether such standards have been appropriately applied in the light of client circumstances • Identification of appropriate courses of action in cases where standards have not been correctly applied
12. Applying the Code of Professional Contact	• Determination whether auditor behavior is acceptable within the dictates of professional requirements and ethical principles
13. Selecting an appropriate audit opinion	• Determination whether the financial statements fairly present results for the period

* Adapted from E. M. Bamber; P. R. Gillet; T. J. Mock; and K. T. Trotman, "Audit Judgment," in *Auditing Practice, Research, and Education: A Productive Collaboration*, T. B. Bell and A. M. Wright (Eds.) (New York, NY: American Institute of Certified Public Accountants, 1995), pp. 57–58.

procedures, evaluating the results of audit testing, considering the materiality of unadjusted audit differences, determining the going concern basis, applying generally accepted auditing standards and accounting principles, applying the Code of Professional Conduct, and selecting an appropriate audit opinion. For example, in applying the Code of Professional Conduct, the auditor makes a judgment as to whether his or her behavior is acceptable within the dictates of professional requirements and ethical principles. This judgment forces the auditor to search for current professional requirements and ethical principles. The research unit of the auditing firm is perhaps the source of this information. The research unit continually monitors the changes in these requirements to assist the auditor with the latest information.

To illustrate the role of judgment in accounting and auditing, consider the fact that both qualitative and quantitative aspects of materiality must be considered in assigning materiality judgments. In August 1999, the SEC issued *SAB No. 99,* "Materiality." This *SAB* indicated that reliance on only a quantitative threshold has no basis in the accounting literature or the law. Qualitative factors as well as quantitative ones must be considered when making a materiality judgment. For example, consider the fact that many entities have established a quantitative threshold, such as 5 percent of net income, to determine materiality as it relates to the preparation of financial statements. Thus, if Company X overstates net income by $2,000 and reports $102,000 as net income, a 2 percent overstatement of net income would be judged by many to be immaterial. However, if Company X had a loan covenant with its major lender that required Company X to report annual net income of $102,000 or more, the $2,000 (2%) overstatement of net income would now be judged by most to be material. Such an overstatement of net income would conceal that Company X is in violation of a loan covenant that potentially could have significant financial repercussions.

Research Quality

Care must be exercised in performing research. This means that research must have certain qualitative characteristics to produce reliable results. A detailed discussion of these qualitative characteristics is beyond the scope of this book.[10] A summary of qualitative characteristics is shown in Exhibit 2–2 in four categories: validity, freedom from bias, variable isolation, and appropriate inferential logic. These qualitative characteristics are described in this section. An accounting example is provided at the end of the section along with a qualifier indicating that, due to various limitations, some qualitative characteristics may be violated in professional research.

---

10. For a detailed discussion of these characteristics, see any research methods book such as U. Sekaran, *Research Methods for Business: A Skill-Building Approach,* 2nd Ed. (New York: NY: Wiley, 1992), pp. 10–14.

Validity

Validity, also called *construct validity*, refers to the care with which the foundation of research is established. It has several components as listed in Exhibit 2–2. The first component is called *purpose*. It refers to the necessity of having a definite purpose for conducting a research project. The question here is why the research should be conducted at all. What is the motivation for the research? Are the questions being addressed just interesting, or do they also have some significant consequences for the problem under consideration? Conducting research without a specific purpose is like trying to find a small object in a dark alley.

Another component of validity is rigor. It means that the theoretical foundation of the research must be sound and valid. Also, the method used to collect evidence must be exact and well controlled so the researcher knows exactly what evidence is collected and what it means in relation to the research question.

The third component listed under validity is testability. Testability indicates that the research question must be one that can be systematically tested with data. That is, a proposition, an expectation, or a hypothesis must be developed beforehand to guide the method of research. If a question is obvious, then testing is a waste of time. On the other hand, if a question is so complicated as to be nearly impossible to plan a test for investigating it, then the research may prove to be a waste of time and resources.

Exhibit 2-2	Characteristics of Good Research	
Characteristic	*Component*	*Meaning*
1. Validity: The care with which the research is constructed	Purpose	A meaningful reason exists for conducting the research.
	Rigor	There is a sound theoretical foundation.
	Testablity	The research question can be tested.
	Replicablitity	The research can be replicated for new evidence.
	Precision	The research provides evidence that is close to reality.
	Confidence	It is probable that research results are close to reality.
	Parsimony	The research process and results are explained in simple terms.
2. Freedom from bias	Reliablity of conclusions	The research is conducted objectively: only facts are presented.
3. Variable isolation	Internal validity	Control for irrelevant variables exists.
4. Appropriate inferential logic	External validity	The results can be generalized for use in similar situations.

The fourth component, replicability, indicates that research can be replicated again to assess the consistency of its results over time. Chapter 6 discusses research models that require many years for sufficient replicative and complementary evidence to develop. However, in many professional research issues, evidence can be collected and replicated with similar results over a short period of time. For example, in addressing operating versus capital leases, the researcher will access the same authoritative sources of guidance no matter how many times the search is replicated in a short period of time. Of course, new standards, interpretations, statements of position, or technical bulletins may be issued that will affect the search over a longer term.

Precision is the next component of validity. It refers to the closeness of the findings to reality. Also called *accuracy*, this aspect of validity is an important criterion in evaluating the research outcome. For example, variance analysis in managerial accounting indicates how close the budget numbers are to actual results. The closer the budget to actual results, the more precise or accurate are the predictions reflected in the budget. Thus, the research process used in the budgetary process is evaluated through the variances discovered after the fact.

The researcher may not have the luxury of time to wait for the actual results to occur in order to measure precision. In some situations, the researcher may never find out the reality. For example, in research involving the assessment of the going concern of an audit client, the auditor does not know the reality of the client's situation until after the client actually ceases operation or files for bankruptcy protection. Some clients who are suspected of going-concern problems may actually continue in existence, and eventually become financially sound. Others may file for bankruptcy perhaps expedited by auditor's going-concern opinion (i.e., a self-fulfilling prophecy may occur).

Confidence as another component of validity is frequently used as a substitute for precision in cases where precision is hard or impossible to measure. We use confidence measured at levels from .01 to .99. Thus, confidence in a going-concern judgment, expressed as a percentage, is the auditor's assessment of the probability that his or her judgment is correct. Alternatively, we may use the consensus of several auditors as a measure of judgment precision.[11] These measures help evaluate the research process ending in the going-concern judgment.

The final component of validity is parsimony. It refers to simplicity in explaining the research. The research questions must be specified clearly and concisely in a simple form that can be easily understood. This does not mean that complex research questions cannot be investigated. In fact, it is for

---

11. For example, A. S. Ashton, "Does Consensus Imply Accuracy in Accounting Studies of Decision Making?" *The Accounting Review* (April 1985), pp. 173–85 provides evidence that consensus is a good surrogate in some accounting and auditing judgment tasks.

the complex problem situations that the accountant needs the research process. In these situations, the research question, however complex, should be broken down into understandable and simple parts for the purpose of scientific research. After parts are well understood, the researcher combines the results to form a judgment about the whole problem.

Freedom from Bias

Freedom from bias, or objectivity, is the next characteristic listed in Exhibit 2–2. It means that only facts should determine the results and form the conclusions from the research. As human beings, we all have preferences and biases. However, if these personal preferences or biases are allowed to influence the research process, undesirable contamination of research results will occur. This contamination will render research results and the conclusions from these results unreliable. Only the evidence collected in the research process should be analyzed for the development of conclusions.

Variable Isolation

Variable isolation is the third characteristic listed in Exhibit 2–2. It simply means that the variable under consideration must be carefully isolated from all other variables. Called *internal validity*, this characteristic determines whether or not the researcher has contaminated the research process by allowing irrelevant variables into the research process. Typically, there are two types of variables in a research. The first is called an *independent variable*. This variable is allowed by the researcher or conditions to vary. The second type is a *dependent variable*. The research analyzes how this dependent variable is affected by changes in the independent variable. The dependent variable must be isolated in a way such that the independent variable's effects on it can be reasonably measured.

For example, the researcher might vary the amount of depreciation expense by the use of various depreciation methods to investigate their effects on the resulting net income. The depreciation method is the independent variable and net income is the dependent variable. If the researcher also allows inventory costing methods to change at the same time, it becomes difficult to determine what independent variable (depreciation or inventory costing methods) caused the change in the dependent variable. Called *confounding*, these variables often contaminate the analysis and the conclusions in ways that make inference about the variable of interest difficult if not impossible. Thus, it is important that independent variables are carefully isolated to measure their effects on dependent variables. This is not always easy due to the dynamic nature of the underlying economic environment. That is, just as you document the economic factors, they may change in ways that might affect your dependent variables. In such cases, one needs to document the environment and communicate the underlying assumptions about and limitations of con-founding variables. It may be possible to find proxies for these variables so that the effects can be measured indirectly. For example, if you were asked to measure the value of a company's intellectual capital, you may decide to document the educational degrees of various employees as a substitute for a measure of intellectual capital.

Appropriate Inferential Logic

The final characteristic of good research listed in Exhibit 2–2 is appropriate inferential logic. Inferential logic is needed if the evidence found is to be generalized to apply to other situations. This is called *external validity* and is determined by whether or not an appropriate method of research was used, a representative sample was selected, and the logic was used appropriately to generalize from the sample to a population of interest.

Types of Logic

Four types of logic can be used for inference. The first is descriptive logic. It simply provides a description of a phenomenon by observing evidence from practice. For example, the AICPA's publication *Accounting Trends and Techniques* provides statistics that simply describe how companies surveyed for the book use various accounting methods, such as the percentage of companies that use the straight-line method of depreciation. The exact opposite of this logic is normative logic, which prescribes a course of action based on some theory. An example of normative theory is an ethical theory such as utilitarianism, which prescribes that a person ought to take action that will result in the most good for the greatest number of people.

The next two types of logic are particularly useful in fields of inquiry such as accounting and law. Deductive logic forms a conclusion by reason-ing from the general to the specific, from a general premise to a particular situation. An example is:

General premise: Every state in the United States has a board
                   of accountancy
Specific situation: Indiana is a state in the United States
Conclusion: Indiana has a board of accountancy

Finally, inductive logic forms a conclusion from a particular situation to a generalized conclusion. Inductive logic is particularly useful as a means of generalizing specific evidence to a general conclusion in empirical research. For example,

Specific situation: *SFAS No. 123* on stock options was issued by the FASB
General Premise: All *SFASs* issued by the FASB must pass the board's
                   due process
Conclusion: *SFAS No. 123* passed the FASB's due process

Note that for the conclusion to be valid in either deductive or inductive logic, both the general premise and the specific situation must be factual. Any error in either invalidates the logic, and its conclusion.

To make a logical inference, the researcher either provides a convincing argument or authoritative support for a selected course of action. In cases where numerical data are collected, an analysis of data must be provided. To do this, we borrow many statistical methods from the field of statistics. Detailed coverage of these methods can be found in standard statistics textbooks. Several methods are briefly discussed in Chapter 5 in relation to the applied research process. This is an area in which computer technology has greatly simplified the use of statistical methods. Complex statistical methods have been programmed in user-friendly statistical software packages such as Minitab, SAS, and SPSS that can be used in professional research. It is not necessary to be a statistician to use the basic, but powerful, statistics in these packages.

External validity is a component of inferential logic, which is based on causality. When a generalization is made concerning the effect of an independent variable on a dependent variable, the researcher must establish a causal relationship between the two variables. A simple association is not sufficient grounds for generalizing unless such an association can also be viewed as causal. For example, an auditor might witness a positive association between some economic indicator and the financial difficulty of a client. Say the economic indicator observed is the rate of growth of the Chinese gross national product (GNP). The association may not be causal if the client is a local company with little or no international business. However, if the client does a significant amount of business in China, then the association can possibly be interpreted as a causal correlation between the Chinese GNP growth rate as an independent variable and the economic well-being of the client as a dependent variable. If the Chinese GNP growth rate dropped in the year that the audit client experienced financial difficulty, the auditor might conclude that one of the independent variables causing the financial difficulty might be the slowdown of the Chinese GNP growth rate. Statistical methods are available that can be used to regress the client's financial difficulty on a number of independent variables and find the degree to which each of these variables contributes to the financial difficulty of the client.

An Accounting Example and a Qualifier

There has always been a question regarding the information needed by various financial accounting information users. In 1994, a special committee of the AICPA identified financial analysts as among the most important users of financial reports. The committee recommended that the needs of these users be determined through systematic research and the quality of their decisions based on accounting information be investigated to assess whether the currently reported accounting information is relevant. Related to this recommendation, research was conducted to examine the relationship between forecast accuracy of financial analysts and specific accounting information items (e.g., the balance sheet and the auditor's report in annual reports) used during financial statement analysis.[12] The study provided a sample of financial analysts with cases in which financial information was provided for a specific company. In general, the study found an association between specific accounting information items and earnings forecast accuracy. The study also indicated that the relatively more accurate analysts used more information items prior to issuing their earnings forecasts than the relatively less accurate analysts.

This study had all the elements of validity. First, it had a purpose for conducting the research. Its purpose was to investigate the relationship between analysts' earnings forecast accuracy and accounting information. Second, the study used prior literature to establish a sound theoretical foundation for the study's purpose and its hypothesis. Third, the research question was testable by observing the behavior of financial analysts. The study used a sample of financial analysts from a major brokerage firm in New York. Fourth, the study can be replicated using a different sample of financial analysts. Fifth, the study provided precise information concerning the classification of analysts into various levels of accuracy. Sixth, using the regression analysis in a statistical software package, the study found the relative importance of various types of information to the analysts' forecast accuracy. However, this analysis is probabilistic in nature (i.e., it provides a confidence interval as compared with a single deterministic number).

The study also was free from the investigators' bias because the researchers conducted the research objectively and focused on facts only. The researchers also isolated the independent variables (accounting information items) by providing specific cases in which levels of independent variables were provided. Thus, no irrelevant variables (e.g., climate in China) were allowed to enter the case studies. This step provided internal validity for the research study. Finally, an inferential logic (simple classification of analysts by degrees of forecast accuracy and the regression analysis) was used to generalize the results, thus providing external validity.

While the research example provided adhered to all qualitative characteristics of research, unfortunately, seldom is an issue so clearly isolated that all the research characteristics can be fully satisfied. In situations where the issue is not clearly isolated and the researcher is making certain assumptions, the consequences of violating such assumptions must be explained when communicating the research results. The researcher must disclose the limitations of the study and provide a statement of the possible effects of the limitations on the research findings. Thus, further investigation

---

12. R. A. McEwen, and J. E. Hunton, "Is Analyst Forecast Accuracy Associated with Accounting Information Usage?" *Accounting Horizons* 13, no. 1 (March 1998), pp. 1–16.

might be needed to add to the reliability (i.e., the internal validity) or the generalizability (i.e., the external validity) of the research results. Practically speaking, the professional accountant seldom has the luxury of time to thoroughly investigate a research issue to a complete resolution. Sometimes, it is necessary to make a professional judgment or decision based on an incomplete information set. Although the role of judgment is briefly discussed earlier in this chapter, a more detailed discussion is presented in Chapter 7.

Types of Research

There are many ways to classify research. A generic classification is discussed in this section. Further information about various research and methods used to carry it out are discussed in Chapter 6. However, since the case analysis method and issue-based professional research are the foci of this book, each of these methods is discussed in a separate chapter: the case research method in Chapter 3 and issue-based research in Chapter 5. Authoritative sources of information needed for the case analysis method and the role of information technology in research are discussed in Chapter 4.

A generic classification of research into scientific and professional research is provided in Exhibit 2–3. In this section, each of these classes of research is further classified into a number of research types as depicted in Exhibit 2–3. Our focus here is to provide general coverage of the most commonly used research types and their purposes. The research methods

Exhibit 2-3	Types of Research		
Class: Purpose	*Type*	*Purpose*	*Method*
1. Scientific: To generate new knowledge	Basic, or pure	To understand fundamental aspects of new knowledge	Descriptive, normative, exploratory, empirical, experimental
	Applied	To use new knowledge to solve contemporary problems	Descriptive, empirical, experimental
	Instructional	To develop methods for dissemination of new knowledge	Empirical, experimental, case studies
2. Professional: To generate solutions to contemporary problems	Applied (but also sometimes instructional and basic)	To use new knowledge to solve contemporary problems	Descriptive library, field research

used to carry them out are also identified. Detailed discussions of various classes of research or more refined research types and methods to carry them out are beyond the scope of this book. The interested reader should refer to specialized research methodology books.[13]

Scientific Research

Scientific research attempts to generate and use new knowledge. Its primary relevance to accounting is in its model building and research on new problems confronting the profession. Standards-setting organizations in general, and the FASB in particular, consult scientific research for suggestions for possible solutions to problems under consideration. Accounting firms have provided support for scientific research for many years and have benefited from the results of this research. KPMG had a program called the Research Opportunities in Auditing Program from the mid-1970s to the mid-1990s. It funded up to 10 projects a year with monetary grants and staff participation in various auditing-related projects. Other accounting firms have had, and continue to have, various types of programs for support of scientific research.

Scientific research is long term in nature. It takes years, even decades, before new knowledge is generated and well understood in some areas. Scientific research is also very costly because of the multiyear nature of its investigation process and complex issues that require rigorous methodologies. Nonaccounting examples include medical research trying to understand the nature of, and to develop cures for, various types of cancer or immune deficiencies such as acquired immune deficiency syndrome (AIDS). This research has been under way for many years with some major breakthroughs, but some disappointments too. It is the dream of many researchers and patients alike that someday the medical profession will have the knowledge and the means to cure these diseases. There is even hope that someday vaccines will be developed to prevent these diseases from occurring in the first place.

An accounting example of scientific research is research on understanding the effects of inflation on financial statements and developing methods to adjust the financial statements for these effects. A reasonable level of understanding has developed over the past decades. However, no overall regulatory or promulgatory requirement exists currently for the disclosure of inflation-adjusted financial statements. Because of the double-digit inflation of the 1970s and pressure from the SEC,[14] the FASB issued *SFAS*

---

13. For example, F. N. Kerlinger, *Foundations of Behavioral Research* (New York: Holt, Rinehart and Winston, 1973) provides a detailed coverage of various research types and methods for behavioral research.

14. *Accounting Series Release no. 190* (Washington, D.C.: Securities and Exchange Commission, 1976).

No. 33, "Financial Reporting and Changing Prices," in 1979, requiring certain disclosures.[15] By 1982, inflation was brought under control and into the single-digit territory, which resulted in the easing of pressure from the SEC. This issue and many compliance problems with *SFAS No. 33* resulted in the FASB's issuance of *SFAS No. 82,* "Financial Reporting and Changing Prices: Elimination of Certain Disclosures," where some of the required disclosures under *SFAS No. 33* were eliminated.[16] The FASB issued *SFAS No. 89,* "Financial Reporting and Changing Prices" in 1986 that eliminated the requirement altogether.[17]

Another accounting example of long-term "scientific" research is the research on understanding the nature and treatment of stock-based compensation plans. It took over a decade for the FASB to consider various research results and to proceed from accepting the issue on its agenda in 1984 to issuing *SFAS No. 123* in 1995.[18] The details of this process are described in an appendix to Chapter 6.

Scientific research, sometimes called *academic research,* can be conducted anywhere, although much of it is conducted in academic institutions by professors trained as researchers. The examples provided above indicate that scientific research can also be conducted in promulgatory organizations such as the FASB. This organization has its own research staff that conducts research on various issues of concern. Of course much of the research that the FASB conducts can be classified as professional in nature as discussed in the next section, but some of the research is scientific in nature. Many research and development units of business entities and accounting firms engage in scientific research as well.

Scientific research can be further classified into three types: basic (or pure), applied, and instructional. These research types are described below.

Basic, or Pure, Research

Basic, or pure, research refers to scientific research that attempts to understand the fundamental aspects of new knowledge. In such research, the researcher investigates the fundamental or theoretical premises of an issue to find out the theories, models, or concepts that can be applied as a foundation to study other areas of concern. The objective of pure research is to understand the building blocks for fundamental theories. For example,

---

15. Financial Accounting Standards Board, *Statement of Financial Accounting Standards No. 33,* "Financial Reporting and Changing Prices" (Stamford, CT, 1979).

16. Financial Accounting Standards Board, *Statement of Financial Accounting Standards No. 82,* "Financial Reporting and Changing Prices: Elimination of Certain Disclosures" (Stamford, CT, 1984).

17. Financial Accounting Standards Board, *Statement of Financial Accounting Standards No. 89,* "Financial Reporting and Changing Prices" (Stamford, CT, 1986).

18. Financial Accounting Standards Board, *Statement of Financial Accounting Standards No. 123 ,* "Accounting for Stock-Based Compensation" (Norwalk, CT, 1995).

while the concept of profit has been around for many centuries, going back to the beginnings of trade and commerce, the modern formulation of profit in the following functional form is a basic research:

$$\pi = px - vx - F \tag{1}$$

Where π is profit formulated as a dependent variable or a function of price (p), volume (x), variable cost (v), and fixed cost (F). From this basic formulation, we have derived many of our accounting concepts. For example, equation (1) can be rearranged and presented as:

$$\pi = (p - v)x - F \tag{2}$$

Where $(p - v)$ represents the concept of marginal profit.

The example provided above is a formulation of a basic model by codifying or describing practice. This indicates that pure research may borrow its knowledge from a description of practice. Exploratory research is a subset of descriptive research. It is used to collect limited data that can be used to describe an issue and to generate basic, or pure, research. Its purpose is to discover new knowledge.

Other research methods useful for basic knowledge include normative and predictive research. The focus of normative research is on the generation of rules and principles that govern the creation of a theory or a model. For example, according to ethical or philosophical concepts, accountants should focus their investigation into the nature of accounting transactions on the truth and its fair presentation by clients. Normative research often requires deductive logic and mathematical formulation of the relationships between dependent and independent variables based on basic assumptions and axioms. For example, a mathematical formulation for break-even analysis can be developed from equation (2) where profit (π) is set to 0 resulting in:

$$(p - v)x - F = 0 \tag{3}$$

Rearranging equation (3) we get

$$x = F / (p - v) \tag{4}$$

Equation (4) provides the normative level of sales (x) that should be achieved in order to generate a sufficient marginal profit $(p - v)$ to cover the fixed cost (F). This is a simple example of a normative mathematical formulation for the generation of basic knowledge. More complex problems require more complex formulations.

Predictive research uses current data and trends to forecast future trends. Weather forecasting is a good example of predictive research. It uses past data and weather patterns to develop sophisticated mathematical computer models that forecast future weather patterns. Of course, as we all know, such forecasts are subject to error. Nevertheless many people have come to depend on weather forecasting for their daily activities. Consequently, weather forecasting has become a daily routine for the media from radio and TV to the print media and the Internet-based information. Another example of predictive research is the research models that predict student success in completing graduate programs. These research models use various input such as undergraduate grade point average and the Graduate Management Aptitude Test to predict a student's success in completing a graduate program.

Forecasting future earnings based on past trends is an accounting/finance example of predictive research. Also, accountants use predictive research models for many of their judgments. For example, auditors and financial analysts regularly use predictive models to assess whether their clients are going to continue as a going concern, or face financial difficulty and ultimately bankruptcy. A specific predictive model produces an index called the Altman Z-score. Based on research studies of key financial ratios of samples of healthy and bankrupt firms in some industries (e.g., manufacturing), professor of finance Edward Altman of New York University developed the Z-score in the late 1960s. The score distinguishes with some degree of confidence bankrupt firms from healthy firms. It predicts potential for bankruptcy in as many as two reporting periods in advance. Using this predictive model, the Z-score of a healthy company would be 2.99 or above, as compared with 1.81 or below for a bankrupt company. Companies that fall between these two points would be considered in the gray area. This range requires the auditors to consider other information and make professional judgment. However, the Z-score is limited in its application because data are not compiled for many industries. This limitation indicates a need for further predictive research to compile such information.[19]

Applied Research
Applied research refers to investigation geared toward the use of existing knowledge to solve contemporary problems. Applied research also refers to the collection and analysis of empirical data to test the validity of a theory or basic knowledge to a specific situation. For example, the basic knowledge represented in equation (2) can be used to investigate the economic viability of special orders and other special decisions as discussed in managerial accounting and cost accounting texts. While the concept of marginal profit can be used to investigate the economic viability of the special order, data may be collected to investigate the reaction of current customers to the special sale. Thus, the consequent behavior of the current customers is investigated through this applied research.

Another example is in the application of professional standards to determine the treatment of acquired in-process research and development

---

19. For more information, see E. I. Altman, *Corporate Financial Distress: A Complete Guide to Predicting, Avoiding, and Dealing with Bankruptcy* (New York, NY: John Wiley & Sons), 1983.

(IPR&D). Public companies increased write-offs of IRP&D during the 1990s. Although acquisitions of technology companies occurred prior to the 1990s, large write-offs of IPR&D were rare until the 1990s. During this time period there was no change in the accounting literature on the treatment of IPR&D. Companies have used existing literature such as *FASB Interpretation No. 4,* "Applicability of *FASB Statement No. 2* to Business Combinations Accounted for by the Purchase Method" to account for these acquisitions. However, the SEC has become concerned about this development and the way companies have accounted for the transactions. The FASB is expected to address this issue through its Emerging Issues Task Force.

Instructional Research

Instructional research is used to develop methods to disseminate new knowledge through education and training. This type of research attempts to understand basic and applied research findings. It also may engage in further research to investigate best methods and practices for dissemination of these findings through education and training of targeted audience. For example, the primary method of teaching intermediate accounting to undergraduate students is through classroom instruction and laboratory setting physically located on college campuses. On the other hand, the graduate intermediate accounting course can be taught using a mix of on-campus and Internet-based pedagogy where the graduate students take more responsibility in learning on their own and at their own schedules. Continuing professional programs geared toward updating the knowledge of professional accountants often take place in group discussion settings at professional conferences and workshops. To prepare the teaching materials for these programs, new accounting or auditing standards are subjected to various instructional research to investigate the best ways in which these standards can be incorporated in accounting and auditing textbooks and courses. While college courses may take a conceptual approach for educating the students, professional courses developed for training of professionals may focus on practical applications.

Professional Research

As stated earlier, scientific research generally requires a long time to bear the fruit of knowledge. Professional accountants seldom have the luxury of time to wait for a new theory to develop and be validated before it can be used to solve a contemporary problem. They face problems in everyday practice that require immediate solutions. Professionals use basic, applied, and instructional research that is currently available as a guide to solving these problems. Thus, professional research can be defined as research that is geared toward generating solutions to contemporary practical problems.

In addition to cost and time, professional research is very different from scientific research in its motivation, method, and communication. The motivation for scientific research is to generate new knowledge while professional research is geared toward finding a solution to a current client problem. The method used to conduct professional research is also different from that for conducting scientific research. For example, by its very nature a tax research conducted for a client may have an advocacy nature (e.g., to save tax cost for the client) and thus be biased toward favorable evidence. In contrast, scientific research must be unbiased and have a method in which both favorable and unfavorable evidence is collected and analyzed. The communication of research results is different for applied professional research and scientific research. While a short report may suffice for the professional communication, scientific research must be carefully written up according to scientific criteria and is often published in competitive journals such as *The Accounting Review*. Papers submitted to these journals go through a rigorous review process by other researchers to ensure validity of the findings.

Professional research also differs from scientific research in its research type. Of the three research types listed for scientific research (i.e., basic, applied, and instructional), professional research uses primarily the applied research type, although large accounting firms also use instructional research for their training programs. Also important to note is that professional research primarily uses a descriptive library or database search for collection of authoritative literature as compared with applied scientific research that often uses empirical/experimental methods to collect data. Professional research also uses case development research (also called field research) to understand the nature of professional engagements. Finally, it is important to note that professional research can result in the generation of new knowledge, thus it can assist basic research. However, this is not a major objective of professional research. Similarly, while instructional benefits might result from professional research, this is not a major objective of professional research.

Other Research Classifications

The classification of research provided in the previous section is not all-inclusive. There are many other classifications as well. For example, research can be classified based on the timing of the research conducted. Pre-facto research (also called *a priori*) refers to research conducted to understand the issues related to a decision or transaction before such decisions or transactions are actually undertaken. The purpose of pre-facto research is to assist the decision-maker in the process of the decision making. On the other hand, post-facto research (also known as *a posteriori*) is conducted after the fact to evaluate the effectiveness of the decision. A confirming bias can be present in post-facto research. That is, the decision-maker might try to find evidence to support the decision that was made rather than objectively evaluate the decision.

Summary

This chapter provided an overview of accounting research. Research was defined as a systematic process of investigating an issue of concern to the accountant. The importance of research was also identified and linked to standards overload, knowledge differentials, the dynamic nature of knowledge, emerging new problems, and legal support. To respond to the need for research, major accounting firms have developed organizational units and Internet-based systems with high levels of participation and authority to conduct professional research and to generate and maintain a knowledge base useful for practice. The new technology has helped accounting firms to develop elaborate systems for this purpose. However, smaller firms have access to technical resources of the AICPA and the FASB for responses to their research issues. The role of judgment was emphasized, particularly in the practice of public accounting, and some examples of judgment were provided. Due to time and cost considerations, the accountant may have to combine professional judgment with research to render a professional service.

The quality characteristics of good research were identified. Validity relating to purpose, rigor, testability, replicability, precision, confidence, and parsimony are major quality characteristics. Other characteristics include freedom from bias, variable isolation, and appropriate inferential logic.

The next issue discussed in the chapter was a dichotomous classification of research into scientific and professional. Scientific research is conducted primarily to generate and/or use new knowledge. It was discussed under three research subcategories of basic, or pure, applied, and instructional. The research methods used to carry them out were also identified. Professional research was identified as primarily applied research geared toward solving contemporary accounting problems facing accountants and their clients. This research is conducted primarily with a descriptive library and/or field research. Also, brief statements were provided concerning the timing of research where research can be pre-facto, post-facto, or predictive. More detailed discussion of the issues in this chapter is provided in the next few chapters.

Selected Additional Reading

For more information on professional research process in accounting, see:

Weirich, T. R., and A. Reinstein. *Accounting &; Auditing Research*, 4th ed. Cincinnati, OH: South-Western College Publishing, 1996.

Ziebart, D. A. *An Introduction to Applied Professional Research for Accountants*. Upper Saddle River, NJ: Prentice-Hall, 1998.

For a skill-building approach to a more general business research orientation see:

Sekaran, U. *Research Methods for Business: A Skill-Building Approach*, 3rd ed. New York: Wiley, 2000.

For detailed discussion of research issues from a scientific perspective, see:

Abdel-Khalik, A. R., and B. B. Ajinkya. *Empirical Research in Accounting: A Methodological Viewpoint*. Sarasota, FL: American Accounting Association, Accounting Education Series, Volume no. 4, 1979.

CGA Canada. *Research Methods in Accounting: Issues and Debates*, ed., A. J. Richardson. Vancouver, BC: CGA-Canada Research Foundation, Monograph No. 25, 1996.

Ryan, B.; R. W. Scapens; and M. Theobald. *Research Methods and Methodology in Finance and Accounting*. Boston, MA: Academic Press, 1992.

Wallace, W. A. *Accounting Research Methods: Do the Facts Speak for Themselves?* Boston, MA: Irwin, 1991.

Questions

1. Define research. What is the difference between scientific and professional research?

2. What is accounting and auditing research and why is it needed?

3. What is standards overload and how does it affect the need for professional research?

4. What are the three levels of expertise and how do they relate to the need for professional research?

5. Why do knowledge differentials exist between specialists and nonspecialists? Is specialization needed if you can find the answer through professional research?

6. Knowledge is said to be a moving target in accounting. How do you plan to manage this situation and keep up with new knowledge?

7. List five examples of new problems facing the accounting professional that did not exist, or existed but were insignificant, a decade ago.

8. What is the benefit of professional research in litigation support for accountants?

9. Describe a typical research unit within an accounting firm.

10. What does a policy committee on research do in an accounting firm?

11. What does an executive research committee do in an accounting firm?

12. What resources are available to smaller accounting firms to support their professional research?

13. What is the role of judgment in professional accounting research?

14. To be reliable, what characteristics must research have?

15. Explain freedom from bias in research. What is wrong with the researcher advocating a given point of view?

16. What is meant by internal validity? Is it possible to isolate variables of interest in research in "soft" fields of inquiry such as accounting?

17. What is meant by external validity? What inferential logic do you use to generalize from sample evidence to a population?

18. List and define various types of inferential logic.

19. Compare scientific and professional research.

20. Define basic, or pure, research and contrast it with applied research.

21. What is the goal of instructional research?

22. Compare normative, predictive, and descriptive research.

23. Compare pre- and post-facto research. What objectives do they serve?

THE CASE RESEARCH APPROACH

Error of Opinion may be tolerated where reason is left free to admit it.
Thomas Jefferson

Objectives

There are two major models of professional research. The first is the case analysis model where issues raised in a case study are subjected to research and analysis. The second research model is issue-based. It aims at understanding and solving contemporary accounting, auditing, and consulting problems via research. In this chapter, we discuss the case research approach, to be followed in the next chapter by a discussion of the sources of information for case analysis. Issue-based research is discussed in Chapter 5. Upon completion of this chapter, you will have learned:

1. A definition of case method research
2. Methods of developing cases
3. The differences between the case and problem approaches
4. Analysis of simple cases
5. A seven-step model for analysis of complex cases

The use of case studies as a research and teaching tool has increased over the past decade. A case study has two distinct parts: case development research and research geared toward case analysis. Case development requires field research where the researcher collects information about a client's problem area for the purpose of documenting and understanding the nature of the problem under investigation. The fieldwork performed by auditors for auditing or management advisory services is an example of this

45

investigation. Once the problem is documented in a case, detailed analysis is performed to solve the problem. In this chapter we define the case approach and provide a brief discussion of case development research. Most of the chapter discusses the nature of case analysis and its differences with the traditional exercise and problem approaches. Two case studies are also discussed to illustrate a simple case situation, as is a complex case study that required a multiple-step approach for its analysis.

A Definition of the Case Method

A case study is a documentation of a real-world situation. It is often used to represent a company with a focus on problem situations in need of research and resolution. Consequently, the case can be very detailed, encompassing many pages in which various aspects of the company are documented. For example, a case study can document the operations, finance, and marketing functions of a given company. Such a case study is useful for discussion of topics in operations research, marketing, accounting, and finance, or all of these combined such as management strategy. Alternatively, the case can be developed to focus on a specific analysis, such as an accounting or auditing application. These cases tend to be shorter and more focused than the more detailed and multifunctional cases.

Regardless of their level of detail, cases are less structured than specific problems used to reinforce various accounting or finance topics. The objective of cases is to explore, describe, and explain a client situation. The researcher then performs research and analysis to address problem areas identified in the case. The focus of this chapter is on the latter. However, a brief discussion of the research process to develop cases is presented below.

Case Development Research

Development of cases from practice is a complicated matter. It takes specialized skills and a detailed plan of action to develop a good case.[1] A summary of these requirements is presented in Exhibit 3–1. The first requirement is that the researcher must have the requisite knowledge and experience of the field, say accounting or auditing, to perform case development research. This is necessary for asking relevant and specialized questions. The researcher must also be able to interpret answers for follow-up questions and searches. Thus, the researcher must be a careful and unbiased listener as well as a good evidence collector.[2]

---

1. For a detailed discussion of the case development research see R. K. Yin, *Case Study Research: Design and Methods*, 2nd Ed. (Thousand Oaks, CA: Sage, 1994).
2. Ibid., pp. 54–59.

Exhibit 3-1	Case Development Research
Requirement	*Examples*
1. Researcher qualifications	Knowledge of the field and experience, good listener, unbiased
2. Case protocol	A detailed plan of action: who should be interviewed and when, what other sources of information should be used
3. Training of staff	Methods of data collection, multiple sources of information
4. Triangulation	Looking for multiple sources of information, coding and recording in databases, developing links between various types of evidence

The second requirement for case development research is a detailed plan of action, also called a *case protocol*. A detailed case protocol provides guidance on various aspects of the case. For example, if a client's personnel must be interviewed for the case development, the protocol must specify who should be interviewed for evidence, and when. Also, while the interviewer must be flexible and alert to ask questions relating to unforeseen issues, the protocol must have a set of questions for inquiry.

The third requirement relates to preparing the staff to conduct the case study research. For example, if there is a need for assistants to collect evidence, such assistants must be carefully selected and trained.[3] Finally, researchers must consult multiple sources, also called *triangulation,* to collect corroborating evidence. They should therefore be trained in various methods of data gathering. Such evidence must then be coded and entered into a case database in which the connections between various types of data can be identified and analyzed.[4]

The client data files of accounting firms provide a rich set of data for case development. However, these data files may not be sufficient for a detailed understanding of contemporary issues facing various clients. To address this issue, the accounting profession has developed programs for case development research. For example, the AICPA has a grant program in which academic and professional accountants team up to develop cases on contemporary accounting issues. Accounting firms also have programs for use of their client databases as well as field research to develop case studies. Through cooperation between the professional accountants in these firms, their clients, and academics, detailed and rich cases are developed for various areas. For example, in cooperation with the University of Illinois,

3. Ibid., pp. 63–77.
4. Ibid., pp. 90–99.

KPMG has a competitive grant program to develop multiple cases per year with a particular focus on strategic audits.

Cases can also be developed from a variety of other sources where detailed company information is stored. A very rich source of information is the archives of the SEC, since all public companies have to file Form 10-K annually, Form 10-Q quarterly, and Form 8-K for other important information as they occur. The information is accessible on the SEC's website (*www.sec.gov*), in its electronic database EDGAR, and the like. The SEC's Enforcement Division is a particularly rich source of data for companies that had been subject to some SEC enforcement action. The cases we have developed for this book are based on a variety of sources including the archives of accounting firms and SEC databases.

A Comparison between the Case and Problem-Solving Approaches

The exercise/problem-solving approach has traditionally been a favorite method of teaching accounting in the past. This approach uses very specific and highly structured exercise or problem sets to demonstrate and reinforce accounting concepts and methods studied in various courses. However, real world problems confronting the accounting professional seldom are as structured as the exercises or problems in various accounting courses. In fact, real world problems are often very complex and unstructured so much so that the professional accountant has to engage in research, analysis, and professional judgment to solve them. The case analysis model is helpful in preparing the accountant to tackle these real world problems and has become increasingly popular in the past decade. In addition, the case model requires the improvement of communication and critical thinking skills because these skills are needed for the analysis and reporting of the conclusions. These issues are addressed in other chapters. Major differences between the case model and the exercise/problem-solving approach are summarized in Exhibit 3–2.

The first major difference between the exercise/problem approach and the case model is the information setup. A problem or exercise is very limited in the amount of information provided. Usually, only specific information that relates to the problem is provided, thus shielding the problem solver from other information. The information is also clearly directed toward answering the questions asked. The case approach provides more information in the setup to indicate the more complex nature of the problem. This information can then be used for multiple objectives such as discussing the implications of the information on various alternative courses of action. Some of the information may even be irrelevant or redundant, requiring the researcher to ignore such information and focus only on relevant information just as the professional accountant has to do in a real world engagement.

Exhibit 3-2	Case and Problem Approaches: A Comparison	
Attribute	*Exercise/Problem Approach*	*Case Approach*
1. Information setup	Simple; short information set	Complex; detailed information set
2. Source of information	Hypothetical situations	Real world situations
3. Nature of questions	Very specific	Generally vague
4. Solution	Single	Multiple
5. Assumptions	Generally not needed	Generally needed
6. Authoritative source	Limited	Extensive
7. Synthesis	Not needed	Needed
8. Discussion	Generally not needed	Needed
9. Cognitive demand	Limited judgement	Extensive judgment
10. Justification	Easy	Complex
11. Report	Only the solution	Extensive report
12. Documentation	Limited	Extensive

The second difference between the two approaches is the source of information. While hypothetical situations are generally depicted in exercises and problems, case materials are adopted from real world situations. This is the reason the case model is said to be more realistic than the simple hypothetical exercises and problems.

The third difference is that in the problem approach, the questions asked are very specific. For example, you are specifically asked to calculate the ending inventory using the LIFO method. In the case model, the questions are generally vague. For example, you might be asked to analyze a company's selection of LIFO inventory pools to determine if management is attempting to manipulate earnings. Thus, to do a case analysis, one of the first challenges is to develop a set of specific objectives to be achieved by analyzing the case.

The fourth difference refers to whether there is only one solution or several alternative solutions. In general, exercises and problems specifically relate to one solution deterministically. The case approach, on the other hand, deals with alternative solutions, each with some degree of uncertainty. A problem that asks you to calculate the depreciation expense of a five-year-life asset with no salvage value using the straight-line method has one and only one solution. A case that presents various fixed assets that might be impaired will have multiple alternative depreciation amounts based on interpretation of the facts and circumstances.

The situation described above often requires making certain assumptions. This is the fifth difference between the case model and problems that generally do not require assumptions. All information is provided in the problem set. This is followed by the sixth difference that relates to the authoritative source. The problem approach often requires reference to a single source such as an intermediate accounting book, while case analysis is based on multiple sources of information and authoritative literature.

Because of the simplicity of the information search in the exercise/problem approach, there is no need for bringing the information search together (i.e., synthesis). On the other hand, the case model requires such a synthesis of information to make sense of the information collected and analyzed. It follows from the synthesis issue that generally there is no need for a detailed discussion in an exercise or problem. The case model, however, requires a discussion of major findings and their implications.

Difference number nine relates to another implication of the complexity of the case model, that of cognitive demand. Because of the need for search, synthesis, and analysis of information in the case model, the analyst must exercise extensive judgment. The case model requires the analyst to engage in much critical thinking and cognitive activity while the exercise/problem approach does not.

The final three differences relate to justification, report, and documentation. Once the judgment is made about a preferable solution in the case model, the analyst needs to support the choice with extensive evidence and justification as compared with a simple justification in the problem approach. The process used in a case model and its findings are written in a relatively extensive report as compared with a specific solution in the exercise/problem approach. While only the required solution is provided in the latter, the rationale, research, sources of information, and conclusions from the case process must be documented in a report. Finally, documentation of the case model is generally extensive, requiring careful filing for later retrieval. In comparison, the exercise/problem approach does not require much documentation in professional archives due to its simple nature.

Models of Case Analysis

Cases differ in many aspects and require different methods of study and analysis. Some cases have specific requirements designed to ensure that certain issues are discussed. These cases are similar to problems and exercises in their objective of reinforcing specific pedagogical issues. However, the differences noted in the previous section still apply. The specific requirements are simply designed to reduce the complexity of the case. Other cases are more complex in their objectives and orientation. They may have multiple objectives and may present information that contains some irrelevant data in addition to relevant data. Consequently, there is a need for different approaches to case analysis depending on the nature of the case. These approaches are discussed below.

Analysis of Simple Cases

We illustrate the analysis of simple cases by analyzing a sample case. The Woodside Recreation, Inc., case that is presented below has four specific requirements. This case illustrates that simple cases do not require extensive analysis of authoritative literature. However, the case does require careful analysis of the data in order to respond to the requirements. These requirements are not as specific as those seen in a typical accounting problem or exercise. Nevertheless, the discussion of the case can be directly tied to the case requirements.

ILLUSTRATIVE CASE	WOODSIDE RECREATION, INC.

Accounting Policies Relating to a Campground Developer/Seller of Campsites

Woodside Recreation, Inc., is an outdoor recreation company that develops campgrounds and sells memberships in them. Woodside buys raw land in areas having a population of at least 1 million within a three-hour drive of the land. It then develops the land to include facilities for tent camping and recreational vehicles. It also constructs a limited number of log cabins available for campers. Amenities typically include at least 300 acres of hiking trails, tennis courts, putting greens, swimming pools, and a clubhouse. Woodside has 60 campgrounds in 20 states located west of the Mississippi River.

Woodside aggressively markets lifetime memberships to its campgrounds at an average cost of $6,000 each and $30 per year in dues. Unlike the concept of resort time-sharing, membership does not convey ownership rights but only the right to use the facilities. Members can use the campgrounds as often as they like but are limited to three weeks at a time. Campgrounds limit the stay of members at any one campground so that members cannot make a campground a permanent home. Memberships are marketed primarily to middle-income families and retirees who as a group constitute 44 percent of the total membership.

Each campground has an average of 300 campsites. Woodside figures that it can sell 10 memberships for each campsite, or an average of 3,000 memberships per campground. To date, for campgrounds in operation more than three years, Woodside has sold an average of 6.8 memberships for each campsite and 5.6 memberships for the total number of planned campsites in all 60 campgrounds. Woodside opens a new campground after selling between 25 percent and 30 percent of all memberships for that campground. Campsite sales during the first three years of a campground's operation average 24 percent of total memberships for each campground. For all campgrounds in operation more than three years, membership sales average 2 percent annually of total memberships available for sale.

New members may pay their membership fee in cash or put as little as 10 percent down and execute an unsecured promissory note due in installments (including interest) over 72 months. During the last three years, 23 percent of new members' fees were received in cash. Woodside records the entire membership amount as membership sales revenue upon receiving a member's signed contract and the minimum down payment. Woodside has no obligation to refund money received or provide additional services to members in the event a membership is canceled for nonpayment of contractual obligations. Membership installment contracts receivable at December 31, 20X3 and 20X2, are as follows:

	(Dollars in thousands)	
	20X3	20X2
Installment contracts receivable	$ 45,600	$ 35,300
Allowance for sales cancellations		
and uncollectable accounts	(8,300)	(4,200)
	$ 37,300	$ 31,100

Approximately 85 percent of Woodside's revenues comes from new membership sales, and marketing expenses average 45 percent of membership sales. Operating revenues for the three years ended December 31, 20X3, 20X2, and 20X1, are as follows:

	(Dollars in thousands)		
	20X3	20X2	20X1
Membership sales	$ 28,000	$ 21,000	$ 16,800
Membership dues			
and miscellaneous	5,000	3,600	3,000
Provision for doubtful accounts	(5,600)	(3,500)	(2,400)
Net Operating Revenues	$ 27,400	$ 21,100	$ 17,400

Land acquisition and improvement costs are charged against membership sales revenue based on the ratio of memberships sold to the total memberships that Woodside estimates it will sell. The total memberships available for sale are based on Woodside's estimate of market demand for memberships of 10 memberships for each campsite. For example, if a campground could support 3,000 members and 300 memberships were sold during the year, 300/3,000 (10%) of costs would be charged against revenues. The unamortized balance of land acquisition and improvement costs is carried on the balance sheet as operating real estate and is stated at cost, net of an allowance reducing reported cost to estimated net realizable value. Operating real estate at December 31, 20X3, 20X2, and 20X1, was as follows:

	(Dollars in thousands)		
	20X3	20X2	20X1
Operating real estate	$162,000	$153,000	$148,000
Allowance for costs of			
membership sales	(82,000)	(70,000)	(62,000)
Operating real estate, net	$ 80,000	$ 83,000	$ 86,000

Woodside pledges substantially all installment contracts receivable as collateral for debt. The current debt to equity ratio is approximately 3.5 to 1.0.

Required
1. Discuss Woodside's accounting policies identified in the case in terms of the quality of Woodside's reported earnings and whether or not you agree with the accounting policies.
2. Identify any financial data that you would change due to a proposed change in an accounting policy. Be specific in your response and support your position with financial data.

3. Evaluate Woodside's cash flows. Support your position with financial data.
4. Discuss any other concerns that you have about
   Woodside's operations.

ILLUSTRATIVE CASE DISCUSSION

There are a number of "red flags" in the case that should raise questions concerning the company's earnings. In particular, the method of revenue recognition and method of allocating land acquisition and improvement costs are reason for concern. Also, liquidity problems are signaled by the data in the case. The case intentionally provides limited financial data in order to raise issues but not become overly involved in detailed calculations.

Requirement 1. The quality of earnings refers to how closely reported earnings correlate to cash flows. The higher the correlation, the higher the quality of earnings is judged to be. Low-quality earnings can mean that the bottom line is padded through the use of liberal accounting policies. When concerns exist over the quality of reported earnings, questions arise about a company's ability to sustain future earnings and the resultant effect on its stock price.

The obvious accounting policy issue is Woodside's method of recognizing revenue on membership sales. Woodside records the entire membership amount as sales revenue on receiving a member's signed contract and the 10 percent minimum down payment. Members execute an unsecured promissory note for the balance due, payable in installments (including interest) over 72 months. During the last three years, only 23 percent of new members paid in cash. Based on reported revenues, approximately 85 percent of Woodside's revenues are derived from membership sales.

Many point out that Woodside's method of revenue recognition is reasonable as long as Woodside makes an appropriate provision for uncollectible accounts and fully discloses the policy. They indicate that the installment method of recognizing revenue is generally not acceptable and cite *APB No. 10,* "Omnibus Opinion-1966," paragraph 12 which states: "Chapter 1A of *ARB No. 43,* paragraph 1, states that 'Profit is deemed to be realized when a sale in the ordinary course of business is effected, unless the circumstances are such that the collection of the sale price is not reasonably assured.' The Board reaffirms this statement; it believes that revenues should ordinarily be accounted for at the time a transaction is completed, with appropriate provision for uncollectible accounts. Accordingly, it concludes that, in the absence of the circumstances referred to above, the installment method of recognizing revenue is not acceptable." However, by analogy, it is interesting to note that according to *FAS No. 66,* "Accounting for Sales of Real Estate," most real estate sales would not qualify for the full accrual method with an initial down payment of 10 percent.

Since the case states that Woodside aggressively markets memberships, it is reasonable to assume that buyer qualification standards are probably minimal in light of the average cost of $6,000. The liberal purchase terms, including the buyer's unsecured note, are not incentives for the buyer to continue making payments on the note if the buyer incurs financial problems or becomes dissatisfied. Other than suspending membership privileges, Woodside does not appear to have much recourse against nonpayment. Therefore, not only do questions exist about the quality of earnings, but they exist about the collectibility of the installment receivables. The allowance for sales cancellations and uncollectible accounts as a percentage of installment contracts receivable is 11.9 percent in 20X2 and 18.2 percent in 20X3. The provision for doubtful accounts as a percentage of membership sales is 14.3 percent in 20X1, 16.7 percent in 20X2, and 20.0 percent in 20X3. These negative trends indicate existing problems and raise the question whether even now there is adequate provision.

The other questionable accounting policy is Woodside's method of allocating land acquisition and improvement costs against earnings. This is based on the ratio of memberships sold to total memberships which Woodside estimates that it will sell. Each campground has an average of 300 campsites, and Woodside estimates that it can sell 10 memberships for each campsite or an average of 3,000 memberships per campground. This method appears to lessen the charge against earnings because for each new membership sold, Woodside charges one-tenth of the campsite cost against earnings.

However, for campgrounds in operation more than three years, Woodside has sold an average of 6.8 memberships for each campsite, and membership sales after three years average 2 percent annually of total memberships available for sale. Woodside has sold an average of 5.6 memberships for the total number of planned campsites in all 60 of its campgrounds. All these facts make one question Woodside's estimate of 10 memberships for each campsite. Historical data suggests that it will take approximately 16 more years for campgrounds in operation more than three years to achieve the 10 memberships for each campsite. For example, if 68 percent (6.8 average per campsite) of 3,000 memberships are sold, then 960 memberships are unsold. At the rate of 2 percent annually of total memberships available, average annual sales of 60 memberships will take 16 years to sell the 960 memberships.

In conclusion, while both policies raise concerns, it is difficult to conclude that the policies are inappropriate. For revenue recognition, the allowance for estimated contract collection losses and sales cancellations should be monitored closely. Some suggest using the installment method for revenue recognition or deferring revenue recognition until a certain percentage of the installment contract (i.e., 25 percent) is collected.

As for the method of allocating land acquisition and improvement costs against earnings, the method appears reasonable but the assumption of 10 memberships per campsite is questionable. Some argue that this assumption needs to be reevaluated. Others note that the operating real estate might be accounted for in accordance with more traditional depreciation methods.

Requirement 2. As indicated in requirement 1, some focus on reporting membership sales on an installment basis or deferring revenue recognition until a certain percentage of the contract is collected. Others focus on increasing the provision for doubtful accounts and the related allowance. For example, an increase in the provision for doubtful accounts to 25 percent of 20X3 membership sales would result in a provision of $7 million and increase the related allowance account to $9.7 million.

As for the allocation of costs, many recommend revising the 10-to-1 ratio. For example, if the ratio is changed to 8-to-1, the 20X3 allowance for costs of membership sales would change from $82 million to approximately $85 million, and 20X3 earnings would decrease approximately $3 million.

Identifiable 20X3 operating data is not that encouraging. If one starts to revise that data, it can become less encouraging. For example, a comparison of 20X3 data with the changes illustrated is as follows:

	(Dollars in thousands)	
	As Reported	*As Revised*
Membership sales	$28,000	$28,000
Dues and miscellaneous	5,000	5,000
Provision for doubtful accounts	(5,600)	(7,000)
Net operating revenues	27,400	26,000
Marketing expenses (45%)	12,600	12,600
Land and improvement costs	12,000	15,000
	24,600	27,600
Income (loss)	$ 2,800	$(1,600)

The income (loss) amounts do not take into account general and administrative expenses, maintenance and operating expenses, and interest.

This case is based on Thousand Trails, Inc., once a high-flying stock on Wall Street that came crashing down. Significant operating losses were reported by Thousand Trails in 1986 and 1987. The company was recapitalized in 1987, and the net carrying value of assets reduced by $38.2 million. Real estate was adjusted in 1986 and 1987 because of the company's reevaluation of membership sales. Membership sales decreased in 1986 by more than 50 percent, and the 1986 provision for doubtful accounts approximated 32 percent of membership sales.

Requirement 3. Because of the fact that Woodside's sales are on an installment basis and its marketing expenses average 45 percent of membership sales, one should be suspicious of cash flow problems. Also, Woodside's high debt-to-equity ratio of approximately 3.5 to 1.0 and its pledge of substantially all installment contracts receivable as collateral for debt are possible signs of cash flow problems.

An analysis of case data supports this suspicion as follows:

	(Dollars in thousands) *20X3 Cash Collected*
Installment contracts receivable 1/1/X3	$35,300
20X3 membership sales	28,000
Total to collect	63,300
Accounts written off	(1,500)*
	61,800
Less: installment contracts receivable 12/31/X3	(45,600)
Cash collected	16,200
Dues and miscellaneous (assumed collected)	5,000
	$21,200

*Beginning allowance $4,200 plus provision $5,600 less ending allowance $8,300.

The $21.2 million must cover marketing costs ($12.6 million accrual basis), operating real estate acquisition costs ($9.0 million), debt service, general and administrative expenses, and maintenance and operating expenses. It is safe to conclude that Woodside has a cash flow problem. Under such circumstances, if possible, a company would continue to borrow and/or raise equity from investors. Some day, the situation is supposed to change and then more cash is supposed to come from sales than creditors and investors. Of course, if that day never arrives, the investors will lose out. In this case the creditors have some protection because the debt is collateralized by receivables.

Requirement 4. This question is open ended and responses vary from financial in nature to operational. In addition to those previously discussed, selected concerns and comments are as follows:

- Marketing costs are too high.
- Financial position could deteriorate quickly in a recession.
- The sales of lifetime campground memberships could be a fad.
- Consumers should think twice about buying a membership. Why spend $6,000 when public campgrounds are inexpensive and readily available?
- If memberships are transferable, there probably is a very limited secondary market for owners to sell their memberships.
- Woodside cannot continue indefinitely to finance expansion by borrowing against receivables.
- As memberships are the primary source of revenues, Woodside will have to continue to add new locations for earnings to grow.
- Woodside is a house of cards ready to fold.

Analysis of Complex Cases

The Woodside Recreation, Inc. case in the previous section illustrated the point that a simple case study still requires analysis that goes well beyond that required for specific accounting problems or exercises. For more complex cases, we need a more detailed case analysis. These cases require that a set of objectives for the case solution be developed so that the discussion will have some structure. The Cullen Provision Corporation case and its related discussion are included in the following section to illustrate these points. Cullen does not require an extensive amount of research, but it illustrates that once the literature is identified and studied, a decision is not necessarily clear-cut. More complex cases are discussed in the following chapters that require significant search of the literature. They also require much professional judgment for analysis.

To facilitate case analysis for complex cases, a general model has been developed over time. This model has seven steps as summarized in Exhibit 3–3. These steps are briefly discussed below and then used to analyze the Cullen Provision Corporation case in the next section.

In the first step, a set of objectives for analysis is identified. The objectives range from the broad topical category of the case, such as revenue recognition, to a more specific objective, such as revenue from software sales. The analyst will then focus on more specific objectives, such as calculation of income and earnings per share, for the specific situation described in the case. Obviously, this step can be skipped if the case has

Exhibit 3-3	Case Analysis and Reporting Method
Step	*Purpose*
1. Identify the objectives of the case	To identify a set of specific objectives for analysis
2. Professional literature search (Begin with a set of key words)	To find the professional literature applicable to the objectives of the case
3. Discussion	To identify linkages between the professional literature and the specifics of the case
4. List alternative solutions	To clearly identify possible solutions
5. Suggested solution	To select a viable solution from the list of alternative solutions
6. Supplements	To provide exhibits, figures, tables, appendices, etc.
7. Addendum	To present additional information of potential importance (e.g., pending exposure drafts, court cases)

already presented the researcher with specific questions. However, failure to establish specific objectives will result in an aimless case analysis.

In the second step, the analyst identifies the professional pronouncements and other literature that are applicable to the case. For example, if the issue relates to the disposal of long-lived assets, then the analyst will identify *SFAS No. 121*, "Accounting for the Impairment of Long-Lived Assets and for Long-Lived Assets to Be Disposed Of."[5] Other related pronouncements and interpretations related to the issue will also be identified, as will similar cases from the literature. For example, a search of the AICPA's *Accounting Trends and Techniques* might provide data on practices by other companies.

This step is perhaps the most crucial in the case analysis. Traditionally, accountants consulted reference books, tables of contents, and indices of professional publications to analyze cases. While these methods are still useful, electronic search has made this process more efficient and complete. Various sources of information are discussed in Chapter 4.

In the third step, the relevant parts of the professional literature identified in step 2 are examined and their relevancy to the case under investigation is discussed. For example, suppose that you have identified *SFAS No. 94*, "Consolidation of All Majority-Owned Subsidiaries," in your discussion of the issues related to a case on consolidations. Now you want to examine the issue of "controlling interest." Your search will identify this paragraph:

> The usual condition for controlling financial interest is ownership of a majority voting interest, and, therefore, as a general rule ownership by one company, directly or indirectly, of over fifty percent of the outstanding voting shares of another company is a condition pointing to consolidation.[6]

Not all sources consulted have the same level of authority. The higher the level of authority, the stronger the level of support for the discussion. In cases where no authoritative literature is found, the analyst needs to consult other sources of information and also make professional judgments.

Step 3 requires most of the analysis and may require a mini-organization of its own. Here, the extant literature must not only be identified, but carefully read, interpreted, and applied to the facts and circumstances of the case. This is not always easy considering the highly technical format of the professional literature.

In the fourth step, the analyst identifies all viable alternative solutions and their impacts. For example, in a case that may be interpreted as a lease

---

5. Financial Accounting Standards Board, *Statement of Financial Accounting Standards No. 121*, "Accounting for the Impairment of Long-Lived Assets and for Long-Lived Assets to Be Disposed Of" (Norwalk, CT, 1995).

6. Financial Accounting Standards Board, *Statement of Financial Accounting Standards No. 94*, "Consolidation of All Majority-Owned Subsidiaries" (Stamford, CT, 1987), par 13.

situation, the analyst may list three alternatives: (1) capital lease, (2) operating lease, and (3) no lease at all. A simple listing of course is not sufficient. The characteristics of each of these alternatives must be identified to ease the process into the next step, suggested solution, in which the analyst selects the most viable solution. The reasons and a summary of the authoritative literature for this selection are then provided to support the choice.

Any supplements or addenda (steps 6 and 7) are presented at the end. Often reference to detailed appendices, figures, charts, exhibits, or tables is necessary somewhere in the discussion of the case or the suggested solution. However, inclusion of the detailed information can divert the readers' attention away from the main issues. For this reason, the analyst includes these sources of information as supplements to the case by placing them at the end of the report. Also, preparation of an addendum is needed to communicate information that is not directly related to the current case but may become relevant in the future. For example, in discussing an issue that is currently being debated (e.g., a bill under debate in Congress or an exposure draft issued by the FASB), the analyst adds a paragraph stating what is likely to happen as a result of such debates. Alternatively, there may be new information on the case that can be shared. For example, suppose that the case under discussion relates to a going concern judgment situation. If new information becomes available indicating that the client represented in the case has filed for bankruptcy protection, then relevant pieces of the information should be provided in the addendum.

While not all steps are relevant or necessary for every case, most are needed for a complete analysis of the case. Many cases in this text do not lend themselves to all seven steps of case analysis. However, case analyses should include the appropriate steps. For example, a case requirement might ask for recommendations concerning a course of action. An appropriate response would include an identification of the relevant literature, discussion of alternatives, and well-supported recommendations. Any supplement or addendum would be presented as needed.

ILLUSTRATIVE CASE	CULLEN PROVISION CORPORATION

Recognition of a Contingent Gain

The Cullen Provision Corporation is a processor and distributor of meats and meat by-products. In 20X1 Cullen sold to the Department of the Army a quantity of precooked hams that failed to meet governmental specifications. The Army Procurement Office delayed in processing the paperwork for return of the purchase, and as a result of the delay, a significant amount of the ham was returned in a spoiled condition. The Cullen Provision Corporation thus incurred a loss on the spoiled ham of $880,000 and wrote the loss off against income in 20X1.

Legal counsel for Cullen advised the company to file a claim through appropriate channels with the Department of the Army, requesting reimbursement for the $880,000 loss due to breach of contract and negligence in the return of the rejected precooked hams. Cullen filed the claim as advised, but as of its year-end December 31, 20X1, and prior to the issuance of the accountants' report on Cullen's 20X1 financial statements, the claim had not been settled. Therefore, the company did not record the claim as a receivable, nor did it disclose the claim, because its collection could not be reasonably assured.

The matter remained unresolved throughout 20X2, but early in 20X3, prior to the issuance of the accountants' report for year end 20X2, Cullen agreed to a settlement of $475,000. The settlement is material in relation to earnings before income taxes for the year ended December 31, 20X2.

The management of Cullen feels strongly that the $475,000 settlement should not be reported in the 20X2 financial statements because the economic event occurred in 20X3, and the payment has not yet been received. Management also opposes recognition in 20X2 because it fears that the deferment of the gain for income tax purposes and not for financial reporting would be challenged by the Internal Revenue Service (IRS) in an attempt to accelerate taxation of the gain into 20X2. Last, management points out that recognition of the gain for book purposes in 20X2 would cause the additional payment of $600,000 of principal on a non-interest-bearing note payable to the previous owners of the Cullen Provision Corporation under the terms of the purchase agreement. The agreement provides that the purchase price would be adjusted and paid by the company to the former owner if a certain level of income is attained as determined in accordance with generally accepted accounting principles.

The managing tax partner of Cullen's independent accountants expressed the opinion that should the IRS challenge the position of recognizing the gain for tax purposes in 20X3, the company would likely prevail. However, he did point out that any such challenge by the IRS would be disruptive and costly for Cullen.

The senior auditor for the independent accountants disagreed with management's position. She maintained that the settlement of the claim was a subsequent event that required adjustment of the December 31, 20X2, financial statements.

Required

1. Discuss how and when this transaction should be accounted for and the basis for your decision. Identify any accounting pronouncements that support your position.
2. Does it make any difference in your response if the settlement involves a contingent gain or loss?

ILLUSTRATIVE CASE DISCUSSION

This case addresses the timing for the recognition of a contingent gain. It is obvious when the company wants to recognize the gain, but the facts indicate some hesitancy on the part of the independent accountants to agree with the company's desire. Depending on the accounting literature that one focuses on, arguments can be made to recognize the gain in either period under consideration.

Students tend to be evenly divided as to when the gain should be recognized. When discussing the case, it is helpful for students to identify all the relevant literature that they have consulted and explain how it entered into their decision. It is important to discuss the fact that disagreement with the company's position means added cost and a possible tax audit for the company. Many students are troubled by being placed in this position, and some are hesitant to make a decision.

The case discussion that follows incorporates the relevant steps of the case analysis model discussed in the chapter. The obvious objective of the case is to determine the timing for the recognition of the contingent gain. Key word searches identifying gains, contingent gains, contingencies, and/or subsequent events should lead to the appropriate sources of literature. The case discussion includes an identification and discussion of the authoritative literature, alternative solutions, and conclusion. Steps involving supplements and an addendum are not needed for this case.

Requirement 1. There are several sources of literature that will be helpful in deciding when the $475,000 settlement should be recognized. As noted in the case, the senior auditor maintained that this was a subsequent event requiring adjustment of the December 31, 20X2, financial statements. *SAS No. 1*, Section 560, "Subsequent Events," indicates that financial statements should be adjusted for any changes in estimates that subsequent evidence indicates is pertinent to conditions that existed at the balance sheet date. An example of such a situation is the settlement of litigation for an amount different from the recorded liability, where the cause of the litigation took place prior to the balance sheet date. Section 560 goes on to indicate that subsequent events with respect to conditions that did not exist at the balance sheet date do not require adjustment of the financial statements. Most of the examples in this *SAS* relate to liabilities or impairment of assets and do not make reference to contingent gains. However, using this standard, one could conclude that the December 31, 20X2, financial statements should be adjusted because the condition existed at the balance sheet date (claim was pending), and the 20X3 settlement agreement confirms the existence of the claim.

Another source of literature is *SFAS No. 5*, "Accounting for Contingencies." The situation at hand fits the definition of a contingency in paragraph 1 as: "an existing condition, situation, or set of circumstances involving uncertainty as to possible gain or loss to an enterprise that will ultimately be resolved when one or more future events occur or fail to occur." *SFAS No. 5*, dated March 1975, addresses loss contingencies, but indicates that *ARB No. 50*, "Contingencies," has not been reconsidered with respect to gain contingencies. *FAS No. 5*, paragraph 17, indicates that the following provisions of *ARB No. 50* shall continue in effect:

a. Contingencies that might result in gains usually are not reflected in the accounts since to do so might be to recognize revenue prior to its realization.

b. Adequate disclosure shall be made of contingencies that might result in gains, but care shall be exercised to avoid misleading implications as to the likelihood of realization.

Based on this, one could argue that agreement to a settlement does not constitute realization, and therefore, recognition of the gain contingency should be postponed until 20X3 when and if realization takes place. This would certainly be the more conservative approach. The argument would appear to find support in *CON No. 5*, "Recognition and Measurement in Financial Statements of Business Enterprises," paragraph 83, which addresses the terms *realized* or *realizable* and *earned*. Keeping in mind that since the concern is over a gain, being earned is not significant in this case.

A third, but somewhat obscure, source of literature pertinent to this case is *SFAS No. 16*, "Prior Period Adjustments," Appendices A and C, dated June 1977. This *SFAS* was issued partly in response to *SAB No. 8*, dated June 1976. *SAB No. 8* responded to the question whether out-of-court settlements meet the criteria for prior period adjustments. This *SAB* indicated "that settlements would constitute economic events of the period in which they occur," rather than a prior period, primarily because they are made at the discretion of management and thus do not meet the criterion that a prior period event "depend primarily on determinations by persons other than management" (criterion C of paragraph 23, *APB No. 9*, "Reporting the Results of Operations"). Accordingly, the SEC opposed treating such settlements as prior period adjustments. It appears that *SFAS No. 16* supports the view that settlements constitute economic events of the period in which they occur. Thus using *SAB No. 8*, as reaffirmed by *SFAS No. 16* limiting prior period adjustments, one can argue that the settlement by Cullen in 20X3 constitutes an economic event of 20X3, and the gain should be recognized in 20X3.

In conclusion, Cullen may recognize the gain in 20X3 because this combination of pronouncements, especially *SAS No. 1*, appears to permit, but does not require, the adjustment of the December 31, 20X2, financial statements. One basis for reporting in 20X3 is that the case involves a gain contingency, and following conservatism, gain contingencies usually are not recognized until realized. Another is the fact that settlements are economic events of the period in which they occur. A third is that the evidence supporting 20X3 recognition is somewhat more current and reflects more recent philosophy than *SAS No. 1*, issued in 1972. Last, as a practical matter, the fact that recognition of the gain in 20X2 would cause Cullen to pay an additional $600,000 on a purchase agreement and might be challenged by the IRS if the gain is deferred for tax purposes cannot be ignored in making this decision. While one might not openly articulate this as influencing their decision, it must be addressed. A number of students have responded to this issue by indicating that the auditor should just agree with the client; end of discussion.

As a post case comment, it should be noted that if Cullen had wanted to recognize the gain in 20X2, a case could probably have been convincingly made to its auditors.

Requirement 2. The point of the question is to recognize that the responses are quite different if the settlement had involved a loss contingency instead of a gain. If a loss, an adjustment of the 20X2 financial statements would probably be required. In that situation, *SFAS No. 5* and *FIN No. 14*, "Reasonable Estimation of the Amount of a Loss," would apply. The key would be that it is probable that a loss had been incurred and the amount could reasonably be estimated.

Summary

We introduced the case research approach in this chapter. We defined cases as scenarios based on real world situations. These cases can be very detailed, encompassing various business functions such as operations, marketing, and finance, or focus on narrower issues in a specific function such as accounting. We distinguished between case development research and the research needed to analyze cases. For case development research, we identified four requirements of researcher qualifications, research protocol, staff training, and research triangulation.

For case analysis, we classified cases as simple or complex, depending on the objectives of the case, and provided illustrative cases for each. For simple cases, we presented analysis that is directly tied to the specific requirements of the case. For more complex cases, we provided a model with seven specific steps for case analysis. These steps begin with the identification of specific objectives and proceed to searching the professional literature for guidance. A discussion of the relevant literature and the listing of alternative solutions follow this step. The final three steps are: suggesting a solution, providing supplements (e.g., exhibits and appendices), and presenting addenda (e.g., pending exposure draft and court cases).

Questions

1. Define the case research approach.
2. What are the two major categories of the case research approach?
3. List four important requirements for case development research and provide an example of each.
4. What are the differences between multifunctional case studies and the more function-specific cases?
5. What is the objective of a case study?
6. Compare simple cases with complex cases.
7. What are the major differences between the exercise/problem approach and the case model of analysis?
8. Why has the case model become so popular in recent years?
9. Distinguish between two types of case models— one with specific requirements and one with more general requirements.
10. What are the steps in a complex case analysis?
11. What would be a consequence of a failure to identify the objectives in a case analysis?

12. To analyze a case, is it sufficient to consult your intermediate accounting book? What should be done?

13. What is involved in the discussion step of a case model analysis?

14. In listing alternative solutions to a case, should you list nonpractical alternatives as well? Why?

15. The suggested solution to a case can be summarized in one or two paragraphs. What type of evidence would you provide to support your choice

16. What is the purpose of providing supplements or addenda in your case model report?

17. Are all seven steps necessary for an analysis of all complex cases?

AUTHORITATIVE SOURCES OF INFORMATION

4

Literature is news that stays news.
Ezra Pound

Objectives

This chapter covers the hierarchy of authoritative literature and the
sources of information for professional research. These sources are useful
for finding the information needed for case analysis as discussed in
Chapter 3. They are also useful for finding information for the remaining
chapters. The volume of information contained in authoritative literature
is detailed and complex. Major sources of information and search methods
for finding the needed professional guidance are identified and briefly
explained in the chapter. While some of the manual sources provide access
to the original texts of authoritative pronouncements, the proliferation of
electronic media in recent years has made the search more comprehensive
and efficient. The chapter provides a discussion of the electronic sources
and their search engines, but a short coverage of manual sources is also
provided. A case study is presented and analyzed using one of the
electronic databases discussed in the chapter. Upon completion of the
chapter, you will have learned the:

1. Primary authoritative sources from promulgatory organizations
2. Primary authoritative sources from regulatory organizations
3. Publications of private organizations and societies
4. Authoritative hierarchy of the professional literature
5. Major electronic sources of information
6. Guidelines for searching the World Wide Web
7. Guidelines for searching accounting-specific databases.

As discussed in an earlier chapter, the model of standard setting in the United States is mixed, covering promulgatory organizations, regulatory agencies, and private associations. These organizations generate a wealth of information for professional research. Indeed, there is such a proliferation of literature that making a decision on what sources to use requires a systematic approach, as well as a good understanding of GAAP and sound professional judgment. Consequently, an issue of concern for research is the extent and the quality of the literature that one needs to consult. In general, it is desirable to conduct an exhaustive search and synthesis of the research literature. However, such an exhaustive search might render the research very costly for the professional accountant. Professional accountants do not always have the luxury of time to conduct an exhaustive search or access to all possible sources of literature for every issue. Instead, they conduct searches for the most authoritative literature that is necessary to make an informed judgment and decision for the research issue under investigation. The authoritative literature is discussed in the first section of this chapter.

The second section focuses on databases and search engines. A summary of major manual sources of authoritative literature is provided first. However, the main focus in this section is on electronic indices, databases, and search engines as powerful tools for finding relevant information. An illustrative case study is also discussed, followed by a word on future electronic search engines and a summary of the chapter.

Authoritative Sources of Literature

What sources of literature have the highest authority for applied research in accounting? The answer to this question depends on the nature of the research question and the type of research to be conducted. For example, for a financial accounting issue, the logical sources that first come to mind are the AICPA, the FASB, and the SEC, as well as many other sources that publish journals and books dealing with financial accounting issues. For tax research, one thinks primarily of the Internal Revenue Code and Regulations as well as court cases and professional journals dedicated to tax research (e.g., *The Journal of the American Taxation Association*). For managerial and cost accounting issues, the Cost Accounting Standards Board's (CASB) publications as well as publications of the Institute of Management Accountants (IMA) and professional journals contain relevant information.

Thus, what is needed is knowledge of the primary publications of these organizations as the sources of professional literature. For financial accounting research, the most authoritative publications of the FASB include the following:

- *Statements of Financial Accounting Standards*
- *Interpretations*

- *Technical Bulletins*
- *Implementation Guides*
- *Emerging Issues Task Force Positions*

Although not published by the FASB, *Accounting Research Bulletins (ARB)* that were issued by the AICPA's Committee on Accounting Procedures before 1959 as well as *APB Opinions* issued by the Accounting Principles Board from 1959 to 1973 still constitute GAAP unless superseded or amended by other authoritative bodies. They are available from the AICPA. Also, the AICPA publishes *Statements of Position (SOP)* that state AICPA's positions on issues under the FASB's consideration. These *SOPs* constitute GAAP unless superseded by an FASB statement. The Accounting Standards Executive Committee (AcSEC) of the AICPA publishes *Practice Bulletins* that provide guidance on how the AICPA believes a transaction should be reported. Similarly, the AICPA's *Audit and Accounting Guides* provide guidance on accounting and auditing practices in a variety of specific situations.

AICPA's industry-specific publications are geared specifically toward providing guidance for accounting and auditing in specific industries. These publications include *Checklist for Defined Benefit Pension Plans and Illustrative Financial Statements, Checklist Supplement and Illustrative Financial Statements for Construction Contractors, Checklists and Illustrative Financial Statements for Banks.* Some of the other industries covered are credit unions, finance companies, and nonprofit organizations. Also, the AICPA has *The Journal of Accountancy,* published monthly, and *The CPA Letter,* published 10 times a year, that provide information on the developments in the profession as well as news and practical articles.

Publications from regulatory organizations are varied and numerous as well. They include publications from the Federal Trade Commission, the Internal Revenue Service, and other regulatory agencies such as the SEC and the CASB. For example, the SEC's authoritative publications include:

- *Financial Reporting Releases*
- *Staff Accounting Bulletins*
- *Accounting and Auditing Enforcement Releases*
- *Concept and Interpretive Releases*

Financial Reporting Releases are issued by the SEC to communicate filing requirements and accounting opinions on a variety of issues. *The Staff Accounting Bulletins* reflect the opinions of the SEC accounting staff concerning financial reporting issues. These bulletins have the power of the SEC behind them and are enforceable. Thus, they form an authoritative guideline. *Accounting and Auditing Enforcement Releases* communicate the SEC's enforcement and disciplinary actions, and *Litigation Releases* provide descriptions of civil and selected criminal proceedings of the SEC in federal courts. Finally, the *Concept and Interpretive Releases* provide a guide on the SEC's positions on concepts and their interpretations.

Perhaps the most publications come from private associations, organizations, companies, and state societies. These publications deal with issues ranging in scope from corporate accounting policy and financial reporting to the impact of standard setting on the society. General examples are the Standards & Poor's publications, Dun & Bradstreet publications, and research reports and journals from public accounting firms, state societies of CPAs, and professional associations. Appendix 4A provides a list of journals published by various publishers, professional associations, and academic institutions.

CPA societies serve their members in a variety of ways. Part of this service is through the publication of newsletters or journals that contain interpretations of standards and practices, personal experiences, case studies, and practice tips. Some of these publications have gained national reputation and prominence for the quality of their contents. *The CPA Journal* published by the New York Society of CPAs, *The Ohio CPA Journal, The Massachusetts CPA Review,* and *The Wisconsin CPA* are examples of these publications.

The American Accounting Association (AAA) is the primary professional organization of accounting professors in the U.S., although it also has a small membership of practicing accountants and international academic members. Its long list of publications includes a number of influential journals, newsletters, research monographs, and statements. In addition to its occasional statements (e.g., *A Statement of Basic Accounting Theory* that the AAA published in 1966 and *Statement on Accounting Theory and Theory Acceptance* that it published in 1977), the AAA has multiple periodic publications for various audiences. For example, its quarterly journal, *The Accounting Review,* publishes papers that are rigorous in nature and deal primarily with fundamental academic research issues. Another quarterly journal of the AAA is *Accounting Horizons.* It deals primarily with issues of interest to both academic and professional accountants, with the bulk of its content related to financial accounting and reporting issues. *Issues in Accounting Education* primarily deals with research issues for accounting education.

Authoritative Hierarchy of GAAP

The success of the researcher in developing a viable solution to the issue or problem at hand depends on the quality and sufficiency of evidence used in the research process. The sufficiency of the evidence is a matter of professional judgment. There has to be enough evidence, and sufficient analysis or synthesis of this evidence, to afford a convincing argument for the course of action selected. However, the professional researcher is not expected to examine every single publication or authoritative pronouncement—only a sufficient sample of those most relevant to the problem or issue. In other words, a reasonable amount of literature search, data collection and analysis (if applicable), and synthesis is needed. What constitutes a reasonable amount is left to the judgment of the accountant. However, the AICPA's Code of Conduct specifies the standards of judgment and due professional care.

The quality of evidence also depends on the authoritative nature of the professional literature used and the care with which data, if any, were collected. Research quality depends on the characteristics that make research reliable, as discussed in Chapter 2. In practical research, where the solution to the research problem depends on the use of appropriate authoritative pronouncements, research quality refers to the position of the literature in the GAAP hierarchy. GAAP hierarchy refers to the authoritative power of the source used. The AICPA has established the hierarchy of authoritative GAAP in *SAS No. 69*, "The Meaning of 'Present Fairly in Conformity with Generally Accepted Accounting Principle' in the Independent Auditor's Report" as presented in Exhibit 4–1.

Exhibit 4-1	GAAP Hierarchy	
Hierarchy	*Pronouncement*	*Source*
First level	*Statements of Financial Accounting*	
	Standards (SFAS)	FASB
	FASB Interpretations (FIN)	FASB
	Accounting Principles Board (APB)	
	Opinions and Interpretations	APB
	Accounting Research Bulletins (ARB)	CAP
Second level	*Technical Bulletins (FTB)*	FASB
	Industry Audit and Accounting Guides	AICPA
	Statements of Position (SOP)	AICPA
Third Level	Consensus positions of the Emerging Issues	
	Task Force (EITF)	FASB
	Accounting Standards Executive Committee	
	(AcSEC)'s *Practice Bulletins*	AICPA
Fourth level	Staff accounting interpretation (AIN)	AICPA
	Implementation guides (Q's and A's)	FASB
	Widely recognized and prevalent	
	industry practices	
Fifth level	*Statements of Financial Accounting Concepts*	FASB
	Issues Papers	AICPA
	AICPA Technical Practice Aids	AICPA
	International Accounting Standards	
	Committee pronouncement	IASC
	Pronouncements of other professional	
	associations or regulatory agencies	Miscellaneous
	GASB statements, interpretations,	
	and technical bulletins	GASB
	Accounting textbooks, handbooks, or articles	

Adapted from *SAS No. 69*, "The Meaning of Present Fairly in Conformity with Generally Accepted Accounting Principle in the Independent Auditor's Report."

The highest level of authority consists of the pronouncements issued by the primary organizations involved with standards setting. For example, the FASB's standards and interpretations form the most authoritative level of literature for financial accounting. The pronouncements issued by the APB and its predecessor, the CAP, if not superseded or amended by other pronouncements also form the first level of authority. Likewise, pronouncements from the CASB form the authoritative literature for cost accounting. The GASB's pronouncements form the authoritative literature for governmental accounting. The Auditing Standards Board's statements and the SEC rules form authoritative literature for auditing.

The second level of authority consists of the FASB's technical bulletins, the AICPA's industry audit and accounting guides, and AICPA's statements of position. The third level of authority is assigned to the consensus positions of the FASB's Emerging Issues Task Force and the AICPA's Practice Bulletins issued by its Accounting Standards Executive Committee. This is followed by the fourth level of authority that is based on the AICPA's accounting interpretations, the FASB's implementation guides, and widely recognized and prevalent industry practices.

The difference between levels three and four authority is that expert bodies in level four publish their guides without prior exposure to public comment. The Accounting Standards Executive Committee (AcSEC), the senior technical committee of the AICPA, publishes bulletins called *Practice Bulletins* that are examples of this level of authority for financial accounting. These bulletins are very practice oriented and assist accountants and auditors in a variety of procedural issues. The Emerging Issues Task Force (EITF) of the FASB also issues its statements on problems too narrow for the FASB's consideration.

Finally, after considering the previous four levels of authoritative literature, if the researcher does not find guidance to resolve the issue, he or she has a host of other literature to search. Examples include *SFACs,* AICPA *Issues Papers,* International Accounting Standards, and other professional associations or regulatory agencies, textbooks, and articles. This literature includes many publications from professionally oriented sources such as *Journal of Accountancy* and *The Practical Accountant* to academic journals such as *The Accounting Review.* The AICPA has research monographs and industry practice manuals that are helpful, as do many other professional organizations in the U.S. and elsewhere in the world.

The GAAP hierarchy presented in Exhibit 4–1 is in the context of financial accounting. Nevertheless, the framework in the exhibit applies well to other areas of accounting and auditing with some modification. For example, the hierarchy that relates to auditing begins with generally accepted auditing standards (GAAS), continues with statements on auditing standards (SAS), the Code of Conduct, interpretations, and industry guides, and ends with academic and professional publications.

It is important to note that the SEC has the coercive legal power to set the form, content, and accounting methods for its financial accounting and reporting requirements. Thus, the SEC's requirements are above the GAAP hierarchy in Exhibit 4–1. However, since the SEC has allowed GAAP to be promulgated by the private sector, the pronouncements of these authorized promulgatory organizations form the highest level of authority subject to occasional SEC overwrite.

Indices, Databases, and Search Engines

Manual Indices

While electronic indices and databases are quickly taking over as the main sources of information, manual sources of information are also available from business libraries and the publishers of these manual indices. Many accounting firms, especially smaller ones, still subscribe to some of these manual sources of information. Since these publications are based on the text of the original pronouncements and their interpretation from the standard-setting organizations, they provide a high level of confidence for many professional accountants using them. A summary list is provided in Exhibit 4–2. The exhibit is presented in four categories: accounting and auditing standards; annual reports and financial ratios; international accounting; and various dictionaries, handbooks, and textbooks. Publication examples are provided for each of these categories.

The accounting and auditing standards are generally published by their originators in a loose-leaf form so that they can easily be updated by their subscribers. For example, the loose-leaf publication of accounting standards by the FASB provides the original text of FASB's pronouncements, thus the loose-leaf is updated every time a new standard is issued. The FASB also publishes *the EITF Abstracts* that cover *EITF's Summaries* and *Technical Bulletins*. Likewise, the AICPA publishes auditing standards in *AICPA Professional Standards*. It also publishes a number of audit and accounting manuals and industry guides.

A number of publishers issue manual reports covering financial reports of many companies in comparison with their corresponding industries. These manuals include the annual publication of *Accounting Trends and Techniques* by the AICPA. In this report, data from surveys of 600 companies are provided as descriptive evidence of prevalent accounting practice. Thus, information is provided on the accounting methods used and the type of disclosure provided by various companies surveyed.

The third category, international accounting, covers publications providing information on various countries in the world. Major international accounting firms provide publications on the accounting, auditing, and tax requirements of doing business in many countries. The AICPA also has a publication providing information on professional accounting in foreign countries. However, generally, the country-specific publications of

---

**Exhibit 4-2   Examples of Major Manual Indices
                   for Accounting Research**

Accounting and Auditing Standards

Accounting Standards, Current Text. A loose-leaf FASB publication of current financial accounting standards, organized by subject

AICPA Professional Standards. Current *Statements on Auditing Standards* issued by the Auditing Standards Board of the AICPA, organized by topic

Audit and Accounting Manual. AICPA's practice aids

Audit and Accounting Guides. AICPA's general and industry guides for specific accounting and auditing issues

EITF Abstracts A loose-leaf publication of the FASB that provides the Emerging Issues Task Force summaries

Annual Reports and Financial Ratios

Accounting Trends and Techniques. AICPA's annual survey of companies concerning their accounting practices, alternative accounting methods used, and types of disclosure

Annual Statements Studies. Robert Morris Associates' five-year comparative ratios for over 300 industries

Industry Norms and Key Business Ratios. Dun & Bradstreet's five-year comparative ratios for over 800 industries

International Accounting

Doing Business in . . . Booklets published by accounting firms such as Ernst and Young and PricewaterhouseCoopers that cover accounting, auditing, tax, and legal issues for doing business in the country covered in the booklet

Professional Accounting in Foreign Countries. AICPA's publication discussing major international accounting and auditing issues

Various Dictionaries, Handbooks, and Textbooks

Numerous entries here. Examples are *Accountant's Handbook* and *Handbook for Accounting and Auditing.* They provide information on topics such as standard-setting organizations, presentation and analysis of financial reports, and specialized accounting for various industries.

---

international accounting firms are more detailed and more specific to the country that the report covers. For example, Ernst and Young publishes booklets called *Doing Business in . . . (a country)*. These booklets cover information about regulatory requirements of accounting, auditing, tax, and general business in various countries from big countries to very small states such as the tiny state of Bahrain in the Persian Gulf.

Electronic Databases and Search Engines

As discussed in the previous section, professional literature is very rich with numerous sources of information and a variety of authoritative hierarchies. It is practically impossible for an accountant to know even the names of all these sources of information, let alone their content. This is

where the information technology has had a major impact. Powerful electronic databases and search engines are now available in which various publications have been indexed for ease of search and retrieval. Typically, the researcher enters a number of key words into the database for search. The database responds by listing the documents in which it has matched the key words. The researcher can then view the documents, narrow the search by specifying additional key words, or switch to a different database altogether. These issues are discussed in this section.

The search by keyword idea is not new. Typically, a hard copy index provided a list of publication names, articles, and authors in alphabetical order. The user found a number of references from this search, but had to search for the hard copies of the references in the library to read. This process took a relatively long time and often resulted in missing references in the index or on the shelves of the library. For example, the AICPA published the *Accounting and Tax Index* in hard copy format for many years before switching to the web-based electronic format as discussed later. The *Accounting and Tax Index* provided an index of the AICPA's own publications as well as other major publications.

The information technology has streamlined this process in several ways. First, due to the abundance of inexpensive storage memory, the index does not have to restrict its content to a limited number of publications. In fact, while theoretical limitations still exist, practically speaking, an unlimited number of publications can be indexed in the same database.

Second, the search engines in these electronic indices are more powerful than the old word indices in hard copy books. These search engines allow the user to search a large number of references in a very short time. Third, the electronic indices have at least the abstract of the publications, and in many cases the full text of the publication in the database. Thus, there is no need for additional library search. Also, disappointments over missing items in the library do not occur because the electronic media can provide access to multiple users at the same time. Many electronic indices allow the user to print the full text of the professional pronouncements and articles, or read them on screen for a fee. Libraries, university systems, accounting firms, or other institutions subscribe to these databases, so the individual users do not have to deal with the fee every time they use the database.

The proliferation of these electronic databases is due to advances in information technology that allow for relatively inexpensive storage and retrieval of huge amounts of information. The technology also has made the retrieval of information research relatively easy. However, the magnitude of information available requires three major criteria for retrieval. The first is the requisite accounting knowledge to understand the volume of information. The technical jargon and the many complex rules in the professional literature clearly require the user to have substantial accounting knowledge just to understand the content. The second criterion is professional judgment that must be brought to bear in choosing relevant information for the research under investigation. As stated earlier, the accountant must use judgment every step of the way to select relevant information and ignore irrelevant information for the research issue at hand. Finally, the accountants must use the authoritative hierarchy of GAAP to guide them in deciding about the level of the authority of the information.

Also interesting to note is that the proliferation of information has resulted in an information overload for an average user. This situation presents business opportunities for accountants in the consulting and assurance services areas where they have a comparative advantage because of their knowledge, training, and professional experience over other professionals. Indeed, accountants are often called upon to assist clients in the development and use of these sources.[1] They are also in a position to provide attestation for the reliability of the information in these databases. The AICPA has developed the WebTrust service in recent years for this purpose. Upon a continuous examination of the reliability of a client's website content, an accountant can issue a WebTrust seal that is displayed on the client's website.

Electronic indices and search engines are numerous and expanding both in number and in content. Newer and more powerful databases provide better and cheaper resources in a competitive marketplace. Many of these indices (e.g., CD Disclosure) used to be published quarterly on compact disks and sent to subscribers. While some of the indices are still available on CDs, the more popular method now is dissemination over the Internet. The Internet provides a cheaper and quicker delivery method. Typically, the user must have a user name and password to access the database from which the search can take place. Due to the importance of the Internet to the delivery of these databases, it is described in the next section, followed by a discussion of accounting-specific databases.

The Internet

The Internet is a virtual network connecting computers across the world. It is the result of much research in the 1970s that was supported by the United States Defense Advanced Research Project Agency. The initial goal of the Internet was to provide a secure network for military communication in which if one segment of the network was damaged, the other segments would continue to work as a reliable means of communication. Like many other advancements in technology (e.g., the invention of the fax machine for military use in the 1930s), the use of the Internet was then extended to nonmilitary organizations such as research institutions, university systems, and government agencies. Today, millions of individ-

---

1. M. C. Francis; T. C. Mulder, and J. S. Stark, *Intentional Learning: A Process for Learning to Learn in the Accounting Curriculum* (Sarasota, FL: Accounting Education Change Commission and the American Accounting Association, 1995), p. 3.

uals and institutions use the Internet across the world. While electronic mail is perhaps one of its greatest uses, also popular are applications in which dissemination and retrieval of massive amounts of information are possible. These applications cover a wide variety of subjects from fashion and sports to news media and professional research and practice that includes accounting. Electronic commerce involving purchases and sales between businesses and consumers has become increasingly popular in recent years.

The Internet is quite extensive and complex. In a nutshell, each user's computer is connected to a server computer that is connected to other servers providing the network of servers that form the World Wide Web, or www. For example, an organization may have 500 computers used by its employees, all connected to a company-owned server or an external server (e.g., America Online) to connect to the Internet. Each computer has an Internet Protocol, or IP, address that identifies the computer within the network.

A site on the Internet is defined as a URL (uniform resource locator) that provides the unique address of the site. Each site may have many pages as well as many links to other URLs. For example, *http://www.AICPA.org* is a URL for the AICPA website. It indicates that the site uses the rules for exchanging files as specified by the hypertext transfer protocol (http). Http provides the rules for the exchange of various files ranging from text to graphics and multimedia. To open an http, you need a web browser such as the Netscape Navigator or the Microsoft Explorer. A web browser builds an http request and sends it to the computer server to connect to the website on the Internet, thus it facilitates the connection from various computers of varying specifications (e.g., a PC or a Mac). A browser also has a number of other utilities to facilitate the use of the Internet. For example, a browser allows the user to bookmark a URL, meaning that it allows the user to add the URL to a list of others and simply click on it to access the site rather than retype the address each time.

AICPA indicates the name of the owner of the URL followed by a domain *org* that indicates AICPA is an organization. Other domains are *com* for commercial enterprises, *net* for network providers such as AT&T, *gov* for government, *mil* for military, and *edu* for educational institutions. U.S. indicates that the URL is a U.S. address. It is generally not necessary to include the U.S. in the URL because the United States is the default country. URLs in all other countries have to specify the country domain at the end of the URL (e.g., .ca for Canada).

The AICPA website is actually a gateway to several websites and web pages covering a host of information about the AICPA as well as many links to other websites for additional information. The gateway concept is an efficient way of providing information on many topics. As discussed later, Rutgers University's website (www.Rutgers.edu/Accounting/raw.htm) has grown over the years into a comprehensive gateway for various accounting information and links.

Searching the Web

The number of websites is already in the hundreds of millions worldwide, and is growing rapidly on a daily basis. To find the information you need, you must have a search engine, something like the alphabetical index of a dictionary or yellow pages, but more powerful. There are many companies whose main product is just that: developing a database of websites and providing a search method called a *search engine* to rapidly search the database using a few key words. These search engines also classify the website into various categories such as autos, real estate, travel, and the like. Netscape and Yahoo! are two examples of these search engines, but there are many more, and they are increasing in number. Generally, when you use key words to access these databases and their search engines, you come to a screen that provides a list, at times lengthy, of sites that the search engine has found. You either narrow the search by providing additional key words or scroll down to take a look at the summary information of the sites found. If the site is of the type that you are looking for, then you can visit the site by pressing the hot link button.

The screen also presents many commercial ads, like the ads in the traditional newspapers but much more extensive in content if you visit the site that is advertised. Advertisers pay for these ads, and they are the reason why the search engines are generally free of charge—they just want your attention, and your purchase of advertised products and services once in a while. They also collect all kinds of information on you based on the sites you visit, the products or services you order, and a host of other information. They can sell this information to negotiate advertising rates, or sell it to anyone interested in the information.

Unfortunately, the web search can be tedious and time consuming because of the unstructured nature of much of the information on the Internet. Any person or business can develop an Internet site and organize the data in any form or shape they desire. Consequently, while using a key word search will find a list, sometimes a very long list of websites, it may not get you the specific information you need. For example, a search for IBM will easily get you thousands of hits. However, if you are interested in a particular piece of information such as the balance of property, plant, and equipment in IBM's 2000 balance sheet, you must do more work. You may want to access IBM's website and its annual report to obtain the information that you seek.

Advances in the communications technology has provided various means of accessing the Internet with differing speeds. Cable and digital subscriber line (DSL) access can be as high as 50 times the speed of a regular analog telephone line. Furthermore, while the analog telephone line occupies the line and is subject to repeated interruptions, DSL and cable are live 24 hours a day and do not get interrupted. However, cable and DSL are also more expensive than the regular telephone access resulting in many households using the telephone as their main source of access to the Internet. Unfortunately, web search can be slow due to the heavy use of the Internet at peak times of the day.[2] Thus, while it is quite possible to reach various organizations' websites by the use of key word searches, the knowledge of specific addresses and their links to other sites is helpful in more pointedly reaching the desired information. For example, information about the Financial Accounting Standards Board can be searched at http://www.FASB.org directly, although it can also be reached via gateway sites such as http://www.rutgers.edu/raw/accounting/.

The AICPA can be searched by reaching its website, http://www.aicpa.org. The Securities and Exchange Commission has a site that provides much information about this regulatory organization including the EDGAR database. This site's address is http://www.sec.gov/. Many other data sources for accounting, auditing, tax, and consulting research have websites as well. These organizations range from the Internal Revenue Service (http://www.irs.ustreas.gov) to the Governmental Accounting Standards Board (http://www.financenet.gov/gasb.htm). If you do not know the URL of an organization you are trying to visit, then search the web by a few key words and then look into hot links. For example, if you search for the FASB, you get a long list of sites that have information on the FASB. One of these sites is Rutgers University's website (http://www.rutgers.edu/accounting/raw/fasb/) that has many links to other sites for information on the FASB.

Much of the information on the web is available at no cost. Other information (e.g., publications) can be ordered electronically. Also, many new entrants to the web may provide opportunities for retrieving information at bargain prices in the future. Typically, these new entrants operate much like newspapers: they charge little or no money for their services because they make the bulk of their revenue from placing ads on their databases and search engines. An example is Pointcast (http://www.pointcast.com) that provides various types of news and stock quotations on the Internet free of charge.

Guidelines for Searching the Web

The rapid increase in the number of websites has resulted in an ocean of information, some of which is redundant, misleading, or useless. The

---

2. In late 1996, America Online (AOL) was very successful in attracting new customers for an unlimited use of its service for a flat monthly fee of $19.95. The problem was that the computer, telephone, and modem capabilities of AOL were insufficient for the success of this promotional pricing model. Frustrating repeated attempts to log on at peak times made customers angry. When they finally logged on, the speed of retrieval was also slow because many users intentionally stayed on line for as long a time as they could. In AOL's Chairman Steve Chase's words, they came to the party and did not want to leave! The effect was inefficiency in retrieval of information, which was costly to those who had come to depend on the service. The problem has been largely mitigated due to AOL's investment in equipment and software.

researcher who does not use the right search engines and/or search strategies can waste much time visiting unwanted sites and gathering unreliable information. To mitigate this problem, it is necessary to have a clear idea about the information needed and to choose an appropriate search engine to find the information. The search engines generally provide alternative ways of searching for the same information. However, each has its own strength and weaknesses. For example, Yahoo! is particularly useful for quick location of company sites and for hyperlinks to other information such as stock quotes. Excite, which claims over 50 million web pages indexed in its database, provides a mechanism for weighting your key words. For example, you can specify that a key word is four times more important than other key words by assigning a four to the important word.

Once you have selected a site as an information source, you need to assess the reliability of the information because websites range from highly accurate to misleading. It is therefore important to analyze the site for its purpose, source, style, and content.[3] Determine the purpose of the website by asking several questions such as "is the web creator trying to sell a product or a service or is it trying to inform or persuade the visitor about something?" The source of the information provides a clue about its possible motives. Generally speaking, business entities create websites to generate business. Many not-for-profit and professional associations may have primary interest in informing you of their existence and publications (e.g., the AICPA) through their websites. Political organizations and advocacy groups are likely to try to persuade you to take a stance on some issue such as birth control. If you have difficulty determining the source and purpose of the site, ask questions by using the e-mail option that is generally provided in the website. If such an option is not available or it is unreliable, find information from other sources or it might be best to leave the site altogether.

The style and functionality of the website is also important. Good organization, good writing, and easy navigational tools are essential for efficient use of the site. Poor organization, unnecessary uses of graphics, and poor writing slow the search process and waste your time.

While the source, purpose, and style of a website give you some information about the motives and design of the site, they do not provide much comfort about its content. The content of the website should be evaluated using the following criteria:

- *Accuracy.* The source of the information should be clearly stated. Also, look for the presence or absence of a third-party verifier. While websites currently lack third-party reliability attestations, accounting firms have begun to provide such a service in recent years.

3. This section is adapted from "Teaching Students to Evaluate Internet Sites," *The Teaching Professor* 11, no. 7 (August/September 1997), p. 4.

- *Comprehensiveness.* Is the information provided comprehensive, or should you look elsewhere for related information? Does the site provide hyperlinks to other sites for information? These hyperlinks are not necessarily the best sources of related information. Sometimes, you should look elsewhere for additional sources.
- *Currency.* Is the information current? Look for the frequency and extent that its creator updates the site. Some websites are created but poorly maintained.
- *Security/Integrity.* Ask questions regarding the security or integrity of the website. For example, if you are providing your credit card number to purchase something on the web, you must be reasonably sure that the information is encrypted and does not end up in the hands of an unintended party. Unfortunately, there have been hack attacks on corporate websites in the past. If you are using accounting information provided on the website of a company, you must make sure that the information is authentic and authorized by the company.

Electronic Sources for Accounting Research

The discussion in the previous section focuses on the use of the web for all types of research. In this section, we focus on the electronic sources, including websites that are specifically useful for accounting research. This is an important distinction because, as stated earlier, due to the unstructured nature of many websites, the search of the web can produce unwanted or irrelevant results. On the other hand, electronic sources dedicated to accounting are helpful to more directly and efficiently get to the desired information. Many of the websites in this category are actually gateway sites in which specialized search engines are provided to find information from various databases in the websites. Also important to note is that unlike the free public websites of the general nature discussed in the previous section, the specialized electronic sources generally cost money to visit because they generally do not make money from other sources such as selling ads. These costs can be based on flat subscription or per search charges. For example, many universities subscribe to use the Lexis Universe database on a flat rate, so that their students, faculty, and staff can access the database free of charge.

We present a summary of the major categories of databases and their purposes useful for accounting research in Exhibit 4–3. After a discussion of these categories, we present and discuss an illustrative case study to show how these databases can be used for case analysis. It is important to note that the information retrieved from any of these databases may need to be augmented with cross references to other sources to make sure that the information is accurate and comprehensive. If in doubt, check the manual sources discussed previously.

Exhibit 4-3   Examples of Major Websites for Accounting Research

Group 1: Accounting and Auditing Standards (Domestic and International)

Accounting Firms Databases. Major international accounting firms have developed professional literature databases for the use of their professionals. These databases are generally available to the public at a fee (i.e., you must receive a user name and a password to use them). An example is Arthur Andersen's Accounting Research Manager. It is available at www.arm.arthurandersen.com.

FARS Database (www.FASB.org). This is Financial Accounting Research System (FARS), published by the FASB. It is currently available on a CD updated quarterly. It provides access to the FASB's and the AICPA's original pronouncements, the Current Text, EITF, FASB's questions and answers (Q&A).

ProQuest (www.ProQuest.umi.com). Provides access and search of various databases such as ABI/Inform Global, Accounting and Tax (newspapers and periodicals). Key word search results in a listing of articles from newspapers and periodicals that provide at least abstracts and in many cases the full text of the article. ABI/Inform also provides information on over 6,000 companies worldwide, updated at least monthly.

Group 2: Annual Reports, Financial Ratios, and Market Data

Bloomberg (www.Bloomberg.com). Financial ratios, market data, and economic and political information in various market sectors. The searcher can print the screens, but cannot download information to files.

Disclosure's Global Access (www.disclosure.com). Market data and company financial statements are provided in this database. However, the files are in pdf format, that can be read and printed only.

EDGAR (www.SEC.gov). Securities and Exchange Commission's Electronic Data Gathering and Retrieval System (EDGAR). Provides a database in which company filings (e.g., 10-K reports) are available for public use. Use PricewaterhouseCoopers' edgarscan (http://bamboo.tc.pw.com) to access EDGAR and download files into the Excel spreadsheet program.

Lexis Universe Financial Information (www.Lexis-Nexis.com). Full text of annual reports that can be copied and pasted into other programs (e.g., word processors).

Market Guide Database (www.marketguide.com). Annual reports, financial ratios, and stock market information. Can be downloaded to the Excel spreadsheet program.

Group 3: Gateways

Numerous useful entries here. Examples are:

Accounting/Auditing/tax (www.taxsites.com). This site provides links to hundreds of sites organized by accounting, auditing, and tax.

Information for accounting students (www.accountingstudents.com). This site is useful for searches on various issues of interest to accounting students ranging from links to accounting firms' websites and information for professional contact and research.

Rutgers University (www.Rutgers.edu/Accounting/raw.htm). This site provides links to many sites ranging from the FASB to the directory of accounting faculty worldwide.

Group 1: Accounting and Auditing Literature

The databases listed in the first group in Exhibit 4–3 provide information on accounting and auditing literature. Some databases (e.g., ProQuest) are integrative and have extensive coverage of information well beyond just accounting and auditing pronouncements. Other databases, such as the

Financial Accounting Research System (FARS) and accounting firm databases, exclusively focus on accounting and auditing pronouncements. Consequently, the latter databases provide more specific and targeted search of the professional literature. The FARS database is described and used in an illustrative case study in this section. Also important to note is that while some of the databases such as FARS are strictly U.S. based, others have domestic and international coverage (e.g., accounting firm databases). However, regardless of the extent of their coverage, the rules of the search are basically the same—you need relevant keywords to search for authoritative pronouncements. The search engines in these databases locate the pronouncements and highlight the key words within each document identified. Thus, the researcher can view, copy and paste, or print the specific passages in which the key words appear.

The FARS Database. The Financial Accounting Research System (FARS) is a product of the FASB. Its content is limited to AICPA and FASB pronouncements on accounting. It has five separate databases called InfoBases as follows:

1. **FASB-OP**—Original pronouncements: contains all AICPA and FASB pronouncements in chronological order, including totally superseded pronouncements.
2. **FASB-CT**—Current text: contains the general standards, industry standards, and the current text sections that have been superseded but are still applicable due to a delayed effective date.
3. **EITF**—Emerging Issues Task Force: includes the full text of each abstract for every issue discussed by the Emerging Issues Task Force since its inception in 1984.
4. **FASB-Q&A**—Staff implementation guides: contains staff special reports and other published implementation guidance. This guidance is for several specific FASB statements, including statements on futures contracts, pensions, and so on.
5. **FASINDEX**: contains the combined topical index for all above databases in FARS.

You need to have a user name and password to access FARS. If you already have a user name and password to access the computer system of your institution and your institution subscribes to FARS, then you may not need a new user name and password. You can access the FARS database by entering a physical computer laboratory where the FARS CD is housed or you can access it by accessing the virtual laboratory from anywhere (via the institution's intranet or the Internet) that your institutional computer system allows you. Once on the system, you simply double-click on the FARS icon on the windows desktop screen to activate the software. Once the program loads, the screen will display the FARS main window containing its five InfoBases as listed above. All available FARS functions that are similar to many other programs (e.g., File, Edit) are accessible from the menu bar. For example, the Open command under the File menu lets you open an existing InfoBase. The Query command opens up a dialog from which you can search any open InfoBase. The Exit command closes the FARS database.

To perform a search in a specific and/or multiple InfoBases, click the Query button and enter your search keyword and click OK. A FARS Query box such as the one replicated below appears.[4] This is a word list in alphabetical order. You can double-click on any keyword to select it for a Query. The screen also shows the number of times the keyword you selected was found in the InfoBase. The Apply to All button will search all open InfoBases.

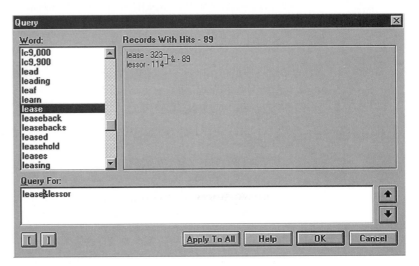

If you search in all FARS InfoBases, you get references from various sources. For example, if you search for keywords Futures Contracts, you receive the following references:

	OP	CT	EITF/Other
FUTURES CONTRACTS			
Hedges			
. . Ongoing Assessment of Correlation . .	FAS80, ¶11	F80.111	EITF.85-6 Q&A.80 #20-21

The search found *FASB Statement No. 80*, "Accounting for Futures Contracts" paragraph 11. F80.111 indicates paragraph .111 of the *Current Text Section F80*, "Futures Contracts." EITF.85-6 indicates *EITF Issue No. 85-6*, "Futures Implementation Questions." Q&A.80 #20-21 refers to questions 20 and 21 of the FASB Highlights, "Futures Contracts: Guidance on Applying Statement 80."

---

4. The screen reproduced here is from a current version of the FARS database. Given the speed of change in the design and content of databases, this screen may already be obsolete by the time you read this section. It is presented for illustrative purposes only.

Group 2: Annual Reports, Financial Ratios, and Market Data
The second group of databases in Exhibit 4–3 provides annual reports, financial ratios, stock market data, and other information for a large number of companies. You can only view or print the financial information from some of these databases (e.g., Bloomberg, Disclosure Global Access, and EDGAR). Others databases such as Lexis Universe Financial Information allow copying and pasting information into other software packages such as word processors. Market Guide's comparative financial reports can be downloaded to the Excel spreadsheet program for additional analysis, tabulation, and reporting purposes. Also, while EDGAR is not directly downloadable, there are software packages that make downloading possible and easy. For example, PricewaterhouseCoopers provides scanning software called Edgarscan that automatically scans EDGAR files and makes them downloadable to Excel spreadsheet programs. The software is free of charge at http://bamboo.tc.pw.com. This site provides a hot link to the EDGAR site as well.

Lexis Universe (www.Lexis-Nexis.com). Unlike FARS, which is a database limited to the AICPA and the FASB pronouncements, Lexis-Nexis is a comprehensive and gigantic database. It covers more than 11,000 news, business, and legal sources, and it adds some 14 million documents to the database each week in addition to its approximately one billion documents already in storage. In comparison with the FARS CD, this database is equivalent to a 14-story stack of CD-ROMs. If printed on continuous paper, the data would stretch 390,000 miles. It has many specialized libraries in various languages covering major fields of practice ranging from taxation and banking to accounting, law, and international issues.[5] To search such a gigantic database, you must have a good search strategy to access the desired information while avoiding the undesirable information.

To access the Lexis-Nexis database through your university, go to the website of the university unit that subscribes to the service. For example, if the library of your university is the unit that subscribes to the Lexis Academic Universe (a new service of Lexis-Nexis), then you can link up to the service via the library's website. If you are a private user or the arrangement is to have a user name and password to directly log onto the database, then go to www.Lexis-Nexis.com and then use your user name and password to log onto the database. A screen appears with five options: News, Business, Legal Research, Medical, and Reference. Select Business. It will give you the following library options:

Business News	Business articles from newspapers, magazines, journals, wires, and transcripts
Company Financial	Detailed financial data about U.S. companies
Compare Companies	Find companies based on a variety of criteria

---

5. D. Campbell and M. Campbell, *The Student's Guide to Doing Research on the Internet* (Reading, MA: Addison Wesley, 1995), pp. 2–3.

SEC Filings and Reports	EDGAR filings, annual and quarterly reports, and proxy statements
Industry	News from over 25 industries
Accounting	Accounting journals and literature
Directories	Trade show information and more

All these libraries have use for accounting research. The accounting library used to provide Authoritative Accounting Literature—US that was similar to, but more extensive than, the FARS database. This library is no longer available because FARS already provides the bulk of the information.

Group 3: Gateways

Finally, the third group of databases listed in Exhibit 4–3 provides gateways to hundreds of useful databases and websites. For example, www.taxsites .com provides links to hundreds of sites organized by accounting, auditing, and tax. Extensive sources of information for accounting students are provided in sites and links at www.accountingstudents.com. Rutgers University has a large number of links to many sites ranging from the FASB to the directory of accounting faculty worldwide. The URL for this site is www.Rutgers.edu/Accounting/raw.htm.

Guidelines for Searching Databases

To search databases efficiently, one can use several search words, called *search operators*, to limit or expand the search. While variations exist between databases, the following brief discussion provides a generic coverage of these operators.

Limiting operators limit the search to a combination of words:

- AND (or the symbol &) is used to look for the word before and after it. Thus, a search for *account* AND *receivable* looks for *account* and *receivable*. It finds only passages where *account* and *receivable* are found somewhere in the passage.

- If you want the two words to be found in an exact order, then use quotation marks around the words in the order you want. For example, "account receivable" indicates that you are looking for "account receivable," but not for "receivable account."

- If you want to find "account receivable" but you don't mind if they are located within *n* (say 10) words from each other, then specify "account receivable"/n. Also if you are looking for "account receivable" or "receivable account" within *n* words, you can specify "account receivable"@n.

- If you want to find one of the terms but not in combination with the other, you can use the NOT (or the symbol ^) operator. For example, *receivable* NOT *account* will find all passages in which receivable appears but not in combination with *account*.

Expanding operators expand the search to be inclusive of two or more words.

- OR (also the symbol |) operator is used to search for all passages that contain a word or another. For example, the search for *receivable* OR *account* will find all passages that have either account or receivable words in it.
- If you want to find all the passages that have both words except when they are together, then use the exclusive XOR (also the symbol ~ but not the lower case xor). This search will find all *receivable* and *account* words, but not *receivable account* or *account receivable*.
- If you want to find all variations of a keyword, then use an asterisk (*) at the end of the word. For example, *account** will locate account, accounting, accountant.

| ILLUSTRATIVE CASE | THE USE OF THE FARS DATABASE: BELL TECHNOLOGIES, INC. |

Recognition Issues for an Installment Sale of Distribution Rights to a Major Customer

Bell Technologies, Inc. is a privately held corporation, with Joseph Bell holding 52 percent of the common stock and family members and friends holding the remainder. The company has been organized primarily to develop database management systems and provide computer-related services. The company has a calendar year-end.

In 20X1 Bell Technologies granted certain specific marketing rights to one of its systems to Hesser Systems, Inc. Subsequent to the grant, disagreements arose between the companies, and Hesser brought suit against Bell for breach of contract. On November 1, 20X1, new agreements and understandings were settled on, and the lawsuit was dropped. The settlement resulted in Bell Technologies agreeing to sell the distribution rights to Hesser Systems for $1 million. The proceeds will be collected in equal amounts of $100,000 every 3 months over 10 successive quarters commencing February 1, 20X2. The parties never reduced the agreement to writing, nor was any interest specified on the payments or even a note executed between the parties.

At the time of settlement, the prime lending rate was 10 percent, and Bell Technologies had recently been granted a loan by a financial institution at a rate of prime plus 2 percent. Also during this time, a private investor approached Joseph Bell and indicated a willingness to lend money to Bell Technologies at one point below prime in exchange for an option to take an unspecified future equity position in the company. It was the intent of Joseph Bell to keep the company in the hands of the present shareholder group and only to consider this private financing option under unusual circumstances.

Hesser Systems, Inc. has always been a major customer of Bell Technologies. As of year-end December 31, 20X1, sales by Bell to Hesser, excluding the settlement, were approximately 70 percent of total sales of $4,700,000. Accounts receivable on December 31, 20X1, excluding any amounts due from Hesser, totaled approximately $240,000. Hesser has always paid its account within a 45-day period and has a good credit rating. However, Hesser, being privately held, will not make any financial information available to Bell Technologies.

Based on some recent tax research, the controller of Bell Technologies has concluded that as an accrual basis taxpayer, Bell Technologies does not have to report the settlement with Hesser until received. The controller's research indicates this to be the case for the portion of a contract that is not due and payable in the year the contract is made and is not evidenced by a note or other negotiable instrument.

For financial reporting purposes, Bell Technologies is planning to record as revenue the 20X1 sale of the distribution rights to Hesser. Bell Technologies will then report a pretax accounting profit in 20X1.

However, due to temporary differences between reporting revenue and expense items for book and tax purposes, Bell Technologies does not expect to have a federal income tax liability for 20X1.

Required

Discuss the various financial accounting decisions that Bell Technologies, Inc. must make and how such decisions will be reported in the company's financial statements in 20X1 and subsequent years. Be specific in your response and state your reasons for each decision. At a minimum, your discussion should include the method of recognizing revenue, the determination of the amount of revenue to be recognized, the balance sheet reporting issues, the tax reporting issues, and any required footnote disclosures.

ILLUSTRATIVE CASE	INTRODUCTION AND SEARCH STRATEGY

The main issue of the case is when revenue should be recognized for an installment sale of distribution rights to a major customer. The timing of revenue recognition is troublesome because the parties were previously involved in litigation over the rights and subsequently agreed to a settlement that was never reduced to writing. No interest rate was specified on the payments and a note was not executed.

The case discussion that follows incorporates the relevant steps of the case analysis model discussed in Chapter 3. In this case, the Financial Accounting Research System (FARS) database as of March 15, 2000, is used to search the professional literature. In order to do this effectively, the researcher must have the requisite accounting and financial reporting knowledge. The objectives of the case are to identify the timing and amount of revenue from an installment sale and the balance sheet reporting implications of said sale. In addition, disclosure issues pertaining to the sale must be addressed. The case discussion includes an identification and discussion of the authoritative literature, alternative solutions, and conclusion. Steps involving supplements and an addendum are not needed for this case.

The FARS database was searched through the Topical Index, using the Advanced Query option. A FARS query identifies the number of hits, which are the number of times the keywords used in the query show up in the database, many of which may be in the same document.

The first part of the search deals with revenue recognition, and the keyword *revenue recognition* was used to begin the search. The search for revenue recognition resulted in 97 hits. To refine the search, the limiting operator AND with the keyword *installment* was used and only 3 hits were identified. *APB No. 10,* "Omnibus Opinion–1966" was then identified as relevant to the case.

Upon analysis of the case for the installment method, other issues were identified. The first was the issue of discounting the installment payments. This issue requires certain accounting knowledge to identify the required keywords for an additional search. For this search, the keywords *present value* were used. This search resulted in 66 hits. Then *present value* AND *interest* were used to narrow the search. This search resulted in seven hits, of which *APB No. 21,* "Interest on Receivables and Payables" was relevant to the case.

A third issue dealt with disclosure requirements for major customers and/or related parties. For this search, the keywords *major customers* were used and six hits resulted. *SFAS No. 131,* "Disclosure about Segments of an Enterprise and Related Information," was quickly identified from the list. Likewise, the keywords *related party transactions* were used and 36 hits resulted. The search was narrowed to include AND *disclosure requirements,* and two hits resulted, and *SFAS No. 57,* "Related Party Disclosures," was identified as the relevant pronouncement.

The last issue is accounting for deferred income taxes. *Temporary differences* were used as the keywords and resulted in 266 hits. However, since the case referred to temporary differences, the conclusion is that deferred income taxes will result. Thus, to narrow the search, *deferred income taxes* was included, and 81 hits resulted. A quick scanning of the hits immediately pointed to *SFAS No. 109,* "Accounting for Income Taxes." Once a document is identified, you can search within the document for specific keywords. The keywords *separate*

AND *deferred tax* were used in this case to identify paragraph 41 of *SFAS No. 109*, which provides guidance on the reporting of deferred taxes in a classified balance sheet.

CASE DISCUSSION

APB No. 10, "Omnibus Opinion–1966," states that revenues should be recognized at the time a transaction is completed, with appropriate provision for uncollectible accounts. Paragraph 12 refers to *ARB No. 43*, Chapter 1, Section A, paragraph 1, which states: "Profit is deemed to be realized when a sale in the ordinary course of business is effected, unless the circumstances are such that the collection of the sales price is not reasonably assured." This provides the basis for much of the present practice of revenue recognition. The revenue recognition alternatives for Bell Technologies becomes whether revenue should be recognized when agreements were reached on November 1, 20X1, or as payments are received, or at some other time.

If, as of November 1, 20X1, Bell has fulfilled essentially all obligations to Hesser, despite there being no written agreement, then the transaction is completed. As to the issue of quarterly payments commencing February 1, 20X2, the installment method of recognizing revenue would be appropriate if collection was doubtful as indicated in *APB No. 10*, paragraph 12. While the tendency of many students is to select the more conservative installment method, the facts indicate that Hesser has always paid its account within 45 days and has a good credit rating. In 20X1, excluding the settlement, Bell made sales to Hesser of approximately $3,290,000 (70% x $4,700,000). The fact that Hesser would not make financial information available to Bell was not significant in this case, because there was no apparent reason to question Hesser's ability or willingness to pay the settlement. As a practical matter, many privately held companies will not make their financial information available to outsiders. Thus, it appears that the installment method of recognizing revenue would not be appropriate, and assuming Bell has no significant future obligations to Hesser, revenue should be recognized on November 1, 20X1. If different assumptions are made concerning Bell's future obligations to Hesser or Hesser's ability or willingness to pay, then certainly arguments can be made for postponing the revenue.

As to matching revenues with costs, any costs associated with the distribution rights have probably already been expensed. Therefore, the distribution rights have a zero basis on Bell's books.

The next issue involves the amount of revenue to be recognized on November 1, 20X1. Bell must determine the fair value of the distribution rights or the market value of the note, whichever is more clearly determinable, and would look to *APB No. 21*, "Interest on Receivables and Payables," for guidance. The facts of the case do not give any indication of the fair value of the distribution rights; therefore, Bell would determine the market value of the note by imputing an interest rate in accordance with paragraphs 13 and 14 of *APB No. 21*.

As to the selection of a rate, at a minimum it should be the prime rate of 10 percent. In the actual case, the prime rate was used, but it is important to keep in mind that this is a contractual right to receive money that is not evidenced by writing or collateralized. It is our opinion that a rate at least two points above prime (12%) is more appropriate and would result in recording revenue of $853,020 at 12 percent ($100,000 x 8.5302) versus $875,210 at 10 percent ($100,000 x 8.7521). Arguments might well be advanced that the facts and circumstances dictate a rate in excess of 12 percent. Whatever rate is used, the imputed interest should be recorded as a discount to the note and amortized as interest income over the life of the note by the effective interest method. As of December 31, 20X1, Bell would have to accrue two months of interest on the note. A final point on the interest rate is that it is irrelevant that Bell had an offer by a private investor to loan money at one point below prime or that Bell recently borrowed money at prime plus 2 percent. It is the debtor that is looked to when imputing an interest rate.

In reporting the receivable on the balance sheet as of December 31, 20X1, the four installments due in 20X2, net of the applicable discount, should be presented in the current asset section and the remaining six installments, net of the applicable discount, should be presented as a long-term receivable. In the actual case, the receivable for the distribution system was not separated from other trade receivables but was disclosed in a footnote to the financial statements. The need for a provision for uncollectible accounts for this receivable and the question of loan impairment are issues raised by some students. In the actual case, a small allowance to cover all receivables was established.

Another issue to consider is the disclosure requirements pertaining to major customers and related parties. *SFAS No. 131*, "Disclosure about Segments of an Enterprise and Related Information," paragraph 39 states: "An enterprise shall provide information about the extent of its reliance on its major customers. If revenues from transactions with a single external customer amount to 10 percent or more of an enterprise's revenues, the enterprise shall disclose that fact, the total amount of revenues from each such customer, and the identity of the segment or segments reporting the revenues." *SFAS No. 57*, "Related Party Disclosures," paragraph 2 requires additional disclosure for related parties which include:

- The nature of the relationship.
- A description of the transactions.
- The dollar amounts of transactions.
- The amounts due from or to related parties
  and the terms and manner of settlement.

This disclosure would be necessary because Bell and Hesser are related parties per paragraph 24f, assuming Hesser "can significantly influence the management or operating policies" of Bell. The facts appear to indicate that Bell is economically dependent on Hesser, but it is possible that Hesser may be equally dependent on Bell. This point tends to be overlooked by most case respondents.

The last issue to be addressed is that of deferred income taxes. Assuming that the controller's tax research is correct as to the tax accounting of the settlement, then deferred income taxes should be provided for the estimated future tax effects attributable to the temporary differences. The point is to note that deferred taxes are an issue relating to the transaction but not to focus on the calculation of deferred taxes. Paragraph 41 of *SFAS No. 109*, "Accounting for Income Taxes," states: "In a classified statement of financial position, an enterprise shall separate deferred tax liabilities and assets into a current amount and a noncurrent amount. Deferred tax liabilities and assets shall be classified as current or noncurrent based on the classification of the related asset or liability for financial reporting. A deferred tax liability or asset that is not related to an asset or liability for financial reporting, including deferred tax assets related to carryforwards, shall be classified according to the expected reversal date of the temporary difference pursuant to FASB Statement No. 37, "Balance Sheet Classification of Deferred Income Taxes." Thus, the deferred tax liability representing the tax effects of the uncollected installment receivables classified as current assets should be classified as a current item and the balance of the deferred tax liability as a noncurrent item.

A Word About the Future of Electronic Search

Professor Robert Jensen of Trinity University, who specializes in technology issues in accounting education, also has a gateway site (http://www.trinity .edu/rjensen). This site provides links to other sites and discussion groups focusing on accounting. In April 1999, Dr. Jensen wrote a piece about the future of electronic search engines. He states that:

> In the future, our searches will extend into the world of queries that extend well beyond "searches" as we know them today. Web bots will conduct diagnostics regarding our learning goals and ask rather sophisticated questions in an attempt to find out what we want to learn about a subject. They will conduct tests on us

to see what it is that we want or need relative to certain goals. The web bots will then canvas cyberspace (actually systems of databases) and assemble a variety of options of meeting our learning goals. These bots may return with modules (not necessarily entire documents or entire data tables) assembled for specific purposes. In more complex situations, they may return recommendations for tutorials and/or complete education programs. The bots may be programmed to make calculations and perform tasks to the limits of artificial intelligence states of the art. They may interrogate experts and bots of experts when assembling our knowledge base.

Should Dr. Jensen's prediction come true, the accountant will have an unlimited knowledge base to draw upon for his or her research. The accountant may be able to do this with relative ease, even in his or her sleep. How far out is this prediction? Only time will tell.

Summary

This chapter provides a discussion of the sources of information for professional research. A five-level hierarchy of authoritative literature for practical research is presented. The hierarchy begins with authoritative pronouncements of the primary standard-setting organizations such as the FASB and ends with a wide variety of academic and professional publications. Major manual indices are also briefly discussed. However, since information technology has made the task of finding information, even full-text material, relatively efficient and easy, the main focus for information search is on electronic databases and search engines.

The Internet and its World Wide Web are briefly discussed and the search engines to find general information from the web are covered. This is followed by a discussion of the databases and search engines specifically useful for professional accounting research. Major databases for search of the authoritative sources of literature were introduced and two of them (FARS and Lexis Universe) were briefly discussed. A search of the FARS database was used to analyze an illustrative case study. Also introduced were databases for comparative annual reports, financial ratios, and market data. Finally, gateway sites were introduced through which one can link to a host of other sources of information. The chapter ends with a view of the databases and search engines of the future.

Selected Additional Reading

Campbell, D., and M. Campbell. *The Student's Guide to Doing Research on the Internet.* Reading, MA: Addison Wesley, 1995.

Cottrell, D. M. *Business and Accounting Research Using Lexis-Nexis.* Boston, MA: Irwin/McGraw-Hill, 1998.

Kogan, A.; E. F. Sudit; and M. Vasarhelyi. *Internet Guide for Accountants: A Living Book.* Upper Saddle River, NJ: Prentice Hall, 1997.

Zeff, S. A. "Commentary: A Study of Academic Research Journals in Accounting." *Accounting Horizons*, September, 1996, pp. 158–77.

Ziebart, D. A. *An Introduction to Applied Professional Research for Accountants.* Upper Saddle River, NJ: Prentice-Hall, 1998, Chapter 4.

Questions

1. Why have authoritative sources of literature become so diverse and complex?

2. What are the primary organizations that issue authoritative literature in financial accounting? Tax? Managerial accounting?

3. Pick five of the general publications of the AICPA and discuss them.

4. What are the purposes for industry-specific publications of the AICPA?

5. What does the AICPA's publication, *Accounting Trends and Techniques*, try to accomplish?

6. List the primary publications of the FASB.

7. Publications from regulatory organizations are many and complex. How does an accountant keep up with them?

8. What are the primary publications of the SEC that concern accountants?

9. Many societies and associations represent the interests of various types of accountants. Pick a state society of CPAs of your own choosing and discuss its publications.

10. How do the publications of the American Accounting Association relate to research issues confronting the accounting professionals?

11. Why is there a need for a GAAP hierarchy in professional research?

12. The electronic indices have revolutionized information search, but what do you do if these searches render too many references for your consideration?

13. The World Wide Web accessed through search engines such as Netscape or Yahoo! can be a frustrating experience due to its still mostly random access structure. Do you think that someday we will see a structured, well-organized web good enough for effective and efficient searches for accounting research? How?

14. List and discuss a general guide for searching the World Wide Web.

15. List and discuss the primary manual indices useful for accounting and auditing pronouncements.

16. List and discuss the primary manual databases useful for corporate annual reports, financial ratios, and market data.

17. List and discuss the primary manual indices useful for international accounting and auditing information.

18. List and discuss the primary websites and databases useful for accounting and auditing pronouncements.

19. Search the FARS database for information on post-retirement benefits. Provide a comparative list of authoritative pronouncements that were identified from FARS.

20. Discuss the concept of a gateway website and provide three examples of gateways for accounting and auditing information.

21. List and discuss three limiting operators for electronic search.

22. List and discuss three expanding operators for electronic search.

Appendix 4A

Accounting Journals Indexed in Popular Indices (e.g., ABI Inform, Accounting & Tax Index, Lexis/Nexis)

The following is a list of journals indexed in some databases. It is not meant to be an exhaustive list of these journals. There are tens, if not hundreds, of other publications ranging from the *Canadian CA Magazine* to the *Indian Journal of Accounting*. Many of these journals are listed on Lexis/Nexis, Infotrac, Accounting & Tax Index, and ABI Inform, but some are not. Some of these journals such as *The Accounting Review* are highly academic in nature, while others are completely practical (e.g., the *Practical Accountant*) or primarily practical (e.g., *Journal of Accountancy*). Some journals are providing a bridge between academic and practical issues of accounting. An example is *Accounting Horizons.*

Abacus

Accounting and Business Research

Accounting and Finance

Accounting, Auditing & Accountability Journal

Accounting Education: An International Journal

Accounting Education: A Journal of Theory, Practice and Research

The Accounting Educators' Journal

Accounting Enquiries: A Research Journal

Accounting Forum

The Accounting Historians Journal

Accounting Horizons

Accounting, Organizations and Society Accounting Research Journal

The Accounting Review

Advances in Accounting

Advances in Accounting Information Systems

Advances in International Accounting

Advances in Management Accounting

Advances in Public Interest Accounting

Advances in Quantitative Analysis of Finance and Accounting

Advances in Taxation

Asia-Pacific Journal of Accounting

Auditing: A Journal of Practice and Theory

Behavioral Research in Accounting

The British Accounting Review

Contemporary Accounting Research

The CPA Journal

Critical Perspectives on Accounting

The European Accounting Review

Financial Accountability & Management

The International Journal of Accounting

International Journal of Intelligent Systems in Accounting

Issues in Accounting Education

Journal of Accountancy

Journal of Accounting and Economics

Journal of Accounting and Public Policy

Journal of Accounting, Auditing & Finance

Journal of Accounting Education

Journal of Accounting Literature

Journal of Accounting Research

The Journal of the American Taxation Association

Journal of Business Finance & Accounting

Journal of Cost Management

The Journal of Information Systems

Journal of International Accounting, Auditing & Taxation

Journal of Management Accounting Research

The Practical Accountant

Public Accounting Report

Research in Accounting Regulation

Research on Accounting Ethics

Review of Quantitative Finance and Accounting

ISSUE-BASED

5

ACCOUNTING RESEARCH

A little neglect may breed great mischief.
Benjamin Franklin

Objectives

In this chapter we discuss a general framework for issue-based applied accounting research. This framework is followed by a brief discussion of major research models that have shaped much of the contemporary accounting thought. The chapter ends with a long list of illustrative issues for research in Appendix 5A. This list can be consulted for the selection of course projects. Upon completion of the chapter, you will have learned:

1. A definition of applied accounting research.
2. A general framework for *hypothetico-deductive* and *inductive-ground-up* logic for applied accounting research.
3. The contemporary accounting research models.
4. The objectives of capital market research.
5. The basics of the capital asset pricing model.
6. Various forms of the efficient market hypothesis.
7. The basics of the option pricing model.

   The focus of this chapter is on issue-based research in accounting. In the first section, we present a framework for conducting applied research along with a broad definition of applied accounting research. An overview of inductive and deductive logic used for research in general, and for professional research in particular, is presented as a part of this general framework. A section in which we identify fundamental research models follows this framework. While primarily academic in nature, these research models form the foundations for much of the literature that is used for applied accounting research. However, due to the applied focus of this book, the details of academic research involved in these models are left out. The methodology of professional accounting research, including the form for communicating the results, is presented in the next chapter.

A General Framework for Applied Accounting Research

Similar to the framework for case research, there is a need for a framework for applied accounting research. Once you identify a specific issue to investigate, you need a theory to guide you through research expectations or hypotheses, a research design, analysis, conclusions, communication, and perhaps new knowledge that can be used to refine the theory used in the research. In this section, we first provide a definition of applied accounting research and then present a discussion of various components of a general framework for applied research.

A Definition of Applied Accounting Research

A general definition of applied accounting research is that it is a systematic process by which defensible answers to specific accounting issues are identified and communicated.[1] A characteristic of this definition is *systematic process*, which indicates a well-organized plan of action in which authoritative literature (Chapter 4) is systematically searched for guidance. Once a solution to a problem or a conclusion for an issue is identified, it has to be defensible by reference to authoritative literature or new evidence.

The process used for professional applied research must be efficient. The professional accountant must find a defensible solution to a problem, or a conclusion for an issue, with the least amount of resources. Thus, the least amount, but the most authoritative, literature must be consulted and used for applied research. Also important is the generalizability of the findings. The research must be well documented so that the findings from one investigation can be used for similar situations in future engagements as well. To achieve these outcomes, the research must have a defensible logic as presented in the next section.

The Framework

Deductive and inductive methods of logic are used in scientific research for drawing conclusions from evidence. In the deductive method, the researcher

---

1. This definition is adapted from S. C. Dilley, R. B. Hayes, and P. Steinebart, "Development of a Paradigm for Applied Accounting Research: A Way of Coping with Subject-Matter Complexity," *The Accounting Review* LVIII, no. 2 (April 1983), p. 410–11.

forms certain expectations or hypotheses from a general premise or theory and collects evidence to investigate those expectations. This method is called the *hypothetico-deductive method* of investigation.[2] In the inductive method, the researcher begins with the data at hand and designs a method to investigate the generalizability of the evidence. This is called generating theories from the ground up.[3] Thus, we call it the *inductive ground-up method* of investigation.

Both hypothetico-deductive and inductive ground-up methods are useful for accounting research. In some problem situations, the hypothetico-deductive method is used to apply generally accepted theories or principles, say GAAP, to specific problem situations. Professional research projects rely heavily on this method. The inductive ground-up logic is used to draw general conclusions from specific evidence, thus building the theories that can be applied to improve current standards and practice. This method is useful for standards setting where evidence from specific practice situations is analyzed for guidance in issuing new standards or interpretations. The method is also useful for professional research where contemporary problems may be solved by reference to examples of practice when professional guidance is lacking or insufficient.

It is important to note that in many problem situations or applied research issues, both the hypothetico-deductive and the inductive ground-up methods of logic are used to arrive at a conclusion. In an applied accounting research, you may begin with the authoritative literature to find a solution to a problem or an accounting research issue. Thus, you use deductive reasoning. However, if the problem or issue is so new or complicated that the authoritative literature is deficient in its guidance, you may collect data from various sources to form a general inductive conclusion, thus using the inductive ground-up method of logic.

A research issue can be identified from personal observation, a referral from a client, or an assignment from a third party. Let's assume that you have identified an issue for investigation. Further, assume that the issue is refined and specific objectives of the research are identified. The next decision is what framework you will use to guide your research process. Exhibit 5–1 presents a general inference logic framework. The framework is set up to show the direction of hypothetico-deductive and inductive ground-up logic. While the direction of the former is top down, the direction used by the latter is ground up, as explained on the next page.

---

2. U. Sekaran, *Research Methods for Business: A Skill-Building Approach,* 3rd ed. (New York: Wiley, 2000).
3. For a detailed discussion of ground-up theory-building, see B. G. Glaser and A. L. Strauss, *The Discovery of Grounded Theory* (Chicago: Aldine, 1967).

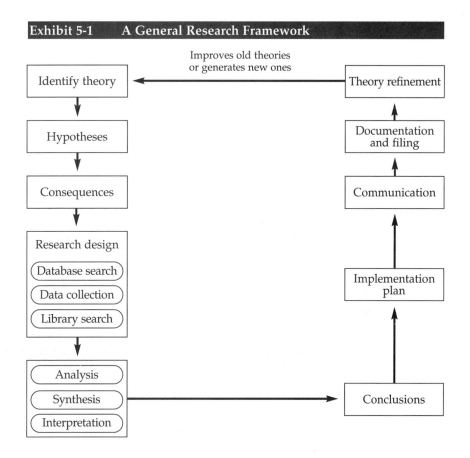

Exhibit 5-1   A General Research Framework

The Hypothetico-Deductive Method

As presented in Exhibit 5–1, in the hypothetico-deductive method, you begin by identifying an appropriate theory. You will then establish hypotheses; assess consequences of these hypotheses; design a research method; perform an analysis, synthesis, or interpretation; and reach a conclusion. Establishing an implementation plan, research report (communication), and filing are also described here because they are the end result of the research process. These components also are used to refine the theory or generate new theories in an inductive ground-up method. These issues are briefly discussed below.

Identify Theory. To begin your research process, you need to identify a theory that has promise in directing your investigation. You identify applicable theories from a host of sources. These sources range from a discussion with knowledgeable colleagues or consultants to a formal search of the literature. The search will hopefully render an applicable theory for the issue under investigation. If such a theory is not identified, a descriptive or exploratory study can be attempted to generate the information needed and to help develop a theory as explained in a following subsection on the inductive ground-up method.

For a contemporary research example, suppose that your interest is to investigate the effects of a dividend policy on a client's stock price. Your search for research theories will lead to the dividend policy decisions research model. For a practical example, consider revenue recognition for a client. Your search for theories of revenue recognition will discover the critical event theory as well as a host of authoritative standards and guidelines from the promulgatory and regulatory sources. To get the references, you select a set of key words and search sources of literature to find the applicable theories, models, or authoritative guidelines.

Hypotheses. The theories selected provide guidance on the set of expectations or hypotheses through the deductive method. Again, if no theory is found to lead to a research hypothesis, a descriptive or exploratory study may be undertaken that will result in a set of expectations. These expectations can be subjected to further research and theory development through the inductive method. For basic or pure research, hypothesis development must be exact and well controlled to provide for internal validity. In professional research, the development of a hypothesis is more like the identification of various courses of action that can be taken to investigate a practical problem. These courses of action and the researcher's expectations about them present the set of testable hypotheses.

Consequences. The hypotheses established or expectations formulated have implications or consequences that must be carefully identified. For example, suppose that a researcher establishes a hypothesis that a 5 percent increase in the dividend payout will have a 10 percent increase in the stock price of the client. The consequences of this hypothesis, if supported by evidence, can be several. Management may have a significant number of shares or call options that will appreciate as a result of this dividend policy. Thus, an issue will be to investigate whether the management is serving its own interest in increasing the dividend payout or is serving the interests of the company as a whole. Similarly, in practical research investigating alternative methods of depreciation, the researcher clearly specifies the impact of the depreciation policy on the net income and cash flows of the company.

Research Design. The method used to investigate the hypotheses or research expectations is called *research design*. There are many different research designs depending on the nature (e.g., fundamental or practical) and the importance of the research. Three general research designs are listed in Exhibit 5–1. Database search is used as a method of data retrieval from databases. For example, the annual report libraries of the Lexis Universe database can be accessed through the Lexis/Nexis online system to search for financial statements and footnotes. Other databases identified in Chapter 3 are also rich sources of both professional literature and empirical data for investigation. Other examples are Moody's Bond Record, Moody's Stock Survey, and Standard & Poor's Corporation Services. These databases and others that have detailed stock and bond prices (e.g., COMPUSTAT and CRSP) provide the raw data used primarily for capital market studies. The vast amount of past observations in these databases can be used in what is called *empirical research*.

Databases are not as plentiful in other accounting fields such as managerial accounting or auditing. Thus, empirical observations are not as readily available for use in these studies. The researcher must select a research design through which empirical data can be collected and library research performed. Several methods of investigation are discussed in Chapter 6.

Analysis/Synthesis/Interpretation. Methods of research such as database search require a method of analysis, synthesis, or interpretation. Most research methods deal with facts in the form of quantitative data that must be coded, analyzed, and tabulated in a form that will be understandable to the audience for whom the research is being performed. The professional research that focuses on library search may also have data to analyze. However, perhaps the most important part of the library search in professional research is to understand and synthesize the authoritative literature around the issue. This understanding and synthesis is important for the purpose of solving the problem under investigation. The synthesis of professional literature is also done in other types of research to understand the extent to which the problem under study has already been subjected to research. Synthesis and data analysis assist the researcher in the interpretation of the results of the study.

Every method of investigation requires some form of data analysis, synthesis, or interpretation. Most methods of investigation require quantitative data analysis using some established statistical method such as mean and standard deviation. Other methods of investigation may indicate qualitative analysis and interpretation. For example, a search of the authoritative literature requires a qualitative synthesis and interpretation of the pronouncements as compared with analysis of quantitative data.

Conclusions. The next item to discuss from Exhibit 5–1 is conclusions. In this part of the study, the researcher summarizes the results and provides conclusions and implications of the findings for further research. For example, a professional accountant studying the nature of a lease transaction might conclude that the lease could be reported as an operating lease. An implication of this conclusion is that the client is allowed to achieve off-balance-sheet financing for the transaction. This is so because neither the lease obligation nor the leased asset is reported in the balance sheet—lease payments are reported as rent expense.

Implementation Plan. Once conclusions are made and implications are specified, an implementation plan is necessary. Such an implementation plan provides a step-by-step process. For example, the operating lease conclusion requires the specification of the journal entries in the books of the client and the requisite disclosure in the financial statements in accordance with *SFAS No. 13,* "Accounting for Leases."[4]

Communication and Filing. The process just outlined will have to be carefully communicated to those concerned. Major format issues relating to communication of research results are discussed in Chapter 6 and illustrated in Appendix 6A. The documentation of the process also needs to be filed for future reference.

Theory Refinement. The process from data collection to forming conclusions from a study may indicate a refinement to an existing theory or suggest a new one for future consideration. There are many examples of this in the accounting profession where frequently the existing standards may prove insufficient to address current problems. While old standards may be used to address these problems in the short run, longer-term standards may be needed to more precisely address those issues. An example of this is accounting for contingent liabilities, addressed in *SFAS No. 5,* "Accounting for Contingencies," issued in 1975.[5] Later FASB statements or other authoritative pronouncements have amended, superseded, and interpreted parts of *SFAS No. 5* to address the specific nature of other liabilities.[6] This process of learning from research to improve existing theories and standards applies as a general rule to all types of research.

The Inductive Ground-Up Method

The top-down hypothetico-deductive method discussed in the previous subsection is useful for many research issues confronting the professional accountant. If the conclusions from this research are consistent with the predictions of the theory, the researcher has found support for the hypotheses. However, if the evidence in the research is inconsistent with the hypotheses, then the conclusions and the implementation plan may result

---

4. Financial Accounting Standards Board, *Statement of Financial Accounting Standards No. 13,* "*Accounting for Leases*" (Stamford, CT: 1976).

5. Financial Accounting Standards Board, *Statement of Financial Accounting Standards No. 5,* "*Accounting for Contingencies*" (Stamford, CT: 1975).

6. For example, paragraph 7 of *SFAS No 5* is amended by *SFAS No. 87, SFAS No. 112,* and *SFAS No. 123*; paragraph 13 is superseded by *SFAS No. 71*; paragraph 18 is amended by *SFAS 111*; paragraph 23 is amended by *SFAS No. 114*; and so on.

in communication of the fact that the theory needs further refinement or testing.[7] If no theory was identified in the first place, the evidence found can result in the development of a new theory altogether. This inductive ground-up method is useful for generating or refining theories useful for standards setting or practices, but it is a by-product of the professional research process. It is of interest more to academic and standards-setting bodies than the professional accountant.

Contemporary Accounting Research Models

Numerous models can be listed as useful for applied accounting research. These models aim at discovering and testing new knowledge, and they are influenced by various economic, environmental, and political realities of their times. In this section, we identify four classes of contemporary research models that have attracted much attention in the past few decades of research in accounting. The purpose is not to provide a comprehensive list of these models, but only illustrative classes with significant applications in accounting. We present a general discussion of one of these classes of research in this chapter, leaving the other three classes for discussion in later chapters. It is important to note that the knowledge base in these models changes as a result of the changes in the economic, promulgatory, and regulatory environment. Nevertheless, as explained below, each of these models presents well-established conclusions that are useful for the professional accountant. Exhibit 5–2 presents these classes of research models and their purposes.

Exhibit 5-2	Contemporary Accounting Research Models
Model	*Purpose*
1. Capital markets research	To understand the effects of accounting information on capital markets (this chapter)
2. Judgment and decision making	To understand and improve human judgment and decision making processes (Chapter 7)
3. Critical and creative thinking and problem solving	To understand new meaning through critical thinking and to create new ideas through creative thinking (Chapter 8)
4. Ethics	To understand and find methods to improve the ethical behavior of accountants and their clients (Chapter 9)

---

7. This conclusion assumes that the research was performed competently and the evidence gathered was reliable. If these assumptions are invalid, then the problem may arise from the research design and implementation rather than from the underlying theory.

The first model in Exhibit 5–2 is the capital markets research. It is discussed in the remainder of this chapter. Model 2 focuses on judgment and decision making. This model is used to assist professionals in improving their judgments and decisions. Details are presented in Chapter 7.

Models of critical and creative thinking and problem solving refer to the understanding of how new meaning can be generated (critical thinking) and how new ideas are created (creative thinking), and how these concepts assist with problem solving. Increasingly more attention has been focused on these issues in recent years as discussed in Chapter 8.

Finally, models of ethics provide the foundation for research in accounting. Attention to these models has increased in recent years to enhance public trust in the accounting profession. Cognitive developmental models of ethics provide a means of understanding stages of ethical cognition in individual accountants. One of the goals of these models is to understand and improve ethical behavior. As such, these models support compliance with the Code of Conduct of the AICPA, but they go well beyond the requirements of the Code to include adherence to higher levels of principles and behavior. Models of corporate ethics relate to the ways in which corporations enhance their compliance with ethical expectations of the society. To assist corporations in this regard, audit firms have developed audits of corporate ethics programs as an area of assurance services. These issues are discussed in Chapter 9.

Models within the Capital Markets Research

Capital markets research deals with the relationship between accounting information on the one hand and asset valuation and security prices on the other. As such, these models provide the vehicles for research in both accounting and finance. The source of the theories used in building these models is primarily in economics, and many of the theories and models have been developed in the fields of accounting and finance. Also, the number of theories and models within the capital markets research is so extensive that several detailed chapters would be needed to describe them. We do not intend to discuss these theories and models of capital markets research in detail. Rather, our objective is to focus on the connection of a number of these models to professional accounting research and standards such as *SFAS No. 123* that deals with the disclosure of the cost of employee stock options and is discussed below. Four major models and their purposes are presented in Exhibit 5–3 and explored in the following sub-sections.

1. Dividend Policy Decision Models

The purpose of dividend policy decision models is to formulate the linkages between dividend, stock prices, and earnings. These research models help

Exhibit 5-3	Major Models within Capital Markets Research
Model	*Purpose*
1. Dividend policy decisions	To formulate the linkages between dividends, stock price, and earnings
2. Firm valuation	To measure the value of a company based on various measures such as future cash flows, earnings, and book values
3. Mix and cost of capital	To formulate the linkages between debt and equity financing and the resulting cost of capital
4. Option pricing models	To formulate the variables in evaluating the cost of options in compensation plans

stockholders to understand and improve their investment decisions. These models also help managers to understand and improve their dividend and capitalization policies. Simply stated, dividend policy has an effect on the firm's market value as reflected in its stock price. The issue is whether the firm should pay out dividends or reinvest the funds in the firm instead. The first option results in cash outflow to stockholders. The second option results in keeping the cash in the company and investing it in productive assets to improve productivity and profitability. Alternatively, excess cash can be used to buy back company shares to enhance overall shareholder value. Of course, cash can be kept and invested in money market funds or savings accounts that pay very little interest. Some cash rich companies opt for this option but are criticized for poor cash management by financial analysts.[8] Other companies invest their excess cash in investment instruments that carry various levels of risk with them, or they use the cash to acquire other companies for vertical or horizontal integration of various business lines.

The stockholder benefits whether the company pays out dividends, keeps the money for further expansion, or invests the cash in prudent investments. However, the nature of this benefit is different. When dividends are paid out, the stockholder receives assets and earns income. When the earnings are reinvested in the business, or invested in prudent investment instruments, the stockholders' wealth is enhanced through an assumed increase in the stock price. Stock price movements, of course, are affected by many factors, only one of which is the dividend policy. This is precisely where dividend policy decision models formulate the effects of

---

8. An interview with financial analysts on January 27, 1997, on CNBC revealed that companies such as Microsoft, Intel, and Chrysler that have billions in cash may be hurting their earnings power by not investing the cash in productive assets or innovative products.

dividend variables as well as other variables to investigate their effects on stock prices.[9]

Dividend policy and the changes made to it over time send a powerful signal to stockholders. One model indicates that dividends send a signal to stockholders about current and future income. For example, suppose stockholders expect a 5-percent increase in dividends every year based on a company's past dividend policy. If the company achieves particularly strong earnings in a given year, should it increase dividends by more than 5 percent? Stockholders might interpret such an increase as a signal that the company's long-term earnings prospects, and the resulting dividends, will continue to grow. A result of this perceived signal might be that stockholders would increase their buying of the stock pushing its price to higher levels. The opposite scenario can also occur when a reduction in dividends signals a decreasing income trend for the future resulting in stockholders selling their shares and pushing the stock price down.[10] This example indicates that changes in dividend policy have significant consequences on the company and its stockholders.

2. Valuation Models

These models provide vehicles for measuring the value of a business enterprise. The dividend policy discussed in the previous section can be used as a valuation model as described below. It was stated earlier that dividend policy has implications for the stock price, and thus the market capitalization of the firm.

The Traditional Valuation Model

A known or assumed stream of future dividends can be used in a mathematical model to measure the current value of the firm that should be close to its market capitalization. This model is called the *traditional valuation model*. A basic formulation of this model is:[11]

$$V_t = \sum_{\Gamma=1}^{\infty} (1 + r)^{-\Gamma} E_t[D_{t+\Gamma}] \tag{1}$$

Where: V_t is the value of the firm at time t

r is the discount rate

$E_t[D_{t+\Gamma}]$ is the dividend at time $_{t+\Gamma}$ expected at time t.

---

9. A classic dividends policy decision model is M. H. Miller and F. Modigliani, "Dividends Policy, Growth, and the Valuation of Shares," *Journal of Business* 34, no. 4 (1961), pp. 411–33.

10. This signal model of dividends policy was developed by J. Litner, "Distribution of Incomes of Corporations among Dividends, Retained Earnings, and Taxes," *American Economic Review* 46, no. 2 (1956), pp. 97–113.

11. See V. Bernard, "The Feltham-Ohlson Framework: Implications for Empiricists," *Contemporary Accounting Research* 11, no. 2 (Spring 1995), p. 741.

Note that equation (1) only focuses on an expected stream of dividends and a discount rate to predict the value of the firm. Each of these variables is subject to estimation error. Furthermore, while the equation does not explicitly specify the underlying accounting earnings and the cash flows that are needed to pay the dividend, it makes the assumption that the earnings and cash flows must be sufficient to support the payment of the stream of dividends.

Also important to note is that there can be many variations of equation (1) depending on the assumptions made. For example, let's look at a situation in which dividend in time t is known. It is also known that the company's dividend policy calls for an increase of g percent every year for the foreseeable future. These assumptions change equation (1) to:

$$V_t = \frac{D_t\,(1+g)}{(1+r)} + \frac{D_t\,(1+g)^2}{(1+r)^2} + \frac{D_t\,(1+g)^3}{(1+r)^3} + \ldots\ldots\ldots + \frac{D_t\,(1+g)^\infty}{(1+r)^\infty} \qquad (1a)$$

Fortunately, there is a mathematical way to reduce equation (1a) to a simple equation as presented in equation (1b).[12]

$$V_t = D_t \,/\, (r - g) \qquad (1b)$$

The assumption in equation (1b) is that the discount rate, r, is greater than the dividend growth rate, g. This is a reasonable assumption because typically companies do not increase the annual dividend by an amount greater than the discount rate (say the corporate cost of capital as described later). Also, providing a dividend growth rate that is greater than the discount rate will result in an infinite stock value because the denominator in equation (1b) will be negative. To illustrate, suppose that Markala, Inc. pays $3 of dividend at time t. Furthermore, Markala's dividend policy is to increase the annual dividend by a rate of 5 percent. Markala uses the prime rate as its discount rate. Let's assume that the prime rate as reported in *The Wall Street Journal* at time t was 10 percent. Consequently, the value of Markala's stock at time t would be:

$$V_t = \$3 \,/\, (.10 - .05) = \$60 \text{ per share}$$

If Markala's outstanding shares were 20,000 at time t, its market valuation at time t would be $1,200,000 (60 × 20,000).

The Fundamental Valuation Model

There is another model called the *fundamental valuation model* that explicitly takes into consideration the future earnings without explicit consideration of future dividends. While an old concept, a contemporary formulation of this model was recently proposed by Professors Gerald Feltham of the

---

12. See a typical financial management text for derivation of this formula.

University of British Columbia and James Ohlson of Columbia University.[13] Consequently, the model is also known as the Feltham-Ohlson model. A basic formulation of the model is:[14]

$$V_t = bv_t + \sum_{\Gamma = 1}^{\infty} (1 + r)^{-\Gamma} E_t[x_{t+I} - rbv_{t+\Gamma-1}] \qquad \text{EQN (2)}$$

Where: bv_t is book value at time t

r is the discount rate

$E_t[x_{t+\Gamma} - rbv_{t+\Gamma-1}]$ is the discounted future expected abnormal earnings at time t.

Note that while equation (1) has dividend in its formulation, equation (2) focuses on future earnings and book values. However, while the book value at time t is taken directly from the company's balance sheet, the expected abnormal earnings and discount rates are subject to estimation errors. For example, suppose that the book value of Markala at time t is $bv_t = \$1,000,000$, its discount rate, $r = 10$ percent, and its reasonably forecasted earnings ($x_{t+\Gamma}$) for the next five years are $110,000, 120,000, 130,000, 120,000, and 110,000. Since the expected earnings based on the discount rate of r (i.e., $rbv_{t+\Gamma-1}$) are $.10 \times 1,000,000 = \$100,000$, then the expected abnormal earnings at time t for the next five years will be: $10,000, $20,000, $30,000, $20,000, and $10,000 respectively. Consequently, the value of Markala at time t according to equation (2) would be:

$$V_t = 1,000,000 + \frac{(10,000)}{(1 + .10)} + \frac{(20,000)}{(1 + .10)^2} + \frac{(30,000)}{(1 + .10)^3} + \frac{(20,000)}{(1 + .10)^4} + \frac{(10,000)}{(1 + .10)^5}$$

$$V_t = 1,000,000 + 9,090 + 16,529 + 22,539 + 13,660 + 6,211 = \$1,068,029$$

If Markala's outstanding shares were 20,000 at time t, its share value would be $53.40 (1,068,029/20,000) as compared with the $60 share value calculated under equation (1).

The point in discussing the two valuation models is that reported dividends and earnings can be helpful in the valuation of companies. However, these variables must also be estimated for the future. While historical data are useful to establish trends, such data must be transformed into future dividends and earnings for input to the valuation models. In addition, an appropriate discount rate must be used to calculate the present

---

13. J. A. Ohlson, "Earnings, Book Values, and Dividends in Equity Valuation," *Contemporary Accounting Research* 11, no. 2 (Spring 1995), pp. 661–88 and G. Feltham and J. A. Ohlson, "Valuation and Clean Surplus Accounting for Operating and Financial Activities," *Contemporary Accounting Research* 11, no. 2 (Spring 1995), pp. 689–732.
14. V. Bernard, "The Feltham-Ohlson Framework: Implications for Empiricists," *Contemporary Accounting Research* 11, no. 2 (Spring 1995), p. 741.

value of future numbers (dividends or earnings) to calculate a current value for the firm.

3. Mix and Cost of Capital

We know that companies have a mix of debt and equity as the source of their capital. What should be the proportion of each in the balance sheet? In other words, what should be the debt to equity ratio? To answer this question, we present a basic formulation of the cost of capital to the firm. We assume a simple structure in which the firm has only one class of common stock and one source of debt. It goes without saying that the formula becomes more complex if the firm has more than one class of common stock with varying return expectations, or has preferred stocks as well as multiple sources of debt with varying interest rates. The basic formulation presented simply states that the cost of capital (COC) is equal to cost of debt (COD) plus cost of equity (COE) divided by total assets (TA):

$$COC = [COD + COE] \; / \; TA \tag{3}$$

Interest expense is a legitimate expense for tax purposes, resulting in the cost of debt being reduced by the tax savings. However, the distribution to stockholders is not accepted as an expense for tax purposes. Thus:

$$COC = [(1-t) \times iD + rE] \; / \; TA \tag{3a}$$

Where: t = tax rate

i = interest rate

r = expected rate of return by stockholders

For an illustration, let's assume that a company has $1,000 total assets financed $600 by debt and $400 by stockholders equity. Thus the debt/equity ratio is 1.5 times ($600/$400 = 1.5). Further, assume that the company pays 10 percent interest to its debt holders, and its shareholders expect 20 percent return on their equity. The marginal tax rate is 40 percent. What is the company's cost of capital? Applying equation (3a), the COC is calculated as:

$$[(1 - 0.4) \times 600 + 0.20 \times 400] \; /1,000 = [36 + 80] \; / \; 1,000 = 11.6\%$$

As this calculation shows, any change in the debt-equity mix will change the numerator of equation (3) and the resulting average cost of capital. For example, the cost of capital for a 50/50 capital structure in the above scenario will be 13 percent.[15]

This simple example indicates that companies have economic incentive to borrow money at a lower rate than the return on equity expected by their

---

15. $[1 - .4][.10][500] + [.20][500] = 130. \; 130/1000 = 13\%$

equity holders because the higher the proportion of the debt to equity, the lower the cost of capital. What will then be the limit of borrowing? What would the model look like when there are different classes of equity holders and debt holders? The cost of capital model formulates these relationships for the purpose of understanding the optimum mix, the cost of capital, and tax effects. However, securities with characteristics of both debt and equity instruments blur the distinctions discussed above. For example, redeemable preferred stock can have characteristics of both debt and equity instruments.

The mix and cost of capital models do not stop at calculating the average cost of capital. They also formulate the relationship between cost of capital and stock prices. In the previous example where the cost of capital was calculated to be 13 percent, if the company earns a return on existing assets of more than 13 percent, one would expect an increase in the firm's stock price because the excess return goes directly to shareholders (debt holders will receive the same fixed rate regardless of the corporate earnings). Management is said to create value for stockholders when this happens. The opposite will occur when the cost of capital exceeds the company's return on assets. Management is said to impair value for stockholders when this happens. Thus, everything else held constant, cost of capital is the rate of return on assets that the company must earn in order to keep the stock price constant.[16]

In its simplest form, return on assets is calculated by dividing the net profit by the net assets. Using the historical accounting numbers, net profit is taken from the income statement and net assets from the balance sheet to calculate the return on assets. For example, the return on assets for a company with $100 million in profits and $1 billion of net assets is 10 percent.

A problem with this calculation is that net profit and net assets are subject to variation due to the effects of inflation or changes in replacement costs of individual assets. Consequently, a number of valuation models have been proposed to adjust the historical cost accounting model for a better measurement of assets and profits and the resulting return on assets. For example, the Consumer Price Index (CPI) or specific replacement costs can be used to adjust the historical costs of assets. Finance professionals use an alternative model called the Capital Assets Pricing Model (CAPM) for the purpose of assessing the value of classes of assets owned by companies. This model is explained in the next subsection.

Another issue is the stock market's ability to capture this information and reflect it in a company's stock price. The Arbitrage Pricing Model has been used to describe this issue. Arbitrage refers to the purchase of securities on one market for immediate resale on another market in order to profit

---

16. R. C. Higgins, *Analysis for Financial Management*, 4th ed. (Boston, MA: Irwin/ McGraw-Hill, 1998).

from market price discrepancies.[17] Investors will benefit from arbitrage only if one stock market is less efficient in capturing the information about a company's true profits or assets and reflecting it in the stock price. The Efficient Market Hypothesis (EMH) has been advanced to address this issue.[18] The EMH is also described below.

The Capital Asset Pricing Model (CAPM). The CAPM captures investors' beliefs about unobservable future returns and incorporates the same in pricing a company's assets.[19] This model uses a mathematical formulation of the portfolio theory. The portfolio theory states that investors diversify their holdings of company shares so as to minimize the effects of the risk of a single stock. The CAPM explains, in part, the risk premium across assets. The risk premium is measured as the difference in a risky return on an asset (called the asset's *beta*) and the risk-free rate of return on Treasury bills as reported in *The Wall Street Journal*.

The research model represented by the CAPM formulates the complex relationships in earnings, capital assets, and cost of capital, taking into consideration the uncertain nature of the risk premium. While its mathematical nature and the subjective determination of some aspects of the risk have been, and continue to be, debated in the literature,[20] it has nevertheless been reported as a useful model for understanding the complex relationships between the variables it uses for asset pricing. A major problem with CAPM is that it cannot accurately measure the value of many assets (e.g., property, plant, and equipment) that are not traded in a market such as the stock market. Thus, it must estimate these assets based on estimated future returns that are subject to estimation errors.

The Efficient Market Hypothesis (EMH). The EMH states that stock markets are efficient in capturing information and reflecting it in a firm's stock price. The question is how efficient. Any inefficiency in getting the latest information by one stock market can result in arbitrage trading because it creates opportunities for investors to gain abnormal returns.

There are three forms of the EMH called the *weak form*, the *semistrong form*, and the *strong form*. These forms are listed and defined in Exhibit 5–4.

---

17. S. A. Ross, "The Arbitrage Pricing Theory of Capital Asset Pricing," *Journal of Economic Theory* 13, no. 3 (1976), pp. 341–60.

18. For detailed reviews of the EMH literature, see E. F. Fama, "Efficient Capital Markets: A Review of Theory and Empirical Work," *Journal of Finance* 25, no. 2 (1970), pp. 383–423 and E. F. Fama, "Efficient Capital Markets II," *Journal of Finance* 46, no. 5 (1991), pp. 1575–617.

19. The CAPM was first developed by Nobel Prize-winning economist, William Sharpe. See W. F. Sharpe, "Capital Asset Prices: A Theory of Market Equilibrium under Conditions of Risk," *Journal of Finance* 19, no. 3 (1964), pp. 425–42.

20. See, for example, R. Jagannathan and E. R. McGrattan, "The CAPM Debate," *Federal Reserve Bank of Minneapolis Quarterly Review* 19, no. 4 (Fall 1995), pp. 2–17.

Exhibit 5-4	Forms of the Efficient Market Hypothesis
Form	*Meaning*
1. Weak	Only historical information is captured and reflected in a company's stock price.
2. Semistrong	All publicly available information (historical and current) is reflected in a company's stock price.
3. Strong	All information (historical, current public, and private information) is reflected in a company's stock price.

Adapted from E. F. Fama, "Efficient Capital Markets: A Review of Theory and Empirical Work," *Journal of Finance* 25, no. 2 (1970), pp. 383-423.

In its weak form, EMH states that only a firm's historical information is captured and reflected in its stock price. In this form, the investor is likely to benefit from arbitrage trading because some markets may have access to some current information that is not shared with other markets. The investor may also have access to private information and use it to his or her advantage.

In its semistrong form, EMH indicates that all publicly available information (historical and current) about a firm is reflected in its stock price. The investor is unlikely in the semistrong form of the EMH to earn an abnormal return by engaging in arbitrage trading because all information is available to all markets. The investor, however, may have access to private information that will help him or her to benefit in any stock market.

In the strong form of the EMH, the investor is unlikely to benefit from arbitrage trading. This can happen because in its strong form, EMH reflects all information (historical, current public and private) in the stock price. Thus, an investor with access to private information cannot earn abnormal returns by engaging in arbitrage trading.

A conclusion from this discussion is that the EMH is a useful model for understanding the dynamics of the stock market's ability to capture information and reflect it in a firm's stock price. As such, it has generated much interest among corporate management as well as academic researchers, investors, and regulators. It is also noteworthy that the information technology has resulted in a much wider access to information. This access can reduce an investor's chances of benefiting from arbitrage trading. Also reducing this chance is the SEC's new ruling concerning selective disclosure of financial information by public companies. In August 2000, the SEC approved a rule, Regulation FD (fair disclosure), that ends selective disclosure of financial information by public companies.[21] Regulation FD essentially requires that companies release material,

---

21. "Mum's the Word in Wake of Disclosure Rule" in *The Wall Street Journal*, August 16, 2000, pp. C1, C8.

sensitive information to all parties at the same time. Companies can no longer selectively disclose such information via private communication to large investors and/or analysts. This rule is expected to reduce chances of arbitrage trading.

A major assumption implicit in the EMH is that capital markets are competitive in the economic sense, and thus they all have equal access to the information. Furthermore, no single investor or trader has the ability to affect the stock price in a significant way. Helping this situation is the popularity of the portfolio theory that indicates that investors strategize by focusing on the risk of a diversified portfolio as compared with the risk of a single stock. Thus, a single stock's ability to influence the market in significant ways is reduced by this strategy. However, in recent years, stocks of many Internet companies such as Amazon.com, Ebay, and Netscape have produced market capitalizations so large that they defy these theories. For example, Netscape with only $16 million of revenue reached a market capitalization of $2 billion in its first day of trading in 1995.

Also reduced is the ability of investors to earn abnormal returns by engaging in arbitrage trading. What then is the value of particular accounting information on a company's stock price? Event studies have been used to investigate the effects of accounting information on stock prices by analyzing the stock prices immediately before and after the release of a particular information (called the event). These studies have generally provided support for the applicability of the EMH models.

Nevertheless, scenarios can be presented that investors have gained abnormal returns by focusing on some aspects of the information that other investors have ignored. While research in determining what is behind this deviation from the EMH continues, it may be stated that an investor with a higher level of knowledge or cognitive complexity may be able to interpret information advantageously than an investor with less knowledge or cognitive complexity. For example, while all investors have access to published financial statements, researchers have shown that some investors can form predictions about future earnings in general, and the EPS in particular, and form portfolios that will have abnormal returns.[22] These studies indicate that detailed knowledge of financial statements is useful for capital markets research. This is particularly important in the age of the Internet, when the speed with which information is widely communicated has dramatically increased. Unfortunately, the Internet does provide the opportunity to quickly spread positive or negative rumors in a chat room style of information sharing that creates unethical opportunities for taking advantage of naïve investors. An investor with knowledge of business

---

22. See for example, J. A. Ou and S. H. Penman, "Financial Statement Analysis and the Prediction of Stock Returns," *Journal of Accounting and Economics* 11, no. 4 (1989), pp. 295–329.

fundamentals and financial information is less likely to become prey to these rumors.

4. Option-Pricing Models

Suppose that a company awards an option to one of its executives to buy 100,000 shares of the company's stock at a given price upon fulfillment of certain contractual terms. How much is the cost of this option to the company as compensation? How should the transaction be recorded in the books of the company? Traditionally, employee stock options have been priced as the difference between the stock price at the time the option is granted and the exercise price of the option. In the past, in order for companies to avoid recognizing compensation expense for stock options, they typically set the option exercise price equal to or greater than the market price on the date that the option is granted. The incentive for the executive is that should he or she increase the shareholder value significantly by improving the share price, there will be significant financial benefits to reap by exercising the options. In most cases, these options have a positive value although the right to exercise the option may be postponed to a later date than the contract signature time.[23]

The measurement of the cost of stock options is a challenging task. Option-pricing models attempt to formulate the variables that must be considered for such a measurement. These models have gained popularity in recent years due to the increasing role of options and other derivatives in the corporate financial picture. This situation presents a complex problem for both accounting and finance.

According to the FASB, a stock option is "a contract that gives the holder the right, but not the obligation, either to purchase or to sell a certain number of shares of stock at the predetermined price for a specified period of time."[24] An option to purchase is called a call option while an option to sell is called a put option. The FASB extensively debated the issue of what the appropriate accounting and reporting for stock options granted to employees should be. Its contention was that these options represented a compensation plan, and the cost of these plans must be recognized as such in the body of financial statements (i.e., as an expense in the income statement). Twelve years of debate resulted in *SFAS No. 123* in 1995 that only required disclosure of the cost of options and left the method of measuring the cost wide open.[25]

---

23. There is a difference here between American and European options. In the U.S., the option can be exercised any time between its initiation and expiration dates. European options generally have to be exercised on the expiration date.

24. Financial Accounting Standards Board, *Statement of Financial Accounting Standards No. 123*, "Accounting for Stock-Based Compensation" (Norwalk, CT: 1995).

25. The details of this process are presented in a comprehensive appendix to Chapter 6 that focuses on the methodology of applied accounting research.

A major problem that confronted the FASB was how to measure the cost of options at the time they were awarded. Such a determination is necessary for recording the transaction as a compensation expense. In an exposure draft, the FASB opted for a popular option-pricing model called the Black and Scholes model.[26] The Black and Scholes model uses six variables to formulate the cost of a call option. The mathematical formulation of this model is quite complex and unnecessary to duplicate here. Basically, the cost of a call option, according to the Black and Scholes model, is a function of six variables as presented in equation (4):

Call option cost $= f(S, T, R, V, X, P)$ $\hspace{2cm}$ (4)

Where:

$S =$ the stock price at the time the option is awarded;

$T =$ the time to maturity
(i.e., time period from the issuance to expiration of the option);

$R =$ the risk-free rate of return;

$V =$ the variability or volatility (i.e., the standard deviation) of the underlying rate of return from the issuance to expiration of the option (i.e., a measure of risk);

$X =$ the option's exercise price;

$P =$ the price of the call option at the issue date.

Of these six variables, three (T, X, and P) are easy to determine because they are contractual between the issuing company and its employees. The first variable, stock price (S), can be adopted from market quotations. The third variable, the risk-free rate of return (R), also can be adopted from market quotations. It is usually the Treasury-bill rate reported in *The Wall Street Journal*.[27]

However, the fourth variable, (V) is the uncertain variable that requires a probabilistic formulation for measurement. The predictive accuracy of the Black and Scholes model is subject to error due to the probabilistic nature of this measurement. In fact, research shows that the model works best when the option's exercise price is at the current stock price at the time of issue, when the duration of the option is three months or less, and when the volatility is neither too high nor too low. Otherwise, the model overvalues the option when the current stock price exceeds the

---

26. F. Black and M. Scholes, "The Pricing of Options and Corporate Liabilities," *Journal of Political Economy* 81, no. 3 (1973), pp. 637–54.

27. D. M. Long and D. T. Officer, "The Relation between Option Mispricing and Volume in the Black-Scholes Option Model," *Journal of Financial Research* 20, no. 1 (Spring 1997), pp. 1–12.

option's exercise price, when there are dividends before the exercise date, and when there is above average volatility in the option price. On the other hand, the model undervalues the option when the current stock price is less than the option's exercise price, and when there is below average volatility in the option price.[28]

These limitations of the Black and Scholes model resulted in difficulty for the FASB in its efforts to justify the use of it in practice. Also, the mathematical nature of the model may be too complex for many practitioners. These and other concerns, such as restricting the ability of small companies to attract executive talent, resulted in the FASB's abandoning of mandatory option cost measurement altogether. As stated earlier, *SFAS No. 123* only requires the disclosure of the cost of options although the reporting entity can elect to report the option cost as a compensation expense in the financial statements if it chooses to do so. Thus, entities not choosing to report cost of stock options can continue to account for stock options in accordance with *APB Opinion No. 25*, "Accounting for Stocks Issued to Employees." Basically, under *APB No. 25*, compensation expense is determined as the excess of the market price over the option price at the date of grant. The method used for option pricing can be as complex as the analytic Black and Scholes model or as simple as a basic numerical analysis—the reporting entity makes the choice, not the FASB.

The FASB's problems with the Black and Scholes option-pricing model indicates the complex nature of derivative instruments and the challenge they present for standard setting. It seems that the FASB has opted for disclosure of these instruments in footnotes as compared with recognition in the body of financial statements. *SFAS No. 133*, "Accounting for Derivative Instruments and Hedging Activities," is another example of this strategy.[29] Nevertheless, research models such as the Black and Scholes option-pricing model help us understand the nature and complexity of measurement and disclosure of these transactions.

Other Models

There are many other models that are used to formulate issues of concern to accountants, management, stockholders, and other stakeholders. They include analytical agency models where the relationships between a company's management (agent) and its shareholders (principals) are formulated. Accounting measures of performance as well as other measures are

---

28. This summary is adopted from P. Brown, *Capital Market-Based Research in Accounting: An Introduction* (Sydney, Australia: Coopers & Lybrand and Accounting Association of Australia and New Zealand: Accounting Research Methodology Monograph No. 1, 1994), pp. 18–19.

29. Financial Accounting Standards Board, *Statement of Financial Accounting Standards No. 133*, "Accounting for Derivative Instruments and Hedging Activities" (Norwalk, CT: 1998).

used to regulate the relationship between the principals and agents in the company. These relationships are very complex, requiring analytical formulation and empirical investigation. Other models formulate the behavior of corporate managers that choose accounting methods and techniques in order to maximize their own personal interests as compared with the interest of the stockholders. A line of research called *positive accounting* deals with these issues. Similarly, information economics and economic consequence models mathematically formulate the effects of accounting numbers on economic decisions. Standard setters in particular pay attention to these models to understand the economic consequences of their standards on various industries and companies within those industries.

One particular research area that has begun to gain attention in recent years in applied accounting research is accounting history. For a long time, researchers ignored this area for model building and research for reasons not completely understood. However, an increasing number of researchers have recently engaged in efforts to understand accounting history. Historical research models help develop an understanding of the relationships between accounting thought and genealogy.[30] For example, the fundamental formulation for corporate valuation in equation (2) can be traced back to 1920 when the Internal Revenue Service (IRS) used the formulation to estimate the impact of Prohibition on the value of breweries.[31] As stated earlier, two researchers published this equation in the mid-1990s. Had research paid more attention to historical events, it would perhaps have taken less than 70 years to develop the equation.

For another example, consider the issue of the auditors' responsibility to uncover management fraud. This issue has been the subject of debate for decades and has recently culminated in the Auditing Standards Board issuing *Statement on Auditing Standards (SAS) No. 82*.[32] This statement requires that auditors plan the audit so that material fraud, if it exists, will be detected. Based on a historical review of fraudulent financial reporting in the U.S. from the late 1800s to the present, researchers have argued that auditors must accept responsibility for detection of management fraud just as they did some 100 years ago.[33] These researchers presented a general

---

30. For a detailed discussion of the issues here, see G. J. Previts and T. R. Robinson, "A Discourse on Historical Inquiry and Method in Accountancy," Chapter 6, in A. J. Richardson, *Research Methods in Accounting: Issues and Debates* (Vancouver, BC, Canada: CGA-Canada Research Foundation: Research Monograph Number 25, 1996), pp. 171–208.
31. V. Bernard, "The Feltham-Ohlson Framework: Implications for Empiricists," *Contemporary Accounting Research* 11, no. 2 (Spring 1995), p. 741.
32. American Institute of Certified Public Accountants, *Statement of Auditing Standards No. 82*, "Consideration of Fraud in a Financial Statement Audit" (New York, NY: 1997).
33. M. J. Abdolmohammadi, M. Iskandar, and P. McMann, "An Historical Perspective on Fraudulent Financial Reporting in the United States" in *Disorder and Harmony: 20th Century Perspectives on Accounting History*, A. J. Richardson (ed.) (Vancouver, BC, Canada: CGA-Canada Research Foundation: Research Monograph Number 23, 1996), pp. 113–31.

model focusing on the linkages between legislation, court decisions, congressional hearings, and private commissions on the one hand, and auditor responsibility on the other. The admission of responsibility in detecting fraud via *SAS No. 82* is welcome news.

Another recommendation made by these researchers is to seek equity in civil liability for auditors. The rapid increase in lawsuits against auditors in the 1980s and 1990s was threatening the very existence of the auditing profession as we know it today. For example, the then seventh largest accounting firm, Laventhal and Horwath, ceased operations on November 21, 1990, due to the pressure from lawsuits.[34] The passage of the Private Securities Litigation Reform Act of 1995 has provided relief by reducing frivolous lawsuits and outrageous settlements.[35] Other recommendations by these authors include redesigning financial statements into customized reports, providing discretionary audit reports with considerable flexibility in wording much like those issued in the early 1900s, conducting random fraud audits such as those conducted by the Internal Revenue Service to catch tax evaders, and establishing regulated audit fees as compared to the discounted rates used in attracting new clients by some accounting firms.

The point in this discussion is that sometimes just looking back into history can suggest solutions to some of our contemporary problems. A focus on research models used in the past or those that can be developed based on historical knowledge can be helpful in putting some of today's problems and issues in perspective.

Summary

In this chapter we provided a general framework for inductive and deductive reasoning in applied accounting research. We first defined applied research and then identified the components of the framework. The framework uses both hypothetico-deductive and inductive ground-up methods for applied research. On the basis of this framework, the process of identifying a theory to establish a set of hypotheses or expectations for the research process to address a specific research question was defined. The need for the development of courses of action and their consequences was also identified, and the research design types and their purposes were discussed.

In the second section of the chapter, we identified four major classes of contemporary research models with particularly significant application in applied accounting research. The first class, called *capital markets research* was briefly described, and four of its major subsets (dividend policy, valuation models, mix and cost of capital, and option-pricing models) were briefly discussed. Brief coverage was provided of capital asset pricing models, arbitrage

---

34. Lee Berton, "Laventhol & Horwath's Ex-Audit Clients Being Forced to Flag Potential Liability." *Wall Street Journal* (Eastern Edition, Feb. 15, 1991), p. A14.
35. Congress of the United States of America, "Private Securities Litigation Reform Act," *Congressional Record* – Senate 104th Congress, 1st Session, 141.106 (1995).

pricing model of securities, and the Efficient Market Hypothesis. The chapter concluded with a brief discussion of the relevance of many other fundamental models of research and of accounting history, which have received much attention in recent years.

Judgment and decision making, ethics, critical and creative thinking, and problem solving models were also listed as contemporary research models. These models are discussed in later chapters.

Selected Additional Reading

Glaser, B. G., and A. L. Strauss. *The Discovery of Grounded Theory*. Chicago, IL: Aldine, 1967.

Sekaran, U. *Research Methods for Business: A Skill-Building Approach*, 3rd ed. New York: Wiley, 2000.

Questions

1. Define applied accounting research.
2. Identify and briefly discuss various components of an applied research framework.
3. Identify and define the two major characteristics of an applied research process.
4. Identify and describe the two major modes of logical reasoning.
5. Identify and define various steps in a hypothetico-deductive method of research.
6. How can the inductive ground-up logic result in the refinement of a theory?
7. Provide a general definition of contemporary accounting research models.
8. List four classes of contemporary accounting research models and discuss their purposes.
9. What is the overall goal of capital markets research in accounting and finance?
10. Four capital market research models were discussed in the chapter. List these models and briefly define them.
11. What is a dividend policy decision model? What types of research has it fostered over the years?
12. Describe two valuation models.
13. Use both the traditional and the fundamental valuation models to calculate a value for Kamper, Inc. An analyst uses Kamper's cost of capital of 15 percent as its discount rate. Currently, Kamper pays a $4 dividend per share and plans to increase the dividend by 6 percent

annually for the foreseeable future. The analyst estimates Kamper's expected abnormal earnings at time *t* for the next five years to be: $100,000, $150,000, $300,000, $500,000, and $200,000, respectively. Kamper has 500,000 shares of stock outstanding.
14. The debt and equity mix in the capital structure of a company has implications for the cost of capital in the company. With a numerical example, calculate the cost of capital for a company.
15. How does the cost of capital and debt/equity mix relate to the stock price of a company?
16. Describe the capital asset pricing model.
17. Describe efficient markets hypothesis and list its three forms.
18. What is arbitrage in equity trading and how can it happen?
19. What is an option-pricing model?
20. Describe the Black and Scholes option-pricing model.
21. Why have option-pricing models proved difficult for the accounting profession as a means of measuring the cost of call options?
22. Briefly describe the economic consequences and the agency models of research.
23. What is research in the history of accounting and how does it relate to contemporary problems facing the profession?

Appendix 5A
Issues for Research

We present a list of research issues in the areas of accounting policy, promulgation, and regulation. Each issue can be selected as a topic of research, say for a term project. For the issue that you select or your instructor assigns as a project, develop a research framework in accordance with Exhibit 5–1 and proceed to conduct the research. You may also need to consult Chapter 6 for information on various methodologies and choose an appropriate methodology for your issue.

A. Accounting policy

1. Accounting policy change: How is it done? What are the considerations in making corporate accounting changes?

2. Information technology has implications for corporate accounting policy. What are these implications and how could they be implemented?

3. Disclosure of accounting information: How is it used? Is it there as a control mechanism or for real use? What arguments are there in the literature regarding the need for disclosure of important financial reporting issues?

4. Environmental accounting and auditing measurement and liabilities: What are the companies doing concerning this problem?

B. Accounting promulgation

1. Post-retirement benefits other than pension plan: What are the cost estimates and accounting issues?

2. What should be the FASB's strategy in setting accounting standards? General? Industry specific? Or general with guidelines for specific industries? What is the role of the SEC in this process (e.g., what method does the SEC prefer)?

3. Stock option accounting: What are the issues and the developments beyond *SFAS No. 123*?

4. Standard setting between accounting and other comparable professions: What are the similarities and differences?

5. What is proportional consolidation and what is the FASB doing regarding this issue?

6. Compare and contrast the pooling and purchase methods of accounting for mergers and acquisitions. What is the FASB's latest stand on these methods?

7. *SFAS No. 87* has provisions for the use of an appropriate discount rate for measurement of certain obligations. Should a different discount rate be used for liabilities (e.g., pension obligations) and expenses (e.g., option pricing)? Is *SFAS No. 69*'s 10 percent discount rate inconsistent with newer FASB statements? What should be done about it?

8. What are the current projects and their status at the ASB, FASB, and GASB?

9. Describe the FASB's current organization. Who are the trustees and what are the criteria for their selection or election? What is the FASB's current budget? How is it funded and how is it spent?

10. Discuss the standards overload problem and provide a history of initiatives to resolve it. What is the current policy of the FASB?

11. Should the FASB consider small GAAP for small companies and big GAAP for large companies? What has been FASB's position on this issue?

C. Accounting regulation

1. Is governmental regulation needed for accounting standard setting or is the profession in a good position to continue setting its own standards?

2. The SEC is the designated accounting regulator (overseer) in the U.S. What is the SEC? What is its organizational structure? Number and function of its employees? Its publications? Its methods of enforcing its authority over public companies and auditors?

3. What authority does the SEC have over foreign registrants and how does it discharge that responsibility?

4. What are the current projects at the SEC? Discuss the topics and their status at this time.

5. What are the current projects at the CASB? Discuss the topics and their status at this time. Include a brief description of the CASB.

6. Environmental accounting and auditing issues, measurement, and liabilities: What are the laws and regulatory rules in regard to this problem?

7. Provide a complete discussion of the SEC's regulations and reporting requirements. What are the penalties for failure to comply with these requirements?

8. How can the SEC's EDGAR system be utilized for retrieving information about companies? Provide specific cases.

D. Future of accounting

1. What will be the shape or form of financial reports in the next decade?

2. What will the accounting firm of the future look like? Stay with the auditing/tax/consulting practices or what?

3. Present a framework of accounting/bookkeeping in an information technology setting.

4. Is the general accounting model broad enough to apply to the information technology setting of the new millennium?

5. How does the new information technology facilitate real-time reporting as compared with periodic reporting of financial and other information by public companies?

E. International accounting

1. International accounting issues (e.g., leases, pension plans, depreciation methods, and EPS) of concern today: What is the set of core standards that the IOSCO has requested from the IASC? Has IASC delivered these standards as yet?

2. Should the U.S. try to (1) influence other countries in accepting its accounting standards or (2) accept international accounting standards for its internal use?

3. ISO 9000 series: What are they? What do they mean? How do they relate to accounting and auditing?

4. Compare inflation accounting in three countries of your choice. Use the U.S. as the base and compare various issues related to inflation accounting.

5. What is hedging in currency transactions and how should it be measured and reported?

6. What are the current projects at the IASC? Discuss topics and their status at this time.

F. Other issues

1. Effects of inflation on accounting reporting: Discuss measurement systems and their implications on financial statements.

2. Accountants in the media: Conduct a historical representation of accountants in the media. Focus on a specific period of time (e.g., 1960–2000).

3. The accounting profession has been actively pursuing litigation reform in recent years to reduce the number and extent of lawsuits leveled against it. What is the extent of auditors' legal liabilities now?

4. Provide a historical account of auditors' responsibility for detecting fraudulent financial reporting.

5. How do you account for the cost of in-process R&D?

6. What types of professional services can be offered by accountants/auditors in the new millennium?

7. What are the sources of information for professional research? Provide a structure and a summary of the literature, databases, and other tools.

8. Internal auditing: What is it? Is the trend toward outsourcing? What personality types are attracted to internal auditing as compared with independent auditing and accounting?

9. Select a contemporary accounting issue and present a research design to investigate it using alternative designs (i.e., deductive-inductive framework, laboratory experiment, and database search).

6

METHODOLOGY OF PROFESSIONAL ACCOUNTING RESEARCH

Every improvement in communication makes the bore more terrible.
Frank Moore Colby

Objectives

In this chapter we discuss the methodology and the process for issue-based accounting research. Upon completion of the chapter you will have learned:

1. The components of a general research methodology.
2. Major evidence-gathering methods and their relevance to professional accounting research.
3. Steps in the professional accounting research process.
4. Communication of research results.
5. Good versus poor quality of professional writing.
6. A format for research reports.

Various data-gathering methods for practical research are discussed in this chapter. The primary focus of the chapter is on an issue-based model of practical research where a specific issue of accounting, auditing, or consulting is subjected to investigation. Various methods of data collection for research are discussed first, followed by a section on the specific steps in the professional research process. This process includes a communication step that is particularly important. Given this importance, we provide some writing guidelines and a report format. To illustrate the whole issue-based research process, we present a research report in Appendix 6A concerning the FASB's option-pricing project.

Methods of Investigation

Methods of collecting data for the purpose of investigating an issue vary depending on the nature of the research issue. They differ primarily in the degree to which they generate internal and external validity as described in an earlier chapter. While some methods may be more desirable from this perspective, the use of other methods may be necessitated by the circumstances. For example, laboratory experiments are generally preferred to mail surveys because the researcher has more control over the variables in the laboratory setting than in a mail survey. However, for many professional research questions, it is impractical to gather a large sample of professionals in a laboratory setting for research purposes. In these cases, the circumstances dictate the use of surveys.

Several primary methods of collecting data are summarized in Exhibit 6–1. The method of research, the type of data collected, and the typical method used for data analysis are presented in the exhibit. They are discussed in the following subsections.

Laboratory Experiments

A laboratory experiment is a setting where a representative sample of participants is given a stimulus, say a case study, and is asked to respond to a number of questions. For example, in one study, a sample of auditors ranging in experience from auditing students to staff to audit partners were given several auditing cases and were asked to make several audit judgments based on the information. These judgments included an assessment of the expected population deviation rate in the control environment of a sales and collection cycle case study. A finding from this study was that in unstructured task situations, experienced auditors outperform inexperienced ones, but for simple, structured tasks and some semistructured tasks, inexperienced auditors do not differ from experienced auditors in their judgments.[1] This finding has implications for task structuring, decision aid development, and training in auditing.

A branch of laboratory experiments that has become popular in recent years is the laboratory markets/experimental economics research design. It is a computerized simulated game in which market variables are formulated in a way to simulate the requisite market. Participants are recruited to use the simulated game to make economic decisions. For example, groups of students may be assigned projects to develop hypothetical companies and

---

1. M. Abdolmohammadi and A. Wright, "An Examination of the Effects of Experience and Task Complexity on Audit Judgments," *The Accounting Review* 62, no. 1 (January 1987), pp. 1–13.

Exhibit 6–1	Professional Research Design	
Method	*Data*	*Analysis*
1. Laboratory experiments	Participant responses to stimuli provided by the researcher	The responses are entered into data sets that can be analyzed using statistical methods (e.g., mean, standard deviation).
2. Survey questionnaire	Participant responses to questions in a questionnaire	The responses are entered into data sets that can be analyzed using statistical methods (e.g., mean, standard deviation).
3. Archival studies	Past experiences such as audits similar to the current engagement	The information from archives is summarized and tabulated for the research objective. Data from adequate samples can be analyzed using statistical methods (e.g., mean, standard deviation).
4. Database search	Various databases such as EDGAR	Reported data from these databases are entered into data sets that can be analyzed using statistical methods (e.g., mean, standard deviation).
5. Library search search of a literature index,	Literature review such as a (e.g., the FASB statements say Accounting and Tax Index	The sources of information and interpretations) are summarized and synthesized for the research objective.
6. Analytical modeling	None, but literature review of analytical work in similar or related research issues	Mathematical formulation is performed using symbols and mathematical conventions.
7. Field research/case study	Detailed information about a real situation is collected by a visit to a company site	The sources of information (e.g., the FASB statements and interpretations) are summarized and synthesized for the reasarch objective.

compete against each other in a simulated competitive market. The simulation game results in a dynamic marketplace in which changes are introduced constantly based on participants' decision inputs concerning marketing, pricing, production, and financial information.

The primary method of analysis for the data collected in a laboratory experiment is statistical analysis and tabulation. As reported in Exhibit 6–1, the responses from these experiments are entered into data sets that can be analyzed using statistical methods. For example, suppose that your class is viewed as a representative sample of all students in your school. You are given a set of six cases representing six different ethical dilemmas for analysis.

Upon your analysis, you respond to 12 questions on each case, covering various aspects of ethical decision making. Collectively, these questions measure your ethical cognition. Upon coding of the responses, the means and standard deviations of various measures can be calculated to compare various sample groups such as male and female students.[2]

The data can also be used to infer the ethical cognition of female and male students at your school by generalizing from the sample to the whole population of the school. The statistics used for this purpose are called *inferential statistics* and require more sophisticated methods than just the mean and standard deviation. Coverage of these statistical methods is beyond the scope of this chapter. A professional researcher benefits from a basic familiarity with the strengths and weaknesses of these methods in order to perform the analysis and to understand the implications of the analysis. However, the researcher does not need to have detailed knowledge of the underlying mathematical or statistical calculations for these models. Software programs are now available that do these detailed calculations for you.

Relatively easy-to-use statistical software packages such as SPSS, SAS, and Minitab that bring sophisticated data analysis within the reach of many researchers are now available for personal computers. This is indeed good news because, more than ever before, the professional researcher needs help from these packages to make sense of the vast amounts of data that are now available through databases and other information technology-generated sources (e.g., accounting systems). The basic knowledge needed for this purpose is modest. Specialized knowledge about these packages and their underlying mathematical and statistical models can be obtained from a library search, software manuals, and consultants. Surveys have indicated that professional accountants view these packages as the third most crucial packages for accountants to know (after word processing and spreadsheet programs).[3]

Survey Questionnaires

Survey questionnaires are useful for collection of data from participants through mail, e-mail, websites, or other distribution methods. In the study of the effects of experience and task complexity on audit judgments mentioned earlier, the authors sent a survey questionnaire to a sample of audit managers and partners from several international accounting firms. These

2. The six cases, the testing procedure, and the ethical cognition measures are the components of a test called the *Defining Issues Test (DIT)*. The test is the property of the Center for the Study of Ethical Development at the University of Minnesota. This test will be further discussed in Chapter 9, "Ethical Considerations in Judgment and Decision Making in Accounting."
3. See S. M. Glover and M. Romney, "Software Survey—20 Hot Trends: The Software Revolution Is Fueling Change and Challenge in Internal Auditing," *Internal Auditor* (August 1997), pp. 28–38.

professionals were asked to classify several audit tasks by their level of task structure using a 1–27 scale (extremely structured to highly unstructured). The results from this survey provided an independent task structure classification for the tasks that were used to collect data in a laboratory setting.

The method of data analysis for data collected in a survey is similar to those used for laboratory experiments. Statistical methods are used to analyze the data where tables can be developed to present a summary of these data. However, the main difference between a survey and a laboratory experiment is the ability of the researcher to control for the variables of interest. In a laboratory experiment, the researcher can isolate the variables of interest from other variables. This control enhances internal validity. Also, participants in these studies are recruited beforehand either randomly (a preferred method) or based on availability and interest (a method necessitated by circumstances). In survey research, not every participant contacted will respond, and often there is a question as to the presence of conditions or variables that the researcher may not have accounted for. The former problem results in a response rate that is low, sometimes well below an acceptable level. The latter problem raises questions about variable isolation or internal validity.

Nevertheless, survey research is a very popular and practical method used in professional accounting. Auditors may use it to survey client personnel concerning a wide range of issues from adherence to control procedures to the level of ethics in the firm. Budgetary practices or preferences may be found by a survey of a company's managers. Given this importance, a detailed survey-based research is provided at the end of the professional research process section to illustrate various steps in the process.

Archival Studies

Archival studies investigate an issue by the use of data from actual situations such as past audits rather than from laboratory studies or surveys. Archival studies go directly to the files containing past information. These studies then code the parts of the information that might be useful for answering a contemporary research question. For example, in a study to understand how auditors identify audit adjustments, two researchers investigated the archives of an international accounting firm and found several procedures that were used as means of directing the auditors' attention to the need for adjustments.[4] Methods of analysis are similar to those in the laboratory experiments and survey questionnaires.

In a more recent paper, researchers used the archives of an accounting firm to investigate the firm's approach to client acceptance. The researchers

---

4. A. Wright and R. H. Ashton, "Identifying Audit Adjustments with Attention-Directing Procedures," *The Accounting Review* 64, no. 4 (1989), pp. 710–28.

focused on the population of 452 proposed clients over a 10-month period. They investigated risk evaluation and risk adaptation strategies used by accountants to accept or reject new clients. Among their findings is that firms with more fraud risk or losses and higher leverage are less likely to be accepted as clients.[5]

Database Search

Databases provide a rich source of data for capital market studies. For example, the Market Guide database provides multiple-year financial statements and ratios for many companies. There are many sources for this search that provide empirical data (i.e., data from past observations). For this reason, the method of investigation is called *empirical research*. The method of analysis in database search is similar to those in the survey and laboratory experiments. Basically, data are tabulated and analyzed using statistical methods.

Library Search

Library search of the literature is used to review the information already available from previous research. This method is the primary method of investigation for many professional research issues where the objective is to find a solution to a contemporary problem in the existing literature. Library search is also an integral part of other research to understand the state-of-the-art knowledge about the research issue before a research design is selected to investigate it further. Without this, a researcher may duplicate something that has already been done, thus incurring research expenses that could have been saved by consulting the existing literature.

The method of analysis for library investigation is primarily a synthesis of the literature around the research objective. This is a qualitative analysis as compared with the quantitative analysis discussed for other methods of investigation. The synthesis of the authoritative literature used for the suggested solutions for various cases in this book is an example of this method of investigation.

Analytical Modeling

Some problems may be investigated by the use of analytical modeling where the relationships between variables are formulated through the use of symbols and mathematical conventions. For example, in a cost-volume-profit study, researchers formulated an analytical model indicating that

---

5. K. M. Johnstone and J. C. Bedard, "Risk Evaluation and Risk Adaptation in Client Acceptance Decisions" (paper presented at the annual meeting of the American Accounting Association: Philadelphia, August 16, 2000).

managers of a firm make investment decisions in risky assets in such a way that their own wealth can be maximized. This occurs when the managers' wealth function depends on vested interests both within and outside the firm, creating a potential for conflict of interest.[6]

Analytical research is not limited to mathematical modeling. It can also be based on deductive reasoning where logical arguments are presented from theories borrowed from philosophy, theology, or other sources. Regardless of its nature as an argumentative or mathematical formulation, analytical research primarily results in the generation of basic knowledge. Other research methods are then used to investigate the validity and applicability of the knowledge to actual situations.

The method of analysis in analytical modeling depends on the source of modeling. If mathematical modeling is used, then mathematical postulates and rules of modeling apply. If ethical or philosophical arguments are used, then the deductive logic is used to draw conclusions from ethical or philosophical theories.

Field Research/Case Study

Field research/case study was discussed in the previous chapter. It is used to collect data in a field setting. In such a setting, the researcher makes a directed search of information within a targeted company to find data for a particular research issue. Field research brings the researcher into contact with a wealth of information on various aspects of the company's operations and financial information generation and reporting. This method is a popular method of information search in auditing applications.

It is often tempting to collect many types of information just because it is interesting. This information collection process may quickly become aimless and confusing because it may result in losing focus on the research question that induced the information search in the first place. This is why the researcher must have a specific objective and focus the search toward collecting data for that objective.[7] The more focused the researcher, the more efficient the search process will be. The issue of efficiency has become increasingly more important in professional settings such as auditing engagements where clients have become much more cost conscious in recent years. Thus, to be competitive in the auditing services market, auditors have to be highly efficient in their information search strategies.

---

6. M. J. Abdolmohammadi, S. P. Kim, and L. Klein, "CVP Under Uncertainty and the Manager's Utility Function," *Review of Quantitative Finance and Accounting* 6, no. 2 (1996), pp. 133–47.

7. The case study research and analysis has gained popularity in recent years. For a reference on the basics of this method see R. K. Yin, *Case Study Research: Design and Methods* (Thousand Oaks, CA: Sage: Applied Social Research Methods Series Volume 5, 1994).

The Professional Research Process

In the previous section, the basics of research methodologies used to collect and analyze data were presented. In this section, a step-by-step process to apply this methodology in issue-based professional research in accounting is presented. While these steps are presented sequentially (see Exhibit 6–2), some steps can actually be performed concurrently by different researchers in a research team. Also, interactions with knowledgeable colleagues, particularly those with extensive experience in issues related to the research topic, could expedite the process significantly or make some steps unnecessary. These issues are discussed below.

Exhibit 6–2 The Professional Research Process	
Steps in the process	*Example: Leases*
1. Identify the problem	A reported rent is identified as a lease transaction.
2. Specify the objectives of the research	To determine the type of the lease.
3. Develop a list of key words	Lease, capital, operating, *SFAS*, etc.
4. Develop alternative courses of action	Capital lease, operating lease, other.
5. Determine the consequences of each of the alternative courses of action	What is the effect of an operating lease on the balance sheet (off-balance-sheet financing)?
6. Collect evidence	Search the professional literature using the key words in step 3.
7. Summarize and synthesize pertinent literature	What are the conditions under which a transaction is a capital lease, an operating lease, or no lease at all?
8. Choose the most appropriate course of action	Given the characteristics of the transaction and the professional literature, is the lease an operating lease or a capital lease?
9. Develop an implementation process	How should the choice of lease option be entered in the books of the client?
10. Communicate your conclusions accurately and concisely	Write a two-page report summarizing the research process.
11. File the research report in permanent files	Code and file the report in a research file both for documentation of the research process and for reference in the future.

Step 1: Identify the Problem

In the first step, the problem under investigation is analyzed and refined. As a result of this analysis, the problem is identified and clearly isolated from other problems or issues to ensure internal validity. Some problems are simple, making the problem identification a relatively easy task. For example, investigating the nature of payment made for a wastebasket and to decide whether it should be treated as an expense or an asset is a simple problem. Due to its immaterial nature, the issue may not even require an investigation—it should be recorded as an expense. However, if the issue is complex, it must be broken into various parts to identify specific problems for investigation. Some issues, such as intercompany transactions, related party transactions, lease agreements, and derivative financial instruments, are very complex. You may need to draw diagrams and flowcharts to help you understand the nature of these problems. As an exercise, draw the relationships in the scenario described in Step 9.

For example, suppose that a client has reported $1.2 million in its income statement as rent expense. An analysis of the nature of the data indicates that this expense relates to the leasing of a warehouse by the client for 10 years, thus the transaction may qualify as a capital lease and not an operating lease. However, depending on the exact nature of this transaction, you may have to identify various aspects of the lease for the purpose of problem identification.

Step 2: Specify the Objectives

The researcher is now ready to take step two, which relates to stating the precise objective of the research. The purpose is to assess more precisely what the nature of the lease is. Thus, the researcher will perhaps set the objective of the research as determining the type of the lease that represents the nature of this transaction.

Step 3: Develop a List of Key Words

In the third step, a list of key words related to the problem is prepared. This step helps the researcher because the key words can be used later to search the professional literature and databases for evidence concerning the topic. The key words for the problem under investigation might be listed as lease, capital, operating, SFAS, and so on. Guidelines about keyword search methods are presented in an earlier chapter.

Step 4: Develop Alternative Courses of Action

Alternative courses of action for the problem are identified in step four. In this step, the researcher tries to identify all viable courses of action related to the problem. While there may be many alternative courses of action, the researcher focuses only on the most plausible alternatives and drops those that are not viable. This will help to contain the research to a manageable level. For example, the alternative means of going to Chicago from Boston include such silly alternatives as walking or riding on a donkey along with more realistic ones such as flying, driving, and taking the train or a bus. The unlikely alternatives are simply not included because they are not plausible, and their inclusion in the research design will result in a waste of time and money. A refined list of alternatives also helps the researcher to develop certain expectations regarding each alternative. The viable alternative courses of action in our lease example are reporting the lease as a capital lease or as an operating lease.

Step 5: Determine the Consequences of Each Alternative

In step five, the consequences of each of the alternative courses of action are specified. It is important for the researcher to have a clear understanding of the specific consequences that each alternative course of action might have. Flying between Boston and Chicago may take only two hours, but the airplane ticket will cost more than a ticket for a bus trip that may exceed 20 hours. The consequences of these alternatives are unclear unless the researcher knows the exact conditions of the traveler. To a professional, the benefit of saving the time is well worth the more expensive plane ticket. A traveler with a limited budget who does not mind the longer travel time in exchange for the cheaper ticket follows quite a different decision model. Also, perhaps a traveler has a fear of flying and as such prefers to take the train for the trip. This example indicates that consequences of alternative courses of action are not always measurable. The judgment and decision making, critical and creative thinking, and ethical models of decision making discussed in later chapters can assist the researcher here. Suffice it to say for now that the researcher has to quantitatively or qualitatively develop a good understanding of the consequences of each of the courses of action. For example, in related-party transactions the accountant must carefully analyze alternatives and account for the substance and not the form of the transaction.

In the lease problem, a consequence of reporting the lease as rent (i.e., an operating lease) will be that only the income statement is affected. The balance sheet is affected only to the extent that the rent expense reduces the net income and thus the retained earnings. On the other hand, if the lease is reported as a capital lease, the balance sheet is affected in a more significant way because the capitalized lease is reported as both an asset and a liability. Reporting a lease as an operating lease, therefore, will reduce the company's debt ratio in a typical client situation when the debt to total assets is less than one. For this reason, treatment of an otherwise capital lease as an operating lease is called *off-balance-sheet financing*.

Step 6: Collect Evidence

In step six, the researcher searches the professional literature using the key words established in an earlier step to find evidence regarding various aspects of the problem and alternative courses of action. These sources include professional pronouncements, literature indices and databases, as well as surveys of current practice (e.g., the AICPA's *Accounting Trends and Techniques*).[8] The sources identified are either directly related to the research issue or have to be used by analogy. In either case, the hierarchy of GAAP discussed in an earlier chapter must be used to assess the authoritative nature of the evidence. If sufficient evidence is not found, the researcher will extend the research to professional and academic journals and other publications that have lower levels of authority. If this search does not render guidance, the researcher may conduct an empirical investigation or a survey of a sample of practitioners deemed to be knowledgeable about the issue. The researcher may also draw upon his or her own knowledge and make a professional judgment.

The search for the lease problem will definitely result in identifying *SFAS No. 13*, "Accounting for Leases," as a primary source. A number of FASB statement amendments will also be identified. According to *SFAS No. 13*, a lease that transfers substantially all of the benefits and risks incident to the ownership of the property should be accounted for as the acquisition of an asset and incidence of an obligation. In other words, it is the substance of the transaction, not its form, that determines the type of the lease. *SFAS No. 13* then specifies four conditions that will determine if the lease is a capital lease or an operating lease.[9] *SFAS No. 13* and related FASB amendments still leave some room for judgment that requires the researcher to look for other sources of literature and professional judgment.

Step 7: Summarize and Synthesize Pertinent Literature

In step seven, the literature and the evidence collected, if any, are summarized and synthesized. In this step the references collected from the professional literature are analyzed for authoritative guidance in the GAAP hierarchy of authority. In other words, not all references are created equal. For example, the researcher begins with *SFAS No. 13* for issues related to leases, but also continues with other less authoritative evidence to find an answer to the problem.

---

8. The AICPA publishes this survey annually.
9. These conditions are: (1) transfer of ownership at the end of the term, (2) existence of bargain purchase option, (3) term of lease being equal to or greater than 75% of the estimated economic life of the property, and (4) the present value of the minimum lease payments being 90% or more of the fair market value of the property, excluding the executory costs.

Step 8: Choose the Most Appropriate Course of Action

In step eight, various courses of action and their consequences are analyzed and related to the professional literature for the purpose of selecting the best course of action. That is, based on the literature summarized in the previous step, the merits of each course of action are identified and evaluated. For example, based on the exact nature of the lease and the information in the professional literature, the researcher makes a judgment as to whether the lease is an operating lease or a capital lease. This choice requires much judgment and is constrained by a number of factors such as ethical and legal considerations in addition to the professional literature. Models of ethical judgment are presented in a later chapter.

Step 9: Develop an Implementation Process

In step number nine, the researcher develops a detailed implementation plan for the selected course of action. The nature of this implementation plan changes depending on the problem under investigation. For example, in the lease problem, once the researcher makes a decision concerning the type of the lease that should be reflected in the client's books, the exact journal entries are also determined and suggested for implementation. A typical intermediate accounting text can be consulted for journal entries.

In a more complex business situation, the client may have devised an elaborate scheme to avoid using the capital lease option. For example, suppose that the client has formed a business relationship with a company, say Supplier, which will build a plant with 100 percent bank financing right next door to the client. A conveyor belt will be constructed to transfer all of Supplier's finished goods into the client's plant for the client's use. The client has agreed to pay Supplier an amount equal to the bank loan payments for the next 30 years, the loan period, as well as a bargain price payment for Supplier's finished goods. The client will also provide management services to Supplier in exchange for a management fee.[10] Is this transaction a capital lease, an operating lease, an unconditional product purchase obligation, or a purchase and sales agreement? What would be the exact nature of the journal entries for this transaction?

If the researcher deems this transaction to be a capital or an operating lease, the requirements in *SFAS No. 13* will apply. If the agreement is viewed as an unconditional product purchase agreement, then *SFAS No. 47*, "Disclosure of Long-Term Obligations," requires a quantified disclosure of the transaction unless the transaction is recorded in the balance sheet as an asset and a liability. If the transaction is deemed to be a purchase and sales agreement, the results will be reflected in the income statement and no

---

10. This is an adaptation from a case in the Trueblood Case Series from Deloitte & Touche Foundation.

disclosure will be necessary unless the researcher views the transactions as a related-party transaction that will require disclosure.

The point is that a seemingly simple lease classification problem can turn out to be a very complex issue for analysis. It will require much research as well as professional judgment to determine the appropriate course of action. Once this is determined, an implementation plan that will require recording of the transactions in the client's books will also be necessary.

Step 10: Communicate Conclusions

This step relates to the communication of the research process in a report. This is a critical step, because unless the research process and the conclusions are effectively communicated, much of the labor and the message can get lost in transition. In general, two types of research reports are developed. One is a detailed report covering all the research steps in the research process for documentation purposes. The other one is an executive summary where the facts about the problem are identified, the courses of action and their consequences are specified, the research used is briefly described, the key authoritative literature is stated, and a conclusion and justification are presented. The reader is then referred to the existence of a more detailed research report for additional information. Given the importance of these issues, they are discussed in the next section.

Step 11: File the Research Report in Permanent Files

The final step in the research process is the filing of the research report in permanent files. Such a file must be set up in a way that will facilitate effective retrieval of the information later. In particular, if similar problems are confronted by the accounting professional, permanent files must be easy to search. An advantage of a well-organized, easy-to-access permanent file is that valuable time and scarce resources are spared from investigating a similar problem later on—perhaps simple updating of the file will suffice. The use of electronic media to store vast amounts of information provides an inexpensive and efficient means of storage and retrieval of the information for reference in the future. A summary header should be attached to the file indicating the name of the client, the problem researched, the date research began and ended, and the contacts in the client firm and the researcher firm. The summary sheet ends with a table of contents of the research report.

Communication Skills for Accounting Research

Effective communication skills are needed for accounting practice and research. While most of these skills are generic in nature, other skills take on a more specialized meaning due to the specialized nature of accounting practice. In an attempt to clarify the meaning of communication skills for accountants, the Accounting Education Change Commission and the American Accounting Association have listed writing, oral presentation, reading and critiquing written work, listening, and understanding interpersonal dynamics as elements of effective communication.[11] In a survey of audit partners and corporate controllers, more than 90 percent of respondents rated listening and writing skills as very important or extremely important for practicing accountants. Speaking skills followed with importance ratings of over 50 percent by the respondents.[12]

Accountants regularly communicate with various constituencies both within and outside of their own organizations. Corporate accountants frequently write memoranda and corporate controllers prepare annual reports. Auditors prepare audit reports and consultants prepare project reports. They communicate both in writing and in oral presentations. For this reason, the AICPA has instituted a method by which CPA candidates are evaluated for their writing skills when they take the CPA examination. The definition of writing skills according to the AICPA is presented in Exhibit 6–3.

According to the AICPA definition, six criteria define effective writing as related to the CPA examination, a definition that can be extended to the practice of public accounting. These criteria are: coherent organization, conciseness, clarity, use of Standard English, responsiveness to the requirements of the question, and appropriateness for the reader. *Coherence* is the orderly presentation of an idea so that the audience or the reader will be able to follow it with ease. *Clarity* refers to the ease with which the audience receives the meaning intended by the communicator. *Conciseness* refers to communicating with as few words as possible. Excess verbiage and digressions make the communication unnecessarily long.

The fourth criterion, *Standard English,* relates to the use of simple words, correct grammar, proper punctuation, and good spelling. *Responsiveness* to the requirements of the question clearly relates to answering the questions asked on the CPA examination. It can also be extended to any situation where the accountant has been asked to work on a problem or decision situation and needs to keep the communication directly linked to the question. The *appropriateness* criterion relates to keeping the audience in mind when communicating to that audience. Audience considerations are also discussed later in the chapter.

The definition provided above is quite generic. However, note that writing is more an art than a science, making an exact definition and a step-by-step process difficult. The definitions provided and the processes

---

11. M. C. Francis, T. C. Mulder, and J. S. Stark, *Intentional Learning: A Process for Learning to Learn in the Accounting Curriculum* (Sarasota, FL: Accounting Education Change Commission and the American Accounting Association, 1995), p. 3.
12. A. M. Novin, M. A. Pearson, and S. V. Senge, "Improving the Curriculum for Aspiring Management Accountants: The Practitioner's Point of View," *Journal of Accounting Education* 8 (1990), pp. 207–24.

Exhibit 6–3	The AICPA's Definition of Writing Skills
Criterion	*Meaning*
1. Coherent organization	Responses should be organized so that ideas are arranged logically and the flow of thought is easy to follow. Generally, knowledge is best expressed by using short paragraphs composed of short sentences. Moreover, short paragraphs, each limited to the development of one principal idea, can better emphasize the main points in the answer. Each principal idea should be placed in the first sentence of the paragraph, followed by supporting concepts and examples.
2. Conciseness	Conciseness requires that candidates present complete thoughts in as few words as possible, while ensuring that important points are covered adequately. Short sentences and simple wording also contribute to concise writing.
3. Clarity	A clearly written response prevents uncertainty concerning the candidate's meaning or reasoning. Clarity involves using words with specific and precise meaning, including proper technical terminology. Well-constructed sentences also contribute to clarity.
4. Use of standard English	Responses should be written using Standard English where, ". . . Standard English is characterized by exacting standards of punctuation and capitalization, by accurate spelling, by exact diction, by an expressive vocabulary, and by knowledgeable usage choices."
5. Responses to the requirements of the question	Answers should directly address the requirements of the question and demonstrate the candidate's awareness of the purpose of the writing task. Responses should not be broad expositions on the general subject matter.
6. Appropriateness for the reader	Writing that is appropriate for the reader takes into account the reader's background, knowledge of the subject, interests, and concerns. The requirements of some essay questions may ask candidates to prepare a written document for a certain reader, such as an engagement memorandum for a CPA's client. When the intended reader is not specified, the candidate should assume the intended reader is a knowledgeable CPA.

Source: AICPA, "Definition of Writing Skills," in *Report of the Testing of Writing Skills Subtask Force of the CPA Examination Change Implementation Task Force* (New York, NY: American Institute of Certified Public Accountants, September 1990).

discussed, therefore, should be viewed as general guidelines. Nevertheless, communication skills can be developed and improved with instruction, practice, and supervision.[13]

An Example of Good versus Poor Writing

To show preferable style and quality considerations that result in good writing rather than poor writing in professional accounting, consider the scenario in Exhibit 6–4. It refers to a dispute between a client and a CPA over the CPA's invoice. The CPA has written a letter to the client to explain the reasons why the amount in the invoice was higher than expected.

---

13. M. E. Adelstein, *Contemporary Business Writing* (New York: Random House, 1971), pp. 6–7.

Exhibit 6–4	Good Writing versus Poor Writing
Poor Writing	*Good Writing*

Poor Writing

Dear Bill:

With reference to your letter of March 8, 1997, please find enclosed herewith an annotated summarized breakdown of work performed for your company during the fourth quarter of last year. With regard to the billing discrepancies which you mentioned in your letter, I would like to remind you that not only the parameters of our projects expanded beyond what we planned in advance, but also it was recently necessary for us to effect an increase in the hourly rates our firm must charge its clients in view of the fact that our operational costs have also increased due to inflation. Obviously, due to this fact, your total quarterly billings were increased substantially over previous totals.

Hopefully, the above explanation and attached summary will resolve some of your questions. If your accountant desires more additional information, he should not hesitate to contact me. Thank you for your cooperation.

Good Writing

Dear Bill:

I can see why you were surprised at our billings for the fourth quarter of last year. Two factors led to the increase:

1. On September 1, our rates increased 12% to $80 an hour.
2. Three unforeseen projects increased the number of hours billed:
   a. We spent an extra 15 hours working on four additional tax returns.
   b. We met with the IRS for 5 hours to discuss last year's depreciation estimates.
   c. We began preparing monthly rather than quarterly financial statements.

The attached annotated summary details the work involved in these projects. If you have any questions, I'm ready to help.

Source: Adapted from G. A. Chaney, "Word Crunching: A Primer for Accountants," *Journal of Accountancy* (March 1990), p. 51.

As shown, the indirect style of writing used in the left column is a poor means of communication for the purpose of the note. It is unclear, wordy, and perhaps incoherent. It is changed to a more direct narrative/descriptive style of writing for effective communication. The narrative/descriptive style provides a more clear description of the reasons why the CPA's invoice reflects a significant increase over the amount billed in the previous quarter. Good punctuation and good narrative (i.e., Standard English) style have changed the poor quality letter into a more informative, more understandable one. Also, note that the tone of the letter is more constructive and pleasant. The client might still have a concern about the increase in the invoice and may even consider switching to another CPA, but such an action will not be prompted by a lack of information and perhaps antagonism that may result from poor writing. To produce the good quality letter, the following guidelines were used:[14]

1. Get to the point quickly.
2. Be natural and conversational, not needlessly formal.
3. Keep words, sentences, and paragraphs short.

---

14. G. A. Chaney, "Word Crunching: A Primer for Accountants," *Journal of Accountancy* (March 1990), p. 53.

4. Plan a logical, easy-to-follow order.
5. Be specific, clear, and brief.
6. Use paragraphs, indentation, bullets, and numbers to make information easy to find and to delineate importance.
7. Read it out loud.
8. Imagine how the reader will read (and misread) each sentence.
9. Make it clear who is to do what by when.
10. Delete needless words and information.

Research Report Format

Research reports are generally written in a formal style. However, all writing quality considerations apply to them. Use letter-size paper and leave one-inch margins for top, bottom, and the two sides. The body of the paper should be double-spaced, but other sections may be written in single-spaced format as explained later. Page numbering must be provided for the main body of the report as well as for charts, figures, and tables. This is accomplished using Arabic numerals as well as Roman numerals depending on the section as also explained later. Various sections of a typical research report are presented in Exhibit 6–5.[15] Appendix 6A provides an example of a professional accounting research report. This report is a generic one, and variations of it can be found in practice.

A. The Quick Reference Section

The first section of the research report provides the information for a quick reference to the background and findings of the study. It usually has four parts. The first part, a transmittal letter, is a summary document to the party for whom the research was conducted. It is a letter or a memorandum, depending on whether the party is outside or inside the organization. It provides a basic statement of the charge, its purpose, major findings, and a statement that the detailed report is attached. It is so brief, you can call it the summary of the executive summary. When a transmittal letter is a memo or a letter to someone you know, you can use the informal style. If the report is written for a course project, generally no transmittal letter is expected.

The second part is a title page. It provides the report title, the name and address of the researcher or researchers, the name and address of the party for whom the report is prepared, and the date of the report. This material is spread over the whole page and is generally centered on the page. Acknowledgments to express gratitude to those who provided assistance, data, or any significant part in the research process are also

---

15. This discussion is heavily adapted from chapters 9 and 10 in C. May, *Effective Writing: A Handbook for Accountants*, 3rd ed. (Englewood Cliffs, NJ: Prentice-Hall, 1992), pp. 148–83.

Exhibit 6–5	A Research Report Format
Part	*Content*

A. Quick reference:

1. Transmittal letter	Cover letter or memorandum giving basic information
2. Title page	Report title, name and address of the preparer and the reader, date
3. Table of contents	A reference list to the sections, figures, tables, etc.
4. Executive summary	A synopsis of the whole report; also called *abstract* or *synopsis*

B. Details:

1. Introduction	Identification of the objective of the report and the need for the research
2. Literature search	Summary of the findings on alternative courses of action
3. Method	Description of the method used to collect evidence
4. Findings	The results from description or analysis of the data
5. Conclusion	The implications of the findings and support for the course of action adopted

C. Supplements:

1. Illustrations	Tables, exhibits, figures, etc.
2. Appendices	Supporting information of secondary importance
3. List of references	Documentation of sources of information, citations
4. End- or footnotes	Footnote or endnote information

provided on the cover page (bottom of the page and left margined). This page is not numbered.

The third part, table of contents, is a reference list of the report material that is placed after the title page. Major sections of the paper are listed and page numbers in which they appear are provided. Also listed are charts, exhibits, figures, graphs, tables, appendices, and so on. This page is single-spaced and either unnumbered or given a Roman numeral.

The final part of the quick reference section is an executive summary. This part gives a synopsis of the whole report for the busy reader. It summarizes the main purpose, method, findings, and recommendations of the research. Some reports call this part an abstract, a synopsis, or just a summary. Its length depends on the scope of the research project and the report length ranging from one short paragraph to two pages single-spaced. Sequential numbering of the report in Arabic numerals begins with this section. The title of the report appears on top of the executive summary section.

B. The Details Section

The details of the research are provided in this section. It begins with an introduction that is very much like the transmittal letter, only more detailed. It identifies the objective of the report and the need for the research and ends with a statement of its findings. Also, it gives a statement of what will follow in the remainder of the paper. This part and the other parts in the main body of the report are double-spaced.

The second part of this section is the literature search. It is used to summarize the most relevant professional literature on alternative courses of action for the research issue. You provide the pros and cons of each course of action with reference to the authoritative literature. Do not overdo this by including insignificant sources. Focus on the significant authoritative literature only. If the literature is insufficient to answer the research questions, you indicate in this section your expectations (also called *hypotheses* or *propositions*) and refer the reader to the next section, method of research, where additional information will be provided.

The third part here is the method of research. It provides information on the method used to collect further evidence. If the research question can be resolved by reference to the professional literature that is reviewed in the previous section, then you do not need this section. However, if additional evidence was collected, it is described in this part of the report. For example, you may have collected evidence from a survey of a sample of professionals, or from an interview of employees, or a detailed plant visit. You simply tell the reader how you designed and executed the research in this section.

The next part is findings. This is a summary of the professional literature that directly relates to the research issue if no additional evidence was collected. If additional evidence was collected via a survey, an interview, or any other method, a description of the data or an analysis of the data is provided here. This section generally uses charts, figures, or tables that are placed at the end of the report but referenced in the body of this part.

The final part of the details section is conclusions. You tell the reader what you believe to be the conclusions from your investigation. What the implications of your findings are and how they relate to the course of action you recommend. Do not leave the reader hanging here. Remember, due to your research, you are viewed as knowledgeable in the subject matter and are expected to take a position. While you do not speculate without support from your findings, you are expected to make educated judgments based on the literature and the data, and take a position. Your client pays you to take educated positions.

C. The Supplements Section

The final section of the report contains supplementary material. The first part of the supplementary material is illustrations. This is where you place charts, tables, exhibits, figures, and so on. One illustration per page (single- or double-spaced depending on the nature of the illustration) is recommended. These documents are numbered using Arabic or Roman numerals or both. For example, tables might be numbered with Arabic numbers, but charts and figures with Roman numerals. These illustrations are referenced in the details section of the research report to tell the reader where they are to be inserted. In published books and articles, all illustrations are already placed in appropriate places in the body of the chapters or articles. In unpublished research reports, however, these illustrations are placed at the end of the report and are referenced within the paper.

The second part in the supplementary section is appendices, if any. Appendices are used to provide supporting information of secondary importance. For example, the research questionnaire, if any, will be presented in an appendix. A copy of a paragraph or several paragraphs from an FASB statement that is particularly relevant to the paper may be presented in an appendix. Appendices are generally single-spaced and numbered sequentially using the alphanumeric style.

The third part, list of references, is used to inform the reader of the details of the sources consulted. In the course of writing your report, you consult many sources of information from authoritative literature to published books, journal articles, and essays. You must cite these references throughout the report wherever you quote from them, and/or paraphrase their statements. You may also state that they have done similar research and give a bit of information about their major findings. Using other's work without giving them credit is plagiarism. It is unethical and illegal. There are several ways you can cite these references, one of which is the footnote method that is adopted for this book. An acceptable alternative is to use the endnote citation that simply groups all citations at the end of the document. Also, at the end of the paper, you provide a list of all those sources cited in the paper. For an example of a format, see the reference list at the end of Appendix 6A. The reference list must not include reference to any work that is not cited anywhere in the report. Also, be sure to include all references that are cited in your report in this list. This section is single-spaced.

Finally, the endnotes or footnotes part provides a method of citation as explained earlier. It is also used to provide additional information that is interesting, but not an integral part of the main text. Whether you use a footnote or an endnote format is a personal choice. Some readers prefer to see footnotes so they can refer to them quickly if they wish. Other readers prefer endnotes because they view footnotes as distracting. Many readers prefer to see as few footnotes or endnotes as possible. On the basis of your reading of your audience, you decide which method to use.

A Survey-Based Example of a Professional Research Issue

The research process described in this chapter was illustrated by the use of the accounting treatment of a lease transaction. The same research process can be used in a large array of other professional research facing the accounting professional. For example, suppose your client is interested in establishing an independent audit committee. The importance of audit committees to corporate governance has been recognized by the AICPA and the SEC's strong recommendations that public companies have independent audit committees. Almost all major stock exchanges now require that listed companies have audit committees. Thus, the issue presents a real business problem to companies, particularly smaller ones, who generally turn to accountants for advice.

Your client asks you for advice on issues related to availability, cost, and responsibilities of audit committees. To relate the issues raised by your client, we provide answers taken from two research reports that have investigated these issues.[16] The problem is identified in the three-part question as previously stated (step 1). The researchers identified the objectives of the research as presenting evidence concerning the three questions asked (step 2). A list of key words was used to search the professional and academic literature to learn about what was already investigated (step 3). Alternative courses of action in this case related to alternative research methods that could be used for investigating the issues (step 4). These alternatives ranged from a survey of current audit committee members to the collection of data on availability and cost of audit committee members and their responsibilities from databases.

Each of these alternatives presented strengths and weaknesses that were considered (step 5). For example, while the use of databases was desirable, the researchers found that compensation data and a detailed list of responsibilities were not available in these databases. The researchers summarized and synthesized the pertinent literature (step 7) and decided on using a survey of current audit committee members to collect data (steps 6 and 8). A detailed implementation process was then developed where the researchers prepared a database of over 1,000 corporate audit committee members and their addresses from various sources as well as a survey questionnaire (step 9). The questionnaire was sent to a sample of audit committee members across the U.S., from which over 30 percent of the recipients responded.

The data were coded, entered into a computer program, analyzed, tabulated, and summarized using descriptive statistical measures such as the mean, the median, and the standard deviation of the responses on variables. This is the only step that is a bit different from the professional research process in Exhibit 6–2, but it relates to the analysis and interpretation of the data collected.

The results from the study were documented and reported in two journal articles (step 10). In one article it was reported that 62 percent of those currently serving on audit committees will agree to serve on additional audit committees, and the average cost per hour of service is $189.60 for typically 17 hours of service per year.[17] Thus, availability and cost questions were answered in this article. In a second article, a long list of responsibilities ranging from safeguarding assets to maintaining a

---

16. The information is adapted from M. J. Abdolmohammadi and E. Levy, "Availability and Cost of Audit Committee Members," *Research in Accounting Regulation* 6 (1992a), pp. 149–62, and M. J. Abdolmohammadi and E. Levy, "Audit Committee Members' Perceptions of Their Responsibility," *Internal Auditing* (Summer 1992b), pp. 53–63.
17. M. J. Abdolmohammadi and E. Levy, "Availability and Cost of Audit Committee Members" *(with E. Levy)*, *Research in Accounting Regulation* 6 (1992), pp. 156–58.

climate of honesty was provided.[18] Thus, the question of what audit committee responsibilities are was answered. As an update to the latter issue, the researcher might also find more current references to the literature by updating the search. For example, relating to maintaining a climate of honesty, a Delaware court ruled recently that such monitoring can insulate board members (audit committee being a committee of the board) from suits by shareholders seeking to hold them personally liable for wrongdoing of company managers and employees.[19] This ruling will be an incentive for audit committee members to take their responsibility more seriously.

The publication of the results in these articles is a means of filing research reports although the researchers keep the details of the research material (step 11). However, publishing papers in journals put them in public domain. This is different from a professional researcher's files that may be viewed as proprietary in nature, thus only accessible by the researcher and his or her professional colleagues.

Summary

In this chapter, methods of evidence gathering as a component of a research methodology were discussed, and laboratory experiments and a survey questionnaire, as well as archival studies, field research, and analytical modeling, were identified. It was concluded that while all methods of investigation are useful in professional research, survey questionnaires and field-based research are particularly popular. Consequently, a detailed example of survey research was provided at the end of the chapter.

Issue-based professional research was then described in an 11-step process. The process begins with identifying the research issue and specifying the objectives of the research and ends with the communication and filing of the research report generated from the process. Given the importance of the 10th step, communication of research results, this issue was discussed in more detail. The AICPA's definition of writing skills was discussed in terms of coherent organization, conciseness, clarity, standard English, responsiveness, and audience considerations. An example of good versus poor writing was also provided for professional writing. This example indicated that the preferred method of professional writing for memoranda and letters is generally the informal style as compared with the more formal style used in research reports. Finally, a general format for research reports was presented. An example of a good report format for issue-based research is provided in Appendix 6A.

Questions

1. Discuss and contrast database search, data collection, and library search.

2. What are empirical investigation and experimental investigation, and what is their relationship?

3. Survey questionnaires are used to collect "perceptual" data about an issue of research. What concerns might you have about the validity of such data?

4. What is an archival study?

---

18. M. J. Abdolmohammadi and E. Levy, "Audit Committee Members' Perceptions of Their Responsibility," *Internal Auditing* (Summer 1992), pp. 58–63.
19. D. Starkman, "Compliance Ruling May Shield Directors," *The Wall Street Journal,* December 24, 1996, p. B5.

5. In a database search, what sources of information are available for capital market research?

6. Library search is used to review and synthesize the literature around an issue of research. What if you do not find an answer to your research question by a review of the professional and/or academic literature?

7. Mathematical and nonmathematical modeling can be used for analytical modeling. What do these mean? As a practicing accountant will you be involved in this type of research?

8. Describe the method of research used for case studies.

9. Test your knowledge of basic statistics. Can you use rudimentary statistical methods such as means and standard deviations to analyze data in a research study?

10. The chapter provided an 11-step process for practical research. List these steps and provide an example for each.

11. Communication of the research process occurs through the research report. What should be included in such a report?

12. What is the definition of writing skills in accounting as provided by the AICPA?

13. What are the general guidelines related to writing good letters and memoranda?

14. List and describe the three sections of a formal research report.

15. List and describe the components of the quick reference section of a formal research report.

16. List and describe the components of the details section of a formal research report.

17. List and describe the components of the supplements section of a formal research report.

18. Why is it important to provide summaries of the research report in the transmittal letter, the executive summary, and the conclusion sections of the research report?

19. What are endnotes or footnotes for?

20. Why is there a need for providing a list of references in your research report?

21. The findings part of the research report presents data and analyses. Why is this necessary?

APPENDIX 6A
AN EXAMPLE OF A RESEARCH REPORT

STOCK OPTION ACCOUNTING:
THE EXPOSURE DRAFT THAT MADE THE FASB [IN]FAMOUS[20]

Table of Contents[21]

---

20. This report is adapted, with significant editing and formatting changes, from Susan List. She was a student in one of the authors' capstone course—Methods and Practices of Professional Research.

21. Transmittal letter and cover page are deleted to save space.

STOCK OPTION ACCOUNTING:
THE EXPOSURE DRAFT THAT MADE THE FASB [IN]FAMOUS

Executive Summary

This paper discusses the issues surrounding stock option accounting and the Financial Accounting Standards Board's (FASB) resolution of this issue. On June 30, 1993, the FASB issued an exposure draft, "Accounting for Stock-Based Compensation." However, it did not anticipate that the exposure draft would generate the amount of controversy that it did. A brief history of stock option accounting is given as well as a discussion of the exposure draft, the controversy surrounding it, and the FASB's final resolution of this issue with the issuance of *Statement of Financial Accounting Standard No. 123*, "Accounting for Stock-Based Compensation," in 1995.

Introduction

In October 1995 the Financial Accounting Standards Board (FASB) issued *Statement of Financial Accounting Standards No 123*, "Accounting for Stock-Based Compensation." The intent of this statement was to:

Establish financial accounting and reporting standards for stock-based employee compensation plans. These plans include all arrangements by which employees receive shares of stock or other equity instruments of the employer or the employer incurs liabilities to employees in amounts based on the price of the employer's stock. Examples include stock purchase plans, stock options, restricted stock, and stock appreciation rights.[22]

This new standard was the final result of the FASB's exposure draft, "Accounting for Stock-Based Compensation," which it issued on June 30, 1993. The original intent of the FASB was to create a new standard that would supersede *Accounting Principles Board Opinion No. 25*, "Accounting for Stock Issued to Employees." However, the FASB backed away from this position due to the controversy, which was generated by the FASB's tentative conclusions in its exposure draft. This paper discusses the issues surrounding stock option accounting and their resolution by the FASB.

The FASB's Definition of a Stock Option

According to *SFAS 123*, paragraph 395, a stock option is "a contract that gives the holder the right, but not the obligation, either to purchase or to sell a certain number of shares of stock at the predetermined price for a specified period of time." For the purposes of this paper, stock options have two main forms: fixed and performance based. A fixed stock option is an option for which the price and the number of shares are set or fixed at the grant date. A performance-based stock option is one that is affected by the achievement of future performance goals.[23]

Literature Search and Method

Research Method

The method used to search for authoritative guidance included the *Price-Waterhouse Researcher*

---

22. Financial Accounting Standards Board, *Statement of Financial Accounting Standards No. 123 "Accounting for Stock-Based Compensation"* (Norwalk, CT: 1995): Summary.
23. Bill D. Cox and John E. Elsea, "Stock-Based Compensation Controversy Heats Up." *The Practical Accountant*, December 1993, 30–31.

CD-ROM; *Accounting & Tax Online; Lexis/Nexis; The Wall Street Journal; Uncover,* a database containing article references; and the Internet.

A Brief History of Stock Option Accounting

Prior to FASB's issuance in 1993 of its exposure draft on accounting for stock-based compensation, *APB Opinion No. 25*, which was originally issued in 1972, gave the authoritative guidance to companies on rules for accounting for stock options. A list of accounting literature, which has given guidance with respect to stock and other supplemental plans, is provided in Exhibit 6A–1. It was in

March 1984 that the FASB instituted the project that resulted in the proposed exposure draft, largely in response to a 200-page paper submitted by the American Institute of Certified Public Accountants (AICPA) requesting, among other things, that stock-option-stock-based compensation programs were not consistent. Time-based options were not valued and expensed, whereas other stock-based compensation was. The AICPA also suggested that certain mathematical models had been developed since 1972 that could measure such options adequately.[24]

Exhibit 6A–1   Accounting Guidance for Stock and Other Supplemental Compensation Plans*

Pronouncement	Date Issued	Title
ARB 43, Ch. 13B (as amended by APB 25)	1953	Compensation Involved in Stock Options and Purchase Plans
APB 15	1969	Earnings per Share
APB 25	1972	Accounting for Stock Issued to Employees
AIN-APB 25	1973	Stock Plans Established by a Principal Stockholder
FIN 28 (as amended by FIN 31)	1978	Accounting for Stock Appreciation Rights and Other Variable Stock Options Award Plans (an interpretation of APB 15 and APB 25)
FIN 31	1980	Treatment of Stock Compensation Plans in EPS (an interpretation of APB 15 and a modification of FIN 28)
FIN 38	1984	Determining the Measurement Date for Stock Option, Purchase, and Award Plans Involving Junior Stock (an interpretation of APB 25)
FTB 82-2	1982	Accounting for the Conversion of Stock Options into Incentive Stock Options as a Result of the Economic Recovery Act of 1981
EITF 84-13	1984	Purchase of Stock Options and Stock Appreciation Rights in a Leveraged Buyout
EITF 84-18	1984	Stock Option Pyramiding
EITF 84-34	1984	Permanent Discount Restricted Stock Purchase Plans
EITF 85-45	1985	Business Combinations: Settlement of Stock Options and Awards
EITF 87-6	1987	Adjustments Related to Stock Compensation Plans
EITF 87-23	1987	Book Value Stock Purchase Plans
EITF 87-33	1987	Stock Compensation Issues Related to Market Decline
EITF 88-6	1988	Book Value Stock Plans in an Initial Public Offering
EITF 90-7	1990	Accounting for a Reload Stock Option
EITF 90-9	1990	Changes to Fixed Employee Stock Option Plans as a Result of Equity Restructuring
FASB Exposure Draft	1993	Accounting for Stock-Based Compensation
SFAS No. 123	1995	Accounting for Stock-Based Compensation

*Source: Adapted in part from *AAR 4295.11,* "Stock and Other Supplemental Compensation Plans."

---

24. William Skaff, "Accounting Challenges Corporate Entrepreneurism: FASB's Proposed Stock Options Rule." *NASDAQ Financial Executive Journal* 3.4 (1993): 10 pages. Online. http://www.law.cornell.edu/nasdaq/v3n4/skaff.html. April 3, 1996.

Exhibit 6A–3 Calculation of EPS*	
Under APB Opinion No. 25	*Under the Proposed Standard*
Calculation of PEPS:	
Proceeds not only include the exercise.	Proceeds are based only on the number of options expected to vest.
Proceeds include the exercise price of the options.	Proceeds not only include the exercise price of the options but also the average prepaid compensation (net of tax) for the current year. Prepaid compensation is calculated as the value of the number of options expected to vest and is allocated to expense over the vesting period.
No compensation expense exists since the options price is equal to the market price at date of grant.	Net income would be reduced for compensation expense (net of tax).
Calculation of FDEPS:	
Proceeds include the exercise price of the options.	Proceeds include not only the exercise price of the options, but also include the year-end prepaid compensation (net of tax).
No compensation expense exists since the option price is equal to the market price at date of grant.	Net income would be reduced for compensation expense (net of tax).

*Source: Adapted from Arlette C. Wilson and Len Weld, "Proposed Accounting for Fixed Stock Options: Financial Statement Impact," *National Public Accountant,* June 1995, p. 26–27.

3. The weighted-average exercise price of options outstanding, granted, and exercised, and the weighted-average fair values of options granted during the year at the date granted.

4. Description of the method and significant assumptions used to estimate the fair value of options, including the risk-free interest rate, expected volatility, and expected dividend yield.

5. Total compensation expense recognized for stock-based compensation awards.

6. Significant modifications to outstanding option grants.[33]

Nevertheless, in spite of the significant changes, the proposed accounting standard for stock compensation can be seen as FASB's response to the perceived inadequacies of existing accounting rules. The development of computerized techniques for valuing nonemployee stock options, which can in turn be easily adapted and applied to employee stock options, provided additional motivation. This technology, which did not exist at the time when *APB Opinion No. 25* was issued, now allows for estimation of the values of stock options.[34]

Findings

The Controversy Surrounding the Exposure Draft

Although the FASB issued its exposure draft on stock option accounting as a result of a reconsideration of perceived deficiencies in *APB Opinion No. 25,* the FASB probably did not anticipate that it would receive such a negative reaction to its proposed accounting changes. In fact, five months before the exposure draft was issued, *The Wall Street Journal* reported that the Washington, D.C.-based Council of

33. Joyce Strawser, "Accounting for Stock-Based Compensation: The FASB's Proposal." *The CPA Journal,* October 1993, pp. 90–91.
34. Ibid., 45.

Institutional Investors would fight an accounting-rule proposal that would require companies to deduct from their earnings the value of stock options granted to executives.[35] Similarly, the Business Roundtable, an influential group of chief executives from 200 major corporations, urged its members to avoid using the FASB-favored method in valuing stock options for proxy reports.[36] In all, the FASB received over 1,700 letters on this issue; most of them were negative.

However, it was not just from the corporate sector that the FASB received criticism on this point in its proposed standard. Opponents to the requirement that stock options be charged against earnings included President Clinton, who felt that it would be unfortunate if the FASB's proposal inadvertently undermined the competitiveness of some of America's most promising high-tech companies.[37] Even the Big Six "accounting firms expressed their objections to the FASB proposal, saying changes in stock prices make it difficult to calculate the value of stock options."[38]

In September 1993, the Nasdaq Stock Market, Inc. "joined the Ad Hoc Stock Options Coalition, whose approximately 45 members include[d] 10 Nasdaq companies, 20 trade associations representing various industries, and 7 staff members of concerned members of Congress. The coalition [met] weekly to develop strategy to oppose FASB's proposed rule."[39] The Nasdaq's key concerns were that stock options were important to the growth of American entrepreneurism and the United States' global competitiveness and the proposed standard would prevent or deter start-up companies from using stock options

as a compensation alternative to cash. The NASD Board of Governors adopted the following resolution on November 12, 1993, which expressed its concerns about the FASB's proposed standard:

WHEREAS, FASB has proposed that companies should be required to account for stock options as compensation based on formulae and conditions contained in the exposure draft;

WHEREAS, for companies that use stock options widely:

• The rule could decrease corporate earnings (for public companies that issue options widely) with no material change to real operating results.
• The rule could increase the cost of capital on both public and private markets.
• The rule could decrease growth companies from attracting and retaining critical employees.
• The rule could negatively impact the country's ability to start and build innovative, potentially high-growth companies that heretofore had these stock options as a major part of getting many or all employees as owners in the company. This would ultimately decrease America's ability to compete on a global scale.

BE IT RESOLVED that the NASD is opposed to accounting for stock options as compensation expense on any basis because such accounting would not be in the best interest of the United States and its global competitive position.[40]

35. Christi Harlan, "Group Opposes Stock-Option Accounting Plan; Institutional Investor Panel Takes Business's Side against Charges to Net Income." *The Wall Street Journal,* January 14, 1993; p. A4.
36. Lee Berton, "Business Chiefs Try to Derail Proposal on Stock Options," *The Wall Street Journal,* February 5, 1993, p. A2.
37. "Clinton Enters Debate over How Companies Reckon Stock Options." *The Wall Street Journal,* December 23, 1993.
38. "Accountants Are Chided over Stock-Option Stance." *The Wall Street Journal,* January 12, 1994, p. A3.
39. "Nasdaq and NASD Oppose FASB's Proposed Rule on Behalf of Nasdaq Companies," *Nasdaq Financial Executive Journal* 3, no. 4 (1993): 16 par. http://www.law.cornell.edu/nasdaq/v3n4/nasdpos.html. April 3, 1996.
40. "Nasdaq."

Exhibit 6A–4	Changes in 1992 EPS Using the Proposed Standard*	
Company	*Reported*	*% Decline†*
Lotus Development	$1.33	−49.6
3Com	0.47	−44.7
Software Publishing	0.93	−40.9
Microsoft	2.41	−18.9
Novell	0.81	−15.0
Alcoa	0.89	−10.0
Amgen	2.42	−8.7
American Express	0.83	−7.0
Paramount Commun.	2.27	−6.9
Allied Signal	3.91	−6.3
McDonald's	2.60	−5.4
Fluor	1.65	−5.0
Disney	2.55	−4.7
Union Carbide	1.39	−4.3
Goodyear	5.35	−3.8
Pogo Producing	0.66	−3.3
Morgan, J. P.	6.93	−3.2
Int'l Paper	1.17	−2.7
Boeing	4.57	−2.5
Rockwell Int'l	2.14	−2.5
Hewlett-Packard	3.49	−2.4
General Electric	5.52	−2.2
Procter & Gamble	3.22	−2.2
Minn. Min. & Mfg.	5.65	−2.0
Westinghouse	0.93	−1.8
Coca-Cola	1.73	−1.7
Merck	3.12	−1.6
Philip Morris	5.45	−1.4
Woolworth	2.14	−1.4
AT&T	2.86	−0.9
DuPont	1.82	−0.9
Exxon	3.85	−0.6
Texaco	3.58	−0.5
Chevron	6.32	−0.4

* Source: Adapted from: Lee Berton, "New Payroll Rule May Eat into 1997 Profits," *The Wall Street Journal*, June 3, 1993, p. C1.
† Based on option values shown in proxy materials, annual reports and estimates made as if FASB's proposal were currently effective. (Sources: Bear, Stearns & Co.; R. G. Associates Inc. of Baltimore.)

Finally, the second major concern expressed by corporations, which would be affected by this proposed rule, was that companies' earnings per share figures would be reduced. Exhibit 6A–4 provides an example of how the proposal to deduct the value of employee stock options could hypothetically affect companies' calendar or fiscal 1992 earnings. In a June 3, 1993, article in *The Wall Street Journal*, several top corporate executives expressed concern that the proposed rule would depress their companies' stock prices because of lower profits.[41]

The FASB's Final Resolution

In 1994 the FASB, bowing to pressure from business and Congress, dropped a two-year-old proposal that would have forced companies to deduct the cost of employee stock options from earnings. Instead, the chief rule-making body for accountants voted 5–2 to require that companies simply disclose in footnotes to financial statements the impact of such options on net profit and per-share earnings. The FASB also voted to encourage companies to voluntarily deduct the cost of options from earnings, though few are expected to do so.[42]

In its final version, *SFAS No. 123:*

> establishes a fair value based method of accounting for stock-based compensations plans. It encourages firms to adopt that method in place of the provisions of *APB Opinion No. 25,* "Accounting for Stock Issued to Employees," for all arrangements under which employees receive shares of stock or other equity instruments of the employer or the employer incurs liabilities to employees in amounts based on the price of its stock.[43]

However, this standard still allows companies to continue using *APB Opinion No. 25,* under the provision that entities that continue to apply *Opinion 25* shall comply with the disclosure requirements of *Statement 123.* If an entity should elect to apply *Statement 123,* that election shall not be reversed.[44]

Conclusion

To date the FASB's exposure draft on stock option accounting has been one of the most controversial financial accounting standards that the FASB has proposed. The main point of contention by those who were opposed to this standard was the FASB's proposal that would require companies to charge compensation expense against earnings. Among the parties who were opposed to this rule were individual corporations and their executives, the Big Six accounting firms, members of Congress, and the Council of Institutional Investors, as well as the president of the United States. In the end, Dennis R. Beresford, chairman of the FASB, "conceded grudgingly . . . that 'there simply isn't enough support for the basic notion of requiring expense recognition.'"[45]

References

Berton, Lee. "Business Chiefs Try to Derail Proposal on Stock Options." *The Wall Street Journal.* February 5, 1993, p. A2.

———. "New Payroll Rule May Eat into 1997 Profits." *The Wall Street Journal,* June 3, 1993, p. C1.

Berton, Lee, and Joann S. Lublin. "FASB Drops Plan to Force Companies to Deduct Option Costs from Earnings." *The Wall Street Journal,* December 15, 1994, p. A2.

Cheatham, Carole; Leo R. Cheatham; and Michelle McEacharn. "ESOPs FABLE: The Goose that Laid the Golden Eggs." *National Public Accountant,* April 1995, pp. 33–35, 45–46.

Cox, Bill D., and John E. Elsea. "Stock-Based Compensation Controversy Heats Up." *The Practical Accountant,* December 1993, pp. 30–31, 33–36, 40–41.

Financial Accounting Standards Board. *Statement of Financial Accounting Standards No. 123,* "Accounting for Stock-Based Compensation" (Norwalk, CT: 1995).

Harlan, Christi. "Group Opposes Stock-Option Accounting Plan; Institutional Investor Panel Takes Businesses' Side Against Charges to Net Income." *The Wall Street Journal,* January 14, 1993, p. A4.

"Industry Board Backs away from Stock-Option Change." *Nation's Business,* May 1995, p. 10.

---

41. Lee Berton, "New Payroll Rule May Eat in 1997 Profits," *The Wall Street Journal,* June 3, 1993, p. C1.

42. Lee Berton and Joann S. Lublin, "FASB Drops Plan to Force Companies to Deduct Option Costs from Earnings." *The Wall Street Journal,* December 15, 1994, p. A2.

43. *SFAS 123,* 1.

44. Ibid, 382a.

45. "Industry Board Backs Away from Stock-Option Change." Nation's Business, May 1995, p. 10.

Means, Kathryn M., and J. Dennis Coates. "What's All the Fuss about Stock Options?" *The Ohio CPA Journal*, June 1995, pp. 29–31.

"Nasdaq and NASD Oppose FASB's Proposed Rule on Behalf of Nasdaq Companies." *Nasdaq Financial Executive Journal* 3.4 (1993), 16 par. Online. http://www.law.cornell.edu/nasdaq/v3n4/skaff.html. April 3, 1996.

Skaff, William. "Accounting Challenges Corporate Entrepreneurism: FASB's Proposed Stock Options Rule." *Nasdaq Financial Executive Journal* 3.4 (1993). Online. http://www.law.cornell.edu/nasdaq/v3n4/skaff.html. April 3, 1996.

Strawser, Joyce. "Accounting for Stock-Based Compensation: The FASB's Proposal." *The CPA Journal*, October 1993, pp. 44–47, 90–91.

Wilson, Arlette C.; and Len Weld. "Proposed Accounting for Fixed Stock Options: Financial Statement Impact." *National Public Accountant*, June 1995, pp. 25–28.

APPLICATION

Section II covers application issues. While applications are numerous and varied, we focus on judgment and decision making in accounting (Chapter 7), critical and creative thinking and problem solving (Chapter 8), and ethical considerations in judgment and decision making in accounting (Chapter 9). The final chapter provides 55 cases on financial accounting and reporting that cover a variety of issues ranging from revenue and expense recognition, to accounting policies, to ethics in financial decision making and reporting.

JUDGMENT AND DECISION MAKING IN ACCOUNTING

The average man's judgment is so poor, he runs a risk every time he uses it.
Ed Howe

Objectives

This chapter covers the role of judgment and decision making in accounting. Upon completion of the chapter, you will have learned the:

1. Meaning of judgment and decision making in accounting.
2. Relevance of judgment and decision making for various types of accounting.
3. Usefulness of judgment and decision-making models in accounting.
4. The Brunswik Lens Model as a conceptual learning model of judgment and decision making in accounting.
5. Applications of Simon's Model of the Decision Process in accounting.
6. Knowledge management: the relationship between task characteristics and knowledge base for judgment and decision making in accounting.

Accountants are often called upon to make difficult judgments and decisions to solve unstructured problems in unfamiliar settings.[1] Several

---

1. M. C. Francis, T. C. Mulder, and J. S. Stark, *Intentional Learning: A Process for Learning to Learn in the Accounting Curriculum* (Sarasota, FL: Accounting Education Change Commission and the American Accounting Association, 1995), p. 3.

frameworks have been developed to model judgment and decision-making processes. For example, economists make an assumption that people are perfectly rational (i.e., they follow a systematic deductive or inductive logic). Consequently, some economic theories argue that decision makers follow a normative-rational path that has a specific and logical direction. Decision scientists and psychologists on the other hand argue that human beings have certain biases that limit rationality. Biases reduce people's ability to be objective. Consequently, these scholars have presented a number of frameworks for judgment and decision making that acknowledge and account for the existence of human biases. For example, Herbert Simon, a Nobel laureate from Carnegie Melon University has argued that people follow bounded rationality in decision making as compared with perfect rationality in economic theories. Bounded rationality is rationality adjusted for people's biases and cognitive limitations. Cognitive limitations relate to people's mental processes such as awareness, perception, reasoning, and judgment that are influenced by many contextual variables.

The judgment and decision-making (JDM) models that have been developed by psychologists and cognitive scientists assist individuals in effectively managing their knowledge, and bringing the knowledge to bear on making judgments and decisions. As such, these models formulate the relationships between the nature of the task for which JDM is needed, the knowledge needed to perform the task, and the decision aids that are useful to perform the task. This chapter presents two complementary models of JDM. The aim of the first model, the Brunswik Lens Model, is to present a conceptual framework for understanding JDM. The second model, Simon's Model of the Decision Process, is an application model that is presented and supplemented with a case study in the context of a going concern judgment. The focus of both models is on JDM from a cognitive developmental perspective, and therefore, they are based on bounded rationality concepts. While there is an ongoing debate in many disciplines such as economics about concepts of perfect rationality and bounded rationality, this debate is not presented in this chapter.[2]

The chapter begins with a definition and discussion of JDM in the context of auditing, managerial accounting, and financial accounting. The relevance of JDM models to accounting is discussed next, focusing on the Brunswik Lens Model. This model is helpful in conceptualizing the JDM setup. It shows how pieces of information are captured and processed through a "lens" to predict an outcome (i.e., make a decision about the future). The second model is Simon's Model of the Decision Process. This

---

2. For an example of this debate, see J. W. Murphy, "Reason, Bounded Rationality, and the Lebenswelt: Socially Sensitive Decision Making," *American Journal of Economics & Sociology* 51, no. 3 (July 1992), pp. 293–304.

model is helpful in presenting the relationships between task characteristics, knowledge base demands, and decision aids applicable to perform JDM in the context of specific tasks. Since the chapter's focus is on understanding JDM issues, an illustrative case study with significant judgment components is provided at the end of the chapter.

JDM Defined

Judgment is defined as the formation of an opinion after consideration or deliberation.[3] It requires the mental ability to perceive information and distinguish the relationships between various cues in the information set. Thus, the quality of judgment depends on the mental ability of the individual to focus on relevant information and ignore irrelevant information to draw sound conclusions from the information. Judgment quality is affected by many factors. These factors include education such as accounting education for accounting judgments or a law degree for legal judgments. Experience and various cognitive abilities such as intelligence as well as skills such as communication also influence judgment quality. We return to these and other characteristics later in the chapter.

Decision making is related to judgment. It signifies the passing of judgment on an issue under consideration and also acting on that judgment. The decision maker then bears the consequences of the action. For example, in an audit setting, an auditor might judge a client as having going concern problems (a judgment) and proceeds to act on issuing an opinion that signals the going concern problem (a decision).

JDM is a terminology popularized over the past decade. It has been used to describe a large body of research with an objective of understanding and improving both individual and group processes involved in judgment and decision making.[4] In earlier writings, JDM was frequently referred to as *behavioral decision theory*[5] or *human information processing*.[6]

---

3. *The American Heritage Dictionary*, 3rd ed. (New York, NY: Dell Publishing), 1994.

4. For recent reviews of this literature see A. H. Ashton and R. H. Ashton (eds.), *Judgment and Decision Making Research in Accounting and Auditing* (New York: Cambridge University Press, 1995) and K. T. Trotman, *Research Methods for Judgment and Decision Making Studies in Auditing* (Melbourne, Australia: Coopers & Lybrand: Accounting Research Methodology Monograph No. 3, 1996).

5. Related to this terminology is *statistical decision theory*, which refers to the formulation of the decision model using optimizing statistical methods. This is not discussed in this chapter—the interested reader is referred to H. Raiffa and R. Schlafer, *Applied Statistical Decision Theory* (Cambridge, MA: MIT Press, 1961).

6. In early synthesis work on the literature, "human information processing" was used extensively. For example, see R. H. Ashton, *Human Information Processing in Accounting* (Sarasota, FL: American Accounting Association: Studies in Accounting Research No. 17, 1982) and R. Libby, *Accounting and Human Information Processing: Theory and Applications* (Englewood Cliffs, NJ: Prentice-Hall, 1981).

The former refers to the theories that formulate aspects of decision making from the behavioral sciences perspective. The latter is concerned with the way people capture and process information in their judgment and decision-making processes.

JDM addresses three major issues:

1. It provides descriptive models of the way decision makers make judgments and decisions. For example, the pieces of information, called *information cues*, used by auditors in their materiality judgments are identified.

2. It provides normative models that prescribe the search processes in collecting additional evidence. For example, the way memory and cognition affect the auditors' search processes for evidence is depicted using theories and models borrowed from cognitive psychology.

3. It attempts to provide measurements of judgment quality. For example, auditors' judgment consistency over time, or their consensus at a given time, is assessed.

JDM in Accounting

The context of JDM differs depending on the type of accounting as presented in Exhibit 7–1. In this section, we present brief statements and examples of JDM applications in managerial and financial accounting and auditing. Nevertheless, it is important to note that the generic models of JDM discussed later in the chapter apply to all areas of accounting. For example, the design, implementation, and assessment of accounting information systems require much judgment and decision making such as what software to acquire or develop internally. Similarly, accounting for income taxes requires the accountant to make many judgments and decisions ranging from the use of an acceptable depreciation method, other than that used for financial accounting, to save on taxes to long-term tax planning issues.

Auditing

Auditing is a professional domain where JDM has a particularly significant role. In fact, it is stated that JDM is the most common area of research in studying auditing and auditors.[7] An AICPA monograph has recently

---

7. M. Gibbins and R. J. Swieringa, "Twenty Years of Judgment Research in Accounting and Auditing," in A. H. Ashton and R. H. Ashton (eds.), *Judgment and Decision-Making Research in Accounting and Auditing* (New York: Cambridge University Press, 1995), p. 233.

Exhibit 7–1	JDM Use and Accounting Type
Accounting Type	*JDM Examples*
1. Auditing	• Establish materiality (e.g., accounting or auditing materiality and acceptable business risk) • Selection of audit tests • Conclusions from audit tests
2. Managerial	• The development and choice of accounting systems • Production costs and variance analysis • Product and service pricing
3. Financial	• Profitability assessment by investors • Creditworthiness evaluations by creditors • Asset impairment assessment by management

documented the significant impact that JDM research has had on auditing.[8] Simply stated, auditors are paid to make professional judgments.

JDM models deal with a wide variety of issues in auditing. The first, and most obvious, is the group of tasks in each of the substantive phases of the audit that requires JDM. The second issue is the consideration of appropriate JDM models ranging from probabilistic models, psychological biases, and cognitive processes to multiperson JDM settings such as those observed in audit teams. The third issue is the consideration of the criteria that can be used to evaluate JDM. A wide range of criteria such as information cue usage, self-insight, accuracy, consensus, stability, and consistency can be used.[9]

To illustrate how JDM is used in auditing, consider the case of an auditor making a going concern decision about a client. Based on evidence collected, the auditor either states that the client will continue to exist or includes a statement indicating that the client will have difficulty continuing as a going concern. Because of the uncertainty in this JDM case, the auditor cannot be sure, thus there is always a degree of risk that the auditor takes in these types of judgments. In realty, the client will either continue to operate or have a going concern problem (e.g., go bankrupt). This setup is depicted in Exhibit 7–2.

As shown in Exhibit 7–2, if the auditor decides that the client will have a going concern problem and in reality the client has such a problem, then the auditor has made a correct decision (Cell 1). Similarly, if the auditor's decision is that the client will not have a going concern problem and

---

8. See T. B. Bell and A. M. Wright (eds.), *Auditing Practice, Research and Education: A Productive Collaboration* (New York, NY: AICPA, 1995).

9. For a review of the studies in auditing JDM see I. Solomon and M. D. Shields, "Judgment and Decision-Making Research in Auditing," in A. H. Ashton and R. H. Ashton (eds.), *Judgment and Decision-Making Research in Accounting and Auditing* (New York: Cambridge University Press, 1995), pp. 137–75.

Exhibit 7–2	Consequences of Judgment and Decisions in a Going Concert (GC) Context	
	Reality	
Decision	GC	No GC
GC	**Cell 1** Correct decision	**Cell 2** Type I Error: Efficiency problem
No GC	**Cell 3** Type II Error: Effectiveness problem	**Cell 4** Correct decision

in reality the client does not have a going concern problem, then the auditor has made a correct decision once again (Cell 4). However, if in reality, the client has a going concern problem, but the auditor decides that the client has no such problem, a serious error called an effectiveness error has occurred (Cell 3). This error can be very costly for the auditor because of his or her failure to make a correct judgment and decision. A consequence of this decision may be a costly lawsuit by investors and creditors against the auditor.

The situation depicted in Cell 2 is also an error, but a less serious one. It indicates that while the client has no going concern problem, the auditor has judged that the client has such a problem. This error is an efficiency error because it indicates that the auditor has either failed to collect sufficient competent evidential matter or has failed to interpret the evidence properly for the decision. A consequence of this error is that the client with no going concern problem will challenge the auditor on his or her going concern judgment. The auditor in turn will have to collect additional evidence to further support or refute his or her initial going concern judgment. Thus, the issue is one of collecting additional evidence for which the client may or may not be willing to pay. The competitive audit environment suggests that the auditor may have to absorb the additional cost of collecting additional evidence or interpreting existing evidence.

Managerial Accounting

Managerial accounting provides information on which managers and executives of an organization base their decisions. These decisions span a wide range from planning and control of operations to budgets and cost of production reports. Product cost allocations, cost of capital calculations, and allocation of profits and costs to various units in the organization require intense JDM by managers. Introduction of new products and services, production facility design and location, extent of production, and cost and price of the products and services also involve JDM that requires managerial accounting information.

An issue of concern then is how managers within an organization make such judgments and decisions. The answer depends on the theory and framework of managerial JDM used. For example, the rational behavior assumption in economic theories and the psychological models of bounded rationality have been used to develop models of behavioral-economics JDM in managerial accounting.[10] Research studies have used these models to investigate (1) the development and choice of accounting information systems, (2) production cost and variance analyses, and (3) product pricing systems.[11] The main issue of research in the first group of studies is the economic and behavioral cost and benefits of various accounting information systems. The other two streams of research focus on particular types of information needed and/or used by managers in their JDM.

Other studies have focused on the effects of incentives on managerial JDM. Incentive contracting is one model that concerns the contractual incentives designed to motivate employees to meet or exceed expected performance. These studies focus on the relationships in an agency theory framework to understand the nature of managerial JDM (as agents of the owners) in relation to owners (also called *principals*) of the firm. For example, some employees might decide to perform a difficult, but not required, task because of an incentive in their employment contract. Others might decide to focus on performing their existing tasks to ensure adherence to budgetary plans.[12]

Financial Accounting

JDM applies to financial accounting as well. The accountant and the users of financial accounting information make a host of judgments and decisions on the basis of financial accounting data. However, the users of financial accounting information are more diverse than those who use managerial accounting and auditing information. The financial accounting information users focus on different areas. For example, investors are concerned with profitability information. Creditors may focus on long-term profitability for long-term loans, but short-term cash flows for short-term loans. Management uses judgment to assess asset impairment.

---

10. Examples of early work in this area are R. M. Cyret and J. G. March, *A Behavioral Theory of the Firm* (Englewood Cliffs, NJ: Prentice-Hall, 1963) and J. G. March & H. A. Simon, *Organizations* (New York: Wiley, 1958).

11. For a detailed review of these studies see W. S. Waller, "Decision-Making Research in Managerial Accounting: Return to Behavioral-Economics Foundations," in A. H. Ashton and R. H. Ashton (eds.), *Judgment and Decision-Making Research in Accounting and Auditing* (New York: Cambridge University Press, 1995), pp. 29–54.

12. For a detailed review of these studies see S. M. Young and B. Lewis, "Experimental Incentive-Contracting Research in Management Accounting," in A. H. Ashton and R. H. Ashton (eds.), *Judgment and Decision-Making Research in Accounting and Auditing* (New York: Cambridge University Press, 1995), pp. 55–75.

The diversity of users and their objectives makes the understanding of the JDM issues in financial accounting very difficult. This is perhaps one reason why JDM research is lagging behind in financial accounting. Financial accounting research models are primarily based on capital market research where the availability of extensive databases has provided an incentive to focus on empirical studies. JDM models normally require the collection of experimental data from survey questionnaires, laboratory experiments, archival studies, or field-based research.

The diversity of the users and their multiple objectives, however, present great opportunities for understanding the applicable JDM models. Our knowledge of this area is limited and there have been calls in recent years for more JDM research in financial accounting issues.[13] Nevertheless, the generic JDM models discussed in this chapter are helpful in assisting decision makers in financial accounting as well as those in the managerial accounting and auditing areas.

JDM Models

The diversity of accounting types, decision makers, and decision contexts requires a multitude of models for JDM. A comprehensive inventory and discussion of these models are beyond the scope of this chapter. Some examples were provided in the previous section in relation to our discussion of the relevance of JDM to various types of accounting. In the next two sections, two generic JDM models that have been used for many JDM contexts are discussed. They are the Brunswik Lens Model and Simon's Model of the Decision Process. The former is discussed in order to illustrate a judgment and decision-making process. The latter model is a more operational model. It is discussed in more detail and followed by a case study.

The Brunswik Lens Model

A framework that is useful for describing the JDM process is the Brunswik Lens model.[14] Its three components are presented in Exhibit 7–3. On the left-hand side of the model is the JDM problem or event (Y_e), say the pre-

---

13. For example, see K. Schipper, "Commentary on Analysts' Forecasts," *Accounting Horizons* 5, no. 4 (1991), pp. 105–21 and L. A. Maines, "Judgment and Decision-Making Research on Financial Accounting: A Review and Analysis" in A. H. Ashton and R. H. Ashton (eds.), *Judgment and Decision-Making Research in Accounting and Auditing* (New York: Cambridge University Press, 1995), pp. 76–101.
14. This model is based on a book by E. Brunswik, *The Conceptual Framework of Psychology* (Chicago, IL: University of Chicago, 1952).

Exhibit 7–3   The Brunswik Lens Model

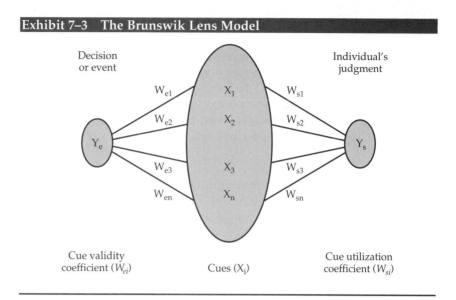

The decision maker observes the information cues (X_i) through the lens and makes a prediction about the future survival of the client (i.e., the going concern judgment). Thus, the information cues must be carefully selected so that they are relevant pieces of information for the judgment. If they are selected so that they all are relevant, then the decision maker's judgment is focused on the right cues. On the other hand, if irrelevant information cues are allowed to enter in X_i, then the JDM quality is adversely affected because the decision maker is using cues that are irrelevant and should not be used in the first place. Irrelevant information cues are said to introduce noise into the JDM process.

The decision maker assigns a weight (W_{si}) for each of the information cues. These weights are called the *cue utilization coefficients*. They influence the decision makers' ultimate judgment of the client's going concern prediction. Thus, it is important for the decision maker to use the right weights for this purpose. The way to assess the propriety of these weights in the Lens model is to compare them with cue validity coefficients (W_{ei}).

diction of the going concern status of a business entity.[15] On the right-hand side is the individual decision maker, say a financial analyst or an auditor who is interested in or charged with the task of predicting the going concern status of the business entity (Y_s). In the middle of the model is a lens that contains the information cues (X_i), say financial ratios such as the current ratio, for the decision maker to use.

---

15. Much of this discussion is adapted from K. A. Houghton, "Accounting: The Stereotype and the Future," *Australian Economic Review* 3, no. 1 (1992), pp. 89–92.

A W_{ei} is a theoretical weight assigned to a variable based on empirical data. For example, financial ratios of many companies have been used to develop theoretical weights for healthy firms in comparison with unhealthy ones. A popular measure, called the Altman's Z-score, has been developed that is used by auditors and financial analysts as a measure of bankruptcy prediction (i.e., Y_e).[16] The Z-score is based on a regression analysis where coefficients of various ratios are found through empirical studies comparing the Z-scores of bankrupt companies over a period of say three to five years before filing for bankruptcy to healthy companies of the same size and characteristics.

The implications of the Lens model for accounting are important and significant. First the information cues (X_i) are based on financial information (e.g., ratios) generated from the accounting numbers. The accuracy, comparability, and reliability of these information cues are vital to JDM. Second, the cue validity coefficients (W_{ei}) are based on the validity of the accounting information provided over a sustained period of time because the theoretical weights are developed over time on the basis of this information. Thus, consistency in reporting is important here. The cue utilization coefficients (W_{si}) represent the decision makers' ability to understand and use the information cues properly by focusing on relevant cues and by assigning correct weights to them. This task requires a clear understanding of the implications of accounting information on decisions.

Lens model is a simple and yet powerful framework that conceptualizes the relationships between information cues and JDM. It also can be used as an application model where predictions can be made by decision makers. For example, the Lens model has been used for decisions to admit students to graduate schools of business. In doing so, admission officers focus on information cues such as applicants' grade point average, their GMAT score, undergraduate school quality, recommendations, and the like to predict a student's success in graduating from college (and professional success upon graduation).[17]

Recently, a study used the Lens model to assess weights (i.e., W_{si}) of certain variables (i.e., X_i) that are associated with effective performance in public accounting. It compared the weights assigned by accounting students with those of recruiters. The authors found that students' pre-employment expectations of job requirements differed from those of recruiters in some important areas. For example, while students placed the greatest weight on communication skills, recruiters placed the least

---

16. This measure is named after E. I. Altman, who proposed the model. See E. I. Altman, "Financial Ratios, Discriminant Analysis and the Prediction of Corporate Bankruptcy," *Journal of Finance* 23, no. 4 (1968), pp. 589–609.

17. R. Libby, *Accounting and Human Information Processing: Theory and Applications* (Englewood Cliffs, NJ: Prentice-Hall, 1981), pp. 4–7.

weight on this cue. On the other side, students placed the least weight on responsibility while this cue received a medium weight by recruiters.[18]

You can use the Brunswik Lens Model to help you decide between job offers. If you have multiple job offers, how do you decide which one to take? As an exercise, identify major variables of interest (X_i) to you, such as salary, flexibility in job assignments, childcare facilities, and the like. Then assign your utility weights to each of these variables (W_{si}) and compare them with validity weights from the recruiters (W_{ei}), if available. This exercise may be helpful to you in making this important decision. If you did this exercise by collecting data from a sample of students and recruiters, you can do formal data analysis such as the correlation between various cue utility weights and cue validity weights. However, at the individual level, such statistical analysis is not possible. The individual decision is made by comparing your own cue utility weights with the recruiters' cue validity weights to help you with the decision.

Simon's Model of the Decision Process

Management scientist Herbert Simon presented a framework that is useful for understanding the relationships between JDM and specific tasks. The framework is called Simon's Model of the Decision Process. The importance of this model is in its explicit inclusion of various phases of a decision. As explained later in the section, these phases of the decision process have implications for consideration of task characteristics such as task structure. The level of task structure has implications for the knowledge base required for performing various tasks, and the decision aids and information technology that can be used to perform the tasks. As such, Simon's model has implications for knowledge management at the individual decision-maker level. It also provides a vehicle for organizing various tasks, such as audit tasks, in a way to manage organizational knowledge, particularly for knowledge-rich organizations such as accounting firms. In this section we describe various aspects of this model.

Phases of the Decision Process

According to Simon's model, each decision has three phases: intelligence, design, and choice. In the intelligence phase, the decision maker performs a few steps to understand and define the problem or the context for which a decision has to be made. In the design phase, the decision maker collects

---

18. R. J. Kirsch, P. E. Leathers, and K. C. Snead, "Student versus Recruiter Perceptions of the Importance of Staff Auditor Performance Variables," *Accounting Horizons* 7, no. 4 (December 1993), pp. 58–69.

Exhibit 7–4	Decision Phases According to Simon's Model of the Decision Process	
Decision Phase	*Steps in the Research Process*	*Purpose*
A. Intelligence	1. Identify the problem	Determine the nature of the problem
	2. Identify objectives	Specify detailed objectives of the problem
	3. Develop key words	Begin the search process
	4. Structure problem	Break the problem into structured components
B. Design	1. Gather data	Collect data about the problem
	2. Code data	Code the data into a form useful for analysis
	3. Generate alternatives	Identify alternative courses of action
	4. Determine consequences of the alternatives	Quantify the risks and values related to the alternative courses of action
C. Choice	1. Analyze data or synthesize literature	Use a quantitative or qualitative process to make sense of the data and the literature
	2. Choose among alternatives	Make a choice among alternatives
	3. Explain choice	Communicate the reasons for the choice
	4. Develop implementation plan	Present a practical, step-by-step implementation plan

evidence regarding the problem and specifies the alternative courses of action and their consequences. Finally, in the choice phase, the decision maker selects the alternative course of action most appropriate for the problem, based on an analysis of the data or a synthesis of the literature. These phases of the decision process and their purposes are depicted in Exhibit 7–4.

For the intelligence phase, the steps of problem identification, objective development, and key words are listed. These steps are consistent with the steps in applied professional research that are discussed in Chapter 6 (see steps 1–3 in Exhibit 6–2). Determination of the nature of the problem and the specification of the problem objectives are the reasons for these steps. The result here is a decomposition of the problem into specific components to facilitate JDM.

In the design phase, the steps of data gathering, coding, alternative solutions, and their consequences are considered. The purpose for these steps is to collect data about the problem, search the professional literature, and code the data into a form that is useful for analysis. These steps are also similar to those in Chapter 6 (see steps 4–6 in Exhibit 6–2). As a result, risks and values related to various alternative courses of action (i.e., consequences) are identified to assist the decision maker in the next phase, choice.

In the final phase of the decision process, choice, the decision maker follows the steps of analyzing the data or synthesizing the professional literature, choosing among alternative courses of action, explaining the choice, and developing an implementation plan. These steps are also similar to the steps in Chapter 6 (see steps 7–9 in Exhibit 6–2). This is where quantitative or qualitative data analysis is performed to make sense of the data or the evidence from the literature. This analysis assists the decision maker in making a choice among alternatives. From this vantage point, the decision maker communicates the reasons for the choice and presents a practical, step-by-step implementation plan.

Decision Phases and Task Characteristics

The decision phases were used to classify the steps in the professional research process in the previous section. This classification provides a useful connection to the professional research discussed in Chapter 6. These decision phases are also useful for a classification of JDM tasks by their level of structure (structured, semistructured, or unstructured). This classification is important because differences in judgments of experienced and inexperienced decision makers (e.g., auditors) have been traced to differences in the task structure.[19] Exhibit 7–5 shows the relationship between decision phases and the levels of task structure.[20]

Structured Tasks
Structured tasks are those for which the problem is well defined in the intelligence phase, alternative solutions are very limited in the design

Exhibit 7–5   Decision Phases and Task Characteristics

	Task Structure		
Decision Phase	*Structured*	*Semistructured*	*Unstructured*
Intelligence: Problem is	Well defined	Reasonably defined	Ill defined
Design: Alternatives are	Well specified	Limited, specified	Numerous
Choice: Requires	No judgment	Some judgment	Judgment and insight

---

19. M. J. Abdolmohammadi and A. Wright, "An Examination of the Effects of Experience and Task Complexity on Audit Judgments," *The Accounting Review* (January 1987), pp. 1–13.
20. The discussion here is based on P. G. W. Keen and M. S. Scott-Morton, *Decision Support Systems: An Organizational Perspective* (Reading, MA: Addison-Wesley, 1978) and H. Simon, *The New Science of Management* (New York: Harper and Row, 1960).

phase, and very little judgment is needed to make a final choice at the choice phase of the decision process. These tasks are generally "simple" and "programmable." An example of these tasks is the computation of depreciation expense for equipment where all aspects of the problem are specified (e.g., use straight-line method of depreciation for a property with an estimated useful life of five years and no salvage value).

Unstructured Tasks
In some tasks, the problem is ill defined at the intelligence phase, and/or the alternative solutions may be numerous at the design phase, thus requiring the decision maker to use considerable judgment and insight to choose an alternative at the choice phase of the decision process. These tasks are viewed as highly complex and nonprogrammable, or unstructured. For example, some exchange transactions involving gain recognition with continuing seller involvement or options make determination of the substance of the transaction extremely difficult.

Semistructured Tasks
Somewhere between the programmable to nonprogrammable or structured to unstructured continuum are tasks with a medium level of structure. These tasks may be called *semiprogrammable* or *semistructured*. The problem in these tasks is reasonably defined at the intelligence phase, alternative solutions are limited and specified at the design phase, leaving some judgment to the decision maker in choosing among the alternatives at the choice phase of the decision process. For example, *SFAS No. 66*, "Accounting for Sales of Real Estate," provides criteria to determine whether profit on the sale of real estate is accounted for by the full accrual method, installment method, or cost recovery method. While the alternative solutions as to when to recognize profit on sale of real estate are limited, the judgment as to what alternative to select is not always clear.

In the task classification scheme just outlined, only one method of task classification—task structure—is presented. Tasks can be classified in a number of other ways as well. For example, a task can be classified as to its level of difficulty, its dynamism, repetitiveness, or the degree to which it can be decomposed into simple parts. While these classification schemes have merits, they require a long discussion.[21]

---

21. The interested reader is referred to review papers by D. J. Campbell, "Task Complexity: A Review and Analysis," *Academy of Management Review* 13, no. 1 (1988), pp. 40–52; R. E. Wood, "Task Complexity: Definition of the Construct," *Organizational Behavior and Human Decision Processes* 37 (1986), pp. 60–82; and J. Shanteau, "Competence in Experts: The Role of Task Characteristics," *Organizational Behavior and Human Decision Process* 53 (November 1992).

Decision Makers' Attributes

In the previous section, we considered the nature of the task. In this section, we discuss general attributes of the decision maker. This is because decision makers' attributes affect the quality of the decision. Borrowing from the psychological literature, we discuss five general attributes of a decision maker as presented in Exhibit 7–6. However, primary focus in this section is on the importance of knowledge for performance.[22] This issue is key to understanding knowledge management as discussed later in this chapter.

Exhibit 7–6 Decision Maker's Attributes	
Attribute	*Meaning*
1. Knowledge	Knowledge of facts, processes, and procedures
2. Psychological traits	Self-presentation attributes such as confidence
3. Cognitive abilities	Abilities to acquire and process information (e.g., intelligence)
4. Decision strategies	Strategies used for decision making
5. Task analysis	Assess the nature of the task

Knowledge

The decision maker is required to have the requisite knowledge of facts, processes, and procedures for the problem under investigation. The insights gained from experience in working on real problems are part of this knowledge base because experience will result in knowledge accumulation and refinement over time. Experience-based knowledge assists the decision maker in understanding and organizing vast amounts of information. This is where experienced decision makers have a comparative advantage over inexperienced ones. Inexperienced decision makers, who have not had the opportunity to practice, lack case-specific knowledge to perform a task, creating a disadvantage for them as compared with more experienced decision makers.

A major issue relating to knowledge is when it would normally be acquired. In general, college education and years of experience have been used as plausible proxies or surrogates for knowledge. Also contributing to knowledge is the in-house technical training that many employersprovide their employees. Finally, supervised instances of practice on specific tasks are important to develop working knowledge.

---

22. There is an extensive body of psychological literature that relates to these issues. Only a brief summary is provided here. The interested reader is referred to M. J. Abdolmohammadi, J. Shanteau, and J. Searfoss, "Importance of Psychological Traits to Expertise in Auditing " (working paper, Bentley College, 2000).

For example, accounting firms typically provide training programs in the first several years of practice and tailor such programs to specific professional ranks such as staff, senior, or manager training programs. Consequently, accounting firms use professional rank as proxy or surrogate for the knowledge necessary for the tasks assigned to auditors of various ranks. They also assign tasks to less experienced staff to perform several times under supervision until the staff is considered capable of performing the tasks independently.[23]

Psychological Traits

The importance of self-presentation for the creation and maintenance of a favorable public image for decision makers has been acknowledged in the literature. For example, experts have higher levels of self-confidence than novices do. They also are more tolerant of stress and ambiguity, more willing to assume responsibility, and more assertive than novices.

Cognitive Abilities

The abilities to accumulate and process information are classified as cognitive abilities. Examples include the ability to connect various types of knowledge and the ability to adapt to new and ambiguous situations. Attention to relevant facts and the ability to ignore irrelevant facts as well as the ability to work effectively under stress are other examples. The behavioral literature indicates that some of these cognitive abilities are innate in nature and transfer between various domains (e.g., intelligence). Other cognitive abilities are specific to a particular domain and relate to the acquisition and processing of certain types of information (e.g., audit evidence).

Decision Strategies

Observations of expert decision makers indicate that they use a variety of formal and informal decision strategies to help systematize decision making. They help decision makers overcome the limitations of human cognition. They range from simple unaided strategies such as decomposition of complex decision problems into several simple problems, to the use of decision aids such as manual checklists or computerized expert systems.

---

23. An important issue here is the extent of knowledge that is necessary to perform specific tasks. For information on professional rank required to perform 332 detailed audit tasks, see M. J. Abdolmohammadi, "A Comprehensive Taxonomy of Audit Task Structure, Professional Rank, and Decision Aids for Behavioral Research," *Behavioral Research in Accounting* 11 (1999), pp. 51–92. For information on years of experience and the number of supervised instances of practice before an auditor can perform each of 453 detailed audit tasks, see M. J. Abdolmohammadi and C. Usoff, *The Assessment of Task Structure, Knowledge Base, and Decision Aids for a Comprehensive Inventory of Audit Tasks* (Norwalk, CT: Quorum Books, 2000).

Task Analysis

The final attribute in Exhibit 7–6 is task analysis, where the decision maker assesses the nature of the task. For example, task structure is a task characteristic that decision makers must assess because of its effects on their JDM. In some tasks, so much knowledge has already been accumulated that decision makers perform well. For example, management's decisions concerning inventory and depreciation methods are easily made keeping in mind uncertain future events (e.g., the future direction of cost of new inventory may be different from the past patterns). Also, new technologies may bring cheaper and more efficient physical assets in the future that may render partially depreciated assets less productive, necessitating a change in future depreciation charges. Yet these tasks are well understood, while our knowledge is limited for other tasks such as accounting for derivative financial instruments, environmental accounting, or accounting for intellectual capital.

Decision Aids Used for JDM

The task structure definitions discussed earlier indicate that while some tasks are programmable, other tasks may be nonprogrammable. This means that a computerized decision aid can be developed and used as an aid to the decision maker for programmable tasks, but not for nonprogrammable ones. This issue has become one of the most important topics in the current environment where information technology affects a large number of tasks in the contemporary organization. For example, task characteristics such as structure or programmability indicate the level and type of information technology that can be used to perform the task. A framework to show how task structure is related to task programmability and decision aids is presented later. In this section, we define the three decision aids and strictly human processing that are presented in Exhibit 7–7.

Complete Automation

Complete automation refers to the development and use of computer programs that completely perform a task. These programs tackle routine tasks and perform them at a high speed. Furthermore, these programs seldom commit any error unless there is an error in the program itself or a programming bug develops in its code. In such a situation, errors occur systematically and repeatedly. In contrast, when routine tasks are performed manually, errors occur randomly as a result of human factors such as fatigue, impatience, or boredom. Accounting examples of the tasks that can be automated are footing, recalculation, and cross checking. Most bookkeeping activities are now typically performed by general ledger software packages.

Exhibit 7–7 Decision Aids Used for JDM	
Decision Aid Type	*Meaning*
1. Complete automation	Some tasks such as footing, recalculation, and cross checking may be done completely by a computer based on some predetermined formula. This is referred to as *complete automation*.
2. Decision support systems (DSS)	A DSS is an interactive computer-based software that assists decision makers. DSSs use certain statistical or mathematical models and data to make inferences for the use of the decision maker.
3. Knowledge-based expert systems (KES)	A KES is an interactive computer-based software that assists decision makers in using expert(s) decision rules to make their decisions. To create a KES, the decision rules of the expert(s) must be elicited and expressed in terms of a number of IF-THEN rules. To employ a KES, the decision maker provides answers to questions posed by the system. The KES then presents a recommendation to the decision maker. The decision maker has the option of accepting or rejecting the recommendation developed by the KES.
4. Strictly human processing	Some tasks may not be suitable for automation, DSS, or KES. These tasks require strictly human processing. It should be noted that all decision aids have a human processing component to them.

Decision Support Systems (DSS)

Some tasks that cannot be programmed completely can nevertheless be partially programmed by software such as decision support systems (DSSs). A DSS is an interactive computer-based program that assists decision makers by addressing certain parts of the problems. These DSSs typically use statistical or mathematical models that process and analyze data for the decision maker. Easy-to-use statistical packages such as *SAS* or *Minitab* can be classified broadly as DSSs. Examples of these tasks are statistical sampling and analytical review procedures in auditing that are typically performed using DSSs.

Knowledge-Based Expert Systems (KES)

There are many other computer decision aids that also assist decision makers. One is a knowledge-based expert system (KES). A KES is developed by the creation of software incorporating the decision rules of one or more experts. These decision rules are elicited and expressed with a number of IF-THEN rules in the software and are provided to decision makers for consultation. It is like having the opinion of an expert at your fingertips. To employ a KES, the decision maker provides answers to questions posed by the system. The KES then presents a recommendation to the decision maker. The decision maker has the option of accepting or rejecting the recommendation developed by the KES. An example of KES is Exper-TAX, a tax-planning expert system developed in the 1980s by Coopers & Lybrand (now PricewaterhouseCoopers).

Strictly Human Processing

Some tasks may not be suitable for automation, DSS, or KES. These tasks require strictly human processing regardless of their nature. For example, research and development contracts can be difficult to account for. Although the decision maker will gather lots of information about the contract, the ultimate decision may be based on an unaided judgment using the available information. The variables may be so diverse and dynamic that their inclusion in a software package in a timely manner may be impossible. Thus, the decision maker performs the JDM primarily as a human processing task.

Knowledge Management

Knowledge management (KM) is a branch of management science dealing with the discovery, documentation, dissemination, evolution, and application of knowledge in an organization. The concept is not new. KM practice can be traced to apprenticeship and family businesses where the knowledge of elders was transferred to others. However, single-office businesses of the past have given way to a multitude of offices scattered throughout the world. Also, the information technology has revolutionized KM, making it necessary for many large companies, particularly service companies such as accounting firms, to invest large sums of money in creating state-of-the-art KM systems. For example, KPMG's annual budget is over $100 million per year. Called KWorld, KPMG's KM system provides an Internet-based information technology that is designed to bring the collective knowledge of the firm to its workforce and clients around the Globe. A KPMG professional in Boston has the same access to this KM system, as does an employee in Ankara, Turkey, or London.

At the organizational level, KM has four components: a domain-specific knowledge base, people, an information technology system, and a process. *Domain-specific knowledge* refers to the knowledge necessary to provide services in an area of specialization (e.g., accounting). *People* consist of those working in the organization in a professional setting (also called *knowledge workers*) as well as those in clerical jobs. For a successful KM, these workers' knowledge must be coded and shared with the rest of the organization. Thus, the benefit of the organization as a whole has become more important as than compared with individuals within the organization. The management of this aspect alone requires much skill and an appropriate reward system to make it happen. Many people still view personal knowledge as a source of power and are unwilling to share it with coworkers.

Information technology is the system consisting of hardware, software, networks, and people that facilitate the discovery, documentation, dissemination, evolution, and application of knowledge in an organization. With the presence of the Internet technology, such an information technology can be highly dynamic, being updated on a real-time basis. Finally, a *process* must be in place to bring the knowledge on specific issues to those in the organization who need it. This process may consist of an automated information technology, as well as the professional staff (e.g., domain specialists) and clerical workers.

Simon's Model of the Decision Process as a KM System

An overall KM system must translate into guidance on performing specific tasks. In this regard, Simon's model of the decision process can be viewed as a KM system. From the discussion of task characteristics, knowledge base, and decision aids in the previous sections, a general JDM framework is presented in Exhibit 7–8 that can be viewed as a KM system. The framework indicates that a low-level knowledge base may be sufficient to perform a structured task. An example is an accounting student who has the knowledge to solve depreciation computations with relative ease. Some psychologists call this a *naive level* of knowledge base. The knowledge base needed to perform semistructured tasks is a medium level. This is generally the knowledge that has been acquired through a few years of experience in addition to college education. Psychologists call this a *novice level*. An example of this is the performance of internal control evaluations by senior auditors. Unstructured tasks require the highest level of knowledge gained from many years of education, experience, and on-the-job training. This is called an *expert level* of knowledge base.

The decision aid applicable for structured tasks is generally, but not always, automation. For example, the task of recalculating the depreciation expense on a test basis for a few items may be viewed as structured in nature, but for an auditor, it may still be a manual task rather than a computerized one. On the other hand, many of the structured tasks such as footing and cross-footing or bookkeeping can be completely automated.

Exhibit 7–8	Relationships between Task Characteristics, Knowledge Base, and Decision Aids		
	Task Structure		
Decision Phase	*Structured*	*Semistructured*	*Unstructured*
Knowledge base:	Low (naive)	Medium (novice)	High (expert)
Decision aid:	Automation	Decision support systems (DSS)	Decision support & expert systems (DSS & KES)

Source: Adapted from M. J. Abdolmohammadi, "Decision Support and Expert Systems in Auditing: A Review and Research Directions, " *Accounting and Business Research* 17, no. 67 (1987), pp. 173–85.

Decision support and expert systems (i.e., DSS & KES) are used to assist the decision maker in a variety of semistructured and unstructured tasks. While the former may be more applicable for semistructured tasks, the latter is used primarily for the unstructured tasks where expertise plays a major role in task performance.[24] For example, internal control evaluation is a semistructured task for which all major accounting firms use DSSs ranging from computerized checklists to expert systems (e.g., Deloitte & Touche's Internal Control Expert). For unstructured tasks such as the going concern judgments by auditors, several expert systems have been developed.[25] These expert systems simply bring the knowledge of the organization to bear on a specific engagement by a professional accountant. It is important to note that decision aids are just that, decision aids. The decision maker still has the responsibility to use professional judgment to make a final decision.

An observation from Exhibit 7–8 is that the more you move from the right-hand side of the exhibit to the left-hand side, the lower the knowledge base required and the more automation that can be developed to perform the task. From an economic perspective, this is a desirable outcome of task-structuring activities. The more that we learn about a specific task and the better that we can describe the nature of the task, the more we can structure the task. This will in turn lower the need for higher-paid professionals and expensive decision aids to perform the task. However, it is also conceivable that regardless of the level of structure, some tasks may require human processing. For example, the task of observing inventory may require human processing even if decision aids (such as electronic eyes) are utilized in the process.

| ILLUSTRATIVE CASE | ESSEX MANUFACTURING COMPANY, INC. |

Ability of a Manufacturer to Continue as a Going Concern

Essex Manufacturing Company, Inc. is a closely held manufacturing company. Thomas Agree, president and chairman of the board of directors, is the majority shareholder and his immediate family owns the remaining stock. Mr. Agree has never paid much attention to internal control systems, nor has he ever been serious about effectively cutting operating costs. He is generally content as long as Essex Manufacturing is able to keep out of financial difficulty, and he can receive a large salary and applicable executive benefits to support his extravagant lifestyle.

---

24. For a recent review of these decision aids and their relationships with task characteristics see W. F. Messier, Jr., "Research in and Development of Audit Decision Aids," in A. H. Ashton and R. H. Ashton (eds.), *Judgment and Decision-Making Research in Accounting and Auditing* (New York: Cambridge University Press, 1995), pp. 207–28.
25. An example of this is GCX expert system developed under a grant from KPMG Peat Marwick's Research Opportunities in Auditing Program. See S. F. Biggs, M. Selfridge, and G. R. Grupka, "A Computational Model of Auditor Knowledge and Decision Process in Going-Concern Judgment," *Auditing: A Journal of Practice and Theory* 12 (Supplement, 1993), pp. 82–99.

Historically, weak operating results of the company's industry have been a lead indicator of an economic downturn. Essex incurred a significant operating loss for the year ended December 31, 20X1, but was marginally profitable in the prior year. This loss was due primarily to a decrease in sales and a substantial increase in fixed manufacturing overhead with little related revenue. In 20X1 Essex put another plant online to expand its present product line and capacity.

Subsequent to year-end, Essex defaulted on long-term debt payments to Harbor City Bank, and as of year-end, was in violation of several long-term debt covenants with Harbor concerning financial ratios. In late January 20X2, Essex was able to renegotiate all of its long-term debt agreements with the bank. Harbor agreed not to call the loan for default, providing Essex made monthly interest payments and minimum principal payments for the next year. Harbor also retained the right to reinstitute a schedule of accelerated principal payments any time during the year that a certain specified earnings level was not achieved. The bank determined the earnings level based on a projected 5 percent sales increase in 20X2 and an assumed rate of return on net sales.

Mr. Agree is concerned that cash flow from operations in 20X2 might not be sufficient to make additional principal payments on the bank loan if they are required. However, he did feel that the 20X1 loss was a one-year occurrence, and the company could continue to operate in the same manner as it did in the past. Sales for the last quarter of 20X1 decreased approximately 25 percent from average quarterly sales for the first three quarters of 20X1. Annualized January 20X2 sales (January sales multiplied by twelve) would meet the bank's projection for 20X2 sales. However, January 20X2 sales were less than the January 20X1 sales, and January has always been the company's leading month for sales volume.

Essex Manufacturing is committed to purchasing an essential piece of equipment in early 20X2 for $300,000. The company anticipates using the Internal Revenue Service refund from the operating loss carryback to pay for most of the equipment. Depreciation expense for 20X2 is estimated to be $500,000.

Exhibits 1 and 2 show Essex Manufacturing Company's balance sheet as of December 31, 20X1, and its statement of loss for the year ended December 31, 20X1.

Required

1. Discuss the structure of the going concern task in an audit setting. Also, identify the knowledge base and the decision aids that can be used to perform this task.
2. Discuss the specific considerations that should be taken into account when deciding if Essex Manufacturing Company's 20X1 report should be modified based on a going concern qualification.
3. Discuss how you would report on Essex's 20X1 financial statements and state the basis for your conclusion.

ILLUSTRATIVE CASE DISCUSSION

This case requires respondents to exercise judgment regarding an entity's ability to continue as a going concern. It requires an identification of the knowledge base and decision aids useful to the rendering of going concern judgment. Its setting is an environment of poor management with no apparent plan of action for dealing with a liquidity crisis. It also demonstrates the plight of many closely held companies confronted with poor economic indicators.

Requirement 1: The JDM in assessing whether a client has a going concern problem is clearly a complex task. The auditor's concern is whether the client has the ability to meet its obligations and to continue its operations over the next operating period. The going concern task can be viewed as somewhere between a semistructured and an unstructured task in Simon's model of the decision process (see Exhibit 7–5). This task is reasonably defined at the intelligence phase. That is, the professional auditing literature has defined the going concern task quite well (see the discussion under requirement 2). Also, the number of alternative courses of action (e.g., issue an unqualified opinion with explanatory paragraph, or a disclaimer of an

EXHIBIT 1

ESSEX MANUFACTURING COMPANY, INC.
Balance Sheet
December 31, 20X1

Assets

Current assets:

Cash	$ 50,000
Accounts receivable	240,000
Income tax refund receivable	200,000
Inventories	600,000
Prepaid expenses	10,000
	1,100,000
Property, plant, and equipment, net	5,000,000
Total assets	$6,100,000

Liabilities and Stockholders' Equity

Current liabilities

Notes payable—bank	$1,500,000
Current maturity of long-term debt	400,000
Accounts payable and accrued expenses	600,000
	2,500,000
Long-term debt	2,450,000
Total liabilities	4,950,000
Stockholders' equity	
Common stock	50,000
Retained earnings	1,100,000
Total stockholders' equity	1,150,000
Total liabilites and stockholders' equity	$6,100,000

EXHIBIT 2

ESSEX MANUFACTURING COMPANY, INC.
Statement of Loss
For the Year-Ended December 31, 20X1

Sales	$10,000,000
Cost of goods sold	7,200,000
Selling, general, and administrative expenses	2,900,000
Interest expense	400,000
	10,500,000
Loss from operations	(500,000)
Income tax benefit from loss carryback	200,000
Net loss	$ (300,000)

opinion) are limited and well specified at the design phase. These two characteristics indicate that the task of going concern assessment can be classified as a semistructured task. However, the choice phase requires significant judgment and insight to make a going concern decision. This aspect of the going concern task indicates that it is an unstructured task. In fact, in two separate research studies over an eight-year period, managers and partners from various accounting firms assessed the task as borderline between semistructured and unstructured tasks.[26]

Due to its complex nature, the going concern judgment also requires specialized knowledge to perform. Clearly, this is a decision that in-charge auditors make in consultation with other knowledgeable colleagues, generally partners. For example, in the two research studies referred to above, professional rank, the number of years of experience, and the number of supervised instances of practice were used as evidence of knowledge. The authors found that generally audit partners with an average of 6.9 years of experience, and 5.8 supervised instances of practice are needed to perform the complex tasks required to issue an audit opinion other than the standard unqualified opinion that includes going concern judgments.[27]

Finally, as stated earlier, the nature of the going concern judgment is so complex that it requires significant judgment and insight to perform. Thus, it is difficult to develop decision aids to assist with this task because every client situation is unique when it comes to going concern issues. For this reason, a vast majority of the managers and partners who participated in the two studies indicated above stated that strict human processing is needed to perform tasks related to issuing an opinion other than an unqualified opinion. A small minority of the managers and partners, however, indicated that knowledge-based expert systems might be useful for this task. No one indicated automation or decision support system to be useful to perform this task.[28]

Requirement 2: The going concern assumption is referred to in *ARB No. 43*, Chapter 3, Section A, paragraph 2, which states that: "financial statements of a going concern are prepared on the assumption that the company will continue in business." When there is uncertainty about an entity's continued existence, *SAS No. 59*, "The Auditor's Consideration of an Entity's Ability to Continue as a Going Concern," specifies the auditor's responsibility. *SAS No. 59* supersedes *SAS No. 34*, "The Auditor's Considerations When a Question Arises About an Entity's Continued Existence," which identifies factors to be considered when such uncertainty exists. In addition to placing greater responsibility on the auditor and changing the assumption about going concern, the general thrust of *SAS No. 59* differs from *SAS No. 34*.

SAS No. 34 focused on solvency, and paragraph 1 states: "When the continued existence of an entity is imperiled, there is heightened concern about the recoverability and classification of recorded asset amounts and the amounts and classification of liabilities." The old standard intentionally used the term *continued existence* and avoided any implication that auditors had a responsibility beyond the consideration of asset recoverability and liability classification. *SAS No. 59* promulgates a new standard acknowledging that even though there may not be a risk of insolvency, there may still persist "substantial doubt" about the entity's ability to continue as a going concern for a reasonable period of time. The term *going concern* replaced *continued existence*.

---

26. This task was studied as FO 23, "For other than unqualified reports, the decision on the type of opinion (qualified, adverse, disclaimer) and wording of the audit report" in M. J. Abdolmohammadi, "A Comprehensive Taxonomy of Audit Task Structure, Professional Rank, and Decision Aids for Behavioral Research," *Behavioral Research in Accounting* 11 (1999), p. 67. It received a task structure mean rating of 6.39 in a 1–9 (structured to unstructured) classification. The same task was also included in a later study by M. J. Abdolmohammadi and C. Usoff, *The Assessment of Task Structure, Knowledge Base, and Decision Aids for a Comprehensive Inventory of Audit Tasks* (Norwalk, CT: Quorum Books, 2001), p. 160. It received a mean structure rating of 5.40.
27. See Abdolmohammadi and Usoff (2001, op cit.), p. 178.
28. See Abdolmohammadi and Usoff (2001, op cit.), p. 196.

According to *SAS No. 59*, paragraph 1, "Continuation of an entity as a going concern is assumed in financial reporting in the absence of significant information to the contrary. Ordinarily, information that significantly contradicts the going concern assumption relates to the entity's inability to continue to meet its obligations as they become due without substantial disposition of assets outside the ordinary course of business, restructuring of debt, externally forced revisions of its operations, or similar actions."

SAS No. 59 uses the same examples as *SAS No. 34* to describe conditions and events that may indicate a going concern problem as well as the mitigating factors. *SAS No. 59*, paragraph 6, provides examples of certain conditions or events that come to an auditor's attention and might indicate that an entity does not have the ability to continue as a going concern.

The following are examples of such conditions and events:

- Negative trends—for example, recurring operating losses, working capital deficiencies, negative cash flows from operating activities, adverse key financial ratios.
- Other indications of possible financial difficulties—for example, default on loan or similar agreements, arrearages in dividends, denial of usual trade credit from suppliers, restructuring of debt, noncompliance with statutory capital requirements, need to seek new sources or methods of financing or to dispose of substantial assets.
- Internal matters—for example, work stoppages or other labor difficulties, substantial dependence on the success of a particular project, uneconomic long-term commitments, need to significantly revise operations.
- External matters that have occurred—for example, legal proceedings, legislation, or similar matters that might jeopardize an entity's ability to operate; loss of a key franchise, license, or patent; loss of a principal customer or supplier; uninsured or underinsured catastrophe such as drought, earthquake, or flood.

SAS No. 59, paragraph 7 considers management's plans to deal with the adverse effects of events and conditions previously discussed.

The auditor's considerations relating to management plans may include the following:

- Plans to dispose of assets
    - Restrictions on disposal of assets, such as covenants limiting such transactions in loan or similar agreements or encumbrances against assets
    - Apparent marketability of assets that management plans to sell
    - Possible direct or indirect effects of disposal of assets
- Plans to borrow money or restructure debt
    - Availability of debt financing, including existing or committed credit arrangements, such as lines of credit or arrangements for factoring receivables or sale-leaseback of assets.
    - Existing or committed arrangements to restructure or subordinate debt or to guarantee loans to the entity
    - Possible effects on management's borrowing plans of existing restrictions on additional borrowing or the sufficiency of available collateral
- Plans to reduce or delay expenditures
    - Apparent feasibility of plans to reduce overhead or administrative expenditures, to postpone maintenance or research and development projects, or to lease rather than purchase assets
    - Possible direct or indirect effects of reduced or delayed expenditures
- Plans to increase ownership equity
    - Apparent feasibility of plans to increase ownership equity, including existing or committed arrangements to raise additional capital
    - Existing or committed arrangements to reduce current dividend requirements or to accelerate cash distributions from affiliates or other investors.

With respect to an entity's ability to continue as a going concern, *SAS No. 59* defines a reasonable period of time in paragraph 2 as "not to exceed one year from the date of the financial statements being audited."

This standard alleviates the auditors of the responsibility of predicting future events. According to *SAS No. 59*, paragraph 4: "The auditor is not responsible for predicting future conditions or events."

The preceding discussion will be considered within the context of this case in requirement 3.

Requirement 3:   In 20X1 Essex incurred an operating loss of $500,000 on $10,000,000 sales. The 20X1 operating loss was attributable to a decrease in sales and a substantial increase in fixed manufacturing overhead. In 20X1 Essex put another plant online to expand its present product line and capacity. Yet, sales for the last quarter of 20X1 decreased approximately 25 percent from average quarterly sales of the first three quarters of 20X1, and January 20X2 sales, Essex's leading month for sales volume, were less than January 20X1 sales. This sales and earnings trend, in light of an apparent economic slowdown and following marginal profitability in the prior year, does not look promising for Essex. A continuation of this trend would appear to indicate a decrease in 20X2 sales. Declining sales coupled with the increased fixed manufacturing overhead and lack of attention to controlling costs would appear to indicate a continuance of operating losses in 20X2.

As of December 31, 20X1, Essex had a negative working capital of $1.4 million ($1.1–$2.5 million) and was in violation of several long-term debt covenants with Harbor City Bank. Subsequent to year-end, Essex defaulted on long-term debt payments to Harbor, but was able to renegotiate all of its debt agreements with Harbor. The renegotiated agreements, providing for interest plus principal payments for the next year, were based on a specified earnings level. However, it appears that Harbor's assumptions as to 20X2 sales and earnings will not materialize; and therefore, Harbor will have the right to accelerate principal payments on the debt. Mr. Agree is concerned not only that cash flow from operations in 20X2 might not be sufficient to cover such payments, but also that accelerated principal payments would probably force even more severe measures. This concern comes from a man who thinks the 20X1 loss was a one-year occurrence and who has never paid much attention to internal control or to effectively cutting operating costs.

A review of several key financial ratios is as follows:

Current ratio	.44:1
Acid-test ratio	.20:1
Working capital deficiency	$1,400,000
Gross margin	28%
Debt to total assets	81%

It is clear that Essex is experiencing an immediate liquidity crisis that probably is going to continue. It is possible that an economic downturn began prior to 20X1 and Essex's management misdiagnosed the problem as insufficient manufacturing capacity, therefore embarking upon an expansion program, when more appropriate financial monitoring would have suggested cost-cutting measures instead. Negative working capital coupled with operating losses have imperiled Essex's ability to meet its short-term obligations. Even if Essex is able to pay interest and the minimum principal on its long-term debt to Harbor, it is still faced with short-term bank notes of $1,500,000 and accounts payable and accrued expenses of $600,000. It does not appear that Essex will be able to meet its short-term obligations unless it is able to restructure its bank debt and work out a payment schedule or obtain concessions from other creditors. Based on its present debt structure, it is unlikely that a financial institution would be willing to make additional loans to Essex. This does not preclude the possibility that an independent investor might be willing to make a loan to Essex or take an equity position, or that the existing stockholders might provide working capital.

Essex should give consideration to postponing the purchase of the $300,000 equipment in early 20X2. Unless the equipment is absolutely essential, its purchase will only exacerbate the present liquidity crisis. In addition, consideration should be given to reducing Mr. Agree's compensation.

It is also a matter of grave concern that Essex's 20X1 gross margin ($2,800,000) did not cover selling, general, administrative, and interest expense ($3,300,000). With anticipated declining sales, high manufacturing overhead, continued incurrence of interest, and no stated plans for improving internal control or cutting costs, it is difficult to be optimistic about the 20X2 operating results and anticipate a sufficient gross margin to cover these costs.

Apart from renegotiating some of its debt with Harbor City Bank, Essex has not revealed any plans to bring in cash or reduce operating losses. Based on the future economic outlook and Essex's anticipated 20X2 operating results, it does not appear likely that a positive cash flow from operations will result.

In the actual case, the auditors concluded that Essex's solvency problems were so pervasive that there was substantial doubt about its ability to continue as a going concern for a reasonable period of time. The factors weighing most heavily in this conclusion were that Essex paid scant respect to internal control systems and effective management of operating costs while faced with declining sales in a period of economic slow-down. The auditors did not have much faith in Thomas Agree's commitment or ability to reverse Essex's present condition. This was especially true in the absence of any formal management plans in response to the situation. The auditors believed that even though Essex had not incurred recurring losses, and it did not have a deficit in stockholders' equity, it soon would be in such a position. However, if Essex were able to restructure its current debt, the argument that Essex is not a going concern would become weaker.

According to *SAS No. 59,* when auditors determine there is a substantial level of doubt about going concern, an explanatory paragraph following the opinion paragraph should be added. *SAS No. 58,* "Reports on Audited Financial Statements," eliminated the "subject to" opinion, however it retained the red flag feature alerting readers to material uncertainties. Paragraph 11 of *SAS No. 58* identifies substantial doubt about the entity's ability to continue as a going concern as a circumstance that may require the auditor to add an explanatory paragraph to his standard report.

The explanatory paragraph must describe in sufficient detail the auditor's doubt and refer to the footnote to the financial statements where the problem is presented. Auditors are not precluded from disclaiming an opinion. *SAS No. 59,* paragraph 13, provides the following paragraph as an example of the appropriate disclosure:

> The accompanying financial statements have been prepared assuming that the Company will continue as a going concern. As discussed in Note X to the financial statements, the Company has suffered recurring losses from operations and has a net capital deficiency that raise substantial doubt about its ability to continue as a going concern. Management's plans in regard to these matters are also discussed in Note X. The financial statements do not include any adjustments that might result from the outcome of this uncertainty.

Finally, some case respondents have proposed that the auditors issue a disclaimer of an opinion in their audit report. They base their conclusion on the complete lack of a management plan, on a past and continued history of weak internal controls, and absence of financial monitoring and cost-cutting consciousness. They argue that failure of Essex is imminent.

Summary

Issues related to judgment and decision making (JDM) in accounting and auditing were discussed in this chapter. JDM was defined and the relationship between judgment and decision making was identified. Decision has an action-taking aspect to it that makes the decision maker responsible for the action. Judgment is the same as decision except that the judge does not bear the consequences, only a judgment. Several examples of tasks in managerial and financial accounting and auditing where JDM is applicable were also provided in the chapter. A conclusion here was that JDM is highly useful, even in financial accounting where JDM research lags behind other areas.

While many JDM models are available in the literature, the Brunswik Lens model was presented as a particularly useful model for understanding JDM concepts. This model is a conceptual framework to use information cues to predict a variable of interest. It shows how information cues form a lens through which a decision maker can assign weights to these cues and predict the variable of interest. The correspondence of these cue utilization weights and theoretical weights (i.e., cue validity weights) was also discussed.

In the next section of the chapter, a detailed discussion of Simon's model of the decision process was presented. Issues of task structure, knowledge base, and decision aids were described. These constructs were then used to develop a general knowledge management framework that shows the relationships between task structure, knowledge base, and decision aids. It was shown that while low knowledge base and automation are useful for JDM in structured tasks, higher levels of knowledge as well as decision support and expert systems are needed for JDM in semistructured and unstructured tasks. Finally, a case was presented to illustrate judgment regarding an entity's ability to continue as a going concern.

Selected Additional Reading

There are many books and journal articles that summarize JDM research, but most have an academic orientation. For a book with chapters on JDM research results in various accounting areas, see:

A. H. Ashton and R. H. Ashton (eds.), *Judgment and Decision-Making Research in Accounting and Auditing* (New York: Cambridge University Press, 1995).

Questions

1. Define judgment and decision making in accounting.
2. The general perception is that accounting is a straightforward problem-solving discipline with little room for JDM. What type of accounting involves JDM in your opinion?
3. What is the general objective of the Brunswik Lens Model?
4. What are cue utilization and cue validity coefficients in the Brunswik Lens Model?
5. Define the three phases of the decision process according to Simon's Model of the Decision Process.
6. How do the three phases of the decision process determine the levels of task structure?
7. Decision makers' attributes affect JDM in many ways. List and describe five categories of attributes.
8. Why is the knowledge base so important in performing a task? How do you assign a person to perform a specific task?
9. An expert without a decision aid is said to be an oxymoron. Why is the use of an appropriate decision aid so important for JDM?
10. What is automation and which tasks are candidates for automation?
11. Define decision support systems (DSS).
12. Define knowledge-based expert systems (KES).
13. What is strictly human processing?
14. Define knowledge management and identify its four general components.
15. Describe three levels of knowledge base and state how these levels relate to levels of task structure.
16. Select five tasks in financial accounting (e.g., deciding FIFO versus LIFO method of inventory). For each task assess:
    - The level of task structure on a 1–9 Likert scale (most structured to most unstructured).
    - Indicate what level of experience is required to perform the task using the following three measures: (1) the number of months of practice; (2) professional rank; and (3) the number of supervised instances of practice before one can perform the task independently.
    - Indicate the decision aid that might be useful to perform each task using the following four categories: (1) automation, (2) decision support system, (3) expert systems, and (4) strictly human processing.
17. For each of the tasks in question 16, assess the level of the following characteristics necessary to performing the task at an expert level:
    - Knowledge
    - Psychological traits
    - Cognitive abilities
    - Decision strategies
    - Task analysis

8

CRITICAL AND CREATIVE THINKING AND PROBLEM SOLVING IN ACCOUNTING

As my knowledge reached its pinnacle, I realized how little I knew.

Ibn Sina (Avi Cena)

Objectives

This chapter covers critical and creative thinking as they relate to problem solving and decision making in accounting practice. Upon completion of the chapter you will have learned the:

1. Definitions of critical and creative thinking.
2. Attributes related to the nature, process, and performance of the tasks that indicate a need for critical and creative thinking.
3. A basic framework of thinking skills and their functions.
4. A complex framework of thinking skills linking critical and creative thinking with problem solving and decision making.
5. Bloom's taxonomy of thinking skills by various levels of cognitive complexity.
6. Problem solving in accounting according to Bloom's taxonomy.
7. Habits that enhance critical and creative thinking.
8. Attributes of good versus poor thinkers.
9. Relationship between critical and creative thinking and communication skills.

The focus of this chapter is on critical and creative thinking. The professional accountant must possess these thinking skills to operate in an increasingly complex environment. These skills assist accountants in problem solving and decision making in general, and in professional research activities in particular. Several attributes such as inquisitiveness, open-mindedness, patience, thoroughness, and perseverance are important for good professional research.[1] Critical and creative thinking go beyond these attributes to include a number of other specialized skills. For example, a critical thinker must have the skill of relating the known to the unknown for effective problem solving and decision making.

It is important for accountants to possess critical and creative thinking skills. Not surprisingly, surveys indicate that over 95 percent of audit partners and corporate controllers view thinking skills to be important for the practicing accountant.[2] The importance of critical thinking to accounting in the professional literature is generally referred to as *professional skepticism*. For example, auditors are required to practice professional skepticism in their audit planning, accounting estimates, and the assessment of clients' management integrity.[3]

The chapter begins with definitions of critical and creative thinking. This is followed by a discussion of the attributes related to the nature, process, and performance of the tasks that require critical and creative thinking. Next, a basic framework for thinking skills is presented in which various skills and their functions are identified. The relationships between problem solving, decision making, critical thinking, and creative thinking in complex environments are discussed next in a complex framework of thinking skills. The activities involved in the thinking process are the subject of the next section where Bloom's taxonomy of thinking skills is presented. This taxonomy arranges thinking skills in an ascending order of cognitive difficulty. A list of habits that hinder critical thinking is presented next followed by a list of desirable attributes that distinguish good thinkers from poor thinkers. The chapter ends with a short discussion of the link between critical and creative thinking and communication skills, as well as a practice case study that illustrates the use of critical and creative thinking skills to accounting.

Definitions

Critical thinking, and its closely related concept of creative thinking, means different things to different people. This situation makes the spec-

---

1. See for example, W. Wallace, 1984, "A Profile of a Researcher," *The Auditor's Report* (American Accounting Association), pp. 1–3.
2. A. M. Novin; M. A. Pearson; and S. V. Senge, "Improving the Curriculum for Aspiring Management Accountants: The Practitioner's Point of View," *Journal of Accounting Education* 8 (1990), pp. 207–24.
3. See *AU Section 316.16–.21* in the *AICPA Codification of Statements on Auditing Standards* (Chicago, IL: CCH Incorporated, 1996).

ification of generally agreed upon definitions of critical and creative thinking difficult. Nevertheless, there are several common clues that can help define these concepts. In this section, these concepts are defined and their differences are identified. Also discussed are the relationships between problem solving and decision making on the one hand, and critical and creative thinking on the other hand.

Critical

Critical has its root in the Greek word *kriticos,* or critic, that means to question, to make sense of, to analyze, and to form judgments of the merits, faults, value, or truth of a matter. It is by questioning and analyzing that you can examine your thinking and the thinking of others. Because of this questioning and analyzing, the word *critical* is sometimes confused with the word *criticize,* which is to find fault with. This confusion results in a negative connotation for the word critical, but this is not the purpose of critical thinking. The word critical in critical thinking is used in a more constructive manner. It is used for making sense of and for analyzing for the purpose of developing a better understanding.

Thinking

Thinking is a mental activity that helps formulate or solve a problem, make a decision, or fulfill a desire to understand. It is a searching for answers, a reach for meaning.[4] Thus, thinking is an active, purposeful, and organized process.[5] It refers to a variety of complex cognitive activities. Examples of these cognitive activities include generating and organizing ideas, forming and applying concepts, designing systematic plans of action, constructing and evaluating arguments, exploring issues from multiple perspectives, and applying knowledge to new situations.[6] All of these cognitive activities are useful in the practice of accounting.

Critical Thinking

It follows that critical thinking is an active, purposeful, and organized process of thinking about one's own thinking.[7] An implication of this definition is that one critically evaluates the logic and validity of information, develops evidence to support or refute his or her views, carefully analyzes situations, and discusses subjects in an organized way. Thus, critical

---

4. V. R. Ruggerio, *The Art of Thinking: A Guide to Critical and Creative Thought* 2nd. ed. (New York: Harper & Row, 1988), p. 2.

5. J. Chaffee, *Thinking Critically,* 3rd ed. (Boston, MA: Houghton Mifflin, 1990), p. 34.

6. J. Chaffee, "Teaching Critical Thinking across Curriculum" in *New Directions for Community Colleges* 77 (Spring 1992), p. 25.

7. J. Chaffee, *Thinking Critically,* 3rd ed. (Boston, MA: Houghton Mifflin, 1990), p. 37.

thinkers do not only seek evidence to support their own views, but also other alternative perspectives.[8]

As an example, suppose that you have gathered all the audit evidence about the financial statements of your client. Now, you must make a judgment concerning the type of audit opinion to issue. Since the vast majority of clients receive an unqualified audit opinion, your thinking may be that an unqualified opinion can be issued in this case as well. Upon an active, purposeful, and organized examination of your current thinking, you realize that a modified, or a qualified, or even an adverse opinion could be issued due to some material misstatements that were discovered.[9] This is where your critical examination of your own thinking and the process of collecting additional evidence will help you make your final decision.

Creative Thinking

Creative thinking refers to original or imaginative thinking to produce innovative solutions or alternative courses of action that are useful for problem solving and decision making. For example, a company might only be willing to acquire another entity if it can account for the acquisition by the pooling of interest method rather than the purchase method. In the pooling of interest method, the acquirer simply combines the financial statements of the acquired company with its own, thereby avoiding recognition of goodwill. In the purchase method, the excess amount paid over and above the acquired company's tangible net worth is recorded as goodwill.

The SEC has made known its opposition to the pooling of interest method, and the FASB has responded by recommending that all business combinations be accounted for by the purchase method, thus eliminating the use of the pooling method. The FASB has also proposed that goodwill should not be amortized but be reviewed for impairment. However, while this situation will make the creative thinking for pooling of interest moot, it makes the judgment of goodwill impairment under the purchase method a topic of creative thinking.[10]

---

8. For a detailed discussion of the issues in this paragraph see J. Chaffee, "Teaching Critical Thinking across Curriculum" in *New Directions for Community Colleges* 77 (Spring 1992), pp. 25–31.

9. The exact proportion of standard unqualified reports to all audits performed is difficult to quantify. However, in a search of annual reports between 1984 and 1994 in the *Lexis/Nexis Research Software* (Mead Data Central Inc., 1995) NAARS database, 15,347 audit reports were found, of which 15,136 (98.6 percent) had unqualified opinions leaving only 193 opinions (1.3 percent) as qualified and only 18 (.10 percent) as adverse opinion (.03 percent) or disclaimer of an opinion (.07 percent).

10. See http://www.rutgers.edu/Accounting/raw/fasb/ for information on Business Combinations Project Summary updated December 20, 2000.

Creative thinking is different from "creative accounting," in which an accountant might try to intentionally manipulate accounting numbers to achieve a desired outcome such as income smoothing. This kind of manipulation is within the realm of fraud and defalcation and is illegal. Needless to say, the SEC will have a negative reaction toward such an approach, and if material, it may initiate an investigation of the company for possible violation of securities laws and regulations with severe penalties.

Differences between Critical and Creative Thinking

To differentiate critical thinking and creative thinking, consider how the human mind works.[11] The human mind has two phases: production and judgment. In the production phase, a person conceptualizes a problem and thinks of various ways to solve it. This phase is creative thinking because it involves the mind in an imaginative and innovative solution-producing mode. In the judgment phase, the person examines and evaluates alternative courses of action, thus making a critical judgment about the merits of various courses of action.

Critical thinking and creative thinking take a highly complex role in problem solving and decision making. As stated in an earlier chapter, many accounting courses use a narrow approach to solving accounting or auditing problems. Typically, the questions asked are direct and simple, and the solutions available to answer the questions are well specified in the textbooks. In contrast, higher levels of critical and creative thinking are needed for more complex problems and decision-making situations. These situations require much judgment and decision making that go beyond simple solutions. As stated by the National Council of Teachers of English, critical thinking is a process that stresses an attitude of suspended judgment, incorporates logical inquiry and problem solving, and leads to an evaluative decision or action.[12]

Attributes that Require Critical and Creative Thinking

The definitions provided in the previous section imply that critical thinking is intertwined with creative thinking, problem solving, and decision making. This relationship is discussed in more detail later in the chapter. What is important to note here is that all of these functions are task dependent. That is, they all occur because of the presence of a context in which critical or creative thinking, problem solving, or decision making is

---

11. This discussion is adapted from V. R. Ruggerio, *The Art of Thinking: A Guide to Critical and Creative Thought* 2nd ed. (New York: Harper & Row, 1988), pp. 3–4.
12. J. N. French and C. Rhoder, *Teaching Thinking Skills: Theory and Practice* (New York: Garland Publishing, 1992), p. 187.

Exhibit 8–1 Attributes that Require Critical Thinking	
Attribute	*Meaning*
Panel A. Nature of the task	
1. Novelty	Tasks are so new that knowledge about them is scarce or incomplete.
2. Significance	Tasks of greater importance require more critical thinking than unimportant ones.
3. Complexity	Tasks are semistructured or unstructured. The total path to perform them is not clearly visible.
4. Uncertainty	Tasks present a degree of doubt and ambiguity; not everything that bears on the task is known.
5. Vagueness	Tasks are unclear in meaning or application.
Panel B. Task process	
6. Imposed meaning	Make some sense out of an apparent disorder, ambiguity, or vagueness.
7. Nuanced judgment	A subtle or slight degree of difference in meaning, feeling, or tone requires judgment.
8. Effortful thinking	Considerable mental work is required for elaborating and making judgments.
Panel C. Task performance is	
9. Nonalgorithmic	The path of action is not fully specified in advance.
10. Multiple criteria	Different perspectives need to be considered.
11. Multiple solutions	No unique solution exists, and each solution has its own costs and benefits to consider.
12. Dissonance resolution	Discrepancy exists between expectation and the reality of the tasks that require inquiry.

Source: This exhibit is based on M. J. Abdolmohammadi and W. J. Read, "Effects of Ambiguity and Vagueness on Auditors' Task Complexity Judgments in Risk Assessment," *Advances in Accounting* 14 (1996), pp. 1–21; and J. Barell, "Removing Impediments to Change," in *Developing Minds*, A. L. Costa, ed. (Association for Supervision and Curriculum Development, 1985); A. A. Glatthorn and J. Baron, "The Good Thinker," in *Developing Minds*, A. L. Costa, ed. (Association for Supervision and Curriculum Development, 1985), pp. 49–53; and L. B. Resnick, *Education and Learning to Think* (Washington, DC: The National Academy Press, 1987).

required. The task attributes, task process requirements, and task performance issues that involve critical thinking are presented in Exhibit 8–1. These attributes are described and supported by various accounting examples.

The Nature of the Task

The attributes related to the nature of the task are presented in panel A of Exhibit 8–1 and are described in the following paragraphs.

Task Novelty
The first attribute listed for the nature of the task is task novelty. Novel tasks are those that are so new that knowledge about them is scarce or incomplete. Thus, the decision maker must use critical thinking to make sense of them. For example, financial markets continually create new

financial products such as derivative instruments. A derivative instrument is a contract to transfer risk from one party to another without transferring the basic underlying instrument. For example, suppose that parties A and B have adjustable mortgages where A's interest rate is 6 percent and B's is 5 percent. In an interest rate swap derivative, party A swaps his high mortgage interest rate of 6 percent with party B's 5 percent for a price. Both parties keep their underlying mortgage obligations, but party A will pay according to party B's interest rate and party B will pay according to party A's interest rate.

The issue is risk management. Party A thinks that interest rates are going to increase in the future and wants to begin with a lower adjustable rate of 5 percent that party B is paying on his or her mortgage. Party B on the other hand thinks that interest rates are going to stay where they are or they are going to fall, so B is willing to accept the higher rate of 6 percent for the mortgage in exchange for a price from party A. Depending upon what actually happens to interest rates in the future, one of the two parties is going to realize a gain and the other party will realize a loss. Accounting for this transaction and the realization of consequent gains and losses presents a novel task for accountants. Several statements on financial accounting standards have been issued in recent years to deal with this issue. For example *SFAS No. 105* (1990), *107* (1991), *115* (1993), *119* (1994), and *133* (1998) are among the authoritative guidance issued in recent years to address various accounting issues related to financial instruments.[13] However, although these *SFAS*s were all issues in the 1990s, later statements have already superseded some. For example, *SFAS No. 133* has already superseded *SFAS No. 105* and *119*.

Task Significance

The second attribute listed under the nature of the task is task significance. If a task is unimportant or immaterial, there is no need to use critical thinking to address it. However, a task with significant or material implication requires critical thinking. In the example of financial derivatives provided earlier, if it affected only a few transactions and people,

---

13. Financial Accounting Standards Board, *Statements of Financial Accounting Standards No. 105*, "Disclosure of Information about Financial Instruments with Off-Balance-Sheet Risk and Financial Instruments with Concentrations of Credit Risk" (Norwalk, CT: FASB, 1990); Financial Accounting Standards Board, *Statements of Financial Accounting Standards No. 107*,"Disclosures about Fair Value of Financial Instruments" (Norwalk, CT: 1991); Financial Accounting Standards Board, *Statements of Financial Accounting Standards No. 115*, "Accounting for Certain Investments in Debt and Equity Securities" (Norwalk, CT: 1993); Financial Accounting Standards Board, *Statements of Financial Accounting Standards No. 119*," Disclosure about Derivative Financial Instruments and Fair Value of Financial Instruments" (Norwalk, CT: 1994), and Financial Accounting Standards Board, *Statements of Financial Accounting Standards No. 133*, "Accounting for Derivative Instruments and Hedging Activities" (Norwalk, CT: 1998).

accountants need not worry too much about it. The fact of the matter is that financial derivatives affect so many people through their investments and retirement plans at such a material magnitude that critical thinking is required. For example, the retirement plan of the employees of the State of California lost some $2 billion in the early 1990s due to investment in risky derivative instruments.

Task Complexity

The third attribute listed under the nature of the task is task complexity. A classification of tasks by their level of complexity for the purpose of problem solving and decision making was provided in an earlier chapter. As stated, simple or structured tasks are those that have very few alternative courses of action. Making a choice between these courses of action requires limited experience or insight. These tasks do not require critical thinking. It is for the more complex tasks (i.e., the semistructured and unstructured tasks) with many possible courses of action that much judgment and insight are required to make a decision. Thus, critical thinking has application for these tasks. For example, financial transactions between companies and investors can be complex and difficult to analyze, especially since they are not always at arms length. If an investor advances money to a company, is this a loan, a contribution to capital, payment for some goods or services, or something else? These transactions often require critical thinking to understand and apply accounting concepts.

Task Uncertainty

The fourth attribute listed under the nature of the task is uncertainty. Uncertain tasks present a degree of doubt and ambiguity for the decision maker. The components of the task cannot be determined with certainty. The interest swap example discussed earlier is an uncertain task because determination of the future directions of the interest rates cannot be stated with certainty. Consideration of uncertainty is a particularly troublesome task for accountants because it requires the use of probabilistic formulas to assist in making future predictions. Critical thinking in the context of probabilistic situations is a challenging proposition for people in general, and for accountants in particular. This is because, typically, accounting is based on past events. However, in recent years, the accounting profession has been under pressure to develop methods that are sensitive to future issues. For example, in a discussion draft, the AICPA Special Committee on Financial Reporting presented a set of detailed recommendations to accounting standard setters and regulators. Among these recommendations was the need for more forward-looking information.[14]

---

14. AICPA, Special Committee on Financial Reporting: *Improving Business Reporting—A Customer Focus: Meeting the Information Needs of Investors and Creditors* (New York: 1994).

Task Vagueness

The final attribute listed for the nature of the task is vagueness. This attribute refers to the unclear meaning of the task. Some tasks have multiple meanings that need to be sorted out. For example, there are hundreds of classes of financial derivatives being traded by financial institutions. Even for a given class of derivatives, say interest rate swaps, there are multiple variations and meanings. Intense critical thinking is required to understand each of these variations to apply the right method of accounting to them.

Task Process

The attributes for task process are listed in panel B of Exhibit 8–1. These attributes are action-oriented in the sense that they are designed to reduce the complexity of some of the task characteristics discussed in the previous section.

Meaning Imposition

The purpose of meaning imposition is to rectify task vagueness and ambiguity. Vagueness and ambiguity present a situation that can be characterized as disorder. By imposing a meaning, you try to make sense of this apparent disorder. To accomplish this, the critical thinker makes certain assumptions as a means of providing a definition for an otherwise ambiguous or vague task. For example, post-employment benefits other than pensions are not very clear as to their meaning and cost determination. Nevertheless, the accountant can use actuarial assumptions about the life expectancy of employees for the purpose of determining pension obligations. Details are provided in *SFAS No. 106*.[15]

Nuanced Judgment

The next attribute in the task process is nuanced judgment. Nuanced judgment refers to understanding a task that presents very subtle or slight differences in meaning from another task. For example, consider the case of an average investor who owns 10 percent of the shares of ABC Company. ABC has declared and issued a 5 percent stock dividend to its shareholders at the end of 2000. On the surface, the average investor might consider the 5 percent stock dividend as a 5 percent addition to his or her wealth. In reality, the stockholder's share of the company has stayed exactly the same: 10 percent. The subtle difference between a cash dividend where a transfer of assets takes place and stock dividend in which only shares of stock are issued requires nuanced judgment to understand.

---

15. Financial Accounting Standards Board, *Statements on Financial Accounting Standards No. 106*, "Employers' Accounting for Postemployment Benefits Other Than Pensions" (Norwalk, CT: 1990).

Effortful Thinking

The final attribute in the task process is effortful thinking. The discussion of the previous attributes indicates that considerable mental work is required for performing tasks that need critical thinking. The assumptions, determinations, elaboration, and judgments involved require much effort in thinking about various issues.

Task Performance

The attributes for task performance are listed in panel C of Exhibit 8–1. These attributes are also action oriented in the sense that they provide the path to task performance as described in the following:

Nonalgorithmic Thinking

The first of the task performance attributes is nonalgorithmic thinking. It means that the path of action is not fully specified in advance. In a simple problem-solving situation, say determination of the depreciation expense, a step-by-step process is available from textbooks. In a problem setting that requires critical thinking, no algorithm may be available to guide the thinker through the procedures. Only general guidelines may be available. For example, while *SFAS No. 133* provides authoritative guidance on financial derivative instruments, a detailed algorithmic cookbook approach is not provided. This is because new and more complex derivative instruments are always being developed and require new algorithms or modifications to previous algorithms to understand, record, and analyze.

Multiple Criteria

The second attribute in the task performance category is multiple criteria. This attribute indicates that many of the tasks requiring critical thinking may require analysis using different perspectives or criteria. The application of multiple criteria is problematic because sometimes these criteria conflict with each other. For example, cost-cutting criterion conflicts with an alternative of improving the quality of, say, a product or service that may require a significant cost to accomplish.

Multiple Solutions

The third attribute in the task performance category is multiple solutions. The presence of multiple alternatives is exacerbated by the fact that multiple criteria need to be applied in the thinking process. The critical thinker needs to consider the costs and benefits of all of these criteria and present a balanced solution. In the example of conflict between multiple criteria, the accountant will perhaps use an alternative course of action where the cost is minimized while at the same time quality of the product or service is improved to an acceptable level.

Dissonance Resolution

The final attribute in Exhibit 8–1 Panel C is dissonance resolution. It refers to lack of agreement or inconsistency, even a conflict between what is expected and the reality. For example, there has been a gap between the public's expectation from auditors to detect financial fraud and the scope of the audit that auditors were undertaking. In an effort to bridge this gap, the AICPA's Auditing Standards Board issued *SAS No. 82*, requiring auditors to plan the audit in such a way that material fraud, if it exists, can be detected.[16] Similarly, the SEC has been very concerned about undesired impact of providing nonaudit services on auditors' independence. While nobody disagrees about the importance of independence to public accounting, it requires dissonance resolution to discern issues of independence in various professional engagements.

Frameworks of Critical Thinking Skills

Many accounting and auditing tasks have the attributes listed in the previous section that require critical thinking. These tasks require professional research by the accountant. A question is what skills must an accountant have to perform such thinking? Since the exact nature of critical thinking skills is not completely understood in the professional literature, it is difficult to list all thinking skills that one needs to perform various professional research projects. However, a common core of thinking skills that applies to social sciences including accounting can be provided. For example, task definition, problem solving, decision making, and creativity are among those mentioned as critical thinking skills for social sciences. These skills are needed for the practice of accounting as well. Nevertheless, the manner in which these skills are used in association with critical thinking is a matter of debate.[17]

Many skills are said to facilitate problem solving, decision making, and creative thinking. For example, argumentation and classification have been suggested to facilitate these activities.[18] Argumentation refers to the skills of distinguishing between convincing and illogical reasoning, deductive and inductive logic, biased and factual reasoning. Classification refers to the skill of organizing information. This skill is becoming increasingly more important due to the abundance of information provided by the new information technology.

---

16. Auditing Standards Board, *Statement on Auditing Standard No. 82*, "Consideration of Fraud in a Financial Statement Audit" (New York: AICPA, 1997).

17. See J. N. French and C. Rhoder, *Teaching Thinking Skills: Theory and Practice* (New York: Garland Publishing, 1992) for detailed discussion of these skills.

18. C. L. H. Knight, "Teaching Critical Thinking in the Social Sciences," *New Directions for Community Colleges* 77 (Jossey-Bass Publishers, Spring 1992), pp. 67–68.

The skills just listed can also be viewed as critical thinking skills, but critical thinking skills are more expansive. To better understand critical thinking skills and their relationships with problem solving, decision making, and creative thinking, a basic framework of thinking skills is presented first. This framework provides the definitions and functions of a standard set of thinking skills. These skills are then linked to problem solving, decision making, critical thinking, and creative thinking in a more complex framework of thinking skills presented in the next section.

A Basic Framework of Thinking Skills

A standard set of basic thinking skills is presented in Exhibit 8–2. These skills are described in the following paragraphs.

Causation

The first thinking skill is causation. It refers to the identification of causal variables (also called *independent variables*) and effect variables (also called *dependent variables*). Formal or informal models to make predictions, inferences, judgments, and evaluations about the cause and effect variables can be used to make a judgment. The behavioral and statistical models of research discussed in previous chapters can help establish these cause and effect relationships. For example, an accountant might establish that capital markets would make changes to the company's stock price (an effect) as a result of changes in the company's inventory costing methods (a cause). However, at this stage the accountant may not know the exact effect. There is a need to use a capital market research model to formulate the cause and effect relationship.

Exhibit 8–2   A Basic Framework of Thinking Skills

Skill	Meaning	Functions
1. Causation	Establishing cause and effect relationships	Prediction, inferences, judgments, evaluations
2. Transformation	Relating the known to the unknown	Analogies, metaphors, logical induction
3. Relationship	Detecting regular operations	Parts and wholes, patterns, analysis and synthesis, sequences and order, logical deductions
4. Classification	Determining common qualities	Similarities and differences, grouping and sorting, comparisons, either/or distinctions
5. Qualification	Finding unique characteristics	Units of basic identity, definitions, facts, problems/task recognition

Source: Adapted from B. Z. Presseisen, "Thinking Skills: Meanings and Models," in *Developing Minds,* A. L. Costa (ed.), (Alexandria, VA: Association for Supervision and Curriculum Development, 1985), p. 45.

Transformation

Once a good understanding of the cause and effect relationship is established, a transformation method is used to relate the known and the unknown. Methods such as analogies, metaphors, and logical induction may be used to make the transformation. For example, the accountant in the above example may use an analogy such as a change in the depreciation method in a previous year caused the income to drop by 5 percent that in turn caused the stock price to drop by 2 percent. Thus, a change in inventory costing that causes a drop of 5 percent in income will result in a drop of 2 percent in the company's stock price. Note that there is no empirical evidence present to support this prediction. It is based only on an analogy that the accountant has used to make the transformation at this point. Metaphors will result in a symbolic transformation. For example, the accountant may assume that the market may see the change in inventory method as a symbol of more serious changes to follow in the company, and therefore, the stock price may change at a higher or lower rate than the 2 percent previously observed. In this particular situation, the critical thinker uses inductive logic to derive a general conclusion from a particular fact or instance.

Relationship

In the third standard skill, relationship, regular operations of the task are detected by focusing on parts, wholes, and patterns. Using analysis, synthesis, sequencing, ordering, and logical deduction, one derives a specific conclusion from a general principle. For example, financial statements have many parts (accounts or groups of accounts) that are first prepared, adjusted, and synthesized before they are put together in a financial statement.

Classification

The fourth skill, classification, refers to determining common qualities. Thus, similarities and differences, grouping and sorting comparisons, and either/or distinctions are developed using this skill. This is where a professional accountant consults the research archives to find the similarities and differences between the research issue at hand and those researched in the past.

Qualification

Finally, using the fifth skill, qualification, one looks for unique characteristics of the task that separates it from other tasks. Thus, basic identity of the task is determined and its unique characteristics are documented. For example, an accountant focuses on basic similarities in accounts before classifying them into various classes of assets, liabilities, or owners' equity.

A Complex Framework of Thinking Skills

The standard set of thinking skills presented in the basic framework is now linked to the complex processes of problem solving, decision making, critical thinking, and creative thinking. Exhibit 8–3 shows this framework.

Problem Solving

In a problem-solving context, the standard-thinking skills needed are causation and transformation. Causation establishes the link between the cause and effect and transformation processes the information from input to output. For example, in a depreciation calculation problem, causation is used to establish that usage (cause) depreciates an asset (effect). The depreciation method used transforms the problem through the depreciation formula to a depreciation expense.

Decision Making

In a decision-making context, the decision maker selects the best course of action from among several alternative courses of action. The standard thinking skills used are classification and relationship. The outcome from this process is the decision. For example, consider the task of choosing an appropriate explanatory paragraph for a going concern communication in the auditor's report. The auditor first investigates the pattern of the going concern uncertainty in the current client situation, using patterns and logical deductions. The auditor will then use the classification skill to establish the similarities and differences between the current client situation and those in the archives to determine common qualities. Once these tasks are performed, the explanatory paragraph can be selected from a list of standard paragraphs. If an appropriate paragraph cannot be found from the archives, the auditor uses professional judgment to develop a new explanatory paragraph.

Exhibit 8–3   A Complex Framework of Thinking Skills

Context	Task	Basic Skill	Result
Problem solving	Resolve a known problem	Transformation, causation	Solution
Decision making	Choose a course of action	Classification, relationship	Decision
Critical thinking	Understand a particular meaning	Relationship, transformation, causation	Reasons, proof, theory
Creative thinking	Create a novel idea	Qualification, relationship, transformation	New meanings, ideas

Source: Adapted by B. Z. Presseisen, "Thinking Skills: Meanings and Models," in *Developing Minds*, A. L. Costa, ed. (Alexandria, VA: Association for Supervision and Curriculum Development, 1985), p. 46.

Critical Thinking

Critical thinking may be required to identify an appropriate explanatory paragraph from the standard examples, or for developing one if standard language is not found. This is because the task requires the understanding of a particular meaning and generation of new knowledge based on established audit standards. The critical thinker uses basic skills of relationship, transformation, and causation to generate new reasons, proof, or theory.

Creative Thinking

Finally, in a creative-thinking context, the thinker is creating a novel idea, say a new method of revenue recognition for a unique exchange transaction or an estimation method to value stock option plans. Basic skills of qualification, relationship, and transformation may be used to generate the new meanings, ideas, or methods.

Bloom's Taxonomy of Thinking Skills

The complex framework of thinking skills as presented in Exhibit 8–3 indicates that it is difficult to develop a step-by-step process for thinking in general, and critical thinking in particular. However, critical thinking can be structured according to cognitive difficulty of thinking skills. A popular taxonomy classifies thinking skills in an ascending order of cognitive difficulty as presented in Exhibit 8–4.[19]

Exhibit 8–4 Bloom's Taxonomy of Thinking Skills	
Thinking Skill	*Function*
1. Knowledge: Recall from memory what you have learned	Define, recognize, recall, identify, label, understand, examine, show, collect
2. Comprehension: Grasp the meaning	Translate, interpret, explain, describe, summarize, extrapolate
3. Application: Apply knowledge to new situations	Apply, solve, experiment, show, predict
4. Analysis: Break the task into subtasks for a better understanding of the task	Connect, relate, differentiate, classify, arrange, check, group, distinguish, organize, categorize, detect, compare, infer
5. Synthesis: Put the parts back into a whole to form a new concept or understanding	Produce, propose, design, plan, combine, formulate, compose, hypothesize, construct
6. Evaluate: Appraise the value based on pre-established criteria	Appraise, judge, criticize, decide

Adapted from B. Z. Presseisen, "Thinking Skills: Meanings and Models," in *Developing Minds*, A. L. Costa, ed. (Alexandria, VA: Association for Supervision and Curriculum Development, 1985), p. 44.

---

19. From B. S. Bloom (ed.), *Taxonomy of Education Objectives* (New York: Longman, 1956) and B. Z. Presseisen, "Thinking Skills: Meanings and Models," in *Developing Minds*, A. L. Costa (ed.), (Association for Supervision and Curriculum Development, 1985), p. 44.

Cognition refers to the mental process of awareness, perception, reasoning, and judgment. Bloom's taxonomy places skills that require lower levels of cognition first, followed by those that require increasingly higher levels of cognition. Thus, while lower levels of cognition are needed for earlier stages of knowledge and comprehension, higher levels of cognition are required for application, analysis, synthesis, and evaluation in Exhibit 8–4. For example, professional research projects involving debt restructuring often involve complexities that require application, analysis, synthesis, and elaboration. The case at the end of the chapter is illustrative of higher levels of cognition.

Bloom's taxonomy specifies the operational skill levels that are necessary for critical thinking at various levels of cognitive difficulty. Thus, depending on the level of work that an accountant is performing, the corresponding level of thinking skill must be used to perform the task. Accounting courses generally focus on the lower cognitive levels of knowledge and comprehension that emphasize facts and accounting standards. Higher levels of application, analysis, synthesis, and evaluation are generally emphasized to a lesser extent. This problem is not limited to accounting education, however, as research shows that most colleges and universities tend to focus their education on the lower levels of knowledge and comprehension in various fields.[20] Yet, the complex environment of accounting practice requires that accountants acquire higher levels of cognitive processes in Bloom's taxonomy to handle the increasingly more complex accounting tasks. This is often termed *meta-cognition*, in which the critical thinker is aware of his or her own thinking and its limitations.[21] Meta-cognitive skills of application, analysis, synthesis, and evaluation have been gaining increasingly more support in accounting education in recent years.[22]

Habits that Promote Critical Thinking

Thus far, critical thinking has been discussed as a holistic approach to the way we make sense of the challenging tasks we undertake. As critical thinkers, we actively use our intelligence, knowledge, and skills to explore and to examine various ideas and different perspectives, be open

---

20. J. Chaffee, "Teaching Critical Thinking Across Curriculum" in *New Directions for Community Colleges*, no. 77 (Jossey-Bass Publishers, Spring 1992), p. 26.

21. B. Z. Presseisen, "Thinking Skills: Meanings and Models," *Developing Minds*, A. L. Costa (ed.), (Alexandria, VA: Association for Supervision and Curriculum Development, 1985), pp. 47–48.

22. See for example, S. L. Gabriel and M. L. Hirsch Jr., "Critical Thinking and Communication Skills: Integration and Implementation Issues," *Journal of Accounting Education* 10 (1992), pp. 243–70.

to the views of others, and not to jump to conclusions.[23] The list can be expanded to include many other skills and attributes. Unfortunately, most human beings have habits and biases that hinder their skills of critical thinking no matter how knowledgeable they are about thinking skills. An awareness of these habits is helpful in mitigating the negative effects of them on critical thinking. A list containing several of these habits and their effects is presented first followed by a discussion of a number of desirable attributes that distinguish good thinkers from poor thinkers.

A List of Bad Habits Hindering Critical Thinking

The major habits that hinder critical thinking are listed in this section.[24] The purpose is to identify ways to promote critical and creative thinking, and to mitigate errors caused by these undesirable habits.

1. *The mine-is-better habit.* Many people have a habit of knowingly or unknowingly thinking that their thinking is better than that of others. This habit impairs objectivity and opens them to accepting errors instead of reality. This is in contrast to the desirable habit of open-mindedness.

2. *Face-saving or defense mechanism.* This habit occurs when a person has done or said something that has an undesirable outcome. The individual then tries to point the finger at someone else or to rationalize his or her own behavior. Thus, one tries to find evidence that confirms prior belief. This is in contrast to the desirable habit of reasoning where belief follows evidence, not personal biases.

3. *Resistance to change.* Laziness, tradition, and insecurity may be the reasons for this habit that hinders open-mindedness.

4. *Conformity.* This habit involves a sense of belonging to a group or profession that reduces a person's tendency to think independently.

5. *Stereotyping.* Fixed, unbending generalizations about race, religion, gender, or ethnicity are habits that hinder rationality.

6. *Self-deception.* This habit results in trying to justify to oneself a wrongful conclusion.

---

23. Many detailed attributes are provided by Chaffee, J., *Thinking Critically*, 3rd ed. (Boston, MA: Houghton Mifflin, 1990), pp. 78–79, and S. P. Norris & R. H. Ennis, *Evaluating Critical Thinking* (Pacific Grove, CA: Critical Thinking Press and Software, 1989), p. 23.

24. For a much detailed discussion of these habits see V. R. Ruggerio, *The Art of Thinking: A Guide to Critical and Creative Thought,* 2nd ed. (New York: Harper & Row, 1988), pp. 38–45, and V. R. Ruggerio, *Beyond Feelings: A Guide to Critical Thinking* (Mountain View, CA: Mayfield Publishing, 1990), pp. 40–93.

There is a need for specific training and practice to overcome these habits and/or to mitigate their undesirable effects on critical thinking. Suffice it to say that a person must be conscious of these habits and try to overcome them in order to improve critical thinking. To help with this issue, we have developed a set of attributes that differentiate between good and poor thinkers as presented in the next section.

Good versus Poor Thinkers

A list of desirable attributes is provided in Exhibit 8–5 to compare good and poor thinkers. These attributes are presented under four classes: general, goal setting, actions, and evidence. For each of these attributes, good thinkers are compared with poor thinkers. It is important to note that we are not providing an exhaustive list under all conditions here. For example, while an accountant may be conscious of various attributes under calm circumstances, he or she might perform completely differently under time-pressure conditions. Rather, we present a list of the most common attributes in this section.

Exhibit 8–5   Attributes of Good and Poor Thinkers

Attribute	Good Thinkers	Poor Thinkers
General:		
1	Tolerant of ambiguity and uncertainty	Intolerant of ambiguity and uncertainty
2	Self-critical	Self-assured
3	Inquisitive, reflective, search extensively	Impulsive, satisfied at first attempt, give up prematurely
4	Value rationality, question intuition	Denigrate rationality, overvalue intuition
5	Honest with themselves, watchful of their own errors	Pretend they know more than they do; assume their views are error-free
6	Welcome controversial tasks	Shy away from controversial tasks
7	Open-minded to others' ideas	Preoccupied with own opinions
Goals:		
8	Are deliberative in discovering goals	Are impulsive in discovering goals
9	Revise goals when necessary	Stick with original goals even if there is need for change
10	Seek balanced goals	Ignore the need for balanced goals; adhere to own goals even if extreme
Actions:		
11	Consider all viable courses of action	Prefer to stay with limited possibilities
12	Analyze possibilities deliberatively	Are impulsive in choosing possibilities
Evidence:		
13	Seek evidence that challenges favored courses of action	Ignore evidence that challenges favored courses of action
14	Seek evidence to refute possibilities that are initially strong	Search only for evidence that favors strong possibilities
15	Base judgment on evidence, not personal preference	Tend to seek evidence in support of personal preference

Source: Adapted from A. A. Glatthorn and J. Baron, "The Good Thinker," *Developing Minds*, A. L. Costa, ed. (Alexandria, VA: Association for Supervision and Curriculum Development, 1985), p. 51; and V. R. Ruggerio, *Beyond Feelings: A Guide to Critical Thinking* (Mountain View: CA: Mayfield Publishing, 1990), pp. 16–17.

General Attributes

The attributes in this category indicate that good thinkers are generally more tolerant of ambiguous or uncertain situations than poor thinkers. In fact, good thinkers might seek ambiguity and uncertainty, while poor thinkers may do all they can to avoid ambiguous situations. Also, while good thinkers constantly critique their ways of thinking, poor thinkers are generally self-assured in their thoughts. Related to this attribute is that good thinkers search extensively for meaning using inquisitiveness and reflective thinking as compared with poor thinkers who generally give up their search prematurely to focus only on the first attempt at thinking. Impulse rather than a systematic process might prompt this thinking. Furthermore, good thinkers value rationality more than poor thinkers, who tend to denigrate rationality. Poor thinkers simply overvalue their own intuition as compared to good thinkers who question their intuition and strive for a more rational meaning.

Also important to note is that good thinkers are generally honest with themselves and consciously watch for errors so that they can detect and correct errors. Poor thinkers, on the other hand, tend to pretend that they know a lot—more than they actually do know. They seldom question whether they have committed any error—they think that they are error-free. A consequence of this attribute is that while good thinkers welcome controversial tasks, issues, or problems, poor thinkers seek standard tasks and shy away from controversial or new tasks, issues, or problems. Finally, good thinkers keep an open mind and even seek ideas from others to improve upon their own thinking. Poor thinkers are so preoccupied with their own thoughts that they frequently ignore ideas generated by others. Simply put, a good thinker knows more and yet asks questions more frequently than a poor thinker, whose knowledge is limited and yet who shies away from asking.

Attributes Related to Goals

Good thinkers use deliberation in discovering goals, are flexible in revising goals, and seek to establish balanced goals. On the other hand, poor thinkers typically are impulsive in goal setting and are inflexible in revising goals even if there is a need for change due to changes in conditions. Poor thinkers also adhere to goals that may be extreme in nature rather than balanced. For example, consider the case of a few accountants who are investigating the treatment of a lease transaction. Good thinking exhibited by accountants establishes research goals systematically after considering all possibilities. The accountants revise the goals as they proceed with the research. They also establish a balanced goal of identifying the true economic substance of the transaction and thus the appropriate treatment (i.e., a capital lease or an operating lease treatment). Poor thinking exhibited by accountants might result in an immediate suspicion of the client's intentions. This suspicion might in turn lead to a decision that the goal of the research is to find reasons why the client should treat the transaction as a more stringent capital lease and not as a more advantageous operating lease from a financial leverage perspective.

Attributes Related to Actions

Good thinkers consider all viable courses of action as compared to poor thinkers who might prefer to stay with a limited number of alternatives even if there are other viable courses of action worthy of consideration. Additionally, while good thinkers use systematic approaches to deliberate about the merits of various courses of action, poor thinkers generally use impulsive approaches to select possible alternatives.

Attributes Related to Evidence

While good thinkers seek evidence that challenges favored courses of action, poor thinkers simply ignore such challenging evidence. Related to this attribute is that good thinkers seek to refute alternatives that are initially strong while poor thinkers might search only for evidence in support of strong alternatives. Finally, good thinkers make their judgment based entirely on the evidence, not personal preferences. Poor thinkers, on the other hand, tend to seek evidence in support of personal preferences. Called a confirmatory bias in search and use of evidence, this bias makes professional judgment one-sided.

A question that arises about the attributes that distinguish good thinkers from poor thinkers is whether these attributes are trainable, developable over time, or innate. Trainable attributes are those that can be taught in an attempt to improve critical and creative thinking. For example, one may be taught to be critical of one's thinking by presenting the steps in which self-criticism can take place. Other attributes may or may not be trainable, but can be developed over time through practice and experience. For example, one can become more tolerant of ambiguity and uncertainty after dealing with a host of ambiguous or uncertain situations. It is of course possible that some of the attributes of good critical thinking are innate in nature. For example, open-mindedness may be innate for some individuals, while others may innately find it difficult to be open minded. It is beyond the scope of this section to develop a list of trainable, developable, or innate attributes of critical and creative thinking. However, being conscious of the desirable attributes and making it a habit to follow the attributes is desirable for their effects on critical and creative thinking.

Critical Thinking and Communication Skills

Thinking skills are closely related to communication skills. It should not be hard to clearly explain ideas in writing or to present ideas orally when one is thinking clearly about these ideas. Conversely, poor thinking results in poor communication—fuzzy writing is said to be the result of fuzzy thinking. Nevertheless, different people have different levels of communication proficiencies and different styles of oral communication or writing. Both critical thinking and communication skills are ways of making meaning out of experience and both require sustained practice for improvement.[25]

Communication skills as related to professional research were discussed in an earlier chapter. We do not wish to repeat the discussion here. Suffice it to say that being specific, distinct, precise, and accurate in both your writing and speaking as well as in your thinking is desirable both from communication as well as thinking considerations. Avoid vague and ambiguous words or clichés. Vague words do not have a distinct meaning. Ambiguous words have more than one meaning. Clichés may have an inaccurate connotation about truth or insight. Use of dialects and slang may limit your message to a smaller audience than desired.[26] Thus, keep the audience in mind and write or speak in a way that is easy for all, not just a portion of the audience to understand.

The FLX Medical Technology case is included in the next section to illustrate the use of accounting literature by analogy, identify alternative solutions, and make judgments. The case also illustrates how poor thinking might result in reaching a quick, but questionable, conclusion.

ILLUSTRATIVE CASE	FLX MEDICAL TECHNOLOGY, INC.

Accounting for a 10 Percent Equity Investment with Venture Capital Funding and a Future Purchase Option

FLX Medical Technology, Inc. was founded 10 years ago by Dr. Michael Ellison and Dr. Samuel Stein. Four years ago FLX successfully completed an initial public offering, selling four million common shares at $7 a share. FLX manufactures and distributes a broad range of respiratory care products used in hospital intensive care units including respirators, ventilators, compressors, and air/oxygen blenders. The company also has emerged as a leading producer of air filtration systems that protect both patient and medical personnel from germ-infested air and the transmission of diseases in operating rooms.

Dr. Ellison and Dr. Stein have decided to expand their distribution of air filtration systems into Europe. However, they are concerned about the risks and costs involved in developing a channel of distribution in Europe. They would like to either share the investment risk or transfer it to an outside party.

25. C. B. Olson, "The Thinking/Writing Connection," *Developing Minds*, A. L. Costa (ed.) (Alexandria, VA: Association for Supervision and Curriculum Development, 1985), pp. 102–7.
26. For detailed instructions see J. Chaffee, *Thinking Critically*, 3rd ed. (Boston, MA: Houghton Mifflin, 1990), pp. 297–395

After discussing their expansion plans with several venture capital firms, Proctor Venture Capitalist Group has agreed to fund the expansion of the air filtration systems into Europe. The agreement specifies that a new company, PS Medical Systems, Inc., will be formed. Proctor will contribute $6 million for a 90 percent equity interest, and FLX will contribute $300,000 and exclusive European marketing rights of the air filtration systems for five years in exchange for a 10 percent equity interest. The agreement provides that PS Medical Systems is required to purchase all its smoke filtration systems from FLX Medical Technology at predetermined wholesale prices, and FLX is required to deliver the systems on a timely basis.

The board of directors of the new company will be composed of seven members. FLX will appoint three members, and Proctor Venture Capitalist Group will appoint the remaining four. After three years, FLX will have the option of purchasing Proctor's 90 percent equity interest in exchange for 600,000 shares of FLX common shares. The FLX common is currently trading at $20 per share. During the first several years of PS Medical Systems' operations, cumulative operating losses of $5 to $7 million are projected. FLX is planning to account for its 10 percent interest in PS Medical Systems by the cost method. However, it is concerned that it may have to record a liability once the investment is made.

Required

1. Discuss the financial accounting and reporting issues that are raised because of FLX's agreement with Proctor Venture Capitalist Group for its investment in PS Medical Systems. Include in your discussion the alternative methods to account for the investment and whether FLX might have to recognize a liability.
2. How would you recommend that FLX account for its investment in PS Medical Systems in the current and subsequent years?
3. If FLX exercises its option to purchase Proctor's 90 percent equity interest, how should FLX account for and report the acquisition? Include in your response a consideration of whether FLX's accounting would be the same regardless of the financial success of PS Medical Systems. Assume pooling accounting is not relevant.

ILLUSTRATIVE CASE DISCUSSION

Accounting for venture capital funding for the expansion of a distribution system raises several accounting issues. The most obvious issue is whether the company's proposal to account for the investment by the cost method is appropriate. From a financial reporting perspective, the company generally would prefer the cost method because it could avoid reporting losses during the initial stages of operation. However, the substantive question is whether the venture capital funding is really at risk. Although this arrangement is not a research and development arrangement addressed in SFAS No. 68, "Research and Development Arrangements," there are enough similarities that warrant consulting SFAS No. 68 for guidance. If the cost method is not used, a determination must be made as to what method is appropriate and how to apply that method.

Requirement 1.   The first issue to be addressed is whether the venture capital funding is really at risk. As previously indicated, *SFAS No. 68* can provide guidance on this issue. Paragraph 5 of *SFAS No. 68* states that: "If the enterprise is obligated to repay any of the funds provided by the other parties regardless of the outcome of the research and development, the enterprise shall estimate and recognize that liability. This requirement applies whether the enterprise may settle the liability by paying cash, by issuing securities, or by some other means." Repayment would be in the form of FLX purchasing Proctor's 90 percent equity interest. However, FLX has the option of purchasing Proctor's interest in exchange for 600,000 shares of FLX common stock. The facts indicate that this is an option, not an obligation.

Paragraph 6 states that: "To conclude that a liability does not exist, the transfer of the financial risk involved with research and development from the enterprise to the other enterprises must be substantive

from a callous disregard of other people's interests or welfare, but from psychological tendencies that foster poor decision making, from both an ethical and a rational perspective.[8] This view suggests that to enhance managers' judgment and decision making, there is a need for training of managers and employees of business entities in ethics and ethical conduct.

This section is a primer on business ethics.[9] A definition of business ethics is provided and the components of business ethics in an organization are identified. This is followed by the accountant's role in providing ethics audit services in which assurance on the effectiveness of various components of business ethics is provided.

Definition

Business ethics is "a management process comprised of programs, management practices, and systems designed to motivate, measure, and monitor the organization's ethical performance."[10] The motivation for such a process is to earn the respect and trust of employees, customers, suppliers, investors, and others by striking an acceptable balance between economic interests and the interests of all affected parties.[11] This process requires an ethics implementation strategy. A survey indicates that the following strategies are being used in corporate America:[12]

	Number	*Percent*
Code of conduct	208	93.3%
Employee training in ethics	99	44.4%
Social auditing and reporting	98	43.9%
Corporate structural changes	46	20.6%
Ethics committees	40	17.9%
Ombudsman	17	7.6%
Judiciary board	3	1.3%
None of the above	2	.9%

---

8. D. M. Messick and M. H. Bazerman, 1996, "Ethical Leadership and the Psychology of Decision Making," *Sloan Management Review* (Winter 1996), p. 9.

9. This section is adapted from M. J. Abdolmohammadi and L. Greenlay. "Corporate Ethics Audit Services: A Detailed Task Model, and Some Methodological Suggestions," *Research on Accounting Ethics* 6 (2000), pp. 67–90.

10. KPMG, "Innovating Best Ethical Practices" (Montvalle, NJ: KPMG Peat Marwick LLP, 1996).

11. F. J. Aguilar, *Managing Corporate Ethics: Learning from America's Ethical Companies How to Supercharge Business Performance* (New York: Oxford University Press, 1994), p. 17.

12. C. Wiley, "The ABC's of Business Ethics; Definitions, Philosophies and Implementation," *Industrial Management* 37, no. 1 (January-February, 1995), pp. 22–27.

Components of Business Ethics

Business ethics has many components. In an effort to understand these components, a classification is provided in Exhibit 9–2. These components are further discussed in the following paragraphs.

Ethical Culture and Climate

Ethics is used to describe issues of good or bad, right or wrong. However, in an organizational context, ethics has an expanded meaning that includes a wide variety of issues ranging from social responsibility to sexual harassment, from affirmative action or empowering workers to hiring the hard-core unemployed.[13] Corporate culture refers to the rules and procedures that have been developed over time to guide the organization's management and employees to respond to contemporary issues and circumstances. Due to the complexity of the corporate environment, identifying all issues and circumstances that require an appropriate response in various circumstances is a challenging task. However, identifying the most pressing issues and circumstances is necessary to develop an elaborate culture capable of handling them.

Exhibit 9–2   The Components of Business Ethics

Component	Purpose
1. Ethical culture and climate	To foster an environment supportive of ethical behavior.
2. Control environment	To institute controls for mitigating unethical behavior.
3. Board of directors	To set an ethical tone at the top.
4. Management	To set an ethical tone at the top and to enforce the ethical tone.
5. Federal and state law issues	To have an effective mechanism to respond to legal requirements.
6. Code of ethics	To provide the ethical principles and general rules of ethics consistent with the corporate mission.
7. Training and development	To increase employees' competence in distinguishing between ethical and unethical behavior.
8. Enforcement	To provide a mechanism for enforcement of the code of ethics.
9. Whistle-blowing	To have an environment where voluntary reporting of unethical behavior is encouraged and whistle-blowers are protected.
10. Ombudsman, ethics officer, ethics committee, judiciary board	To have a specific office or individual responsible for the development and enforcement of the code of ethics.

13. A. W. Singer, "Can a Company Be Too Ethical?" *Across the Board* 30, no 3 (April 1993), pp. 16–22.

Corporate climate is a subset of the overall corporate culture. It relates to the perceptions of employees and customers regarding a company's organizational norms and structure that support values such as providing warmth and support to peers and subordinates.[14] Corporate climate therefore determines whether employees treat each other and customers with respect or with jealousy and aggression. A major part of the corporate climate is its ethical climate, which refers to the shared perceptions that employees hold concerning ethical procedures and policies existing in their organization.[15]

Control Environment

A company's control environment has been viewed as the most influential in establishing and enforcing an effective control system in that company. The Committee of Sponsoring Organizations of the Treadway Commission (COSO) emphasized the importance of the control environment by stating that the tone of an organization influences the control consciousness of its people and provides the foundation for all other components of the internal control system. The COSO also emphasized the impact that an effective control system will have on providing discipline and structure. Integrity, ethical values and competence of employees, and management's philosophy and operating style were also emphasized.[16] This list of desirable attributes, particularly integrity and ethical values, implies that a company needs to develop and implement codes of conduct and other policies to enhance its ethical standing.[17] It is important to note that accountants and auditors (both internal and independent) are concerned with the strength of the system of internal controls. Thus, this component of business ethics is particularly relevant to the practice of accounting. Accountants are generally involved in the design, implementation, and audit of control systems in business entities.

Board of Directors

A business entity should have a mechanism to consider board of director candidates with a reputation for personal integrity and to eliminate those individuals with possible conflicts of interest or undue influence.[18] Such an approach should result in recruiting board members that will serve the

---

14. For a detailed discussion, see B. Victor and J. B. Cullen, "The Organizational Bases of Ethical Work Climates," *Administrative Science Quarterly* 33 (1988), 101–25.
15. J. C. Wimbush and J. M. Shepard, "Toward an Understanding of Ethical Climate: Its Relationship to Ethical Behavior and Supervisory Influence," *Journal of Business Ethics* 13, no. 8 (1994), pp. 637–47.
16. COSO (Committee of Sponsoring Organizations of the Treadway Commission), *Internal Control: Integrated Framework* (Harborside, NJ: AICPA, 1992), p. 2.
17. Ibid., p. 27.
18. Adapted from D. M. Driscoll, W. M. Hoffman, and E. S. Petry, *The Ethical Edge* (New York: MasterMedia Limited, 1995), Chapter 18.

company with integrity and honesty and will help establish an ethical tone at the top.

Management

The importance of management integrity is recognized in professional standards. *SAS No. 53*, "Auditor's Responsibility to Detect and Report Errors and Irregularities," for instance, indicates that management is above the controls that constrain employees, or can override them easily—thus management integrity is important. In addition, management must exercise constant vigilance and timely intervention to foster the firm's ethical standards.[19] For example, suppose you discover that the president of the company for which you work as an accountant has borrowed money from the company. It is unclear when the money will be paid back, but the president wants you to record the note receivable as a current liability so that the long-term debt to equity ratio is not affected. What will you do?

Federal and State Law Issues

The U.S. Sentencing Guidelines require judges and prosecutors to take into consideration aggravating and mitigating factors when they determine the fines and the length of probation for organizations convicted for serious legal violation in federal courts. "The mitigating factor receiving the most attention from business ethicists is the one that states that if an organization had in place, prior to the offense, 'an effective program to prevent and detect violation of law,' this program can reduce its fines by up to 60 percent."[20] Thus, some federal and state laws have direct impact on ethical performance in the sense that they either provide positive rewards (e.g., fine reduction in the U.S. Sentencing Guidelines) or negative rewards (e.g., fines for unlawful conduct).

Code of Ethics

"Normally, an ethical code provides an organization with a frame of reference, defining the areas of ethical concerns and the core values that are to guide action. At best, it can also be highly inspirational, inducing employees' pride and outsiders' admiration. What is important to understand is that ethical codes are just one of the many managerial tools for motivating corporate ethical behavior."[21]

---

19. F. J. Aguilar, *Managing Corporate Ethics: Learning from America's Ethical Companies How to Supercharge Business Performance* (New York: Oxford University Press, 1994), p. 95.
20. D. M. Driscoll, W. M. Hoffman and E. S. Petry, *The Ethical Edge* (New York: MasterMedia Limited, 1995), Chapter 10.
21. F. J. Aguilar, *Managing Corporate Ethics: Learning from America's Ethical Companies How to Supercharge Business Performance* (New York: Oxford University Press, 1994), pp. 61–62.

Training and Development
One of the means of an effective ethical process is a formal training program. Such programs are required for developing employees' understanding, competence, and commitment with respect to ethical behavior on the job.[22]

Enforcement
Credible enforcement of ethics is necessary to assure adherence to the code of ethics. Penalties for violating codes of ethics include termination, suspension, demotion, probation, performance appraisal notes, and other forms of penalty.

Whistle-Blowing
Whistle-blowing is defined as "The disclosure by organization members (former or current) of illegal, immoral, or illegitimate practices under the control of their employees, to persons or organizations that may be able to affect action."[23] It is argued that "Co-workers who are willing to monitor their peers' behavior and report violations to management represent a potentially important supplemental control resource for organizations."[24] Accountants and auditors are particularly positioned to engage in whistle-blowing activities in organizations. The protection of whistle-blowers is an important dimension to make it effective, but it is a very sensitive issue. For example, as an accountant what will you do if you discover that the company you work for has violated some state or federal laws? Will you keep quiet or will you blow the whistle?

Ombudsman, Ethics Officer, Ethics Committee, and Judiciary Board
Ethics committees, ombudsmen, ethics officers, or judiciary boards play an important role in the development and enforcement of ethical processes. These authorities bring ethical dilemmas into the open for the purpose of discussion and resolution. Also, they provide a mechanism as a report-receiving office for whistle-blowers. Approximately 25 percent of the major public companies surveyed in one study indicated that they have established this function.[25]

---

22. F. J. Aguilar, *Managing Corporate Ethics: Learning from America's Ethical Companies How to Supercharge Business Performance* (New York: Oxford University Press, 1994), p. 104.
23. J. P. Near and M. P. Miceli, "Effective Whistle-Blowing," *Academy of Management Review* 20, no. 3 (1995), pp. 679–708.
24. L. K. Trevino and B. Victor, "Peer Reporting of Unethical Behavior: A Social Context Perspective," *Academy of Management Journal* 35, no. 1 (1992), p. 38.
25. C. Wiley, "The ABCs of Business Ethics; Definitions, Philosophies, and Implementation," *Industrial Management* 37, no. 1 (January-February, 1995), pp. 22–27.

The Accountant's Role in Enforcing Ethics in Business

Accountants who are also trained in ethics and ethics audits can play a major role in business entities to help improve ethical conduct. An ethics audit service is a new area of assurance services. Internal auditors, independent auditors, or others can provide this service. In fact, some CPA firms have developed ethics audit practices in recent years. An example is the ethics audit program at KPMG, LLP that has four components.[26] The first component is an assessment of the ethical climate of the client, encompassing culture, environment, motives, and pressures. This is followed by an assessment of performance incentives. The issue is whether the performance incentives provide a motivation to behave outside the moral norm. The third component is the communication of the message about what is acceptable or unacceptable ethical behavior. This communication covers issues of ethical policies, procedures, and training downstream from management to employees. It also covers the nature of upstream communication from employees to management. The final component of KPMG's ethics audit is compliance. Compliance refers to the assessment of the effectiveness of policies, procedures, and offices involved in the client's ethics program.

The ethics audit is a service provided to identify vulnerabilities and to provide suggestions to upper management about these vulnerabilities. It typically results in a management report, not an audit opinion. For example, the auditor might find that the top management has integrity and also has good ideas about ethics, but that these ideas are not effectively communicated downstream. Consequently, the auditor develops suggestions for the downstream communication of these issues.

To perform such a service, auditors must be sensitive to ethical issues, must be trained in ethical reasoning, must have motivation to behave according to ethical norms, and must have the ethical character to engage in ethical behavior and resist unethical action. These issues are explained in the next section. Auditors also need specific audit tasks that relate to ethics in organizations. These tasks can be documented in a questionnaire or in a free-format interview process with client employees individually or in focus groups. For example, related to ethical culture and climate, a relatively simple task is to determine whether the corporate culture is in congruence with the formal internal control system.[27] A more complex question is whether or not the client has a positive moral atmosphere with a diverse group of individuals in terms of individual ethical beliefs, values, and

---

26. KPMG Peat Marwick, "Creating the Moral Organization," *KPMG Internet Web Site* (Montvalle, NJ: 1997).

27. L. Falkenberg and I. Herremans, "Ethical Behaviours in Organizations: Directed by the Formal or Informal Systems?" *Journal of Business Ethics* 14 (1995), p. 135.

ethical reasoning (i.e., is individual diversity tolerated, encouraged).[28] Similarly, an example of a task related to internal control and its effects on ethical conduct of a business entity is to determine whether the internal audit function is effective as a mechanism for responsiveness to reporting of unethical acts.[29]

An ethical item or audit task related to the board of directors is whether the board is actively involved in the evaluation of management's enforcement of its corporate ethics code. Or whether the board of directors meets without any insider members to discuss accountability of the management for enforcement of the corporate ethics code.[30] Related to management, the auditor may be interested in knowing whether management has undesirable ethical attitudes that indicate a possible willingness to commit an illegal or unethical act.[31] Thus, management's ethical behavior is an important variable to assess because the knowledge that the CEO has done the right thing ethically when faced with a tough business decision sends a strong message to all levels of the organization.[32] Note that such assessments are very difficult to perform and highly sensitive. The auditor needs much training and experience to handle such delicate tasks.

To assess the adherence of the client to federal and state laws, the auditor might be interested in determining whether the client has in place a clear-cut policy to ensure that hiring decisions are made without regard to race, color, age, religion, national origin, or marital status. Also important is the existence of a clear-cut policy that provides reasonable assurance that the company accommodates individuals with disabilities under the provisions of the Americans with Disabilities Act.

Corporate codes of ethics are varied in terms of their level of detail (some are only statements of principles while others are more specific). Thus, the audit tasks that the auditor might want to perform depend on the nature of the code. For example, the auditor might be interested in knowing whether the code of ethics has guidelines for accepting gifts from vendors, or accepting gifts/favors in exchange for preferential treatment.

For training and development, an important question is whether a business entity has a systematic, periodic, or continuous program of employee ethics training or whether the training program is a one-time shot.

---

28. L. A. Ponemon, "Comment: Whistle-Blowing as an Internal Control Mechanism: Individual and Organizational Considerations," *Auditing: A Journal of Practice and Theory* 13, no. 2 (1994), pp. 118–30.

29. COSO (Committee of Sponsoring Organizations of the Treadway Commission), *Internal Control: Integrated Framework* (Harborside, NJ: AICPA, 1992), p. 84.

30. POB, *Strengthening the Professionalism of the Independent Auditor: Report of the Public Oversight Board of the SEC Practices Section, AICPA* (New York: 1994).

31. K. L. Hooks, S. E. Kaplan, and J. J. Schultz, Jr., "Enhancing Communication to Assist in Fraud Prevention and Detection," *A Journal of Practice and Theory* 13, no. 2 (1994), pp. 86–117.

32. COSO (Committee of Sponsoring Organizations of the Treadway Commission), *Internal Control: Integrated Framework* (Harborside, NJ: AICPA, 1992), p. 21.

Many audit tasks are also relevant to other components of business ethics such as enforcement, whistle-blowing, ombudsman, ethics officer, ethics committee, and judiciary boards. For example, the level of moral reasoning of key employees can be used to assess the likelihood of employees taking a strong stance against ethical violations (i.e., employees with higher levels of ethical cognition have more propensity to report unethical behavior). An important issue here is whether the business entity assures anonymity of whistle-blowers. Similarly, it is important to determine if the business entity has an ethics officer or similar body and whether or not the body has authority to discharge its responsibility.

Some of these ethics items or audit tasks are controversial in nature and complex in their application. They relate to the issue of what is ethics in the first place and whose ethics should determine whether or not an individual or an organization is ethical. It is important to note that the Auditing Standards Board of the AICPA has recently issued *Statement on Auditing Standards No. 82*, "Consideration of Fraud in a Financial Statement Audit," which is a formal recognition of the auditor's responsibility to audit for one class of unethical behavior—fraud. It requires the auditor to plan and perform the audit to obtain reasonable assurance about whether the financial statements are free of material misstatement, whether caused by error or fraud. Fraud is defined in *SAS No. 82* as fraudulent financial reporting or misappropriation of assets. While the scope of *SAS No. 82* is limited to fraud only, its guidelines may be useful in developing audit procedures for other types of unethical issues ranging from sexual harassment to unethical hiring and firing practices.

As stated earlier, the ethics of individuals engaged in accounting and auditing play a big role in the success of corporate ethics programs. For example, suppose that you are an accountant for a company that uses the LIFO method of inventory. The company's code of ethics indicates that income manipulation is not allowed. However, confronted with a lower gross margin at the end of the year, a manager wants your help to realign LIFO inventory pools so that the cost of goods sold can be understated resulting in a higher gross margin. How will you respond to this request? The ethical sensitivity, reasoning, motivation, and character needed to make these types of judgments and decisions are the subjects of individual ethics as presented in the next section.

Individual Ethics

Definition

Individual ethics can be defined in many different ways depending on the philosophy adopted. In general, it is the study of what is right in human behavior.[33] It focuses on the ultimate goals that ought to be pursued and the actions that ought to be taken to achieve those goals. Notice that the key phrase is *ought to be,* not *what is.* What ought to be depends on the philosophy adopted. For example, in the free market economy of most Western cultures, this is interpreted as respect for individual rights and concern for fairness and the common good. In a socialist system, ought to be is interpreted as the good of the society as a whole even if it is at the expense of the individual. The discussion in this chapter is focused on the Western democratic tradition.

The significance of ought to be is its effect on an individual's ability to recognize other individuals' experiences and feelings as real and important. Individuals who have no such recognition are said to have no conscience, but the degree to which such a recognition materializes depends on the ethical principle adopted. This is where the study of religion and philosophy is helpful. Five general individual ethical principles are briefly discussed here.

Principle of Self-Interest

Following this principle, an individual focuses on his or her self-interest because maximization of self-interest is said to be good for the maximization of the interests of the society as a whole. To achieve this, however, the individual does not advance his or her interest selfishly. Selfishness is referred to as the practice of advancing one's interest to the point that the interests of others are unduly harmed. Thus, the principle of self-interest is moral to the extent that it is controlled and not harmful to the self-interest of others. It is not difficult to imagine how complex the ethical dilemmas can become when this principle is followed. Trading of stocks on inside information is an example of an unethical behavior even if one adopts the principle of self-interest, because it harms the self-interest of others.

Principle of Harm Minimization

This principle is based on the notion that it is relatively easy to discern what is physically or psychologically harmful to others. The ethics of this principle is that the individual is obliged to follow a degree of self-control (as compared with self-interest in the previous principle) so that his or her actions will not harm others. For example, an accountant who discovers irregularities in his company can minimize the harmful effects on stockholders by disclosing the irregularities to the company's board for corrective action. While this whistle-blowing disclosure may be undesirable for the

---

33. This discussion is adopted from a handout by Philosophy Professor M. Francis Reeves, "Some Commonly Accepted Ethical and Professional Principles" (Bentley College, 1995).

accountant due to its possible effects on his job at the company, the disclosure will have the effect of catching fraud early and thus minimizing the financial harm on stockholders.

Principle of Utilitarianism

According to this principle, the individual acts in a way in which public interest is optimized. Thus, the individual takes actions that will result in the greatest good for the greatest number of people. Note that there may be a pareto-optimality in this principle. Pareto-optimality refers to the situation where even though the greatest good may result for the greatest number of people, there are still other people who lose financially or psychologically as a result of others' actions. In the example provided for harm minimization, suppose that the company management is holding significant, but minority, ownership of the company. Further, suppose that the company's board takes corrective action by disclosing the fraud to the public. The board also reminds management that it is illegal to sell its stocks on insider information (i.e., before the fraud is fully disclosed to the public). Thus, a consequence of the accountant's fraud disclosure is that it may be good for a majority of stockholders but not for management, which is minority stockholder. Management will suffer significant financial losses if other stockholders sell out their stocks and force the stock price to fall.

Principle of Universality

This principle refers to a consistency in actions under similar circumstances. Thus, the individual adhering to this principle asks a question such as: Do I want others to take the action that I took under similar circumstances? Or, is it that I want preferential treatment where I want others to treat me in a more advantageous way than I am willing to treat them? Consider the previous example once again and assume that the accountant has shares of stock in the company. If he sells his stock at market price before disclosing the fraud to the board, he has committed an unethical act according to the principle of universality.

Principle of Human Rights

Here the individual follows a global justice principle where the freedom and human rights of others are fully respected. This principle is based on the premise that rights such as freedom of speech are sacred in nature and ought to be respected at all costs even if they conflict with other important rights or principles. For example, the production and dissemination of sexually explicit material are viewed as undesirable from several perspectives ranging from religious laws and moral principles to the laws protecting the rights of minor children. However, freedom of speech has been used to argue against banning this material in many countries.

The ethical principles just outlined vary in their degree of desirability. They form different levels of ethical cognition or reasoning, and they have been the subject of much research and model building. A model, called the

Kohlberg Stage Model of Moral Development, uses a mix of these principles for representing various stages of moral reasoning. This model in its basic form is presented in the next section.

Kohlberg Stage Model of Moral Development

Cognitive developmental models propose that moral judgment is developed over time in various stages. Thus, these models facilitate a training process through which ethical judgment can be improved. The late Harvard University professor, Lawrence Kohlberg, developed a general stage model based on moral development of children that was first proposed by the noted child psychologist, Jean Piaget.[34] Through a process of telling a story to a group of children, questioning and observing them, Piaget developed a stage model of child development.

Kohlberg extended Piaget's work with children into the moral judgments of adolescents and adults. He proposed a sequence model that has three levels of moral development with each level subdivided into two stages for a total of six stages.[35] This model is presented in Exhibit 9–3. Each of the six stages is viewed as qualitatively higher than the previous stages in terms of ethical reasoning.

Exhibit 9–3   Kohlberg's Stage Model of Ethical Cognition

Level	Stage	Action	Reason for Action
I. Preconventional: Self-centered	1.	Avoid breaking rules	Avoid punishment
	2.	Follow rules	Serve own self-interest
II. Conventional: conformity	3.	Group membership (do what is expected by others)	Need to be accepted as a good person in the eyes of group members
	4.	Obey laws, rules, and regulations	Keep social institutions going
III. Post-conventional: conviction	5.	Upholding nonrelative obligations first	Obligation to law
	6.	Follow self-chosen ethical principles	Belief in ideal as a rational person

Source: Adapted from L. Kohlberg, "Stages and Sequences: The Cognitive Developmental Approach to Socialization," in D. Goslin (ed.), *Handbook of Socialization Theory and Research* (Chicago: Rand McNally, 1969).

---

34. Piaget's book, originally published in 1932, presents his major contribution to the cognitive developmental theory. See J. Piaget, *The Moral Judgment of the Child*, M. Gabain (trans.), (New York: Free Press, 1965).

35. Kohlberg did his doctoral dissertation at the University of Chicago in 1958 on moral development of children. He later extended his work to adolescents and adults in L. Kohlberg, "Stages and Sequences: The Cognitive Developmental Approach to Socialization," in D. Goslin (ed.), *Handbook of Socialization Theory and Research* (Chicago: Rand McNally, 1969), and in L. Kohlberg, *Essays on Moral Development: vol. II, The Psychology of Moral Development* (San Francisco: Harper & Row, 1984).

The Preconventional Level

The first level of moral development is called the *preconventional level*. It refers to the principle of self-interest and is the ethics of convenience. A stage 1 individual avoids breaking rules simply to avoid punishment. This reasoning indicates that if the person can find a way not to be punished, he or she is not inclined to obey rules. A stage 2 individual, on the other hand, obeys rules willingly, but seeks personal rewards through manipulation of others. Thus, the stage 2 individual has a greater awareness of the feelings of others than a stage 1 individual.

The Conventional Level

The second level of moral cognition is called the *conventional level*. It is the ethics of conformity. At its elementary stage (i.e., stage 3), the individual has group loyalty and seeks to be accepted by members of the group as a good person. Thus, the stage 3 individual does what is expected by others in the group, say the AICPA membership. In stage 4, the individual obeys civic and/or religious laws, rules, regulations, and professional codes because he or she believes in the importance of obeying such laws, not just for acceptance by peer groups.

The conventional level implies that obeying professional codes of conduct, such as that of the AICPA, needs only stage 3 (membership loyalty) or stage 4 (belief in law and order). Thus, one can argue that only a conventional level of moral cognition is necessary for accounting practice. While this level may be necessary for practice, the increasingly higher levels of public expectation in recent decades indicates that it may no longer be sufficient. Contemporary accountants of today may be held to higher levels of ethical reasoning than his/her predecessors.

The Post-Conventional Level

The third level of moral cognition is called the *post-conventional level*. At this level, an individual has achieved the ethics of conviction. The individual reasons based on principles to which he or she is committed. There are two stages in this level, classified as stages 5 and 6 in the Kohlberg model. At stage 5, the individual is attracted to the ethics of some high-order ethical principle such as utilitarianism. At the final stage, the individual follows the ethics of unwritten global ethical principles. This stage is found in ethical principles of justice, duties, and equal human rights.

Kohlberg's stage theory predicts that generally individuals progress throughout life from lower stages to higher stages of moral cognition. However, the rate of progress depends on many factors such as age, education, and training. A question is how to measure an individual's stage of ethical cognition and his or her progress toward higher levels. This issue is discussed in the next section.

Measures of Ethical Cognition

Kohlberg developed an instrument called the *moral judgment interview (MJI)* to measure ethical cognition. MJI utilizes a series of dilemmas that an individual verbally resolves in response to an interviewer's questions. An elaborate scoring system is then employed to analyze the individual's responses and to establish the stage of the individual's moral development. The MJI takes a long time to administer and has a relatively subjective coding process.

To overcome these disadvantages, a measure called the *defining issues test (DIT)* has been developed by Professor James Rest of the University of Minnesota. It is a self-administered, multiple-choice questionnaire where six dilemmas are used, each written as a scenario and stated in the third person. The individual is asked an overall question of what one ought to do in each of the circumstances. Each scenario is accompanied by twelve questions (for a total of 72).[36] The subject indicates the importance of each item in the resolution of the dilemma by using a four-level scale (much importance, some, little, or none). Appendix 9A provides an abridged version of the DIT with only one dilemma and 12 questions. In describing the DIT, Rest explains that:

> The DIT is based on the premise that people at different points of development interpret moral dilemmas differently, define the critical issues of the dilemmas differently, and have intuitions about what is right and fair in a situation. Differences in the way that dilemmas are defined therefore are taken as indications of their underlying tendencies to organize social experience. These underlying structures of meaning are not necessarily apparent to a subject as articulate rule systems or verbalizeable philosophies—rather, they may work 'behind the scenes' and may seem to a subject as just common-sensical and intuitively obvious.[37]

While several indices have been developed from the scoring of the DIT, the most commonly used score is the P-score, P standing for principled moral thinking. A measure between 0.00 and 1.00, the P-score represents the weight that an individual assigns to items that are included in the DIT to measure stages 5 and 6. Thus, the P-score measures an individual's standing on Kohlberg's post-conventional level ethics of conviction.

The University of Minnesota controls the distribution and scoring of the DIT instrument. A result of this is a huge database at the university that has been developed over the years from numerous administrations of the DIT

---

36. According to Rest, these questions were designed to represent the different considerations that are diagnostic of different schemes of fairness. See J. Rest, *Moral Development: Advances in Research and Theory* (New York: Praeger Publishers, 1986), p. 196.
37. J. Rest, *Moral Development: Advances in Research and Theory* (New York: Praeger Publishers, 1986), p. 196.

worldwide. This database can be used to develop P-score averages for many strata of the society. For example, a subset of the database indicates that the average P-score for high school graduates is 31.03 (with a standard deviation of 13.90). Thus, a high school graduate who achieves a higher P-score is viewed as one having a better than average ethical cognition. Conversely, a high school graduate who achieves a lower P-score is viewed as one having a lower than average ethical cognition.

A General Model of Moral Behavior

Moral cognition is necessary for moral behavior; however, it may not be sufficient. A person with a high level of moral cognition as measured by the DIT P-score may still choose to engage in immoral or amoral behavior. In fact, empirical studies show that only 10 to 15 percent of moral behavior is explained by moral cognition.[38] To engage in moral behavior, components other than moral judgment are also necessary. Reviewing the psychological literature on various aspects of moral judgment and behavior, Professor James Rest has developed a model that encompasses four components, only one of which is moral judgment. These components are discussed below.[39]

Component I: Moral Sensitivity
Moral sensitivity refers to the degree of awareness of how one's actions affect other people.

> It involves imaginatively constructing possible scenarios, and knowing cause-consequence chains of events in the real world: it involves empathy and role-taking skills.[40]

An implication of this component is that individuals must consciously and imaginatively assess their moral sensitivity when they consider taking an action on an ethical dilemma. Training programs specifically designed to enhance moral sensitivity in professional schools such as dental, nursing, and sports have resulted in gains in students' moral sensitivity.[41]

---

38. See S. Thoma, "Moral Judgments and Moral Action," in J. R. Rest and D. Narvaez (eds.), *Moral Development in the Professions* (Hillsdale, NJ: Erlbaum, 1994), p. 201.
39. See J. R. Rest, "Background: Theory and Research," in J. R. Rest and D. Narvaez (eds.), *Moral Development in the Professions* (Hillsdale, NJ: Erlbaum, 1994), Chap. 1, pp. 1–26.
40. J. R. Rest, "Background: Theory and Research," in J. R. Rest and D. Narvaez (eds.), *Moral Development in the Professions* (Hillsdale, NJ: Erlbaum, 1994), p. 23.
41. See Chapters 3 (by L. J. Duckett & M. B. Ryden), 7 (by M. J. Bebeau), and 10 (by B. J. L. Bredemeier & D. L. L. Shields) in J. R. Rest and D. Narvaez (eds.), *Moral Development in the Professions* (Hillsdale, NJ: Erlbaum, 1994).

Component II: Moral Judgment

Moral judgment is the component of moral behavior where the individual chooses the more morally justifiable courses of action from the alternative courses of action generated from component I. Many studies of moral judgment involve cases where alternative courses of action are given in the case and the subject is asked to make a judgment as to which course of action is morally more justifiable. This is in contrast to the situation where the subject independently generates the alternative courses of action in component I and then makes a judgment about which course of action is more ethical.

Component III: Moral Motivation

Moral motivation is the comparative importance assigned by the individual to moral values (e.g., lack of interest in falsifying reports in accounting) other than self-interest values (such as wealth maximization at any cost to others). There is little research in this area of moral reasoning. Researchers, however, have linked moral motivation to professionalism in professional schools where motivations such as service to the society and professional responsibility have been linked to component III. For example, dental students were lectured on professional motivations such as service to society and patient well-being and were then asked to write essays on the ethics of the dental program in their midterm and/or final examinations. While difficulties such as students' failure to see limits of obligation and a narrow interpretation of the obligation were observed, the need for explicit instruction was also indicated.[42]

Component IV: Moral Character

Moral character refers to the ego strength, perseverance, backbone, toughness, strength of conviction, and courage that is needed for moral behavior.[43] To have this strength, the individual needs to have many virtuous characters. For example, an accountant must have virtues such as trustworthiness, benevolence, altruism, honesty, integrity, impartiality, and open-mindedness in serving the public interest. The accountant also must have the characters such as reliability and dependability, faithfulness, and trustworthiness in serving clients' interests.[44] In a national survey of accounting professors, accounting students, independent auditors, and internal auditors, a list of 40 virtues was subjected to an importance rating

---

42. See Chapter 7 (by M. J. Bebeau) in J. R. Rest and D. Narvaez (eds.), *Moral Development in the Professions* (Hillsdale, NJ: Erlbaum, 1994).
43. See J. R. Rest, "Background: Theory and Research," in J. R. Rest and D. Narvaez (eds.), *Moral Development in the Professions* (Hillsdale, NJ: Erlbaum, 1994), p. 24.
44. See S. M. Mintz, "Virtue Ethics and Accounting Education," *Issues in Accounting Education* (Fall 1995), pp. 247–67.

for the practice of auditing. Not surprisingly, the top 20 attributes included honesty, conscientiousness, objectivity/impartiality, trustworthiness, fairness, compliance with rules of conduct, professional skepticism, compliance with auditingstandards, diligence, and lack of interest in illegal activities.[45]

These results indicate that we have a fairly good idea about what ethical characteristics are needed for practice. However, training to develop the characteristics is the challenging part. Moral failure can occur because of deficiency in any of the four components in the model. Thus, it is important to provide training for ethics as discussed in the next section.

Ethical Training: The Case Method

It has been suggested that while moral dilemmas in professional judgment are highly complex, business school graduates are ethically naive and unprepared to deal with these dilemmas.[46] This problem is often blamed on shortcomings of ethical training in business schools. For example, business schools have been criticized for their singular focus on what it takes to get ahead without a sufficient focus on what is right.[47] In response, many business schools have begun integrating ethical issues in various courses in functional areas such as accounting. An approach that is used to improve ethical reasoning of students is the case method. Typically, cases or video vignettes depicting ethical dilemmas are presented and discussed to sensitize students to the delicate nature of ethical issues and to improve their ethical reasoning.

The analysis of a case on an ethical dilemma is similar to the case approach used for analyzing accounting and auditing issues as presented in Chapter 3. The analysis typically is done in four distinct steps as presented below:

1. Identify stakeholders.
2. Identify ethical issues.
3. Identify alternative solutions.
4. Make a decision: select a preferred solution.

To begin analyzing the case, you must understand the facts of the case. Thus, it is helpful to list the most significant facts before you begin your analysis. Once you have a good understanding of the facts, you identify and

---

45. See M. J. Abdolmohammadi, "Attributes of Ethical Audit Decision Making," *Research on Accounting Ethics* (forthcoming).
46. See V. E. Henderson, "Can Business Ethics be Taught?" *Management Review* 77, no. 8 (1988), pp. 52–54 and L. A. Tansey, "Right vs. Wrong," *Managing Your Career* (Spring/Summer, 1994), pp. 11–12.
47. See R. H. Schwartz, S. Kassem, and D. Ludwig, "The Role of Business Schools in Managing the Incongruence between Doing What Is Right and Doing What It Takes to Get Ahead," *Journal of Business Ethics* 10 (1991), pp. 465–69.

discuss the primary stakeholders of the case in step 1. For example, in a case involving questionable financial reporting, at a minimum, stakeholders would include shareholders, creditors, employees, and the general public.

In the second step, ethical issues, the focus is on identifying the morally questionable issues and their magnitude. Is the ethical issue a contained problem that only requires an internal investigation within the company, or does it relate to various stakeholders outside the organization? From this vantage point, various viable alternative solutions (step 3) are identified. The focus here is on the strength and weaknesses of the alternatives and the moral consequences of each alternative. Based on this analysis, the preferred alternative is selected in step 4.

The preferred solution identified in step 4 is then further discussed for the purpose of developing an action plan. For example, if questionable financial reporting has occurred, a preferred alternative might be to acknowledge the problem and proceed to develop an implementation plan so that the chances of it happening again in the future are minimized. The implementation plan may call for changes to the code of ethics, new or revised policies, procedures, training, and enforcement processes. This is in contrast to other alternatives such as a lawsuit that might take many years and significant resources to resolve. It should be noted that action plans under these sensitive circumstances can draw strong opposition and significant obstacles that may require decisive and timely managerial response to overcome.

For the preferred course of action, you also must have a morally justifiable argument. Arguing that the selected course of action and its implementation plan is the least costly plan is not a moral justification. Making the argument that the course of action is the right thing to do under the moral principle (say utilitarianism) is a morally justifiable argument.

To illustrate the ethical case analysis approach, a practice case is provided in the next section. Additional cases are provided in Chapter 10.[48] The cases focus specifically on various ethical dilemmas in financial reporting.

ILLUSTRATIVE CASE	ANTELOPE FINANCIAL

Revenue Recognition: Gain-on-Sale Accounting

Ethical reasoning in accounting comes in handy when making judgments and decisions in gray areas for which rules and regulations are insufficient or vague. Generally, the lapses in ethics are attributed to poor judgment as compared with intentional fraud. Antelope Financial is a case study of this kind.

During the course of the last 25 years, the economy has witnessed an explosion in financial engineering. Financial firms have been busy creating, swapping, and owning financial instruments that did not exist

48. Edward Bernardo developed all ethics cases in an independent study under the authors' supervision. We thank him for his contribution to this book.

before. With this financial evolution, however, it has become increasingly difficult to value and account for these financial assets and transactions, adding uncertainty and risk to investors. The practice known as *gain-on-sale accounting* exemplifies these difficulties. First made popular in the early 1990s by Wall Street, this practice involves borrowing money at a low rate, usually available through the money markets, and lending at a higher rate for a specified period of time, much like a bank. Over time, the firm recognizes the spread (i.e., the difference between its financing costs and its lending rate) as profit. Although this in and of itself represents nothing new, Wall Street added a twist: firms now package (securitize) these loans, sell them, and recognize their profit today by discounting to present value all scheduled future cash flows for a given asset (bond) sale. This practice usually works well in calm markets and growing economies. There can be difficulties, however.

Antelope Financial has for years been building a solid business as a provider of syndicated loans and commercial finance. Although not a bank, this multiline financial company enjoys ongoing relationships with many small but growing firms, meeting nearly all their financial needs with a variety of financial products and services. An aggressive but well-managed player, Antelope has grown to become one of the largest players in its niche, penetrating the market of small to midsized firms nearly to the point of saturation. Although well rewarded by investors with a healthy stock price and earnings multiple, the firm's management is concerned about future growth in this mature market and has been exploring ways to grow beyond its narrow focus and to move into consumer home finance. At the suggestion of its board, Antelope begins to pursue strategic acquisitions. One firm, Put-You-In-Housing Financial (PYIHF), appears to offer Antelope an ideal fit in both business mix and client base. The company lends to individuals for the purchase of trailer homes, manufactured housing, and small houses. This type of company offers ongoing relationships at above average rates with a profitable client base. The potential for supplemental financing through other lines like auto loans and credit cards represents a tremendous source of untapped revenue. To finance itself thus far, PYIHF has relied on gain-on-sale accounting, securitizing all of its loans for sale, booking profits, and loaning the proceeds to additional customers. PYIHF has over $1 billion on the books in this manner.

After initial scrutiny, Antelope's board grants its CEO's request to allow him to pursue the acquisition of PYIHF, provided the deal does not dilute Antelope shareholders or expose it to significant risk. Antelope's stock jumps when the news of the takeover is made public; the market fully grasps the benefit of the synergies and additional customer base Antelope will profit from. The financial press proclaims it to be a great move on the part of Antelope's CEO. At that point, PYIHF was trading at a price-earnings multiple (P/E) slightly lower than Antelope's, and would therefore not dilute its earnings. As Antelope proceeds with the due diligence process, you are asked to closely inspect PYIHF's books. As the CFO in charge of all financial matters and head of the due diligence inspection, you will report your findings to the CEO.

Upon close inspection of the books, you immediately realize that PYIHF's practice of gain-on-sale accounting presents several risks to your firm. Although profitable, most of PYIHF clients represent what is known as the subprime market for lending; these people have poor credit histories with high rates of default. Although these facts have been accounted for with loss loan provisions and reserves, the rate of loss has been erratic and difficult to predict statistically. The revenues booked from these sales look suspect to you. Also, the residences are at risk to fire and hurricane due to their small size and construction, yet few homeowners have fire and casualty insurance. The assets backing your loans are therefore greatly at risk. Furthermore, PYIHF has many loans on the books yet to be securitized. These fixed rate loans are currently being financed by the company's own short-term variable rate bank lines. The market for these securities has dried up, and the firm is now in a highly leveraged position, presenting risk to Antelope should it acquire this firm. Although not exactly fraudulent, PYIHF's accounting practices are highly "optimistic" and leave little margin for error. Based on these facts alone, do they violate the rules of conservatism?

Being an ethical person, to say nothing of the fact that you are bound by duty in a publicly traded corporation regulated by the SEC, you approach your CEO and voice your concerns over the viability of revenues booked, the quality of assets, and the risks associated with this significant acquisition. He scoffs at you, asking if you are really a member of "the team." He restates his complete confidence in the acquisition and questions your ability to hold down such a high-profile (paying) position within the company. "Successful businesses take measured risks and educated guesses every day," he says. "We're well within our bounds." You suggest writing down the overall valuation a bit, recognizing the potential for loss of earnings and assets. He reminds you that a write-down like that would increase dramatically the multiple that Antelope pays for PYIHF. This would dilute earnings, and the board would stop the acquisition immediately. To cover yourself, you ask that a note be added to the financials and to the SEC Form 8-K. Again, he reminds you that the board would bar the acquisition due to the apparent risks to the firm. Furthermore, he reminds you that this acquisition has been announced publicly, with his name all over the papers. To back out now would be embarrassing. He asks that you agree to the acquisition, and sign off on the Form 8-K. "What's the worst that could happen? Those events are unknown and unforeseeable." What do you do? What other large, over-riding risk is associated with the PYIHF portfolio? How could that blow up?

Required

Provided that precious few cases and real-life situations have absolute answers, the four-step case analysis framework introduced in the chapter can help you work through difficult situations and ethical dilemmas.

1. Identify Stakeholders
List the parties involved. First list those parties directly affected by the various results of these accounting transactions and the way they are reported. List the size and scope of each party (e.g. an individual, a population). Then list those parties indirectly affected in the same manner. Next to that list, note the extent to which they stand to benefit or be harmed under the various transactions and their various interpretations.

2. Identify Ethical Issues
From an ethical context, what are the moral issues involved? Here, you should take a step away from accounting and auditing standards and focus on the argument from a greater perspective of *right versus wrong*. Although, ideally each proposed solution could be classified as good or bad, rarely will this be the case; resolutions are usually characterized by various shades of gray. Some may have both a good and bad connotation depending upon the viewpoint of the treatment.

3. Identify Alternative Solutions
In a cost/benefit analysis, the materiality and the impact of the various treatments should be closely examined. Here, common sense and prudence should be your overriding thought process. In those seemingly all too frequent cases where the treatment could go either way and the impact be equal on both sides, clearly the accountant should choose the method that he or she feels will provide the clearest picture of a given transaction or organization.

4. Make a Decision: Select a Preferred Solution
The hardest part requires your judgment and decision with a morally justifiable explanation. That's what you will be paid (and evaluated) for.

ILLUSTRATIVE CASE DISCUSSION

1. Stakeholders
Many stakeholders can be listed. Examples are the CFO, the CEO, creditors, investors, suppliers, customers, and the general public. As the CFO, you are responsible for the decisions related to the financial management of and reporting for the company. Not only do you have power to effect change, but a fiduciary responsibility to do so for the benefit of shareholders. You are responsible for the financial engineering that occurs in takeovers, especially at financial firms. You focus on the internal makeup and financial gearing of the firm,

determining how the various pieces should be put together financially. You are in charge of risk management.

The CEO can be ultimately held responsible for all decisions that the company implements. Especially at the strategic level of decision making where mergers and acquisitions are consummated, the CEO has an outward focus.

Creditors as stockholders have lent significant sums of money to the firm and, therefore, have financial ties to the firm. In doing so they depend on their ability to assess risk. By extending credit, creditors depend on the success of the firm so that they receive payments on their loans.

Investors risk their personal assets and life savings. They entrust the stewardship of their assets to the CEO and CFO of the firms in which they have invested. The expectations are that these officers will work to grow their businesses, take prudent risks, and provide competitive returns on the equity they manage. Suppliers depend on the firm to meet production schedules, and promptly pay bills when due. Customers depend on the firm to meet schedules to deliver quality content, products, and intermediate goods that fit into their own production cycles.

Finally, the general public makes decisions based on the faith and trust it places in the companies issuing shares and financial statements to the public. This trust is furthered by the publicized work of outside auditors and regulators, thus these parties can also be viewed as stakeholders.

2 **Ethical Issues**

The five ethical principles in the chapter can be listed and related to each of the stakeholders. For example, in relation to the CFO, the principle of self-interest indicates that the CFO should use the greatest self-interest in delivering accurate financial statements. The CFO generally has responsibility for managing firmwide financial risk. Minimization of these risks benefits the CFO.

For harm minimization, consider the fact that the CFO has the responsibility for the company's financial reports. His interests in producing reliable financials and minimizing harm are one and the same. As a manager of risk, the CFO must be able to recognize and take prudent risk, while not being reckless with the firm's capital.

In regard to utilitarianism, as a key contact to the financial community, the CFO understands the need for consistent and practically functional financials. The CFO, however, answers to the CEO, and therefore sometimes faces a difficult task of balancing disparate needs to find a working common ground. Thus, the CFO maintains a difficult balance between risk and return.

The principle of universality indicates that the CFO may want to satisfy needs and comply with accepted standards so that investors and creditors may closely look at, and hopefully invest in, the firm.

The principle of human rights may have limited applicability for the CFO unless one considers the availability of reliable information about the company to be a human rights issue. Also, given the stewardship function of the CEO, the ethical issues related to this stakeholder are similar to those of the CFO.

The ethical issues related to creditors and investors can be summarized as follows: The principle of self-interest indicates that creditors and investors seek financial returns, hopefully from a successful and growing company, with the potential for future growth. For harm minimization, generally creditors prefer the most conservative approach, as they develop a picture of a worst-case scenario and make decisions from there. Investors' capital is at risk, making them the parties most subject to harm.

For utilitarianism, it can be argued that creditors and investors need and demand the most accurate and up-to-date information in order to make informed decisions with their capital based on risks and potential rewards. Universality indicates universal standards and accepted accounting practices allow for greater transparency and better assessment of risks, allowing firms to employ capital in the most productive and efficient manner. Thus, these standards are helpful as universal standards for creditors and investors.

Finally, from the human rights perspective, it can argued that any firm engaged in the extension of credit effectively invests in the success of its client. Behind these creditors, the employees, their families, and the investors depend on firms to be up front and play by the rules. Fraud hurts all parties involved. Similarly, investors are the innocent bystanders to what goes on with their money and investments. As these investments represent people's futures and life savings, special care and attention are given to its trust and the manner in which it is deployed.

The rights of the suppliers and customers can also be analyzed under the five ethical principles. Most of the discussion, however, applies to creditors and investors.

For the general public as a stakeholder, consider the fact that the stock market crash of 1929 and, to a lesser extent, the crash of 1987 demonstrated the extent to which the general public has an interest in proper financial conduct. American citizens with no direct investment or relationship with the stock market lost their jobs and felt the brunt of the ensuing economic decline. Thus, the principle of self-interest can be used to argue for the interest of the general public in prudent financial acquisitions.

Harm minimization implies that proper management of risk through reliable financial reporting reduces volatility and unexpected stock fluctuations, promoting growth and employment stability. Unreliable financial reporting results in misappropriation of capital and destroys value. When management takes imprudent risks, it not only jeopardizes its own future, but the small part of the economy it has control over. When poor management bankrupts a previously healthy business, it really destroys value that otherwise was a part of, owned by, and contributed to the overall economy. There can be no excuse for this erosion of value due to irresponsible management or ethical lapses.

For utilitarianism, one can argue that accurate financials allow all participants in the economy (investors deploying capital and corporations making business decisions) to seamlessly interact and conduct financial transactions in a highly efficient manner due to consistency of standards and protocol. In this way, economies of scale through valid standard comparisons (e.g., ratio analysis and universal measures of profitability) lead to faster and sounder decisions, and therefore lead to greater efficiencies and higher risk-adjusted returns.

Universality implies that the promotion of reliable and *conservative* financials promotes the economy and allows all to benefit through growth in GDP and a higher standard of living. This is true for the general public, including even those not invested directly (through stocks) or even indirectly (through loans made by their company or bank). A higher standard of living benefits all, from the rich (for obvious reasons) to the poor, through greater availability of charitable funds and government programs due to higher tax receipts.

Finally, the principle of human rights implies that human rights of the general public depend upon the financial ability of all parties involved in all sectors from government to corporate to private. The more successful these entities are financially, the greater their resources to effect change for the better. Reliable financial reporting serves as the building block for this growth.

3. Alternative Solutions

As the executive in charge of consummating this acquisition, an acquisition brought to you by the CEO, there appear to be few attractive options, if any. One would hope that a frank conversation with your CEO, especially if you were not consulted before the deal was announced, might lead to more options. Personalities and egos appear to be driving this deal, however, things that rarely lead to prudence and options. If your CEO refuses to reexamine the deal and recognize the significant risk of failure brought about by this acquisition, then you have a hard decision to make.

One option that some firms pursue would be to acquire PYIHF and immediately spin off the undesirable assets. Ideally, the firm can then use the proceeds of the sale to pay down some of the debt, and be left with only those assets it wanted, leaving the firm less leveraged and holding less risk. This can be both risky and expensive. Much of the benefit of this strategy depends upon two things: what Antelope paid for the assets, and the price Antelope can obtain by reselling them. Generally, we operate in an efficient market. Depending on the skills and market knowledge of its investment bankers, Antelope may sell these assets at a loss. Although this may be fine to a certain extent, it does increase the price of the acquisition, potentially to a prohibitive extent. Beyond even this rosy scenario, many of the assets may be illiquid (cannot be sold); either they may not stand on their own or a buyer may not emerge. Already, PYIHF has grappled with this problem in its loan portfolio; the firm comes to Antelope with loans on the books it has been unable to sell. To buy these loans in anticipation of resale would be to assume that Antelope knows more about the secured loan market than PYIHF, a player competing in this market for years. This is usually a dangerous proposition. If the acquisition were to be contingent upon these sales, Antelope takes on significant market risk by doing so. This seems to violate the terms put forth by the board of directors, and the spirit of the fiduciary responsibility the CFO has to shareholders.

Assuming that the CEO will refuse to reconsider the acquisition, one overriding factor may sway you one way or another: the relative size of the acquisition. Should the acquisition be relatively small compared to Antelope in terms of market capitalization, assets, debt (enterprise value), and total cost, you may consider completing the acquisition, provided that certain conditions are met. The less material the impact, the easier it may be to swallow the acquisition (and any baggage that comes with it). Can you extricate yourself from the situation by voicing an official concern, at least to the board? That way, you've made it known that this acquisition does not meet your approval. Stated as such in absolute terms, this is probably not an option. Perhaps you can sign off on the deal with reservations, citing certain caveats, at least privately to the board and executive team, if not publicly. You probably can cite reservations privately in a discussion/debate during a meeting of the board with key executives present. Public commentary, however, probably will not be an option. At least this way you have voiced reservations in front of the board, *partially* removed yourself from potential blame should the deal eventually falter, and you may even persuade the board to reconsider the acquisition entirely. This would undoubtedly bring the ire of your CEO upon you, however, making life at work difficult, if not impossible. In light of this fact alone, you may reconsider your position within the firm, and begin shopping your resume. Unless there are significant benefits and extenuating circumstances, this may ultimately be the best option. Furthermore, before signing off on the acquisition, you must be able to justify that the acquisition provides at least a minimum level of benefit to the firm without taking on too much risk. Your fiduciary duties to shareholders as an executive require that you be able to meet this test. This requirement alone really may lead you to the only other option.

One other overriding risk looms large on the balance sheet of PYIHF. PYIHF has a portfolio of completed loans on its books, loans representing money the firm has lent to many individuals over the last several months that cannot be reversed. When PYIHF booked these long-term loans, the rates they lent at were higher than the short-term rates the firm was borrowing at in the financial markets. The longer the firm holds these loans, however, the more risk the firm takes on due to the following reason: a change in the level or term structure of interest rates can cause a firm's liabilities to rise more than the value of its assets. Hedging this risk, a process known as *managing the gap*, can be very difficult. In this case, the firm has lent long, and borrowed short. If short-term interest rates go up, their cost of financing can exceed their lending rate. This would be catastrophic to both PYIHF and Antelope. An astute CFO should be cognizant of the risks associated with such an acquisition.

4. A Preferred Solution

If the favorable circumstances above do not present themselves, especially if this acquisition is very large relative to your firm, the only real option may be to politely remove yourself and begin shopping your resume as soon as possible. That way, the weight of any guilt you may carry, to say nothing of the fear of a ticking financial time bomb, will not haunt you (after work, as well as during). You also protect your good name and take with you all the experience and contacts gained while at Antelope. Furthermore, should you remain with the firm, this stay may still prove temporary. When the risks of the deal become apparent, and even begin to take their toll on the firm's equity and capital base (to say nothing of its stock price), you may still find yourself shopping your resume, under less favorable terms.

Summary

In this chapter, a primer on four areas related to ethics in financial reporting was provided. The first was the AICPA's Code of Professional Conduct. A discussion of the principles, rules, interpretations, and enforcement process of the Code was included. A conclusion from this section was that CPAs have the responsibility to serve the public interest to the best of their ability in order to gain the public trust.

The second issue discussed was business ethics. The public's expectation of ethical business practices links the first issue with this one. Business ethics and its complex components were introduced. Major areas of concern were then identified and the role of the accountants to assist business entities was discussed. The broadly defined "ethics audit" service was identified as a part of the emerging area for assurance services.

Given the importance of ethical cognition for performing the ethics audit, individual ethics issues were discussed next. Broad ethical principles ranging from self-interest to ethics of utilitarianism and justice were introduced. A six-stage model of ethical cognition and methods to measure it followed this. One of these, the *defining issues test (DIT)* generates a number of scores for the six stages including the P-score that measures one's standing relative to stages 5 and 6. There is already a large database of the DIT scores at the University of Minnesota that can be used as a benchmark to compare the P-scores of individuals within a number of population strata (e.g., college graduates). An interpretation of the six-stage model is that only a stage 3 or 4 is needed to practice as an accountant in accordance with the AICPA's Code of Professional Conduct. However, the public expectation of ethical audits (such as fraud audits per *SAS No. 82*), indicates that higher stages may be needed for the practice of accounting and auditing.

As a part of this discussion, ethical cognition was said to be only one of the four components necessary for ethical behavior. The other three components according to a popular theory are moral sensitivity, moral motivation, and moral character. Finally, the discussion of the previous issues indicated a need for ethical training. A complete discussion of this issue was considered beyond the scope of the chapter. However, a four-step process for a case-based training with an objective of improving one's ethical reasoning through dilemma-based case analysis was provided, followed by an illustrative case study.

Selected Additional Reading

Ponemon, L. A., and D. R. L. Gabhart, 1993. *Ethical Reasoning in Accounting and Auditing* (Vancouver, BC, Canada: CGA-Canada Research Foundation Monograph no. 21).

Questions

1. Present and briefly discuss the four components of the AICPA's Code of Professional Conduct.

2. Discuss the six principles in the AICPA's Code of Professional Conduct.

3. Present and discuss the rules and interpretations of the AICPA's Code of Professional Conduct.

4. How does the AICPA enforce its Code of Professional Conduct?

5. Define business ethics.

6. It is said that good ethics is good business. Do you agree? Is there a trade-off between ethics and profit in business?

7. How do business ethics relate to organizational culture and climate?

8. How can an ethically trained accountant contribute to ethical conduct in a business entity?

9. If the board of directors is not vigilant enough to monitor an entity's ethical conduct, can an accountant be effective in helping the business stay ethical?

10. The assessment of the internal control system as an ethical monitoring system is a complex task. Who should be involved in performing this task?

11. Could federal sentencing guidelines result in good ethical conduct in business entities?

12. Who is an ethics officer? How can you make such officers effective in enforcing ethical conduct in a business entity?

13. List and discuss five ethics items/audit tasks that can be performed in an ethics audit.

14. Define individual ethics and list five ethical principles that relate to this definition.

15. How do ethical principles form levels of ethical cognition?

16. Describe Kohlberg's stage model of ethical cognition. Where in the model does an accountant who adheres to the AICPA's Code of Professional Conduct belong?

17. Is ethical reasoning alone sufficient for ethical behavior? If not, what other components are needed for ethical behavior?

18. List five ethical characters and discuss them as they relate to accounting or auditing. How can accountants be trained to have these characters?

19. Discuss the steps in case-based ethical training.

APPENDIX 9A
THE DIT INSTRUMENT

(One Dilemma, 12 Questions Only)
HEINZ AND THE DRUG

In Europe a woman was near death from a special kind of cancer. There was one drug that doctors thought might save her. It was a form of radium that a druggist in the same town had recently discovered. The drug was expensive to make, but the druggist was charging 10 times what the drug cost to make. He paid $200 for the radium and charged $2,000 for a small dose of the drug. The sick woman's husband, Heinz, went to everyone he knew to borrow money, but he could only get together about $1,000, which is half of what it cost. He told the druggist that his wife was dying and asked him to sell cheaper or let him pay later. But the druggist said, "No, I discovered the drug and I'm going to make money from it." So Heinz got desperate and began to think about breaking into the man's store to steal the drug for his wife. Should Heinz steal the drug?

Heinz and the Drug: ○ Should Steal   ○ Can't Decide   ○ Should not steal

Great / Much / Some / Little / No

○○○○○ 1. Whether a community's laws are going to be upheld.

○○○○○ 2. Isn't it only natural for a loving husband to care so much for his wife that he'd steal?

○○○○○ 3. Is Heinz willing to risk getting shot as a burglar or going to jail for the chance that stealing the drug might help?

○○○○○ 4. Whether Heinz is a professional wrestler, or has considerable influence with professional wrestlers.

○○○○○ 5. Whether Heinz is stealing for himself or doing this solely to help someone else.

○○○○○ 6. Whether the druggist's rights to his invention have to be respected.

○○○○○ 7. Whether the essence of living is more encompassing than the termination of dying, socially and individually.

Great	Much	Some	Little	No	
○	○	○	○	○	8. What values are going to be the basis for governing how people act towards each other.
○	○	○	○	○	9. Whether the druggist is going to be allowed to hide behind a worthless law which only protects the rich anyway.
○	○	○	○	○	10. Whether the law in this case is getting in the way of the most basic claim of any member of society.
○	○	○	○	○	11. Whether the druggist deserves to be robbed for being so greedy and cruel.
○	○	○	○	○	12. Would stealing in such a case bring more total good for the whole society or not.

	1	2	3	4	5	6	7	8	9	10	11	12
Most important item	○	○	○	○	○	○	○	○	○	○	○	○
Second most important item	○	○	○	○	○	○	○	○	○	○	○	○
Third most important item	○	○	○	○	○	○	○	○	○	○	○	○
Fourth most important item	○	○	○	○	○	○	○	○	○	○	○	○

Source: The Defining Issues Test, Center for the Study of Ethical Development at the University of Minnesota, 1979.

10

CASES ON FINANCIAL ACCOUNTING AND REPORTING

Objectives

This chapter provides an inventory of cases for use in various areas of financial accounting and reporting. For each case, the primary area of coverage is identified, although the case can be used in relation to other topics as well. The primary objective of this chapter is to provide the opportunity for discussion of various issues covered in the book by matching cases to the topic of interest. The cases are based on real world situations and require research of the authoritative literature. The cases allow one to experience many unique situations that accounting professionals must deal with when a solution is unclear. All amounts in the cases should be treated as material. The dates of 20X1, 20X2, and so on are used to represent current dates, but the most current accounting pronouncements should be applied to any case analysis.

List of Cases

Revenue and Expense Recognition

C10–1   Aztec Laboratories, Inc.
   (Recognition alternatives in accounting for a research and development contract)

C10–2   Bleaker Fruit Company
   (Accounting for contingencies)

C10–3   Caltron Computers, Inc.
   (Revenue recognition for a computer hardware company)

C10–4   Dover Books, Inc.
   (Revenue recognition from a membership program of a bookstore chain)

Revenue and Expense Recognition

C10–1	Aztec Laboratories, Inc.

Recognition Alternatives in Accounting for a Research and Development Contract

Aztec Laboratories, Inc. is a biotechnology company organized to develop and commercialize innovative pharmaceutical products. The company has been successful in developing a number of therapies to treat neurodegenerative diseases, and several Aztec scientists are recognized specialists for their work in this field.

In March 20X1, Tenneyson Pharmaceuticals, Inc. approached Aztec to research a therapy for Alzheimer's Disease. After many months discussing the project, the companies signed a collaborative research and development contract. Significant points relating to the contract are as follows:

- Aztec Laboratories will conduct the research to develop a therapy for Alzheimer's Disease.
- If the research is successful and a therapy is developed, Tenneyson Pharmaceuticals will obtain worldwide marketing rights to the therapy. Aztec will maintain all manufacturing rights to the therapy and will receive royalties on units sold.
- A project team will be responsible for directing the research. The team will be composed of three Aztec employees and two Tenneyson employees. The team will submit quarterly written research progress reports to Tenneyson and monitor the project operating budget.

- Tenneyson will make equal quarterly payments to Aztec totaling $27 million over six years. Payments are not tied to costs incurred by Aztec, and if Aztec spends less than budgeted amounts, Tenneyson is still obligated to pay the $27 million.
- Timing and continuation of payments are dependent upon Aztec achieving eight specified technical benchmarks, which are outlined in the contract. If Aztec fails to meet a benchmark, it has an additional six months' time to meet the technical specifications. Funding will continue by Tenneyson during this six-month period. If Aztec still has not met the benchmark, it will have a second six-month period without Tenneyson funding to rectify the problem. If, after the second six-month period, Aztec is still not in compliance with the technical benchmark, the contract becomes voided.
- If the contract becomes voided, Aztec is not obligated to refund any of the payments received to date, and Tenneyson is not obligated to pay the unpaid balance of the $27 million contract. Aztec's obligation under the contract is to perform on a best efforts basis in researching the therapy for Alzheimer's Disease.

The nature of this contract is different from other research contracts entered into by Aztec. Julia Gartside, Aztec's vice president of research and development, views this contract as Tenneyson's prepayment for future worldwide marketing rights to any Alzheimer's Disease therapy developed by Aztec. She indicates that Tenneyson negotiated for payments to be made on a quarterly basis in order for it to monitor the research progress while reducing its overall financial risk. Gartside further notes that Aztec's management considers the $27 million contract amount to be what Tenneyson was willing to pay for the marketing rights rather than being associated with or related to actual costs incurred. Gartside states that total development costs are anticipated to exceed Tenneyson's $27 million of funding.

Required
Discuss the alternative methods Aztec Laboratories could use to account for the contract with Tenneyson Pharmaceutical. Include in your discussion the pros and cons of each alternative considered and your recommendation as to how Aztec should account for the contract.

C10–2	BLEAKER FRUIT COMPANY

Accounting for Contingencies

Bleaker Fruit Company is a privately held company that distributes fresh fruits and vegetables to supermarket chains, independently owned food markets, and restaurants. In 20X1 Lawson Baylor, an employee and shareholder, retired from Bleaker and his 15 percent ownership interest was redeemed for cash and notes. Per the terms of the redemption agreement, Bleaker paid cash of $600,000 to Baylor at the time of redemption and issued an installment note for $600,000. Quarterly payments of $30,000 would be made on the note, with interest based on *The Wall Street Journal* (*WSJ*) prime lending rate. In addition, if Bleaker's 20X1 or 20X2 earnings, exclusive of shareholders' salaries and income taxes, exceeded $1,000,000, Bleaker would be required to increase the total redemption price of Baylor's stock to $1,500,000. The additional $300,000 would be payable in quarterly installments of $25,000 plus accrued interest at the *WSJ* prime lending rate. The first quarterly payment would be due on March 31, 20X3, and interest would begin accruing as of January 1, 20X3. The redemption agreement specified that earnings, exclusive of shareholders' salaries and income taxes, be determined in accordance with generally accepted accounting principles.

Bleaker reported 20X1 earnings, exclusive of shareholders' salaries and income taxes, of $475,000. Since Bleaker did not achieve the specified earnings in its agreement with Lawson Baylor, no adjustment was made in 20X1 for the stock redemption agreement with Baylor. Bleaker reported 20X2 earnings, exclusive of shareholders' salaries and income taxes, of $950,000. The 20X2 earnings were reduced by a $250,000 accrued charge for a 20X3 agreement with Marcia Forbes.

Effective January 3, 20X3, Marcia Forbes's employment as a sales consultant with Bleaker was terminated because of her alleged inability to get along with customers. Also effective on January 3, 20X3, Marcia Forbes and Bleaker entered into an agreement to settle several counter claims and legal threats, including sexual harassment, by Marcia Forbes concerning her employment and termination. The agreement provides that Bleaker will pay Marcia Forbes or her estate $50,000 annually for the next five years. The first payment will be due on January 3, 20X4. The *WSJ* prime lending rate on January 3, 20X3, was 7.5 percent.

In 20X1 Bleaker sold a quantity of fruit to Healthway Supermarkets that Healthway alleged had been treated with a certain pesticide. Bleaker had purchased the fruit from Holly Farms, which agreed to accept return of the fruit if returned within three days. Bleaker immediately informed Healthway to return the fruit directly to Holly Farms within three days. Apparently, Healthway delayed in returning the fruit, and Holly Farms alleged that the fruit was returned in a damaged condition four days after the return period expired. Since Bleaker was liable to Holly Farms for the $320,000 cost of the fruit, it incurred a loss of $320,000 on the transaction in 20X1. Bleaker requested that Healthway reimburse it for the $320,000 because it had failed to return the fruit in a timely manner and returned it in a damaged condition. Healthway refused Bleaker's request and the matter was unresolved as of December 31, 20X1.

In 20X2 Bleaker threatened Healthway with legal action but was not able to resolve the matter. Finally, in late 20X2 Bleaker filed suit against Healthway to recover damages caused by Healthway's delay and negligence in returning the fruit. In early February 20X3, prior to the issuance of the accountants' report for the year ending December 31, 20X2, Healthway agreed to a settlement. The agreement specified that Healthway would reimburse Bleaker $160,000 within 60 days for 50 percent of the loss on the damaged fruit and each party would be responsible for its own legal costs.

Bleaker's 20X2 financial statements did not include the $160,000 settlement, but a note to the 20X2 financial statements did disclose the nature of the claim and that a settlement agreement was reached in February 20X3. Bleaker's accountants have not completed their examination of Bleaker's 20X2 financial statements.

Required
1. Discuss whether Bleaker has determined earnings for the year ending December 31, 20X2, in accordance with generally accepted accounting principles. Be specific in your response and identify all alternatives considered and accounting pronouncements that support your position.
2. Discuss other concerns, besides the financial statements being prepared in accordance with generally accepted accounting principles, the auditors have in dealing with Bleaker as a client.

| C10–3 | CALTRON COMPUTERS, INC. |

Revenue Recognition for a Computer Hardware Company

Caltron Computers, Inc. is a publicly held company with a total market capitalization in excess of $450 million. Caltron manufactures minicomputer systems that are designed to achieve the power of a mainframe at a fraction of the cost. The minicomputers are Unix-based and use multiple Intel Pentium chips.

Caltron generally recognizes revenue when minicomputers are shipped. During the fourth quarter of 20X1, Caltron recognized revenue from four transactions that were questioned by its auditors, Peale, Gower & Quill. The auditors are concerned not only about the impact that these transactions will have on 20X1 reported earnings but the impact on Caltron's proposed secondary public stock offering in early February 20X2.

The first transaction involved the recognition of $400,000 of revenue on two systems shipped to Elegant Housing, Inc. on a trial basis for six months. Elegant paid Caltron $20,000 at the time of shipment, November 15, 20X1, which would be applied to the purchase price if Elegant accepts the systems or forfeited if Elegant returns the systems. Preliminary reports from Elegant are that they are quite satisfied with the systems.

The second transaction involved the recognition of $250,000 of revenue on a system not shipped as of December 31, 20X1, under a bill and hold arrangement with Alation Electronics. Alation paid $175,000 to Caltron on December 15, 20X1, and requested Caltron to hold the system for shipment until the first quarter of 20X2. Once Alation notified Caltron where to ship the system, it would pay the $75,000 balance due in 20X2.

The third transaction also involved a bill and hold arrangement with BTO Computer Leasing, a lessor of computer equipment. On November 1, 20X1, BTO ordered five systems from Caltron and paid $190,000 down, on the condition that Caltron would hold the systems at its warehouse and assist BTO in finding lessees for the systems. Caltron recognized $950,000 of revenue in 20X1 on the BTO transaction. As of December 31, 20X1, Caltron identified an end user to lease one of the systems from BTO. The lease terms were still being negotiated between BTO and the end user.

The last transaction involved the fourth quarter 20X1 recognition of $220,000 of revenue and a related $110,000 allowance for sales returns for a system shipped to Harvey Industries on a trial basis for four months. The system was shipped to Harvey on November 27, 20X1, and Harvey paid 50 percent of the purchase price at that time. If Harvey accepts the system, the balance would be due March 27, 20X2. If Harvey returns the system, its down payment of $110,000 less any shipping costs would be returned. Caltron had previously entered into two similar transactions with Harvey. On one occasion Harvey purchased the system, and the other time Harvey returned the system. Based on these previous results, Caltron recorded the $110,000 allowance for sales returns.

Required
1. In general, evaluate Caltron's revenue recognition policy and the quality of Caltron's earnings.
2. Discuss how and why Peale, Gower & Quill should recommend that Caltron account for and report the four transactions in the fourth quarter of 20X1. Include in your discussion specific reference to bill and hold arrangements and accounting pronouncements that you used to formulate the basis of your recommendation.

| C10–4 | DOVER BOOKS, INC. |

Revenue Recognition from a Membership Program of a Bookstore Chain

Dover Books, Inc. is a publicly held chain of 40 bookstores located throughout Florida, Georgia, and South Carolina. Dover specializes in children's books and carries a complete line of best-selling titles. Dover has expanded at the rate of five new stores during each of the past three years and is planning on opening twelve new stores in the coming year. Gross revenues during the past year were approximately $60 million, and net earnings were less than $1 million.

Dover is concerned about its ability to finance the opening of future retail outlets and has pursued a secondary public offering with its investment banker. The investment banker is of the opinion that Dover will need to report higher earnings in order to receive a favorable stock market price from the public offering.

To supplement revenues and increase unit sales, Dover is planning to institute a chainwide membership program. The nonrefundable membership fee will cost $15 annually and entitle members to a 10 percent discount off the retail price of any book purchases. The membership also will entitle members to additional special discounts on selected titles. Each member will receive a membership identification card with an identification number and expiration date embossed on it.

Based on a research study conducted by Dover's marketing department, 80,000 to 100,000 memberships are projected to be sold within the next 12 months. The incremental costs of promoting the memberships will be insignificant. Dover is planning on recognizing the membership fees as revenue when received. Dover's position is that since the fee is nonrefundable, it is earned on receipt.

Required

1. Discuss the alternatives available to Dover Books, Inc. for recognizing revenue from membership fees.
2. What is your recommendation to Dover Books, Inc. for recognizing revenue from membership fees? Include a discussion of your reasons and cite any accounting pronouncements that support your recommendation.

C10–5	JASPER MANUFACTURING COMPANY

Recognition of a Gain on the Sale of Real Estate with Seller-Provided Financing

Jasper Manufacturing Company is a manufacturer of lighting fixtures and related electrical products. Jasper has twelve manufacturing facilities located throughout the country. During the past two years, Jasper has incurred material operating losses and has experienced significant cash flow problems. In an effort to return to profitability and improve cash flow, Jasper has decided to consolidate some manufacturing operations. This decision will leave Jasper with real estate no longer needed in its operations. Jasper has decided to sell one parcel of real estate at a significant gain in order to boost 20X1 earnings immediately and help alleviate the cash flow problems.

After lengthy negotiations, Jasper has reached an agreement with Tuttle Company, Inc. for the sale of the real estate. The terms of the agreement are as follows:

- The sale price is to be $4,500,000.
- A down payment of $300,000 is to be paid by Tuttle to Jasper.
- A payment of $300,000 is to be made by Tuttle to City National Bank to pay in full Jasper's existing mortgage on the property.
- A mortgage note of $3,900,000 is to be issued by Tuttle, payable to Jasper. Tuttle is required to make only interest payments during the first 6 years at 14 percent and principal and interest payments in years 7 through 14.

Jasper had originally hoped to be able to generate more immediate cash from the sale, but had unexpected difficulty in finding a qualified buyer. Jasper reached the agreement with Tuttle, even though Tuttle had a history of operating losses and was unable to obtain conventional financing with acceptable terms. Thus, Jasper essentially ended up financing Tuttle in order to consummate the sale. The carrying value of the real estate in Jasper's accounts was $1,100,000.

Required

1. Discuss whether Jasper should recognize a gain of $3,400,000 in 20X1 on the sale of the real estate.
2. Discuss how Jasper should account for the transaction in years subsequent to 20X1.

| C10–6 | OCM TECHNOLOGIES, INC. |

Accounting and Reporting a Corporate Restructuring

OCM Technologies, Inc. designs networking technologies and products such as switches, interface cards, and modems. At the end of the third quarter of 20X1, OCM's management adopted a plan to restructure its modem products division. The plan provided for changes in how it designs, manufactures, and distributes those products. It will include the termination of 500 employees over the next 15 months, the retraining of the employees, and the closing of a leased manufacturing facility.

The modem products division reported an unaudited pretax loss of $7.9 million for the first three quarters of 20X1 and an unaudited pretax loss of $3.4 million for the fourth quarter of 20X1. OCM estimates that the modem products division will report a pretax loss of $8.0 million for 20X2. Included in the 20X2 estimated operating results is a charge of $9.6 million for operating salaries to be paid to employees that will be terminated.

As of December 31, 20X1, OCM notified employee groups that will be part of the termination, and to date 300 employees have voluntarily accepted a special termination benefit for past services of $5,000 each to be paid upon employment severance in 20X2. The other 200 employees to be terminated, whether voluntary or not, also will receive a termination benefit of $5,000 each in 20X2. OCM has not accrued any termination benefits as of December 31, 20X1, or included them in the estimated 20X2 pretax loss of $8.0 million. OCM's effective tax rate for 20X1 and 20X2 is 30 percent.

At the end of 20X2, OCM will close one of its modem products division's manufacturing facilities. The facility to be closed is under an operating lease that requires OCM to pay a $1 million lease cancellation penalty in January 20X3. Since OCM will have no future use for this facility, OCM plans to pay the penalty.

OCM has engaged a management consulting group for 20X2 to work on the implementation of new manufacturing technologies for modem products. The estimated costs for these services are $400,000. This includes $100,000 for retraining of employees in the modem products division. Costs for the management consulting group, as well as the lease cancellation penalty, have not been included in the unaudited pretax loss for 20X1 or for the estimated pretax loss for 20X2.

Due to the restructuring of the modem products division, OCM will dispose of certain manufacturing equipment in 20X2. As of December 31, 20X1, the equipment has a carrying value of $300,000 and an estimated fair value of $200,000 at the time of disposal. OCM has not included an impairment loss in any of the data for 20X1 or 20X2.

OCM's management is concerned about reporting the restructuring of the modem products division in the 20X1 and 20X2 financial statements. After much discussion, management concluded that it would be best for OCM to report all charges related to the restructuring in the 20X1 financial statements. One opinion of an OCM officer was that the restructuring could be reported as discontinued operations in 20X1.

Required
1. In general terms, how would companies prefer to account for and report a restructuring similar to that of OCM's?
2. Discuss whether OCM could report the restructuring as discontinued operations in 20X1 and/or 20X2. Include in your discussion what, if any, differences there are between reporting a restructuring and discontinued operations.
3. How would you recommend that OCM account for and report the restructuring plan in its 20X1 and 20X2 financial statements? Include in your response the basis for your recommendation and make sure that you specifically address all the data in the case.

C10–7	SMART SECURITY SYSTEMS, INC.

Recognition of a Gain on the Sale of Customer Contracts with a Repurchase Option

Smart Security Systems, Inc. (Smart) is a closely held company that monitors, through telephone lines, residential and commercial security systems. Smart has been in operation for five years, and revenues have been increasing at a compound annual rate of 50 percent. Smart's revenues are derived from monthly security monitoring fees, systems servicing fees, and sales of security equipment. Smart's revenue and customer-base growth has been generated through its own sales efforts and financed by operating cash flows, bank loans, shareholder loans, and shareholder equity contributions.

On June 1, 20X1, Smart purchased accounts from Safeco Monitoring, Inc. for $230,000. The accounts will provide Smart with recurring monthly security monitoring fees of $19,000 and any fees from servicing the systems. Smart believed that this was an excellent opportunity to increase its customer base and revenues at a very reasonable cost. Typically, a transaction of this nature would cost 20 times monthly monitoring fees. To finance the purchase of the Safeco accounts and to obtain some needed working capital, Smart approached Bendix Finance Company. Bendix has provided funds for some of Smart's competitors by arranging for the purchase of customer accounts.

On June 30, 20X1, Bendix agreed to purchase some of Smart's security monitoring accounts for $610,000. The accounts provide Smart with monthly security monitoring fees of $27,000. Smart will collect the monthly fees and at month-end remit the fees to Bendix. In addition, the agreement provides that Smart will monitor and operate the security systems for the accounts that Bendix purchased. For this service Bendix will pay Smart a monthly fee equivalent to 25 percent of the recurring monitoring fees for a period of three years. At the end of this period, Smart can repurchase the accounts from Bendix for $160,000. Bendix has structured the agreement based on an assumed interest rate of 12 percent.

All responsibility to customers will be assumed by Smart. The accounts sold to Bendix included all the Safeco accounts acquired on June 1, 20X1, and some accounts generated through Smart's own sales efforts. If one of the accounts sold to Bendix terminates Smart's monitoring services, Smart will replace that account with an account of equivalent value.

Smart's controller, Florence Cedrone, proposes that in 20X1 Smart recognize a gain of $380,000 on the sale of accounts to Bendix. Florence Cedrone has based the gain on the difference between the $610,000 selling price of accounts to Bendix and the $230,000 purchase price of accounts from Safeco. According to Ms. Cedrone, the accounts sold to Bendix that were generated by Smart's own sales efforts had a zero basis.

Required
Discuss how Smart should account for the transaction with Bendix in 20X1 and subsequent years. Indicate any alternatives considered and the basis for your conclusion.

Accounting Policy Issues and Overview Cases

C10–8	AMERICAN PHYSICAL AND SOCIAL PROGRAMS FOR CHILDREN, INC.

Cash or Accrual Basis of Accounting, Accounting Year-End, and Miscellaneous Policy Issues

Harvey Acker and Jane Clemens, child psychologists, have started and are operating American Physical and Social Programs for Children, Inc., a sports-oriented school year and summer camp program for children. The program was started one year ago and has four operating locations. With assistance from their book-keeper, Harvey and Jane have prepared a balance sheet as of June 30, 20X2, and an income statement for the year then ended, on a modified cash basis (Exhibits 1 and 2).

Harvey and Jane have decided to seek the advice of an accountant and revealed the following about their operations:

- Harvey and Jane are the sole shareholders, and each paid $20,000 for no par common stock of American. On July 31, 20X1, the corporation borrowed $100,000 at 12 percent from a local bank. Equal principal payments plus interest are due monthly on the bank loan over the next five years, beginning August 31, 20X1. The corporation executed an agreement, effective July 1, 20X1, through which it purchased the operating assets of Fun Time Programs, Inc., an organization that ran similar programs for many years. The agreement provided for payment of $30,000 for furniture and fixtures and $50,000 for sports equipment. These values were determined by an outside independent appraiser and agreed to by all parties. The agreement further provided for an additional payment of $80,000 due on July 1, 20X3, and that as consideration for such payment, Fun Time Programs, Inc. and/or its share-holders would not compete in a similar business for five years within a distance of 200 miles of any American operating location. American then negotiated new leases, purchased additional fixed assets, and expanded operations.
- The organization costs to incorporate were $15,120 and were paid primarily for legal services.
- The school-year programs run from mid-September to mid-June for 10-week periods and most customers prepay for each 10-week period. As of June 30, 20X2, customers owed $28,800, of which a $4,000 allowance would be adequate to cover uncollected accounts.
- The summer camp program runs from the last week of June through the last week of August. Each camper pays in advance. Camp deposits started coming in about the beginning of March, and as of June 30, 20X2, camp receipts collected in advance but not earned totaled $224,200. All operating facilities are leased. Summer camp programs are operated on local college campuses. The summer rents are 20 percent of the gross camp receipts and become due and payable to the lessor the month following the month that the facilities are actually used. Camp revenues collected and earned the last several days of June 20X2 totaled $85,400.
- Depreciation for financial reporting and income taxes are the same. The combined federal and state income tax rate is 30 percent and the company has made no estimated tax payments as of year-end.
- Program supplies on hand as of June 30, 20X2, total $17,700.
- The only significant unpaid liabilities as of June 30, 20X2, are salaries of $16,000, employee payroll taxes of $3,500, and utilities of $2,000.
- Advertising costs paid during the year were incurred to gain market recognition, and normal advertising costs are expected to be approximately $30,000 per annum.
- American is presently being sued for gross negligence due to injuries sustained by a child while participating in a gymnastics program. It is the opinion of American's legal counsel that the case can be settled out of court at a cost of anywhere from $10,000 to $50,000 to the company. Harvey and

Jane are worried about the unfavorable publicity that the suit could bring and would like to settle the matter as quickly as possible.

- Harvey and Jane believe that they made a fantastic deal with Fun Time Programs, Inc. It is their opinion that Fun Time mismanaged their business affairs and then sold out to them for virtually nothing. They have been able to use basically the same programs and expand on them, enabling the company to be profitable immediately. They anticipate that the business will be very profitable for many years, and that the major moneymaker is summer camps.

Harvey and Jane inform the accountant that they need financial statements prepared for the bank and corporate income tax returns filed.

Required
1. Discuss the company's selection of June 30 as its fiscal year-end and the apparent implications of such a decision.
2. In order to prepare financial statements, many accounting policy decisions must be made. List the areas in which accounting policy decisions must be made, your choice of each accounting policy, and your reasons for selecting such.

Exhibit C10–8:1

AMERICAN PHYSICAL AND SOCIAL PROGRAMS FOR CHILDREN, INC.
Balance Sheet
June 30, 20X2

Assets

Current assets		
Cash		$ 28,292
Money market funds		288,177
Total current assets		316,469
Fixed assets		
Furniture and fixtures	$33,509	
Sports equipment	65,047	98,556
Less: Accumulated depreciation		9,856
Total fixed assets		88,700
Other assets		
Deposits		8,500
Total assets		$413,669

Liabilities and Stockholders' Equity

Current liabilities	
Notes payable	$ 20,000
Payroll taxes withheld	14,196
Total current liabilities	34,196
Long-term liabilities	
Notes payable	61,663
Stockholders' equity	
Common stock, no par	40,000
Retained earnings	277,810
Total stockholders' equity	317,810
Total liabilities and stockholders' equity	$413,669

Exhibit C10–8:2

AMERICAN PHYSICAL AND SOCIAL PROGRAMS FOR CHILDREN, INC.
Statement of Cash Receipts and Disbursements
For the Year Ended June 30, 20X2

Receipts	
Program fees	$2,052,620
Interest	11,395
	2,064,015
Disbursements	
Salaries	1,073,142
Rent	342,026
Program supplies	95,897
Payroll taxes	89,387
Interest	10,918
Advertising	40,958
Organization costs	15,120
Utilities	20,575
Insurance	73,405
Miscellaneous	14,921
	1,776,349
Excess receipts over disbursements	287,666
Depreciation	9,856
Net income	$ 277,810

3. Based upon your recommendations in question 2, prepare a balance sheet as of June 30, 20X2, and an income statement for the year then ended.
4. If you had been retained as the accountant prior to the time that American incorporated, what would you have advised American to do differently and why?

C10–9	FINAL CARE, INC.

Accounting for an Exchange Transaction, Revenue Recognition, and Payment to a Former Shareholder

Final Care, Inc. is a privately held company in the "after-life" industry. It sells cemetery lots, provides cemetery and funeral services, and constructs and sells crypts. Final Care's shareholders are extremely concerned about increasing reported earnings in anticipation of a future initial public stock offering. Final Care's new auditors, King, Sproule & Hunt, in a cursory review of the current year financial statements, have expressed concern over some of the accounting policies.

The first policy that King, Sproule & Hunt questioned involves revenue recognition. Final Care recognizes revenue on the sale of crypts when the buyer signs a purchase contract and makes a 20 percent down payment. Because at that time construction on the crypts has not yet started, Final Care accrues the estimated costs of construction to achieve a matching of costs with revenues. The costs to construct crypts can be reasonably estimated by Final Care. Selling expenses average approximately 40 percent of the sales price of crypts.

The time from the signing of the purchase contract to the completion and installation of the crypt is usually one year. Final Care is obligated to construct the crypt at the location specified in the contract. If the use of the crypt is required prior to completion of construction, Final Care will provide temporary interment in another crypt until completion of the contracted crypt.

The second policy that the auditors questioned concerns the accounting for a tract of land. In addition to owning cemetery land, Final Care owns several tracts of unimproved land that it either converts to cemetery land or sells. In the current year, Final Care exchanged a tract of unimproved land for "barter credits" that represent future advertising services from Bucknell Associates. The land has a carrying value of $800,000 and an appraised value of $2,200,000. The barter credits have a face value of $2,600,000, and assuming that the barter credits are all used as expected in the future, a discounted present value estimated to be $1,700,000. If for any reason Bucknell Associates sells the land prior to Final Care using all the credits, Final Care can exchange with Bucknell the lesser of 25 percent of the original $2,600,000 in credits or the balance of unused credits for cash. Any remaining credits can still be exchanged for future advertising services.

Final Care initially recognized a gain on the exchange of land of $1,400,000 (appraised value of land $2,200,000 less carrying value of land $800,000). However, at the time of its own internal review, Final Care reconsidered the accounting for the transaction and changed the reported amount of the gain to $900,000 (discounted present value of barter credits $1,700,000 less carrying value of land $800,000).

The last policy that concerned King, Sproule & Hunt involves the deferral of certain payments to a former shareholder/employee. In the current year a dispute arose between Howard Washington, a 1 percent shareholder, and Karl Selest, the largest shareholder and chief executive officer of Final Care, over the management of the company. Each party threatened the other with litigation. Finally, the dispute was settled by Final Care paying $500,000 to Howard Washington. Washington then resigned from the company and sold his shares to the remaining shareholders. The settlement agreement specified that the payment was for lost income. Final Care deferred the $500,000 payment to Washington and is amortizing it over five years. Final Care views the payment as providing a future economic benefit because it purchased future peace for the company. Final Care believes that this is especially relevant with an initial public offering being anticipated.

Required
1. Discuss the accounting policies that Final Care selected and any alternatives that they should consider.
2. Discuss the accounting policies that King, Sproule & Hunt should recommend and the basis for their recommendation.

C10–10	FRANTEK, INC.

Revenue Recognition, Inventory Valuation, and Liability Recognition Issues

Frantek, Inc. is a manufacturer of microcomputer parts and components. At the beginning of its fiscal year, Frantek entered into an agreement with Conte Technologies to manufacture microcomputer accessory boards according to Conte's specifications. The agreement provided that within the next 12 months Frantek was to deliver a minimum of 100,000 boards to Conte at a stipulated price per board. If Frantek failed to perform per the terms of the agreement, financial penalties were provided. In addition, the agreement required that Conte make royalty payments to Frantek on the basis of a predetermined schedule of units shipped. The royalty payments actually constitute a deferral of the selling price. The agreement stipulated that in no case would the royalty payments be less than $2 million. To assist Frantek with its working capital needs during the development stage of the boards, Conte loaned Frantek $6 million, payable in 36 months with accrued interest.

Frantek encountered some technical difficulties in developing the boards according to Conte's satisfaction and was not able to meet the agreed-on timetable for the shipment of boards. The problem was that boards equipped with a certain manufacturer's chip did not meet Conte's operating standards. Frantek was able to solve the problem by having a third-party contractor replace the chip with a different manufacturer's chip that met Conte's standards. The contractor charged Frantek $7 per board to replace the chip.

As of Frantek's current year-end, Frantek had shipped only 38,000 boards and had 41,000 boards, with the unsatisfactory chip, in its year-end inventory. No royalty payments had been paid by Conte to Frantek. Conte recognized that Frantek had made a good faith effort to perform under the terms of the agreement and agreed to amend the agreement, effective as of Frantek's current year-end, as follows:

1. Conte would waive its rights to impose any financial penalties under the agreement.
2. Frantek would cease manufacturing the accessory boards per the agreement and not fulfill the 100,000 minimum.
3. Conte would purchase the 41,000 accessory boards in Frantek's inventory at 110 percent of Frantek's cost.
4. Any Conte purchases of boards would be paid for by reducing the $6 million loan from Conte to Frantek.
5. Conte has the right to order Frantek to replace the unsatisfactory chip in the remaining 41,000 boards. The cost of replacement is to be paid by Frantek. Any boards not ordered for chip replacement will be shipped to Conte at some specified future date.
6. Conte will pay Frantek the minimum royalty amount of $2 million specified in the original agreement. Conte will not be liable for any additional royalties.

Concurrent with the signing of the amended agreement, Conte ordered 20,000 of the remaining accessory boards held in Frantek's inventory to have the chip replaced.

Required
For Frantek's current year-end as well as subsequent year-ends, discuss the accounting issues raised by the amendment to the agreement between Frantek and Conte. Your discussion, at a minimum, should include a recommendation as to how Frantek should resolve issues relating to revenue recognition, inventory valuation, and liability recognition and classification.

C10–11	INFOMIX TECHNOLOGY, INC.

Accounting and Reporting for Related Party Transactions

Infomix Technology, Inc. is a closely held corporation that distributes computer graphics components and develops database management software. Sondra Tate owns 75 percent of Infomix and the remaining 25 percent is owned by an unrelated management group of seven individuals. Sondra Tate also owns 90 percent of TSK Consulting, a software consulting company, and 100 percent of Trask Enterprise, Inc., a wholesaler of microcomputer parts and supplies. Infomix is required to have separately prepared audited financial statements for its bank in accordance with the terms of existing debt covenants. The debt is secured by Infomix's assets and not guaranteed by shareholders.

In preparation for its year-end audit, Infomix identified for its auditors the following related party transactions and its proposed accounting for them:

1. During the year, Clay Software initiated a copyright infringement suit against Infomix. Although Infomix denied the charges, Sondra Tate, in her desire to avoid any adverse publicity for the company and to protect her investment, personally interceded and reached an out-of-court settlement with Clay Software for $200,000. Because the settlement was initiated by Sondra Tate and did not require the use of Infomix's assets, Infomix has disclosed the settlement by a footnote but did not include its affects in the financial statements.

2. TSK Consulting provides Infomix with computer, accounting, and management services for a fee of $18,000 per month. TSK and Infomix have a written agreement identifying the services and the monthly fee. All fees were paid on a timely basis. Infomix accounted for the fees according to the terms of the agreement.

3. Sondra Tate conveyed title to a parcel of land to Infomix for $100. At the time of conveyance, the land was appraised for $100,000, but the appraiser indicated in a written appraisal report that with certain easements and zoning variances the land would be appraised for $225,000. Infomix has commenced procedures to obtain the easements and zoning variances, and its real estate attorney indicated that they probably will be granted. Infomix reported the land at $225,000 in its balance sheet but is uncertain whether it should report a gain of $224,900 or $125,000.

4. Infomix had excess inventory of certain computer graphics components having a cost of $900,000. Due to technological changes, the net realizable value of these parts was $600,000. However, at year-end Trask Enterprise, Inc. purchased all the parts for $900,000 cash. Infomix recorded the sale at $900,000 and did not believe that any loss recognition on the transaction was appropriate.

5. Infomix had a $2.8 million note payable to Sondra Tate. The loan was originally granted to provide working capital and research funds for new products. Due to delays in product development and increased competition, Infomix has been experiencing cash flow problems and is now unable to meet debt principal payments to Sondra Tate. Consequently, Sondra Tate has decided to forgive $1.3 million of the debt and defer remaining principal payments. Infomix has recorded the forgiveness of the $1.3 million debt as an extraordinary item.

Required

Discuss Infomix's proposed accounting for the related party transactions. If you disagree with any of Infomix's accounting, identify alternatives considered, your recommendation, and the basis for your conclusion.

C10–12	WENDELL SYSTEMS, INC.

Deferring versus Expensing Costs in the First Year of Operations

Wendell Systems, Inc. was incorporated on February 2, 20X1. It was organized by 10 shareholders who contributed a total of $250,000 in exchange for common stock. Two of the shareholders, Marty Mahoney and Cecila Shriberg, will be actively involved in the business. Wendell Systems plans to distribute and install high-end home audio and video entertainment systems. Wendell anticipates obtaining future financing from a second placement of stock to venture capitalists in 20X2.

In anticipation of seeking financing from venture capitalists, Marty Mahoney and Cecila Shriberg are concerned about first-year operating results. Marty Mahoney states that the higher the reported earnings, the better their chances are of obtaining financing on favorable terms. Cecila Shriberg is not certain that she totally agrees with Marty. However, she indicates that some 20X1 expenditures could be capitalized instead of expensed to increase 20X1 earnings. Cecila thinks that the costs of organizing Wendell Systems and starting up its operations could either be capitalized or expensed. She indicates that if these costs are capitalized and subsequently amortized, Wendell would achieve certain tax benefits and 20X1 operating results would improve.

After investigating the issue further, Cecila informs Marty that for tax purposes Wendell Systems can elect to capitalize and amortize over a period of 60 months or more start-up expenditures and organizational expenditures. She states that these provisions are contained in Internal Revenue Code Sections 195 and 248, respectively. If Wendell Systems does not make these elections, then for tax purposes the expenditures are permanently capitalized. She also informs Marty that according to her understanding there is limited authoritative guidance on the financial accounting for organization costs and start-up costs. Thus, she concludes that Wendell Systems would be justified in following tax law and capitalizing both organizational and start-up expenditures and amortizing them over the minimum period of 60 months.

Marty Mahoney and Cecila Shriberg then compile the following list of 20X1 expenditures:

Newspaper and radio advertising prior to commencing operations	$ 60,000
Training of installation technicians	27,000
Legal fees for incorporation	6,000
Accounting fees for incorporation	2,000
Accounting fees for business and tax consulting	20,000
Promotion and commission fees paid for the sale of stock	15,000
Market research surveys prior to commencing operations	50,000
Fees paid to executive search firm to hire a marketing director	20,000
	$200,000

They plan on capitalizing these expenditures as organization costs and start-up costs and amortizing them over 60 months.

In addition, Cecila Shriberg notes that Wendell Systems incurred $100,000 for direct-response advertising costs in 20X1. These costs were incurred because of the results of the market research surveys prior to commencing operations. The costs relate to print advertisements in trade publications with an 800 number included. Cecila informs Marty that direct-response advertising costs can be capitalized. She recommends that Wendell Systems capitalize these costs and amortize them over 60 months to be consistent with the amortization of the organizational and start-up costs. Marty agrees that this sounds like a reasonable plan.

Required
1. What are organization and start-up costs? Give examples of each.
2. In the absence of authoritative sources of accounting guidance, is it appropriate to base financial accounting on federal tax law?
3. Is Wendell Systems' proposed accounting treatment of the organizational and start-up expenditures and direct-response advertising costs in accordance with generally accepted accounting principles? Be specific in your response and identify how you are treating all the expenditures in the case. Cite any literature that you base your decision on.
4. Discuss whether Wendell Systems' proposed accounting and reporting for organizational and start-up expenditures and direct-response advertising costs will likely influence the decision of future investors.

C10–13	**WHITESTONE BANK CORPORATION**	

Ability of a Bank to Continue as a Going Concern

Whitestone Bank Corporation, a member of the Federal Deposit Insurance Corporation (FDIC), reported total deposits of approximately $20 million at year-end December 31, 20X2. As a federally insured institution, Whitestone is subject to regulation by the FDIC which requires minimum regulatory capital maintenance of 6.0 percent of adjusted assets to be maintained. At December 31, 20X2, Whitestone's regulatory capital was 4.5 percent. Whitestone's violation of an applicable FDIC law, regulation, rule or order of, or condition could result in its termination as an FDIC insured institution, the assessment of certain monetary penalties, the entry of a capital directive against the bank, or other enforcement actions.

In 20X2 Whitestone incurred a net loss of $800,000 after a realized tax benefit of $50,000. The 20X2 loss included a $650,000 charge for settlement of litigation. A draft note to Whitestone's 20X2 financial statements concerning the litigation read as follows:

> In 20X1 a borrower of the bank filed suits against the bank and its former president. The suit against the bank included intentional and negligent misrepresentation in connection with loan financing commitments and breach of contract. During 20X2, a verdict of $650,000 was returned against the bank for negligent misrepresentation and breach of contract.
>
> The suit against the former president of the bank included intentional and negligent misrepresentation. An attachment has been sought against the former president in the amount of $2 million. The former president has sought entitlement to indemnification including legal costs, pursuant to the bank's by-laws, and the bank has agreed to indemnify the former president for any actions to which he is entitled to indemnification under the bank's by-laws. Since additional discovery remains to be taken, it is not possible for the bank to presently determine the outcome of the litigation or the range of any potential loss which might result from these actions, and no provision for any liability that may result has been made in the accompanying financial statements. The bank intends to vigorously defend these actions.

When Whitestone's current president, Paul Mallory, was discussing 20X2 operations with Sandra Rubinsky, managing partner of the accounting firm Holt, Rubinsky, Gerson & Swanson, P.C., Sandra raised the question about Whitestone's ability to continue as a going concern. She pointed out that 20X2 was the second consecutive year that a loss was incurred, and 20X2 resulted in approximately $450,000 net cash being used in operations. Sandra acknowledged that management forecasted improved operating results for 20X3, but such results would not bring the bank into compliance with minimum regulatory capital requirements. Sandra also reminded Paul Mallory that Whitestone had already received the tax benefit of all loss carrybacks, and as of December 31, 20X2, Whitestone would only receive additional tax benefits by being able to use the net operating loss carryforwards of approximately $600,000.

Paul Mallory agreed that while 20X3 operating performance would not likely bring Whitestone into compliance with minimum regulatory capital requirements, the bank should be able to sustain operations on a day-to-day basis throughout 20X3. He also noted that on January 18, 20X3, Whitestone's board of directors approved a plan to issue up to 200,000 shares of its $1 par value common stock at a public offering price of $8 per share, subject to the approval of various regulatory agencies.

Sandra Rubinsky indicated that she was aware of the board's action. However, she cautioned Paul not to forget that the offering price was determined by the board without regard to the bank's assets, earnings, book value per share, or other generally accepted criteria of value.

Required

1. Discuss the structure of the going concern task in an audit setting. Also, identify the knowledge base and the decision aids that can be used to perform this task.
2. Discuss the specific considerations that Holt, Rubinsky, Gerson & Swanson, P.C. should take into account when deciding if Whitestone bank's 20X2 report should be modified based on a going concern qualification.
3. Discuss how you would report on Whitestone's 20X2 financial statements.

Current Assets

C10–14	LUTHER STORES, INC.

Valuation and Reporting for an Investment in Equity Securities

Luther Stores, Inc., a publicly held corporation, holds as of December 31, 20X2, an investment of 200,000 shares of Willowby Manufacturing Company. Willowby shares are traded on the American Stock Exchange and closed at $30 per share on December 31, 20X2.

Luther Stores, Inc. began acquiring Willowby shares in January 20X1 and as of May 31, 20X1, had acquired 300,000 shares (approximately 10 percent of the outstanding shares) at a weighted-average cost of $48 per share. During 20X1, Willowby stock traded from a low of $34 to a high of $52 per share. On June 15, 20X1, Luther signed a letter of intent to acquire Willowby for $56 per share, subject to due diligence. After completion of the due diligence, Luther reduced its offer to $52 per share. Willowby's board of directors rejected Luther's offer and in turn made a self-tender offer to acquire 1,000,000 shares of its outstanding stock for $54 per share. The self-tender offer was on a prorated basis and was completed for the 1,000,000 shares in November 20X1. Luther participated in the offer and sold 100,000 shares of Willowby back to the company. As of December 31, 20X1, Willowby stock was trading at $36 per share.

Luther incurred significant costs in its takeover attempt of Willowby, which were recorded in the investment account, bringing the average cost per share to $62 for 300,000 shares. When Luther sold the 100,000 shares back to Willowby, it recorded an $800,000 [100,000 shares x ($62–54)] charge against earnings. Luther accounted for the remaining 200,000 shares of Willowby as available-for-sale securities and recorded an unrealized loss of $5,200,000 [200,000 shares × ($62–36)].

During 20X2, Willowby stock traded from a low of $28.50 to a high of $49.25 per share. Willowby's net earnings increased from approximately $1.90 per share in 20X1 to $2.80 per share in 20X2. Luther does not believe the market price of Willowby's stock reflects the improving operating results. The price to earnings ratio decreased from approximately 19.0 at the end of 20X1 to 11.0 at the end of 20X2. When Luther conducted its due diligence process in 20X1, an independent appraiser reported the fair value of Willowby's land and buildings to be $15.0 million in excess of the recorded book value. When this $15.0 million excess over book value is combined with Willowby's net book value at December 31, 20X2, the net book value becomes approximately $37 per share.

Required

1. Discuss whether you agree with Luther Stores, Inc.'s accounting for its investment in Willowby Manufacturing Company in 20X1.
2. Discuss whether as of December 31, 20X2, Luther should be concerned that the decline in value of the Willowby stock is other than temporary.
3. How should Luther account for its investment in Willowby in 20X2?
4. Discuss, with respect to equity securities, what the term *gains trading* means, and whether it can occur within the framework of generally accepted accounting principles.

C10–15	MORGANTOWN SAVINGS BANK

Accounting for a Short-Term, Fixed-Income Mutual Fund Portfolio

Morgantown Savings Bank is a Federal Deposit Insurance Corporation insured savings bank. Morgantown is engaged primarily in the business of attracting personal and institutional deposits from the general public, originating residential and commercial mortgages, making personal and commercial loans, and investing in debt and equity securities.

From 20X1 through 20X3, when interest rates were declining, Morgantown sold in excess of $150 million of its fixed-rate mortgages. The sales were undertaken to realize a profit on the appreciation of the fixed-rate mortgages and to better match the bank's assets and liabilities. Morgantown's management was concerned that the declining interest-rate cycle would eventually turn around, and that if it did not sell some of its fixed-rate mortgages, it would have a significant mismatch of assets and liabilities. Therefore, during this period of declining interest rates, the bank implemented a strategy to sell long-term fixed-rate assets.

Beginning in early 20X3, the bank decided to build a short-term, high-quality, fixed-income investment portfolio. Some of the proceeds from the sale of the fixed-rate mortgages became part of this portfolio and were reinvested into short-term, fixed-income mutual funds. Given the size of the investment portfolio, the lack of in-house staff with investment management experience and expertise, and the difficulty in hiring an independent investment manager, the bank decided to use mutual funds. Morgantown constructed a diversified short-term portfolio from funds offered by Dreyfus, Fidelity, Scudder, and Vanguard. From these four investment management companies, the bank invested in eight funds in 20X3. The largest investment in any fund was $9.2 million and the smallest was $3.5 million. The total cost of the portfolio was $54.0 million. Morgantown does not consider this a trading portfolio, and to date none of the funds have been sold. As of December 31, 20X4, the market value of the eight funds is $49.2 million. The underlying securities held by the funds have credit ratings, according to Morningstar, Inc., between A and AAA. The weighted-average maturity of these funds is 2.75 years, and it is the bank's policy not to own funds with a weighted-average maturity of more than five years.

Beginning in early 20X4 and extending through December 31, 20X4, the Federal Reserve Board increased the federal funds rate six times. Only once in the past 50 years has the Federal Reserve Board increased interest rates six times in a year. Correspondly, in 20X4 the market value of the eight fixed-income funds declined significantly. As of December 31, 20X4, the eight funds had an unrealized loss of $4,800,000. Exhibit 1 presents the schedule of quarterly unrealized losses for the fixed-income portfolio from December 31, 20X3, through December 31, 20X4.

Morgantown's auditors have raised the issue of whether as of December 31, 20X4, the unrealized losses on the fixed-income portfolio are "other than temporary." The unrealized losses were accounted for as temporary in Morgantown's 20X3 financial statements and 20X4 quarterly reports through September 30, 20X4. Morgantown believes that the portfolio should be evaluated with respect to impairment relative to share-price movement of funds in correlation with the direction of short and intermediate-term interest rates, the length of interest rate cycles, and the likely appreciation or depreciation over an interest-rate cycle. Morgantown notes that a lag time (i.e., one to two years) is typical before the economy reacts to a major Federal Reserve Board action.

Morgantown states that an analysis of the share price appreciation of the eight fixed-income funds for the 36 months ending December 31, 20X1, revealed a range of appreciation from 4.8 percent to 9.57 percent. During this 36-month period, the Federal Reserve Board raised rates 4 times and lowered them 21 times.

In conclusion, the bank believes that as of December 31, 20X4, it is impractical and premature to reach a conclusion on impairment of the portfolio until sufficient time has passed to evaluate the effectiveness of the Federal Reserve Board action. The bank proposes that December 31, 20X6, be a reasonable time to determine impairment of the portfolio.

Exhibit C10–15:1			
MORGANTOWN SAVINGS BANK			
Fixed-Income Portfolio			
Schedule of Unrealized Losses			
December 31, 20X3, through December 31, 20X4			
(000 omitted)			
Date	*Portfolio Cost*	*Market Value*	*Unrealized Loss*
12/31/X3	$54,000	$53,480	$ 520
3/31/X4	54,000	52,020	1,980
6/30/X4	54,000	50,915	3,085
9/30/X4	54,000	50,535	3,465
12/31/X4	54,000	49,200	4,800

Required

1. Discuss in general terms how Morgantown Savings Bank should account for and report its portfolio of short-term, fixed-income mutual funds.

2. Discuss whether you agree with Morgantown's accounting and reporting for its portfolio of short-term, fixed-income mutual funds for the period December 31, 20X3, through September 31, 20X4. Include in your discussion Morgantown's proposal to determine impairment of the portfolio at December 31, 20X6.

3. How would you recommend that Morgantown account for and report its short-term, fixed-income mutual funds as of December 31, 20X3, and throughout 20X4, including December 31, 20X4? Include in your response the basis for your recommendation.

C10–16	ROLLINS MACHINE, INC.

Accounting for an Investment in an Available-for-Sale Equity Security

Rollins Machine, Inc. (RMI) is a manufacturer of precision bearings and tools for the industrial market. RMI is a calendar-year corporation. Its common stock is registered with the Securities Exchange Commission (SEC) and traded on the New York Stock Exchange.

In the first quarter of 20X1, RMI purchased 2,500,000 shares of Willow Winds Nurseries (WWN), a national chain of retail nurseries whose stock is traded on the American Stock Exchange. RMI's aggregate cost of its investment in WWN totaled $14,500,000 ($5.80 per share). RMI's investment represented 5.1 percent of the outstanding common stock of WWN, and RMI categorized the investment as an available-for-sale equity security. On March 31, 20X1, the quoted market price of WWN common stock on the American Stock Exchange was $5.00 per share, which represented an aggregate market value of $12,500,000 for RMI's investment in WWN. In its March 31, 20X1, quarterly report filed with the SEC, RMI reported the investment in WWN as a current asset of $12,500,000 and reported an unrealized loss of $2,000,000 in other comprehensive income and as a separate component of stockholders' equity.

At the close of the second quarter, June 30, 20X1, the quoted market price of WWN common stock on the American Stock Exchange was $5.80 per share, which now represented an aggregate market value of $14,500,000 (equivalent to RMI's original cost). In its June 30, 20X1, quarterly report filed with the SEC,

RMI reported the investment in WWN as a current asset of $14,500,000 and reported an unrealized gain of $2,000,000 in other comprehensive income for the second quarter of 20X1.

In early September 20X1, RMI and WWN entered into discussions about the possible sale of RMI's investment in WWN to WWN. The discussions resulted in WWN verbally offering to acquire all of RMI's holdings in WWN at $5.80 per share when the stock was trading at $5.125 per share. The offer was never reduced to writing or accepted by RMI. RMI disclosed to the SEC the substance of the verbal offer and the fact that it was outstanding on and after September 30, 20X1.

On September 30, 20X1, the quoted market price of WWN common stock on the American Stock Exchange was $4.875 per share, which now represented an aggregate market value of $12,187,500 for RMI's holdings. In preparing its September 30, 20X1, quarterly report filed with the SEC, RMI used as market value the verbal offer from WWN of $5.80 per share in determining carrying value. Thus, RMI reported the investment as a current asset of $14,500,000 and did not report an unrealized loss of $2,312,500 in other comprehensive income and as a separate component of stockholders' equity in the third quarter of 20X1. RMI's disclosure in its September 30, 20X1, financial statements concerning the WWN investment was as follows:

> Marketable equity securities consist principally of the common stock of Willow Winds Nurseries and are stated at cost at the balance sheet date. The company holds 5.1 percent of the outstanding common shares of Willow Winds Nurseries. During the third quarter of fiscal 20X1, the company entered into discussions with Willow Winds Nurseries concerning the possible sale of its investment in Willow Winds Nurseries at an amount equivalent to the company's total cost. An agreement for the sale of stock has not been reached, as of balance sheet date.

Required
1. Discuss whether you agree with RMI's accounting and disclosure of its investment in WWN. Include in your discussion whether *FASB Statement No. 115*, "Accounting for Certain Investments in Debt and Equity Securities," makes a provision for a market price other than a quoted market price.
2. Would your response be different if the offer was in writing and/or a designated time for acceptance was specified?
3. If you disagree with RMI's accounting and disclosure of its investment in WWN, indicate any proposed changes in the accounting and disclosure.

Investments

C10–17	BAYCO, INC.

Carrying Value of an Investment in an Affiliate's Preferred Stock Acquired in Exchange for a Long-Term Receivable

Bayco, Inc. manufactures and markets equipment for commercial air cooling and heating systems. Bayco has a calendar year-end, and its only class of outstanding stock is owned by 10 individuals. In 20X1 Bayco began research into the development of a new technology for commercial solar heating systems and related products.

In late 20X1, several shareholders of Bayco formed Solar Systems, Inc. to conduct Bayco's activities relating to solar systems. Solar Systems agreed to reimburse Bayco $107,116 for product research and development costs incurred to date. Bayco reported this amount as a current account receivable in its December 31, 20X1, balance sheet and disclosed in a footnote that it was from a related party. Bayco is required to prepare separate financial statements for its operations because of a debt covenant for its bank loan. The bank will not accept combined financial statements of Bayco and Solar Systems.

Throughout 20X2 and 20X3, Solar Systems was engaged primarily in the research and development of solar products. Sales during this period were minimal, but operating losses and shareholders' deficit were significant. Solar Systems's operating losses and working capital needs were funded by advances from Bayco. Bayco charged Solar 12 percent interest for all advances, which totaled approximately $25,000 in 20X2 and $49,000 in 20X3. Bayco recognized the interest, none of which was paid, as revenue in both years.

As of December 31, 20X2, Bayco reported in its balance sheet $292,100 (including interest) as a current account receivable from Solar, and as of December 31, 20X3, reported the entire amount as a long-term account receivable from Solar of $521,400 (including interest). In its footnotes to the 20X2 and 20X3 financial statements, Bayco disclosed that the receivables were from a related party and stated that "interest was realized from advances to Solar Systems, Inc. of $24,800 in 20X2 and $49,600 in 20X3." There were no other significant disclosures in 20X2 or 20X3 concerning the receivable from Solar.

On November 30, 20X4, Solar Systems, Inc. issued to Bayco, Inc. $100 par value, 10 percent, nonvoting, noncumulative preferred stock in exchange for its debt to Bayco. The stock was issued in the ratio of 1 share of preferred stock for each $100 of debt and is redeemable at the option of the holder at par value any time after December 31, 20X7. At the time of the exchange, Solar owed Bayco $691,400 (including an additional $60,600 of unpaid interest for 20X4). Bayco canceled its receivable from Solar and recorded the investment in Solar's preferred stock at $691,400. As of December 31, 20X4, Bayco reported Solar's preferred stock as a $691,400 long-term investment.

Solar Systems's operating results are not expected to change significantly in 20X5. Solar is going to continue to be dependent on Bayco to fund its operating losses and working capital needs. Presently, no independent investors or financial institutions appear willing to make loans or take an equity position in Solar Systems.

Required
For each year 20X1 through 20X4, discuss Bayco's accounting and reporting of its business activities with Solar Systems and any alternatives considered on a year-by-year basis. If you disagree with Bayco, state your proposed accounting and reporting and your reasons for such treatment.

C10–18	HESSON OFFICE SUPPLIES, INC.

Exchange of a Wholly Owned Subsidiary for a 50 Percent Interest in a New Corporation

Hesson Office Supplies, Inc. (HOS) is a distributor of office equipment, furniture, and supplies. HOS has a wholly owned subsidiary, Belknap Equipment Company, a manufacturer of office equipment. HOS has been discussing with Tykes Office Equipment the possibility of forming a new business entity. Tykes also has a wholly owned subsidiary, Reddington Office Furniture, a manufacturer of office furniture and fixtures.

HOS and Tykes have tentatively agreed that they will exchange their entire interest in their wholly owned subsidiaries, Belknap Equipment Company and Reddington Office Furniture, for a 50 percent interest in a newly formed corporation. Thus, the new corporation would receive the two subsidiaries and issue 50 percent of its stock to HOS and the other 50 percent to Tykes. The fair value of the net assets of each subsidiary exceeds its book value, and the relative net book values and fair values of the two subsidiaries are not proportional. However, through negotiation HOS and Tykes believe that their contributions to the newly formed corporation would be equal in value in spite of this disproportionate relationship.

The fair value of a 50 percent interest in the new corporation would exceed the carrying value of HOS's investment in Belknap.

Required
1. Discuss how HOS should account for the exchange of its wholly owned subsidiary, Belknap Equipment Company, for a 50 percent interest in the newly formed corporation.
2. Discuss how HOS should account for its 50 percent interest in the newly formed corporation subsequent to the exchange.
3. Discuss how the newly formed corporation should account for the assets it received in the exchange transaction.

 C10–19   METROTRONICS, INC.

Exchange of a Wholly Owned Subsidiary for the Company's Outstanding Stock

Metrotronics, Inc. is a defense contractor that has a wholly owned electronics subsidiary, Eagle Electronics Company. The common stock of Metrotronics is held by 10 individuals. Ellis K. Marsh owns 87,603 shares (approximately 20 percent) of Metrotronics' common stock. During the past several years, Marsh has become increasingly dissatisfied with Metrotronics' operating results and its failure to diversify. Therefore, Marsh has been seeking a way of divesting his investment that would be acceptable to all of Metrotronics' shareholders.

On December 2, 20X1, Metrotronics and Marsh reached an agreement that enabled Marsh to divest his stock ownership. By the terms of the agreement, on December 31, 20X1, Metrotronics would exchange all of its stock in Eagle Electronics Company for the 87,603 shares of Metrotronics' common stock held by Ellis K. Marsh. In addition, Metrotronics would assume all the liabilities ($2,500,000) of Eagle Electronics Company and pay $500,000 directly to Marsh.

As of December 31, 20X1, the fair market value of Eagle's assets was determined by an independent appraisal to be $4,000,000. Marsh and the other shareholders of Metrotronics agreed that the $4,000,000

Exhibit C10–19:1

Balance Sheet
December 31, 20X1
(000 omitted)

	Metrotronics	Eagle Electronics
Current assets	$ 8,000	$ 200
Investment in Eagle Electronics	300	
Fixed assets	10,200	2,600
	$18,500	$2,800
Liabilities	$11,200	$2,500
Common stock	6,300	100
Retained earnings	1,000	200
	$18,500	$2,800

was a fair and reasonable appraisal of the total assets. In early January 20X2, Marsh sold for $4,000,000 all the assets of Eagle Electronics, Inc. to Marsh Associates, a limited partnership of which Ellis K. Marsh is the general partner.

Exhibit 1 shows an abbreviated balance sheet of Metrotronics and Eagle immediately prior to the transaction.

Required
1. Discuss how Metrotronics should account for the December 31, 20X1, transaction with Marsh. Include in your discussion all alternatives considered and why you have accepted or rejected them.
2. Prepare the balance sheet of Metrotronics as of December 31, 20X1, immediately after the transaction between Metrotronics and Marsh.

C10–20	NEWSON COMPANIES, INC.

Exchange of a Division for the Company's Outstanding Stock

Newson Companies, Inc. is a publicly held diversified company, the stock of which is traded on a national exchange. Newson has entered into an agreement, dated May 31, 20X1, with Jessica Bryant to sell her a division that manufactures adult games, in exchange for some of the Newson common stock she holds. The market value of the stock to be received exceeds the book value of the manufacturing division. Newson will continue to operate a division that manufactures children's games, as well as its many other diversified business operations. Bryant is a major stockholder and director of Newson. At the time of signing the agreement she owned approximately 4.2 percent of Newson's outstanding stock, having a market value of $8 million. After the sale was completed on August 1, 20X1, Bryant owned 2 percent of the stock.

Subsequent to the signing of Newson's agreement with Mrs. Bryant, Felton Industries made a tender offer on July 18, 20X1, to acquire the stock of Newson Companies, Inc. This offer significantly increased the market value of Newson's stock. The market value of Bryant's stock that was transferred in the exchange with Newson increased over $1.2 million between May 31, 20X1, the date of signing the agreement with Newson, and August 1, 20X1, the date of sale. Bryant did not attempt to renegotiate the number of shares to be paid for the division even though the tender offer significantly increased the value of the stock. At the time the agreement with Bryant was signed, Newson was not aware that Felton was planning on making a tender offer to acquire their shares.

Required
1. Discuss whether the sale of the manufacturing division of adult games qualifies as the disposal of a segment of a business. Identify in your discussion the differences between reporting the sale as the disposal of a segment or not reporting it as the disposal of a segment.
2. Is it appropriate for Newson to recognize a gain on the sale of the division for its own stock?
3. Without prejudice to your response in question 2, assuming that it is appropriate for Newson to recognize a gain on the sale, discuss the appropriate date to be used for each of the following:
   a. Date to be used for determining the proceeds of the sale for the purpose of measuring the gain.
   b. Date to be used for recording the gain in the accounts of Newson.
4. Discuss the amount that Newson should report for the stock it received in the sale in its 20X1 financial statements.

C10–21	Tosco Companies

Accounting for a Joint Venture Partnership and Issues Relating to Research Funds and Expenditures

Tosco Companies has entered into an agreement with Hermitage, Inc. to form a joint venture partnership for the purpose of developing advanced laser products. The main points of the agreement are summarized as follows:

1. Hermitage will provide for the cash needs of the joint venture and Tosco will provide the technology.
2. Hermitage will immediately contribute $6 million to the joint venture to be paid to Tosco according to the following terms:
   a. $1 million to be retained by Tosco with no obligation to return said funds in the future.
   b. $5 million to be used by Tosco to conduct research in Phase I of the joint venture. Phase I is to research, engineer, and design the products.
3. If, during the initial part of Phase I, Tosco's research findings do not meet certain criteria specified in the agreement, then Hermitage will contribute an additional $2.5 million to the joint venture. The additional funds will be paid to Tosco to conduct more extensive research with the anticipation of meeting the specified criteria.
4. Phase II of the agreement provides for the input of an additional $30 million by Hermitage to construct a manufacturing facility if Phase I is successful.
5. Phase III is the manufacturing of the new products.
6. During Phases I and II, all losses will be allocated to Hermitage. If any gains result during this period (which is not expected), they will be shared 51 percent by Hermitage and 49 percent by Tosco. During Phase III, gains and losses will be shared in accordance with percentages specified in the partnership agreement.
7. The agreement requires the joint venture to maintain its records in accordance with generally accepted accounting principles and requires that financial statements be audited. Tentatively, it is planned for Tosco to have an initial capital credit of $22 million for the technology it contributed and Hermitage to have a capital credit of $6 million for the cash it contributed.
8. If Tosco is unable to meet the specified criteria at the end of Phase I, Hermitage can then require Tosco to issue shares of its common stock as payment for its equity in the partnership. The number of shares issued will be determined by dividing the amount expended by Tosco for new product research and development by the greater of either Tosco's market value per common share or $20 per share.

Through the years, Tosco has been involved in several similar projects with other companies. In these projects, either Tosco has been unsuccessful in completing the projects or the other companies have terminated the projects in accordance with the agreements.

Required
1. How should Tosco account for the $1 million it received when the joint venture was formed?
2. Discuss the alternatives available to Tosco in accounting for the $5 to $7.5 million received from the joint venture for research and development activities and indicate what alternative you recommend. Also, include in your discussion how Tosco should account for the actual expenditures it makes for research and development of the new products.
3. Discuss the accounting and reporting implications for the joint venture partnership in crediting Tosco's capital $22 million for the technology it contributed.

Fixed and Intangible Assets

C10–22	PACKARD TRADING COMPANY, INC.

Accounting and Reporting for Export Rights—Quota

Packard Trading Company, Inc. is an international importer of household goods, electronic equipment, and computer equipment. Packard has several wholly owned foreign trading subsidiaries that act as its purchasing agents throughout the world. Osian Enterprises, Inc. is Packard's subsidiary covering the Far East markets. In order to operate in many of these markets, Osian Enterprises must have a license or right to export a stated quantity of a particular product. This license or right is referred to as *quota* and can be purchased from a foreign governmental agency or other parties holding quota. Quota purchased from a foreign governmental agency is referred to as *permanent quota*, while quota purchased from other quota holders is temporary quota.

Permanent quota holders pay a one-time fee to obtain the right or license to permanently export a stated quantity of a product for an indefinite period of time. To retain their right or license, permanent quota purchasers must use at least 90 percent of their quota amount annually, either by exporting product or selling temporary unused excess quota so that another party can export product. Permanent quota holders are also restricted from selling more than 30 percent of their quota.

Temporary quota is traded in an active secondary market between permanent quota holders needing to sell temporary excess and parties in need of additional quota to export products. Temporary quota usually trades at 50 percent less than the cost of permanent quota. Companies with stable or increasing export volume for their products are often willing to incur the increased cost of permanent quota over temporary quota in order to minimize the risk of products not being exported due to a lack of quota.

In prior fiscal years, due to the immateriality of quota transactions, Osian's purchases of permanent and temporary quota were all expensed in the year of acquisition and reported as such in the consolidated financial statements of Packard Trading Company, Inc. However, on review of the current purchases of quota and projected levels of exporting from Far East markets during the next five years, Packard is concerned that quota transactions will no longer be an immaterial amount. Therefore, Packard is considering several alternative accounting policies for quota. One such policy is to write off 50 percent of the cost of quota over a three-year period. At each fiscal year-end, Packard will evaluate the carrying value of all quota (including prior year purchases) by comparing the market value to the carrying value and reporting the lower amount. The market value is readily available through published quotations or quota brokers.

Required
1. Discuss whether Packard should change its accounting and reporting for quota and how any change should be reported.
2. Discuss the policy Packard is considering of writing off 50 percent of the cost of quota over a three-year period and reporting at the lower of carrying value or market value. Does this appear to be a rational policy or arbitrary in nature?
3. If Packard wrote the carrying value of quota down in one period to a lower market value, could it write the carrying value back up in another period? Why or why not?
4. If some or all of the cost of quota is capitalized, how should it be reported in Packard's consolidated balance sheet?
5. Discuss other alternatives that Packard might consider in accounting and reporting for quota. What policy would you recommend and why?

| C10–23 | POTOMAC SAVINGS BANK, INC. |

Accounting for the Write Off of Goodwill

Potomac Savings Bank, Inc. is engaged primarily in the business of attracting retail and wholesale deposits from the general public and investing those deposits in various types of residential and commercial mortgages; consumer, construction, and commercial loans; and debt and equity securities. The bank conducts its business from 11 locations and is a member of the Federal Deposit Insurance Corporation.

On July 1, 20X1, Potomac paid $45 million cash to acquire all the outstanding stock of Williamstown Savings Bank in a transaction accounted for under the purchase method. Goodwill of $7 million was recognized at the time of acquisition and will be amortized over a 20-year period by the straight-line method. Potomac was willing to pay a premium to acquire Williamstown because it believed that the merged entities would give it a competitive market advantage and increase earnings.

Williamstown was deemed to have a highly visible and strong presence in its local market. Williamstown's senior management was extensively involved in community affairs and was instrumental in attracting and maintaining a favorable mix of low-cost deposits to total deposits. Williamstown's underwriting policies were perceived to meet high standards that limited risks with its loan portfolio. At the time of the merger, Williamstown's total assets of $300 million were projected to increase to approximately $425 million by December 31, 20X3.

Subsequent to the merger, many of Potomac's assumptions regarding Williamstown did not come to fruition. Within 10 months of the merger, six senior officers of Williamstown terminated their employment with the bank. Three became officers of a competing bank, and one became president and chief executive officer of another competing bank. The former officers were able to attract a number of Williamstown's customers to their new banks and a significant amount of low-cost deposit accounts.

The anticipated asset growth for Williamstown was not achieved. In fact, the combined entities shrunk in asset size from $750 million in July 20X1 to $625 million at December 31, 20X3. While some of this was attributable to the officers' leaving, market conditions had changed dramatically since the merger. The overall economy was in a recession, and the regional real estate market was experiencing an unprecedented downturn. The once-perceived high-quality asset base of Williamstown was now loaded down with nonperforming real estate loans and other assets declining in value. Consequently, this has caused significant increases in loan loss provisions and write-downs of asset carrying values. Thus, the Williamstown operations contributed to Potomac's reported 20X2 loss of $11.3 million and estimated 20X3 pre-audit loss of $26.4 million.

Prior to Potomac's December 31, 20X3, year-end audit, Winston Fedo, chief financial officer, questioned whether the unamortized goodwill of $6.125 million from the Williamstown acquisition was permanently impaired. After consulting with several other bank officers, Winston concluded that Potomac should write off the remaining goodwill and report a 20X3 net loss in excess of $32 million. He did not think that the additional write off would depress the bank's stock market price any further.

When discussing this matter with Potomac's auditors, Winston Fedo pointed out that the original purchase price of Williamstown was based on a discounted cash flow analysis that has not been realized. In fact, if current circumstances were known, no premium would have been paid, and it is doubtful whether the acquisition would have been made. Fedo also indicated that he attributed approximately 40 percent of the 20X3 loss to Williamstown, and this would not justify a carrying value of goodwill. Fedo determined the 40 percent based on the fact that Williamstown's assets were 40 percent of the total assets at the date of the merger.

Finally, Fedo indicated that the future operations of Williamstown on a stand-alone basis, once projected to be profitable, are now projected to continue for the next several years at a loss in excess of $700,000 per year. The merged operations are projected to incur a $1.5 million loss in 20X4 and break even in 20X5. Fedo concluded by pointing out that the future profitability did not support the $6.125 million carrying value of goodwill at December 31, 20X3.

Required

1. Discuss whether it is ever appropriate to write off goodwill in its entirety. Include in your discussion the long-term implications of writing the goodwill off in its entirety. *Can't restore it*
2. Discuss the alternatives in accounting for the goodwill in Potomac Savings Bank's financial statements for the year ending December 31, 20X3. Include in your discussion arguments that support each of the alternatives.
3. Which alternative in accounting for the goodwill do you support and why?

C10–24	ROARK MEDICAL EQUIPMENT, INC.

Accounting for the Impairment of Long-Lived Assets

Roark Medical Equipment, Inc. is a manufacturer and distributor of medical equipment. Its stock is publicly traded in the over-the-counter market. In 20X1 Roark started a medical pocket lights division (EENT Division) which manufactures and distributes pocket lights used in the examination of eyes, ears, nose, and throat. Roark purchased a building for $1,000,000 to manufacture the lights and paid $450,000 for custom designed manufacturing equipment.

The EENT Division has sustained operating losses since its inception, and continuing operating losses are forecasted for the next four years. As of the end of 20X4, the carrying amount of the building and equipment is $840,000 and $270,000, respectively. Roark's management is concerned that it might not be able to recover fully the carrying amount of the EENT Division's assets. Management estimates that the assets will generate total cash flows in the range of $800,000 to $1,200,000 over the next four years. The present value of the range of projected cash flows discounted at 10 percent is $634,000 to $951,000. Management does not believe that it is able to obtain any reliable market prices for the assets.

In preparing financial statements for the year ended December 31, 20X4, management is concerned whether an impairment loss must be recognized for the EENT Division's assets. Thomas Woodson, Roark's chief financial officer, indicates that internal data and analysis suggest the likelihood of assets generating cash flows of $800,000 is twice as great as is the likelihood of assets generating $1,200,000. Margaret Calley, Roark's president, asserts that it would be premature to recognize any impairment loss at this time, and accounting standards are flexible enough to allow Roark discretion as to when recognition should take place, if ever.

Without consideration of any impairment loss in 20X4, Roark will report net earnings of $10,000,000. However, because of increased competition, a changing economic environment, and increased research and development costs, Roark anticipates reporting a loss from continuing operations in 20X5.

Required

1. What is the practical difficulty of applying the accounting standard for the impairment of long-lived assets to be held and used in a business? In applying the standard, do opportunities exist for earnings management?
2. Discuss whether or not you agree with Margaret Calley's assertion that it would be premature to recognize any impairment loss in 20X4, and accounting standards are flexible enough to allow Roark discretion as to when recognition should take place, if at all.

3. What concern, if any, would you have if Roark did not recognize any impairment loss in 20X4?
4. Discuss your recommendation as to how, or if, Roark should account for any impairment of assets in 20X4. Be specific in your response and use data from the case to support your position.
5. Without prejudice to your response in requirement 4, if Roark recognizes an impairment loss in 20X4, could it write up the assets in a subsequent year? Does it matter whether the impaired assets are to be held and used in a business or to be disposed of?

C10–25	WEBSTER PAYNE, INC.

Accounting for Noncompetition Agreements

Webster Payne, Inc. is a closely held company that manufactures and markets precision nautical instruments. During the year Webster Payne redeemed the shares of two shareholders/employees. They were Joseph Landon, age 44, and Marge Webster, age 65, 3 percent and 15 percent shareholders, respectively. The former shareholders entered into noncompetition agreements with Webster Payne.

The agreement with Landon was reached under less than amicable circumstances. For the past several years Landon had been extremely dissatisfied with the management and direction of the company. After many heated discussions with other shareholders, an agreement was reached to redeem Landon's stock and pay him to refrain from engagement or participation in the business conducted by Webster Payne, Inc. for a period of six years. The noncompetition agreement requires Webster Payne to make monthly payments of $3,000 to Landon or his estate, commencing the first month of the next fiscal year and continuing for a period of six years.

Marge Webster was one of the original shareholders of the company and had been planning to retire for several years. She reached an agreement quickly and without any disputes. Besides having her stock redeemed, she agreed to receive total payments of $800,000 for entering into a noncompetition agreement. The agreement, signed the last day of the current fiscal year, requires that Webster Payne, Inc. make annual payments to Marge Webster of $100,000, commencing the first day of the next fiscal year and continuing for a period of eight years. The agreement requires that Marge Webster refrain from engagement or participation in the business conducted by Webster Payne, Inc. for a period of three years from the date of the first payment. In the event of Marge Webster's death, all payments shall terminate, but in no instance shall Marge Webster or her estate receive less than five periodic payments of $100,000 each. In structuring the agreement, Marge Webster essentially allowed Webster Payne, Inc. to determine the length of the noncompetition clause and the payment terms for whatever time periods that it deemed reasonable.

In accounting for these noncompetition agreements for the current year-end, Simon Cross, chief financial officer of the company, is planning on disclosing the existence of the agreement with Joseph Landon in the notes to the financial statements. However, he is planning on recording an intangible asset and a liability for the agreement with Marge Webster. Simon Cross believes that as the agreement with Landon was entered into under less than amicable circumstances, it is probable that Landon will not abide by the agreement. He thinks that Landon's age and recognized expertise in the design of nautical instruments will eventually lead him into a competing business venture.

On the other hand, Simon Cross believes that asset and liability recognition are appropriate for Marge Webster's agreement because of her desire to retire and willingness to allow the company to significantly influence the structuring of the agreement. Simon Cross also thinks that because of Marge's age and loyalty to Webster Payne, it is unlikely that she will not abide by the agreement. Mr. Cross is planning on recording the noncompetition agreement at $601,040 which represents the present value of the $800,000 discounted at the prime rate of 10 percent for three years. The liability and the unamortized discount will then be recorded at $800,000 and $198,960, respectively.

Required

1. In general, discuss the appropriate accounting and reporting of noncompetition agreements. Include a discussion of any alternatives for accounting and reporting noncompetition agreements, and the rationale for each position.

2. Discuss what might have been the reasoning for Webster Payne, Inc. in the way that it structured the agreement with Marge Webster and the accounting proposed by Simon Cross.

3. If it is deemed appropriate to record an intangible asset as of the current year-end for the noncompetition agreement with Marge Webster, discuss how you would account for it. Be specific as to amounts and include a discussion of subsequent years' accounting.

4. Discuss your specific recommendation to Webster Payne, Inc. in accounting and reporting for each of the noncompetition agreements.

Current and Long-Term Liabilities

C10–26	ABBOTT ELECTRIC COMPANY, INC.

Accounting for Postretirement and Post-Termination Employee Agreements

Abbott Electric Company, Inc., a supplier of electrical parts and motors, is wholly owned by George Abbott. The company has annual sales of $14 million and employs a staff of 80. Mr. Abbott has reached a tentative agreement to sell 50 percent of the stock in his company to Nicholas Wagner. The agreement provides for a selling price of the stock based on a stipulated multiple of 1.25 times 50 percent of the fair market value of the net identifiable assets of Abbott Electric, Inc. as of the current year ending September 30, 20X1. The fair market value of the net identifiable assets will be determined in accordance with generally accepted accounting principles.

At issue in the determination of the fair market value of the net identifiable assets are two agreements George Abbott entered into with three employees. The first agreement was entered into at the beginning of fiscal year 20X1 with Jennifer Bostic, age 55, and Richard Wilson, age 56. Mr. Abbott has characterized this agreement as a management security program to provide postretirement benefits to Bostic and Wilson of $60,000 per employee, per year for an eight-year period, and payable in semiannual installments of $30,000.

The agreement provides that payments will be made if Bostic and Wilson remain in the employment of Abbott Electric Company, Inc. until their normal retirement date (on attaining the age of 65) or on their actual date of retirement, if later. If either employee dies after payments commence, the company is required to make the remaining payments to the employee's beneficiary. If either employee dies while in the employment of the company but before retirement, the company is required to pay to the employee's beneficiary a $60,000 lump sum. The agreement is neither funded nor guaranteed and does not preclude the company from terminating either employee. Although the plan is unfunded, the company has purchased two whole life insurance policies that would provide for the funding of the agreement if either or both of the employees become vested in the benefits.

The second agreement was entered into with Miles Stillwagon two days after the current September 30th year-end. Effective October 2, 20X1, Mr. Stillwagon's services with the company were terminated due to his alleged inability to get along with his co-workers. In settlement of several counterclaims and legal threats by Mr. Stillwagon over his termination, a financial agreement was reached. The agreement provides that the company will pay Mr. Stillwagon or his beneficiary $30,000 annually for the next six years. The first payment will commence one year from the date of the agreement.

George Abbott believes that generally accepted accounting principles do not require the recognition of liabilities for either of these agreements as of September 30, 20X1. On the other hand, Nicholas Wagner believes that as of September 30, liabilities of $960,000 for the first agreement and $180,000 for the second agreement should be recognized.

Required
1. Discuss the arguments in support of and against liability recognition as of September 30, 20X1, for each of the agreements.
2. Discuss your recommendation for how each agreement should be accounted for. Include in your discussion what year(s) the effects of the agreement (including specific dollar amounts) should be reported in the company's balance sheet and income statement. Identify any accounts to be reported in the financial statements.

| C10–27 | CALICO FASHIONS, INC. |

Forgiveness of a Lessee's Debt as an Inducement Not to Terminate a Lease

Calico Fashions, Inc. is a retailer of high-fashion women's apparel. Calico operates 12 retail stores in California. All operations are conducted out of rented premises, located primarily in shopping malls.

Calico's most recently opened store is located in a new marketplace in a major industrial city. This marketplace was developed by B. G. Developers, Inc. as part of an urban renewal project to revitalize the downtown shopping section of the city. Calico was one of the first tenants in the marketplace and signed a 10-year lease with B. G. Developers to commence in January 20X1. The lease provided Calico with several termination options at various intervals during the lease term if Calico did not attain certain sales volumes. Separate from the lease agreement, B. G. Developers loaned Calico $100,000 as an inducement to enter into the lease and to be used for making renovations to the premises. The loan provided for interest-only payments at prime plus 2 percent, due annually each December 31, and for the principal to be repaid at the end of 10 years.

The new marketplace did not develop into as thriving a retail shopping area as B. G. Developers had projected, and consequently several lessees who had termination options in their leases exercised them. B. G. Developers was concerned that Calico might also exercise one of its termination options and therefore in 20X2 offered in writing to ratably forgive the loan and any interest over the remaining eight years of the lease term if Calico remained a tenant. If Calico terminated the lease at any time prior to the expiration date, the applicable balance of the note at such time and interest would be owed pursuant to the original terms of the note. This offer was to become effective January 1, 20X3.

Calico's management considered the offer and decided that at this point in time it intended to remain a tenant for the duration of the lease term. In planning to prepare their financial statements for calendar year 20X2, management intended to report on the income statement a $100,000 gain from restructuring of debt. Calico's management believed that, as their intention was to remain a tenant for the duration of the lease, the $100,000 was not a contingent gain and should be recognized immediately. Alternatively, management felt that if its auditors disagreed with recognizing the $100,000 gain in 20X2, the auditors would agree to recognizing the gain in 20X3.

Required
1. Discuss whether the substance of B. G. Developers' offer to ratably forgive the loan is separate and independent from the lease with Calico. Include in your discussion any implications for financial reporting purposes.

2. Discuss whether or not you agree with Calico's proposed accounting for the $100,000 and its assessment of how the auditors might react. State your reasons for your position and give your proposed accounting treatment if you disagree.

C10–28	CHANDLER STORES, INC.

Accounting for a Junk Bond Restructuring from a Leveraged Buyout

Chandler Stores, Inc. is a regional grocery store chain. In late 20X1 Chandler went through a leveraged buyout. A significant part of the purchase price for the buyout was financed through the issuance of 10-year, 14 percent, $20 million face value bonds. No principal payments are due on the bonds until maturity, and interest payments are deferred for the first four years.

Throughout 20X2 and 20X3, Chandler concentrated on increasing individual store size to approximately 50,000 square feet, compared with the chain average of 30,000. In the increased selling space, Chandler added higher-margin departments such as delicatessens, salad bars, and bakeries. Besides enlarging stores, operating hours of many stores were extended to 24 hours a day, seven days a week. During this time, gross margins increased from 22 percent to 24 percent, and cash flows from operations improved to a break-even point. Operations are not yet profitable but are projected to be in the near future.

Each year Chandler plans to add five new stores and upgrade two or three older ones. Plans call for the expansion to be financed through internally generated funds, equity contributions from owners, and bank borrowings. Chandler is about to close on a $25 million line of credit at prime plus 1.5 percent.

As part of its overall financing plans, Chandler is considering a restructuring of its $20 million face value bonds issued in 20X1. The marketplace has valued the $20 million debt as being of junk bond quality, and the market value is currently only $11 million. At the beginning of 20X4, Chandler is proposing to offer to the holders of the bonds a package of cash, common stock, and notes in exchange for the $20 million face value bonds and the $6 million accrued interest due on the bonds. The package, valued by an independent investment banker, totals $18 million and includes cash of $8 million, common stock of $3 million, and notes of $7 million. The notes will be due in seven years and require annual interest payments of $900,000, or approximately 13 percent annually.

Required
1. Assuming that the investment banker's estimate of the value of the package is correct and the proposal is accepted, discuss the accounting alternatives for Chandler in reporting the 20X4 restructuring.
2. Based on your response in question 1, discuss the financial reporting implications for each alternative in 20X4 and subsequent years.

C10–29	CLEARTRONICS, INC.

Accounting for a Troubled Debt Restructuring

Cleartronics, Inc. is a 90 percent owned subsidiary of Bridgestone Industries, a publicly held conglomerate. The remaining 10 percent of Cleartronics is owned by a management group. Cleartronics develops and distributes plain-paper and full-color copiers. Cleartronics recently entered the full-color market and believes that it will be competitive in both price and quality.

On July 1, 20X1, Cleartronics' management group was able to negotiate a management buyout of the company with Bridgestone. The buyout was partially financed with senior term debt from States Bank and Trust. Cleartronics also issued a subordinated debenture with a common stock purchase warrant to Bridgestone in the exchange for its 90 percent equity interest. The debenture has a face value of $10 million and was subordinated to the States Bank and Trust debt. The warrant issued contained both a put and call feature. The warrant was valued at and recorded as $4,967,000 on July 1, 20X1. The valuation was mutually determined by Cleartronics and Bridgestone as the put price of $8 million on June 30, 20X6, discounted at approximately 10 percent to the July 1, 20X1, acquisition date. The call feature allowed Cleartronics to call the warrant at the current fair market value of its common stock. If Cleartronics exercised the call, the due date of the debenture would be accelerated.

In years subsequent to the buyout, Cleartronics incurred operating losses and cash flow problems that caused it to be in violation of certain debt covenants with States Bank and Trust. Management attributed its financial problems to shrinking margins in the plain-paper copier market and quality control problems with its full-color copiers. Management believed that operating results would improve within the next 12 to 18 months, but States Bank and Trust indicated its intent to call the debt. Therefore, Cleartronics approached Carlson Bank Corporation about becoming senior lender. Carlson agreed to new financing contingent on the removal of the put feature on the common stock purchase warrant held by Bridgestone Industries.

Cleartronics then requested that Bridgestone allow them to restructure the debt. It pointed out that in the absence of the Carlson Bank financing, the likelihood of its continuing as a going concern was in doubt. In addition, Cleartronics indicated that with the existing call feature it could call the warrant at the current fair market value of the common stock, which had essentially no value at this time.

Bridgestone realized that it was jeopardizing its subordinated debenture position unless it agreed to the removal of the put feature, and so it reluctantly agreed to restructure the debt. On July 1, 20X4, Cleartronics issued to Bridgestone a new $10 million subordinated debenture replacing the original $10 million debenture. The new debt required interest payments of $4.1 million over the next four years. Cleartronics also issued a new subordinated debenture of $2.1 million representing the unpaid accrued interest on the original $10 million debt. This debt required interest payments of $864,000 over the next four years. Last, Cleartronics issued a new common stock purchase warrant for the same number of shares and price as the original 20X1 warrant, except that it did not contain a put and call feature. The discounted value of the original warrant as of July 1, 20X4 was $6,611,000.

Required

1. Discuss how, or if, Cleartronics should account for the common stock purchase warrant on the date of issuance, July 1, 20X1, and in subsequent years 20X2 and 20X3. Your discussion should include at what amount, if any, the warrants should be reported for each period, how they should be reported in the financial statements, and how changes in the value of the warrants, if any, should be reported in the financial statements. pg 540,542
2. Discuss how Cleartronics should report the restructuring agreement of July 1, 20X4, and how it should account for the agreement in subsequent periods.

| C10–30 | COMPTO MANUFACTURING, INC. |

Balance Sheet Classification of Debt Not in Compliance with the Borrowing Agreement

Compto Manufacturing, Inc. is a publicly held defense contractor with annual revenues in excess of $1.1 billion. Compto entered into a number of borrowing agreements, one of which is with Wilshire National Bank for $150 million payable over the next seven years with interest at $1\frac{1}{2}$ percent above prime.

According to the term of the Wilshire National Bank agreement, Compto must be in compliance at the end of each calendar quarter with a number of debt covenants. If Compto is not in compliance, Wilshire has the right to call the debt immediately. One such covenant requires Compto to maintain a current ratio of 1.5 or better. Compto's current ratio decreased every quarter for the past five quarters, and as of September 30, 20X1, Compto is perilously close to being in violation of this debt covenant with a 1.51 current ratio. During the fourth quarter of 20X1, Compto continued to experience liquidity problems, and its current ratio as of December 31, 20X1, is 1.46.

Wilshire National Bank, on receiving notification from Compto that it is in violation of its borrowing agreement as of December 31, 20X1, entered into discussions with Compto's president and treasurer. Wilshire indicated that it would be willing to waive its right to call the debt with respect to the current covenant violation as of December 31, 20X1, for a period of 9 to 15 months. However, Wilshire indicated that it is not waiving its right to call the debt for any future covenant violations pertaining to the current ratio.

Required
1. If Wilshire waives its right to call the debt with respect to the current covenant violation for a period of nine months, what should be the December 31, 20X1, balance sheet classification of Compto's debt to Wilshire National Bank?
2. What would your response be to question 1 if the period was 15 months?
3. Assume that Compto was not in violation of the current ratio covenant as of December 31, 20X1, but that it is probable that Compto would be in violation of the current ratio covenant as of March 31, 20X2. What should be the December 31, 20X1, balance sheet classification of Compto's debt to Wilshire National Bank?
4. If Wilshire National Bank refuses to waive its right to call the debt with respect to Compto's violation of the debt covenant as of December 31, 20X1, is there any alternative for Compto to avoid classifying the debt as a current liability as of December 31, 20X1?

intent + Ability

| C10–31 | GLEASON CANDY, INC. |

Accounting for a Right of Return

Gleason Candy, Inc. has been manufacturing candy for more than 30 years. The company has an August 31 year-end; 25 percent of its total sales volume is Halloween candy, which contributes 30 percent to the net earnings. Sales are made directly to wholesalers, who then sell to retailers. The terms of the sales have always been net 30 days with no right of return after receipt by the wholesaler. On average, Gleason has always shipped 95 percent of its Halloween candy prior to year-end.

Since several publicized incidents of tampering with Halloween candy and other product tampering incidents, management has become concerned about the impact this might have on their business. Management anticipates that there might be some softening of Halloween sales volume but does not anticipate any significant decline. However, the real impact appears to be coming from their wholesalers, who are starting to demand some right of return with respect to the purchase of Halloween candy. The wholesalers are being squeezed by some large retailers who are refusing to place purchase orders for Halloween candy unless they have a right of return after Halloween.

After extensive discussion, the management of Gleason Candy is convinced that they will have to make concessions to the wholesalers with respect to the right of return of Halloween candy. If concessions are not made, it is highly probable that many wholesalers will do business elsewhere. Gleason Candy is not willing to take that chance and will grant its wholesalers the right of return of Halloween candy up through November 30.

The budgeted sales of Halloween candy for the coming year is $15 million, the same as the prior year's actual sale. However, management is uncertain as to what percentage might be returned as they have no historical experience or other basis for an estimate.

To offset the potential loss of revenues and decrease in earnings, Gleason's management has decided to increase the price of all Halloween candy by 10 percent; this will increase their projected gross margin to 45 percent. They believe that their market will absorb such a price increase and that the increase will cover any decrease in earnings due to returned sales. They do not plan to record any year-end provision in the accounts for returned sales because they have no experience to base their estimate on and because they believe the price increase will cover the returns. They also point out that, as financial statements are issued early in October, they won't have the benefit of hindsight to know what the returns will be until after the financial statements have been issued.

Required
1. Discuss whether you agree with management's assessment of the situation and comment on their logic.
2. As outside independent auditor for Gleason Candy, Inc., what are the accounting issues involved, and how do you recommend they be resolved? State the basis for your recommendations.
3. Without prejudice to your previous responses, assume that actual Halloween candy sales are $15 million and that Gleason records a 10 percent provision for estimated returns at year-end. Also assume that in November of the next fiscal year, credits are given for actual returns of $1,350,000. How would these facts be reflected in the current year and subsequent year financial statements?

Leases and Pensions

C10–32	CARLY MACK CORPORATION

Accounting for a Building Lease on Land Leased to the Building's Lessor

Carly Mack Corporation (CMC) is a manufacturer and distributor of cellular telephones and paging equipment. CMC's operations have expanded in recent years, and CMC is now in need of additional office space for its administrative and sales personnel. CMC owns a large tract of land near its manufacturing plant and plans to build an office building there for its administrative and sales personnel.

CMC contacted several real estate developers about its plans to develop the land. Houston Real Estate Developers, Inc. proposed that CMC lease the land to Houston, which will construct an office building that CMC can lease. CMC found Houston's proposal to be financially attractive and entered into an agreement with Houston. The significant points relating to the agreement are as follows:

- CMC will lease the land to Houston for 40 years. Houston will pay a nominal land rent to CMC for any period that CMC leases the office building from Houston.
- Houston will lease the office building to CMC at a fair market rent for an initial term of 10 years. The lease contains several fixed rate renewal options that allow CMC to extend the lease up to an additional 30 years. At the inception of the lease, the fixed rate renewal options are not considered to be bargain renewal options.
- After the initial 10-year term of the lease, the lease provides CMC with an option to purchase the building for $7.2 million. At the inception of the lease, the purchase option is not considered to be a bargain purchase option. If CMC exercises the purchase option, Houston's land lease is automatically terminated.

- Houston estimates that the office building will cost $9 million to construct and have a useful life of 40 years.
- The lease provides that if CMC does not exercise its purchase or renewal options, Houston will pay CMC fair market rent for the remaining term of the land lease.

Required
1. Discuss the considerations that CMC must take into account when it classifies the office building lease with Houston on land that it is leasing to Houston. Be specific in your response and identify how you would classify the lease.
2. Discuss whether your considerations in classifying the office building lease in question 1 would change if (answer parts *a* and *b* below independently of each other):
   a. CMC leases the land to Houston for 20 years.
   b. Houston pays a nominal land rent to CMC for the entire 40 years. If CMC exercises the purchase option, Houston's land lease will still automatically be terminated.

C10–33	HOME HEALTH CARE, INC.

Accounting for Settlement and Curtailment Gains of Employer's Defined Benefit Pension Plan

Home Health Care, Inc. (HHC) is a distributor of health care products and equipment. It sells primarily to hospitals, nursing homes, and health maintenance organizations. HHC has over 2,000 employees and maintains a defined benefit pension plan for them.

HHC has become increasingly concerned over the escalating cost of maintaining its defined benefit pension plan. After an extensive analysis of its pension plan, HHC concluded that as the plan was significantly overfunded, now was the opportune time to terminate the plan. Accordingly, HHC froze all benefits related to its defined benefit plan effective October 1, 20X1, and terminated the plan effective December 31, 20X1, the last day of its 20X1 fiscal year. Simultaneously, HHC adopted a defined contribution plan effective January 1, 20X2. The new plan covers essentially all the employees of HHC, and HHC's contributions to the plan represent a percentage of each participating employee's annual contribution.

On termination of the defined benefit plan, all participants were considered fully vested. The accumulated plan benefits associated with the terminated plan were settled through the purchase of annuity contracts in 20X2 or through lump-sum distributions to participants in 20X2 with remaining lump-sum distributions to be made in 20X3.

HHC determined that on plan termination a gain on curtailment and settlement would result. As a result of overfunding, residual plan assets would revert to HHC. The curtailment gain and settlement gain were $5.75 million and $6.25 million, respectively. HHC planned to report the curtailment gain in 20X1 and the settlement gain in 20X2.

Required
1. Discuss why HHC would want to terminate its defined benefit plan and adopt a defined contribution plan.
2. Discuss when, if at all, HHC should recognize the $5.75 million curtailment gain and $6.25 million settlement gain.
3. If several years ago HHC had funded prior service costs, discuss how HHC should account for the unamortized balance of the prior service costs at the date that it terminates participation in the defined benefit plan.

C10–34	HOWARD DISTRIBUTORS, INC.

Lessor's Accounting for an Operating Lease

Howard Distributors, Inc. is a distributor of industrial cleaning products. Howard recently constructed new warehouse space for its operations and will lease its old warehouse space, which has an estimated remaining useful life of 10 years. Howard has entered into an agreement to lease 75,000 square feet of its old warehouse space to GVT Markets, Inc. The significant terms of the lease are as follows:

1. The lease term is for six years at $10.00 per square foot. However, GVT will receive a rent holiday the first six months and pay no rent. In addition, since GVT needs only 50,000 square feet of space during the first year, it will pay rent of $250,000 (50,000 square feet $\times$ $10 $\times$ 1/2 year) for the second half of the first year. The annual rent for the second through the sixth year will be $750,000.
2. GVT has 15 months remaining on its existing lease with Jonas Realty at $15,000 per month. Howard reached an agreement with Jonas Realty to settle GVT's lease for a lump-sum of $150,000. Howard will pay the $150,000 directly to Jonas and not be reimbursed by GVT.
3. Howard will reimburse GVT $18,000 for moving expenses. GVT will be responsible for all other moving expenses, which are estimated to be $12,000 to $15,000.
4. Howard will spend $80,000 to make structural changes to the building in accordance with GVT's specifications. GVT will not reimburse Howard for these expenditures.
5. GVT will pay on a quarterly basis its proportionate share (based on 75,000 square feet) of taxes, insurance, and common area maintenance charges.
6. GVT has a three-year renewal option tied to the change in the consumer price index.

Required
1. Discuss how Howard Distributors, Inc. should account for the lease terms with GVT Markets, Inc. Include in your discussion how much rental income and any related expenses that Howard should report in each year of the lease.
2. Discuss why lessors and lessees are often in conflicting positions when negotiating a commercial real estate lease. Consider some of the terms in the Howard/GVT lease.

C10–35	LANGSTON STACEY, INC.

Accounting for an Automobile Lease with a Residual Value Deficiency Clause

Langston Stacey, Inc. recently entered into an agreement to lease a new 20X1 luxury automobile from Shiretown Motors. The fair market value of the automobile was $40,000 at the inception of the lease. Significant terms of the lease are as follows:

- The lease is for 18 months.
- The monthly rental payable at the end of every month is $1,284.
- The lessee is responsible for insurance, maintenance, and taxes.
- The lessee at the end of the lease will be required to make up any residual value deficiency on the automobile between $9,333 and $22,666, or a maximum of $13,333.
- The lessee is limited to 24,000 miles driven over the 18 months. The lessee will pay an additional charge of 25 cents per mile for all miles in excess of the 24,000 mile limit.

Langston Stacey estimates that the economic life of the leased automobile is three or four years. Langston has requested from Shiretown the implicit rate of interest used in the lease, but Shiretown has refused to make that information available. Langston's incremental borrowing rate is 1 percent per month, which approximates the actual implicit rate in the lease.

Required
1. Discuss from the standpoint of each party how it should account for the lease and why.
2. Did your response to question 1 appear to meet the objectives of *FASB Statement Number 13,* "Accounting for Leases"?
3. Discuss how the parties should account for the lease if, instead of requiring Langston to make up any residual value deficiency, the lease required Langston to pay a fee to an unrelated third party to guarantee a $22,666 residual at the conclusion of the lease.
4. Why would Shiretown Motors be willing to agree to the residual value deficiency clause, which holds Langston Stacey potentially liable for only a maximum of $13,333?

C10–36	LEFTIS, COHEN AND BLUM ASSOCIATES

Accounting for Lease Termination Costs, Lease Inducements, and Related Issues

Leftis, Cohen and Blum Associates (LCB) is an advertising agency with offices in New York, Atlanta, Los Angeles, and London. LCB recently entered into a lease agreement with Tyler Realty Development, Inc. for new office space for its New York office. The agreement is for five years at a base rent of $100,000 per month plus a proportionate share of taxes, insurance, and common area maintenance charges. The lease provides LCB with a five-year renewal option tied to the change in the consumer price index. If LCB does not renew the lease, it shall be subject to a $50,000 penalty.

As an inducement to enter into the lease, Tyler Realty has agreed to pay LCB $200,000 to offset the costs of terminating its old lease. In addition, Tyler Realty has agreed to reduce the monthly rent by $40,000 for the first 9 months of the lease. The costs of any build out to adapt the space to LCB's needs will be LCB's responsibility.

LCB will incur a $100,000 termination penalty to buy out its old lease. At the time of termination, the remaining book value of leasehold improvements at the old leased property totals $150,000. LCB estimates that it will incur moving expenses of $20,000 to relocate to the new space. The costs of adapting the new space to its needs will be approximately $300,000, and the improvements are estimated to have a useful life of 15 years.

LCB has been conducting preliminary discussions with several advertising agencies about a possible sale of its agency. Recent advertising agency sales have been consummated on the basis of a multiple of gross revenues or net earnings with certain modifications and adjustments. LCB believes that if it decides to sell the agency, increases in earnings will enable it to command a higher selling price. Thus, with respect to the lease transactions, LCB is planning on selecting the accounting treatment that will maximize earnings.

Required
1. Discuss the accounting treatment that would enable LCB to maximize earnings from all the lease-related transactions.
2. Discuss your recommendation about how LCB should account for all the lease-related transactions and identify the effect on LCB's earnings.

C10–37	VALCOR GAMES COMPANY

Sale and Leaseback of Real Estate with Majority Shareholder

Valcor Games Company, a manufacturer of children's toys, is a closely held corporation. Janet Townsend, the president, owns 70 percent of the outstanding no par common stock and 50 percent of the $100 par value, 7 percent, cumulative, nonvoting preferred stock. The remaining 30 percent of the common stock is owned equally by Townsend's three children. The other 50 percent of the preferred stock is owned by Townsend's husband.

Several years ago Valcor had a new manufacturing building custom designed and constructed on its land. The new facility has significantly contributed to Valcor's operations by reducing its manufacturing costs. During the current year, Valcor sold to and leased back from Janet Townsend this facility, both the land and building, from which it conducts all its manufacturing operations. The property was sold for fair market value of $2,000,000 and resulted in a $900,000 gain, which will be included in Valcor's taxable income in the year of sale. Janet Townsend paid Valcor $1 million in cash and issued a $1 million promissory note that required monthly principal and interest payments for eight years. The fair value of the land was estimated to be 10 percent of the total fair value of the leased property at the inception of the lease. The remaining estimated economic life of the building was 20 years.

The leaseback is for an initial term of four years; the company has options to extend for three successive terms of four years each. The lease requires minimum lease payments of $20,000 monthly during the initial lease term. The minimum lease payments during each extension period are to be redetermined by agreement between the parties when the options are exercised. In addition to the minimum lease payments, Valcor is obligated for maintenance, insurance, and taxes on the real estate. The $20,000 monthly rent is considered to be a fair market rent, and the present value of the monthly payments discounted at the implicit rate for the initial four-year lease term is $760,000.

For financial reporting purposes, Valcor proposes to defer the $900,000 gain and to amortize it ratably over a 20-year period as a reduction of rent expense.

Required

1. What reasons would Valcor and Townsend have for entering into the sale and leaseback agreement?
2. How would you recommend that Valcor account for the sale and leaseback transaction, and what is the basis for your recommendation? Include in your response an evaluation of alternatives considered.

Accounting for Income Taxes

C10–38	ELLIS SYSTEMS, INC.

Accounting for the Tax Consequences of Electing Out of Sub-Chapter S Status

Ellis Systems, Inc. is a contractor of commercial building energy systems and a consultant for the design of energy savings systems. From its inception through June 30, 20X2, Ellis has not been subject to federal income taxes. The company had properly elected Sub-Chapter S status, which resulted in the income of the company through the year ended June 30, 20X2, being included in the taxable income of the shareholders. Ellis terminated the Sub-Chapter S election on July 15, 20X2. Therefore, for the fiscal year beginning July 1, 20X2, Ellis Systems, Inc. will be subject to federal income taxes as a corporation. The company was not subject to any state income taxes.

Due to Ellis's change in tax status as of July 1, 20X2, material temporary differences were created. The differences were attributable to the financial reporting of long-term construction contracts on a percentage-of-completion basis versus a completed contract basis for tax purposes. Consulting income was accounted for on an accrual basis for financial reporting purposes, but on a cash basis for taxes. The resultant tax effect of electing out of Sub-Chapter S status is that some income recognized for financial reporting purposes in the year ending June 30, 20X2, and prior years will become taxable income to the company in the years ending June 30, 20X3, and later. This income will not be taxed to the individual shareholders.

In years ending prior to June 30, 20X2, there were no provisions for federal income taxes, nor were any federal income tax liabilities or deferred tax assets or liabilities reported in Ellis's financial statements. The major accounting issue facing the company since electing out of Sub-Chapter S status is whether deferred federal income taxes should be provided for in the financial statements for year ended June 30, 20X2, and if so, how said taxes should be reported. If deferred taxes are not provided as of June 30, 20X2, the question then becomes how or whether to report the tax effects of terminating Sub-Chapter S status in the June 30, 20X3, financial statements. Ellis's financial vice president, Linda Tarabelli, and its controller, Bryan Joseph, discussed these matters at length.

Bryan Joseph believes that it is preferable to report the tax effects in the June 30, 20X2, financial statements as an extraordinary item. He thinks that it would be more informative to report the deferred tax liabilities in the June 30, 20X2, financial statements. He also believes that the criteria for extraordinary item treatment are met because this is an unusual one-time event in the company's existence which would not recur in the foreseeable future. Joseph notes that on termination of an S election, a new election cannot be made for five years unless the Internal Revenue Service consents to an earlier election. Linda Tarabelli acknowledged Joseph's approach but indicated that there were other alternatives to be considered.

By applying the enacted marginal tax rate to all the temporary differences existing at June 30, 20X2, Joseph calculated Ellis's expected future federal income taxes payable to be $780,000. The $780,000 represents $340,000 of taxes pertaining to consulting income, expected to be payable by June 30, 20X3; and $440,000 of taxes pertaining to construction contracts, of which $250,000 is expected to be payable by June 30, 20X3, and the remainder in subsequent years.

Required

1. Discuss whether you agree with Bryan Joseph's proposed accounting and reporting for the termination of Ellis's Sub-Chapter S election.
2. Discuss the other alternatives that Linda Tarabelli referred to in accounting and reporting for the termination of Ellis's Sub-Chapter S election. Include in your discussion the specific accounting period that you are considering.
3. How do you recommend Ellis account for and report the termination of its Sub-Chapter S election, and what is the basis for your recommendation?
4. Do you agree with reporting deferred tax assets and deferred tax liabilities in a classified statement of financial position as current or noncurrent based on the classification of the related assets or liabilities which give rise to the temporary differences? State your reasons.

temporary difference

| C10–39 | WESTIN SUN INSURANCE COMPANY |

Accounting and Reporting for the Tax Benefit of an Operating Loss Carryforward

Westin Sun Insurance Company is a diversified insurance and financial services company. Westin also has interests in real estate development and technological enterprises. Beginning in the fiscal year ending November 30, 20X1, Westin began recognizing the tax benefit of a tax loss carryforward generated in the same fiscal year in its financial statements. Westin reported $17 million of tax benefits recoverable in its November 30, 20X1, balance sheet and a like amount in its earnings statement for the year then ended. The tax benefit represented approximately 30 percent of net income and was measured by using the enacted marginal tax rate applicable in the period that Westin expected to realize the tax benefit. Westin could not carry back the current year net operating loss because taxable income in the prior years eligible for carryback had previously been offset by a net operating loss deduction.

For financial reporting purposes, Westin has reported net income in 7 of the past 10 years. However, for income tax purposes, Westin reported a net operating loss for the year ended November 30, 20X1. The primary differences, excluding temporary differences, between pretax accounting income and taxable income are tax-exempt interest and excludable dividends earned by Westin. Westin's management further explained that the tax-exempt interest and excludable dividends could not be used to offset losses generated by nonlife insurance operations of Westin. Westin has earned a substantial amount of its tax-exempt interest and excludable dividends from funds held for future casualty and property claim payments.

Westin's management believes that it is appropriate to recognize the tax benefit of the loss carryforward arising in the fiscal year ending November 30, 20X1, in its November 30, 20X1, financial statements. The company points out that it has elected consolidation for income tax purposes. This will mean that profitable life insurance company operations will offset nonlife insurance company losses. Also, it is expected that future operations of nonlife insurance companies will become profitable and start generating taxable income. Westin does not anticipate a problem in the realization of the tax benefit of the operating loss carryforward within the newly enacted 20-year period.

Required
1. Discuss the circumstances when it is appropriate to recognize a deferred tax asset for an operating loss carryforward.
2. Assuming that it is appropriate for Westin to recognize the tax benefit of the operating loss in its November 30, 20X1, financial statements, identify how the tax benefit should be reported.
3. What tax-planning strategies are available to Westin for realizing the tax benefit of the operating loss carryforward?
4. What should Westin do if it recognizes the deferred tax asset for the operating loss carryforward and then concludes it is more likely than not that realization of some or all of the deferred tax benefits will not occur?

Accounting Changes

| C10–40 | BECKER ELECTRICAL SUPPLY COMPANY, INC. |

Change in Inventory Reporting

Becker Electrical Supply Company, Inc. is a discount wholesale distributor of electrical supplies. Becker, a closely held company, has been operating for over 20 years. Sales have increased every year since inception and were over $14 million for the year ended December 31, 20X1.

Becker has been receiving an adverse opinion from its outside auditors due to the fact that it has been valuing inventories under the constant price method, which is not in accordance with generally accepted accounting principles. The following footnote from Becker's 20X1 financial statements explains this method.

Inventories

The company has consistently valued its inventories using a constant price method under which individual items are valued at their initial purchase price regardless of any changes in their price when replaced in subsequent years. In an inflationary period and a period of increased inventory volume, under the constant price method inventory valuations are generally lower than actual cost or market price, and net income is generally understated to the extent of the difference in actual cost and constant cost of current year increments in inventories, net of income tax effect; and year-end inventories, income tax liability, and stockholders' equity are likewise understated. The opposite result is obtained in a deflationary period and a period of decreased inventory volume.

Becker also valued its inventories for federal income tax purposes by using the constant price method. Because this method is not acceptable for federal income tax purposes, Becker applied to the Internal Revenue Service for permission to change its method of accounting for valuing inventories from its present method to cost or market, whichever is lower, on a first-in, first-out (FIFO) basis, beginning with the taxable year ending December 31, 20X2 (year of change). Becker indicated that the inventories as of the beginning of the year of change were as follows:

Inventories valued at FIFO cost or market, whichever is lower	$2,010,654
Inventories under constant price method	959,822
Adjustment-increase in income	$1,050,832

The Internal Revenue Service granted permission for Becker to change its method of accounting for inventories as requested and indicated that the amount of adjustment is to be taken into income for tax purposes over a 10-year period (adjustment period). In addition, the service provided:

1. That Becker is to take one-tenth of the adjustment into account in computing taxable income each taxable year of the adjustment period beginning with the year of change.
2. That Becker's inventories at the beginning of the year of change, the end of the year of change, and for later taxable years shall be valued at FIFO cost or market, whichever is lower.
3. That during the adjustment period, if the value of Becker's inventories related to this change is reduced as of the last day of any year by more than 33 1/3 percent of the inventory at the beginning of the year of change, the balance of the adjustment not previously taken into account in computing taxable income will be included in income in the year of the inventory reduction.

Becker also adopted the FIFO method, effective January 1, 20X2, for financial reporting purposes. In preparing financial statements for 20X2, Becker is uncertain as to the financial reporting requirements as a result of the change in the inventory method. Becker estimates the total tax effect of the adjustment over the 10 years to be $357,000.

Required
1. Discuss how this change should be accounted for and reported in Becker's 20X2 financial statements and explain the basis for your conclusions. Be specific in your response as to how the effect of this change is reported. pg 825
2. Discuss why Becker might have been willing to accept an adverse opinion on its financial statements for years prior to 20X2.

C10–41	OCTOVAN CONSTRUCTION, INC.

Changes in Depreciation Accounting and Long-Term Construction Contract Accounting

Octovan Construction, Inc. is a small privately held construction company. Over 60 percent of its revenue is derived from the design and construction of industrial and residential septic systems. Octovan's earnings have steadily declined over the past several years while its working capital and debt to equity ratio have deteriorated. Octovan is investigating operational and financial strategies to mitigate these trends.

One of Octovan's primary creditors, Broadmoor County Bank, has become increasingly concerned over Octovan's $600,000 unsecured demand note that it is holding. Subsequent to the current year-end, but before the issuance of any financial statements, Octovan and Broadmoor reached an agreement in principal that allows Octovan to refinance the $600,000 demand note. The refinanced debt will include 60 equal principal payments of $10,000 per month with interest at the prime rate plus 1½ percent. Octovan's motor vehicles, machinery, and equipment will be assigned as collateral. Octovan is planning on reporting the debt as a noncurrent liability in the current year balance sheet.

In reviewing its accounting policies, Octovan believes that changes are warranted for depreciation accounting and long-term construction contract accounting. In prior years, Octovan reported depreciation for both tax and financial reporting purposes based on the modified accelerated cost recovery system (MACRS) as provided for by the Internal Revenue Service code. However, for the current year, Octovan changed its method of depreciation accounting for financial reporting purposes to obtain a better matching of revenue and expense. The newly adopted method provides for depreciation by the double-declining-balance method using longer useful lives. The estimated useful lives of the assets are as follows:

Category	Life
Motor vehicles	3–5 years
Machinery and equipment	5–10 years
Office furniture and equipment	7–10 years
Buildings and leasehold improvements	18–35 years

The effect of this change is to reduce beginning of the year accumulated depreciation $250,000 and to reduce current year depreciation expense $100,000. Tax depreciation will continue to exceed book depreciation for the next several years.

Octovan also changed its method of accounting for long-term construction contracts. In previous periods, revenue was recognized whenever customers were billed for both tax and financial reporting. The timing of billings was specified in each contract. Now for financial reporting purposes, Octovan has adopted the percentage-of-completion method of accounting for long-term construction contracts in order to obtain a better matching of revenue and expense. The effect of this change increases costs and estimated earnings on uncompleted contracts (not yet billed) by $200,000 as of the beginning of the current year and increases current year revenues by $80,000.

Octovan is planning on reporting both of these changes prospectively in the current year financial statements. Octovan's effective federal tax rate is 30 percent for the current and prior years. Octovan does not anticipate a change in its future effective federal tax rate.

Required

1. Discuss whether you agree with Octovan's plans for financial reporting as of the current year-end.
2. If you disagree with any of Octovan's plans in question 1, discuss your recommendation for financial reporting. Be specific as to financial statement impact and presentation.
3. Based on your response in question 2, draft a footnote to Octovan's financial statements for its change in depreciation accounting and long-term construction contract accounting.

C10–42	PILGRIM CORPORATION

Change in Classification of LIFO Inventory Pools

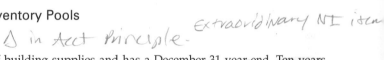

Pilgrim Corporation is a manufacturer of building supplies and has a December 31 year-end. Ten years ago the company adopted the dollar value last-in, first-out (LIFO) method of inventory valuation for all its inventories. LIFO valuations have always been determined by six LIFO pools corresponding to the company's six operating product divisions.

In early 20X2, Pilgrim embarked on a project to change its method of LIFO inventory valuation by expanding the number of LIFO pools. The concept was to classify pools on the basis of product similarity rather than operating divisions. Pilgrim's management calculated the impact on earnings of various proposed pools and finally settled on a classification of 92 product pools that appeared to enhance 20X2 earnings the most.

After agreeing on the new classification of LIFO pools, Pilgrim's management met with key operating employees to explain the change. During the course of this and subsequent meetings, employees were informed of the positive impact LIFO liquidations would have on earnings. Employees were also informed that it was company policy to maximize earnings and that LIFO liquidations would help achieve this goal.

The effect of the change in classification of LIFO pools on 20X2 net earnings was material. Net earnings increased $4.7 million due to the change; this represented approximately 18 percent of net earnings. The only disclosure regarding inventories and the change in inventory pools in the company's 20X2 financial statements was included in the following footnotes:

Note 1: Summary of Significant Accounting Policies
Inventories—Inventories are stated at cost determined on the last-in, first-out (LIFO) method of inventory–valuation. Market value of domestic inventories is not lower than LIFO cost. Inventory costs include raw material, labor, and manufacturing overhead.

Note 5: Inventories
Inventories consisted of the following categories at December 31 ($000 omitted):

	20X2	20X1
Finished products	$29,235	$30,678
Work in process	10,120	7,002
Raw materials and supplies	42,811	39,313
Total inventories	$82,166	$76,993

During 20X2, the company reclassified its LIFO pools to correspond to similar product groups rather than divisional operating product groups. LIFO inventory costs are now assigned to small groups of similar products and provide a better matching of current costs against current sales. The effect of this change was to increase 20X2 net earnings by $4,712,000, or $.18 per share.

Required
1. Describe how a LIFO liquidation can maximize earnings.
2. Discuss whether you agree with Pilgrim's change in its LIFO pools and its disclosure of the change. Include in your discussion any proposed changes in reporting or disclosure and the reasons for your changes.

Stockholders' Equity

| C10–43 | A. F. HALL, INC. |

Accounting for Redeemable Convertible Preferred Stock

A. F. Hall, Inc., a privately held company, is a supplier of flexible packaging for the food and beverage industry. Hall produces labeling for soft-drink bottles and packaging for such products as frozen foods, cheese, meat, snack foods, and candy. Hall reported sales of $47 million in 20X1. Hall's board of directors has been contemplating a public offering of its stock and has contacted an investment banker to investigate this possibility.

On May 15, 20X1, in a private offering, Hall issued 400,000 shares of redeemable convertible Series A, $1.00 par value, 6 percent cumulative preferred stock at $10 per share. The offering was made to fund new product development and expand manufacturing capacity. Each Series A share is convertible into one and one-half shares of common stock at the option of the holder and is subject to mandatory conversion at the earlier of a public offering or mandatory redemption May 15, 20X4, at a price of $14.50 per share. No accumulated dividends are due on the Series A preferred stock when converted.

In preparing its draft December 31, 20X1, financial statements, Hall's controller reported the Series A preferred stock in the stockholders' equity section. She did not adjust the carrying amount of the preferred stock for the periodic accretion of the difference between issue price and conversion price. On review of the 20X1 draft financial statements, Hall's assistant controller expressed the opinion that in substance the preferred stock was really debt financing. He recommended that the preferred stock be reported as long-term debt and the periodic accretion be reported as interest expense in the income statement.

Required
1. Discuss whether the A. F. Hall, Inc. Series A preferred stock is an equity or debt instrument.
2. Discuss what might have been the motivating factors for A. F. Hall, Inc. to issue the Series A preferred stock.
3. Discuss how A. F. Hall, Inc. should account for the Series A preferred stock. Include in your discussion all the alternatives considered and the pros and cons of each alternative.
4. Discuss any other accounting issues that are raised when deciding how to account for and report the A. F. Hall, Inc. Series A preferred stock.

| C10–44 | INTILEXT TECHNOLOGY, INC. |

Accounting for Stock Option Plans

Intilext Technology, Inc., a publicly held company, is a supplier of advanced performance printheads, specialty printers, and printer mechanisms. Its products are primarily used by ticketing, office automation, lottery, labeling, and specialty printing industries.

On January 1, 20X1, Intilext implemented a stock option plan for certain key employees. Under the plan to be accounted for by the intrinsic value method, employees were granted 200,000 stock options which have an exercise price equal to the $10 market price on the January 1, 20X1, grant date. Effective December 31, 20X1, employees were fully vested in the options and the options were exercisable for 12 years. If as of December 31, 20X5, an employee has not yet exercised his stock options, he can elect to receive one share of restricted stock in exchange for every four stock options held. The election to exchange options for restricted shares cancels the options and does not require any cash from the employee.

The restricted shares carry all the rights of ownership as unrestricted shares except that the employee cannot sell them until after December 31, 20X8. If a holder of restricted stock terminates his employment or is terminated by Intilext prior to December 31, 20X8, the restricted shares must be redeemed by Intilext for $1.00 per share.

Through December 31, 20X5, none of the stock options were exercised, forfeited, or canceled. The quoted market price of Intilext Technology, Inc.'s stock during this period was as follows:

Date	Market Price Per Share
January 1, 20X1	$10
December 31, 20X1	12
December 31, 20X2	13
December 31, 20X3	15½
December 31, 20X4	13¼
December 31, 20X5	16½

Required
1. What is the nature of the Intilext stock option plan?
2. Identify what amount, if any, Intilext should report as compensation expense for the stock option plan for years ending December 31, 20X1, through December 31, 20X5. Provide a schedule that supports your response.
3. How would your response to question 2 be different if the restricted stock alternative can be settled December 31, 20X5, at the employee's election in either stock or cash equivalent to the market value of the stock?
4. What would be the nature of the stock option plan described in question 3?

| C10–45 | KELSO CORPORATION |

Accounting for Stock to Be Issued

Kelso Corporation is a manufacturer of home telephones. Kelso was incorporated in 20X1 and its shares are held by 10 individuals. The company has a calendar year-end.

During 20X2, Kelso's president and major shareholder has been attempting to obtain additional capital from investors. In September 20X2, he was able to obtain $300,000 from two investors with the understanding that 300 shares of voting common stock would be issued to them only if an additional $700,000 could be raised from other specified investors. If the additional capital is not raised, Kelso will repay the $300,000. Kelso anticipated receiving the additional money by the end of October 20X2, but at the request of the individuals providing the $300,000, he issued them a 30-day promissory note for the money. It was the intent of all parties to convert the debt to stock once the additional capital was obtained.

However, unexpected delays arose in receiving the additional capital. Finally, on December 24, 20X2, agreements for the $700,000 were signed, the money was received, and 700 shares of voting common stock were issued to the investors. Kelso then notified its attorney to issue the 300 shares to the individuals holding the promissory notes, which had been renewed at every 30-day interval. The attorney in turn informed Kelso that due to blue sky state laws to which the two investors are subject, stock subscriptions must be published 10 days prior to the issuance of the stock. Accordingly, the subscriptions were published and the 300 shares of stock were issued on January 7, 20X3.

In preparing its December 31, 20X2, balance sheet, Kelso is planning on reporting the $300,000 as equity rather than debt.

Required
1. Discuss the alternatives in reporting the $300,000 as of December 31, 20X2.
2. Discuss which alternative you would recommend and the basis for your recommendation.

C10–46	WBM MEDICAL CORPORATION

Accounting for Purchase Warrants with Put and Call Features Issued in a Stock Acquisition

WBM Medical Corporation designs, develops, manufactures, and markets medical devices and systems for use in specialized surgical and diagnostic procedures. On June 1, 20X1, WBM acquired all the outstanding voting stock of Cion Technology, Inc., a manufacturer of laparoscopy equipment for less invasive surgery. The purchase price was in excess of the fair market value of Cion's net identifiable assets.

In connection with WBM's acquisition of Cion's stock, WBM issued a warrant to Aldolfo Cion, Cion's sole shareholder, for 800,000 shares and a warrant to Karlin, Zenger & Zinn (KZZ), investment bankers, for 1,600,000 shares. WBM also paid $600,000 to KZZ. The warrant and cash were compensation for KZZ's investment banking services for the acquisition of Cion Technology. The warrant holders can purchase common stock of WBM for $1.50 per share through December 31, 20X8, or during the period from July 1, 20X6, through December 31, 20X6, put the warrant to WBM at 93 percent of its fair market value. The warrant also provides for WBM to call the warrant at 109 percent of its fair market value during the period from July 1, 20X4, through June 30, 20X6. On June 30, 20X1, based on KZZ's appraisal and the appraisal of an independent third-party investment banker, the warrants to Cion and KZZ were assigned values of $50,000 and $100,000 respectively.

At the time of the acquisition, KZZ arranged temporary financing for WBM and received an additional fee of $225,000. The loan agreement provides that as a condition precedent to WBM receiving the financing, WBM issue the warrant for 1,600,000 shares, and the warrant itself specify that it is issued to satisfy the loan agreement provision. The loan agreement lists only the $225,000 as the fee for obtaining the loan.

In December 20X1, KZZ arranged permanent financing for WBM's acquisition. At this time WBM issued another warrant to KZZ to purchase 500,000 shares at $3.75 per share through December 31, 20X8. This warrant has comparable put and call features as the $1.50 warrant issued on June 1, 20X1. This warrant, like the previous one, is not listed as part of the fees to be paid for obtaining the loan, but the issuance is a condition precedent to the borrowing.

Required
1. Discuss the 20X1 and subsequent year accounting and reporting issues raised for WBM by its issuance of the $1.50 warrant to Aldolfo Cion, the $1.50 warrant to KZZ, and the $3.75 warrant to KZZ. Your discussion should include the impact on the financial statements.
2. What is your recommendation in accounting and reporting for each warrant at the date of issuance, at the current December 31, 20X1, balance sheet date, and at subsequent balance sheet dates? State the basis for your recommendation.

Business Combinations

C10–47	A. C. EDWARDS ELECTRONICS

Acquisition of Treasury Shares and the Impact on the Pooling Method of Accounting

A. C. Edwards Electronics (ACEE) is a closely held electronics company. ACEE's stock has historically traded in a limited market, primarily between existing shareholders. Recently a group of shareholders expressed concern to the board of directors about the liquidity of their investment in ACEE.

ACEE's board is sympathetic to the shareholders' concern and is considering two options to assist in establishing more trading activity in the limited market for its stock. The options are as follows:

1. ACEE would act as a market maker in its own stock by making a tender offer to purchase its stock and then attempting to sell any tendered shares. Several years earlier, ACEE made a similar tender offer for its shares; no shares were in fact tendered, but the offer had the effect of stimulating stock trading among shareholders, at prices in excess of that offered by ACEE.
2. ACEE would pay a fee to an independent third party to make a market in their stock. The fee would be based in part on any losses realized by the party as a result of being a market maker in ACEE's stock. This option would enable ACEE to improve the marketability of its stock without being in the position of reacquiring its own shares.

ACEE is concerned that if it elects either of these options, shares would be considered tainted for purposes of applying the pooling method of accounting for possible future business combinations. At this time ACEE is not contemplating any business combinations, but that does not preclude the possibility in the future.

As a separate issue, ACEE is also considering the establishment of an employee stock ownership plan (ESOP). Under the plan, ACEE would purchase treasury stock and hold the stock for future funding of the ESOP.

Required
1. What is the concern over treasury shares in a business combination accounted for as a pooling of interests?
2. Discuss whether, if shares were purchased by ACEE and subsequently not resold (option 1), the shares would be considered tainted for purposes of applying the pooling method of accounting for possible future business combinations.
3. Discuss whether, if ACEE paid a fee to an independent third-party market maker (option 2), that would cause any of the shares owned or sold by the market maker to be considered tainted for purposes of applying the pooling method of accounting for possible future business combinations.

4. Discuss whether, if ACEE were to purchase treasury shares to fund the ESOP, such shares would be considered tainted for purposes of applying the pooling method of accounting for possible future business combinations.

C10–48	CROCKER INDUSTRIES, INC.

Pooling versus Purchase Accounting

Crocker Industries, Inc. manufactures and distributes health and beauty aid products which are primarily sold to drug chains, food chains, and mass merchandisers. Many of its products are individually trade-marked. Crocker has expanded its product line and market through selective acquisitions, and annual sales now exceed $800 million.

Crocker targeted JD Company, Inc., a manufacturer of skin care products, as a potential acquisition and made a tender offer to acquire JD Company. Subsequent to the offer, the parties reached a tentative agreement, which provides for Crocker to acquire all of the 1,000,000 outstanding shares of JD Company voting common stock. Crocker would acquire 910,000 shares of JD Company by exchanging 1.3 shares of its voting common stock for each share of JD Company and would acquire the remaining 90,000 shares of JD Company by paying cash. In addition, Crocker agreed to the cash buyout of 20,000 outstanding JD Company stock options. These options are held by JD Company's management who also are shareholders.

Prior to making the tender offer, Crocker's analysis of the potential acquisition of JD Company revealed that a significant amount of goodwill would result if the purchase method is used to account for the business combination. Crocker structured its tender offer to enable it to account for the potential acquisition of JD Company by the pooling of interests method.

Required

1. Do you agree with the concept of pooling of interests accounting? State your reasons and the basis for your position. Include in your response whether Crocker's proposed acquisition of JD Company appears to be in agreement with the concept of pooling.
2. Why might Crocker want to account for the proposed acquisition of JD Company by the pooling of interests method?
3. Discuss whether Crocker's proposed acquisition of JD Company can be accounted for as a pooling of interests.
4. Without prejudice to your response in question 3, assuming that it is not appropriate to account for the proposed acquisition as a pooling of interests, discuss possible ways Crocker might restructure the proposal in order to qualify the acquisition as a pooling of interests. Specifically address the issue of the outstanding stock options.

C10–49	HAVOLINE ENTERPRISE, INC.

Accounting for a Business Combination

John Havoline, Carla Mendoza, and Jason Garoux were the sole shareholders of Havoline Enterprise, Inc., a manufacturer of metal castings, and held 80, 15, and 5 percent, respectively, of the outstanding voting common stock. John Havoline was the president, Carla Mendoza the vice president, and Jason Garoux the chief financial officer of Havoline Enterprise.

John Havoline wanted to consummate a business combination between Havoline Enterprise and another company in order to step up the book values of Havoline's assets to market value. He also wanted the combination to be with a public company in order to make other acquisitions easier, to possibly make a public offering in the future, and to provide himself, Mendoza, and Garoux with an investment that would be much more liquid than Havoline Enterprise common stock. The combination will not qualify for the pooling of interests method of accounting because Havoline Enterprise was recently the subsidiary of another corporation.

Thus, early in 20X1, John Havoline entered into discussions about a possible business combination with David O'Shanley, the controlling shareholder of Briggs Baton, Inc., an inactive public company. Briggs Baton formerly was a manufacturer of industrial machinery until it ceased operations two years ago. At the time that it entered into discussions with John Havoline, Briggs Baton's only assets were cash and marketable securities totaling approximately $600,000.

After several months of negotiations, an agreement was reached wherein the shareholders of Havoline Enterprise would be issued 80 percent of the outstanding common stock of Briggs Baton, Inc., in exchange for 100 percent of the outstanding common stock of Havoline Enterprise, Inc. After the business combination, Havoline Enterprise became a wholly owned subsidiary of Briggs Baton, Inc., and John Havoline, now a 64 percent shareholder in Briggs Baton, became president and chairman of the board of directors of Briggs Baton. Carla Mendoza and Jason Garoux, now 12 percent and 4 percent shareholders in Briggs Baton, also became officers and board members of the company. Three other individuals associated with Havoline Enterprise were named to the nine-member board of directors of Briggs Baton.

In preparing consolidated financial statements for the year ended December 31, 20X1, John Havoline and Carla Mendoza increased the carrying value of Havoline Enterprise's fixed assets from $3,898,200 to an appraised value of $6,690,700. Depreciation in the financial statements was based on the $3,898,200 carrying value of the assets with a useful life of 20 years for machinery and equipment. Prior to 20X1, the useful life of Havoline's machinery and equipment had been eight years, which was always considered reasonable.

The 20X1 consolidated balance sheet also presented as a current asset a $210,000 account receivable of which no provision had been made for losses due to uncollectible amounts. The receivable resulted from a 20X1 transaction in which Havoline Enterprise sold obsolete inventory previously written down to a zero basis. The sale was to Greta Manufacturing Company, which was controlled by John Havoline. Greta's financial statements for the year ended September 30, 20X1, reported an operating loss of $806,129 on sales of $4,021,290 and a deficit stockholders' equity of $1,233,541. The 20X1 auditor's report on Greta included an explanatory paragraph about Greta's ability to continue as a going concern for a reasonable period of time.

The only disclosure in the consolidated statements prepared by Havoline and Mendoza pertaining to the machinery and equipment indicated that they were being depreciated by the straight-line method over 20 years. There was no disclosure in regard to the receivable from Greta.

The 20X1 consolidated financial statements prepared by Havoline and Mendoza received an unqualified opinion from the accounting firm of Kelp, Shatner and Company.

Required
1. Discuss whether you agree with how John Havoline and Carla Mendoza prepared the 20X1 consolidated financial statements. State the reasons for your position and give your proposed accounting treatment if you disagree.
2. If you indicated any proposed changes in question 1, discuss the impact such changes would have on the consolidated balance sheet and income statement.

C10–50	JUBILANT COMPANY, INC.

Accounting for a Preacquisition Contingency

Jubilant Company, Inc., a food processor and operator of a chain of retail supermarkets, had been negotiating over the past several months to acquire Fido Foods, Inc., a processor of canned and dry pet foods. The net book value of Fido Foods was $40 million and Fido has been profitable the past 5 years, with an annual average sales increase of 7 percent. An agreement was finally reached and Jubilant was to acquire all of the outstanding voting common stock of Fido for $50 million. The parties agreed that $87 million should be assigned to the identifiable assets of Fido, but there was a question regarding $2 million of the $40 million in liabilities reported by Fido.

The $2 million had been accrued by Fido the previous year for the estimated loss in settlement of a lawsuit. The suit charged that Fifi, a 10-year-old Great Dane, owned by Mrs. A. Hazelton Abrahams, was poisoned by Fido dog food and subsequently died. Mrs. Abrahams, a 75-year-old widow, sought damages of $10 million in total for suffering caused by the loss of her only companion and protector, and for the pain and conscious suffering that Fifi endured. After many hours of research and discussion, the management of Fido and their legal counsel, Jasper and Jasper, concluded that Fido had some liability exposure in this case. One batch of Fido dog food was recalled, and it was possible that Mrs. Abrahams's dog might have eaten some. Also, several years ago the company settled a similar suit out of court for $1 million.

Jubilant's management, legal counsel, and accountants expressed reservations about the validity of this claim and felt that the recording of a $2 million liability was going overboard. They were also aware that Fido's accounting policies were very conservative and that Jasper and Jasper had a reputation for being extremely conservative. Jasper and Jasper in turn gave Jubilant's management a written legal opinion stating their position. They estimated that the range of liability was from $1 million to $4 million, and their best estimate was for a $2 million settlement.

In late 20X1, Jubilant Company, Inc. completed the transaction and acquired all of the outstanding voting common stock of Fido Foods, Inc. for the agreed-on $50 million. The acquisition required the use of the purchase method of accounting and was accounted for as such. Jubilant's December 31, 20X1, consolidated statement of financial position did report the $2 million liability. Management finally concluded that the lawsuit was probable and that $2 million was a reasonable estimate.

In June 20X2, Jubilant's legal counsel, Geller, Harriman and Mann, settled the lawsuit out of court for $100,000. It seems that Mrs. Abrahams's dog had been known not only to eat the contents of Fido canned dog food but also on occasion to eat the can too. Once confronted with this information, Mrs. A. Hazelton Abrahams felt that the $100,000 would more than console her and buy a new puppy with a few cans of dog food to boot.

On being informed of the settlement, Jubilant's president, Colin W. Downing, was ecstatic and informed the controller, Hank Zorri, that pretax earnings would now be $1.9 million more than anticipated. Hank responded that he wasn't so sure that the adjustment was income; it might even be a prior period adjustment or something else. At this point Downing screamed, "Call the CPAs—I don't want to lose $1.9 million of income because you think it's something else."

Required

1. As the independent CPA for Jubilant Company, Inc., how are you going to advise them to account for the settlement of the lawsuit and why? Include in your discussion the alternatives considered and their effect on Jubilant's December 31, 20X1, and subsequent years' consolidated financial statements.
2. Would it make any difference in your response to question 1 if the lawsuit was settled in June 20X3 instead of June 20X2?

3. Assuming Jubilant did not allocate the $2 million liability as part of the purchase price, how are you going to advise them to account for the June 20X2 settlement of the lawsuit and why? Include in your discussion the alternatives considered and the basis for your conclusion.

C10–51	KENDALL BANK & TRUST COMPANY

Dividend Policy and the Impact on the Pooling Method of Accounting

Kendall Bank & Trust Company is a publicly held company. Several years ago, Kendall's board of directors articulated a policy of achieving higher returns on equity and maximizing shareholder value through the leveraging of its excess capital position. This policy included cash and stock dividend distributions.

On December 10, 20X7, Kendall's board declared its regular quarterly dividend of $.22 per common share. In addition, on that date the board declared a special cash dividend of $.22 per common share and a 5 percent common stock dividend. Kendall's board also declared a 5 percent common stock dividend in the fourth quarter of 20X5 and 20X6. These dividends are all part of the board's plan of achieving higher returns on equity and maximizing shareholder value. Currently, the return on equity is 11.2 percent but is projected to increase to 15.0 percent in 3 years.

On November 21, 20X7, Olympic Trust Company contacted Kendall's management about a possible merger. At the December 10 board meeting, Kendall's management advised the board that it had been contacted by Olympic, and it provided some summary data to Olympic's management on December 2, 20X7. At the conclusion of the meeting, Kendall's board was uncertain whether Olympic would pursue a merger, and if it did, whether it would want to enter into a merger with Olympic.

In late December 20X7, merger discussions between Olympic and Kendall resumed and escalated quickly. On January 7, 20X8, Kendall signed a definitive agreement to acquire all of the outstanding common stock of Olympic in exchange for Kendall's common stock. Kendall is planning to account for the business combination by the pooling of interests method. Prior to entering into the agreement with Olympic, Kendall's board reviewed its recent earnings (loss) and dividend history. A summary of the Kendall's earnings (loss) and dividends per share from 20X1 through 20X7 is as follows:

	20X7	20X6	20X5	20X4	20X3	20X2	20X1
Earnings (loss) per common share	$1.45	$1.09	$.92	$.68	$.36	$(.22)	$.81
Common cash dividends per share	$1.10	$ .72	$.48	$.40	$.44	$.68	$.68

Adverse regional economic conditions contributed to Kendall incurring a loss in 20X2. These conditions resulted in Kendall holding a larger percentage than normal of nonperforming assets in 20X2 through 20X4. Due to uncertainties caused by the regional economic downturn, Kendall temporarily reduced cash dividends in 20X3 and 20X4. As economic conditions improved, Kendall's percentage of nonperforming assets declined by 20X5, and Kendall systematically began to increase cash dividends.

Required
1. What is the concern over dividends in a business combination to be accounted for by the pooling of interests method? How does that concern specifically relate to Kendall?
2. Discuss whether you agree with Kendall's proposal to account for the business combination by the pooling of interests method. Assume that any criteria for pooling accounting not mentioned in the case are met. Support your response with an analysis of the facts and data presented in the case.

3. Without prejudice to your response in question 2, assume the SEC informs Kendall that the business combination does not qualify as a pooling of interests. Can you recommend any action that Kendall might take in 20X7 to "cure" the situation and have the SEC agree with Kendall's use of the pooling of interests method?

C10–52	PRESTONE, RILES & NYE ASSOCIATES

Consolidation versus the Equity Method of Accounting for an Investment

Prestone, Riles & Nye Associates (PRN), a marketing communications company, has offices throughout the United States and a wholly owned subsidiary in the United Kingdom. In an attempt to expand its international presence, PRN has been looking to acquire a marketing communications company having ties to the expanding eastern European market.

PRN has identified such a company and entered into an agreement to acquire all of the outstanding stock of Broadwick Communications, Inc., a marketing firm with excellent contacts throughout eastern Europe. Broadwick is a closely held company with three shareholders each owning 25 percent of the stock and eight individuals owning the remaining 25 percent. The agreement provides that in exchange for Broadwick's stock, PRN will pay $14 million cash to the Broadwick shareholders (Sellers) and form a new entity, BPRN International, Inc. BPRN will conduct the former activities of Broadwick. BPRN will have two classes of stock, Common A and Common B, owned by PRN and the Sellers. The ownership distribution of BPRN will be as follows:

	PRN	Sellers
Common A	48 percent	52 percent
Common B	80 percent	20 percent

Common A is voting stock and Common B nonvoting stock. The Sellers believed that it was important for them to maintain voting control of the new entity so that their existing clients did not perceive them to have sold out. The agreement provides that all significant operational and financial decisions of BPRN require a 67 percent affirmative vote of the Common A shareholders. The agreement stipulates that income distributions or loss incurrences will be shared in accordance with the ownership of Common B shares. The ownership percentages of Common B shares also determine the ratio in which shareholders would be responsible for future capital contributions, loans, or guarantees of indebtedness.

The agreement provides the Sellers with a put option to sell 4 percent of the Common A stock of BPRN to PRN at any time during the next four years. The exercise price will be $2.2 million for each 1 percent sold during the first two years and $1.8 million for each 1 percent sold during the last two years. PRN will be required to pay the exercise price if the Sellers exercise the put option. The exercise price currently is estimated to be significantly in excess of the fair market value of each 1 percent of Common A stock.

The three former majority shareholders of Broadwick also have entered into executive management contracts with BPRN. The contracts call for each executive to receive an annual base salary of $200,000 and be eligible to participate in PRN's management bonus program. The value of this benefit is estimated to be almost equal to the base salaries. However, the executives will not receive any cash bonuses until such time that the Sellers exercise put options resulting in PRN acquiring at least 2.1 percent of the outstanding Common A stock.

PRN has made arrangements for BPRN to obtain a significant bank loan to help finance its expansion in eastern Europe. PRN will provide administrative and account support for BPRN in consideration for a fee of 1/2 of 1 percent of net account billings. PRN is planning to account for and report its investment in

BPRN using the equity method until such time as it has a controlling interest in the voting Common A stock. PRN anticipates that the Sellers, in order to minimize individual taxes, will not exercise their put option until the next calendar year at the earliest. The fiscal year-end for PRN is November 30.

Required
1. Discuss the reasoning and support that PRN has in using the equity method to account for and report its investment in BPRN.
2. Discuss whether you agree with PRN's plan to account for and report its investment in BPRN using the equity method. If you disagree, state your proposed accounting and reporting for the BPRN investment and your reasons for such treatment.

| C10–53 | UNIVERSAL SOFTWARE, INC. |

Accounting for Purchased Research and Development

Universal Software, Inc., a publicly held company, is a software developer of a wide range of business applications programs. Universal serves the materials-management needs of all major industries, including manufacturers, distributors, health care, financial institutions, and transportation. Its primary products are software for purchasing, materials control, inventory management, and financial modeling and forecasting. Revenues increased 15 percent in the prior fiscal year ending December 31, 20X3, and compound earnings growth exceeded 20 percent in each of the last three years. Universal's stock currently trades at a multiple of 35 times current earnings.

In early December 20X4, Universal acquired the net assets of Ozark Software for $120 million. Universal purchased Ozark for its technology and business applications products. In accordance with the purchase method of accounting, Universal allocated $64 million of the purchase price to the tangible assets acquired and $20 million to the liabilities assumed. Universal allocated the remainder, $76 million, to the identifiable intangible assets acquired, primarily purchased in-process research and development. The sum of the tangible and identifiable intangible assets acquired less liabilities assumed exceeded the purchase price, hence Universal did not record any goodwill.

The valuation of tangible and intangible assets was based on an independent appraisal by a nationally recognized firm. The purchased in-process research and development was appraised at $65 million through the application of a discounted income approach. Projected debt-free income, consisting of revenues less operating expenses, income taxes, and returns on assets, was discounted to a present value amount.

Universal is very concerned that with its stock trading at such a high multiple of earnings, any disappointment in future reported earnings could severely impact its stock price. Due to this concern, Universal concluded that it would certainly be better not to charge the $65 million of purchased in-process research and development against future earnings. Therefore, Universal decided to take a one-time fourth quarter 20X4 charge of $65 million for the write-off of the purchased in-process research and development.

Required
1. Discuss whether Universal's allocation of $65 million to purchased in-process research and development might be a way to avoid recording goodwill. Include in your discussion reasons why Universal might want to avoid recording goodwill.
2. Discuss whether it is appropriate for Universal to write off the entire amount allocated to the purchased in-process research and development in 20X4. Include in your discussion a recommendation as to how Universal should account for the purchased in-process research and development and the basis for your recommendation.

Ethics

C10–54	ARTISAN ENTERTAINMENT

Purchase versus Pooling Accounting: The Value of Eroding Intangibles

The entertainment industry has grown increasingly concentrated over the last 20 years. Driven primarily by technology, as well as a need for increasing economies of scale through size and integration, the pace of this consolidation has only accelerated over the last five years. Firms now fall into two broad categories: content originators—creators of the actual entertainment itself in the form of manuscripts, movies, editorial commentary, and so on, and distributors—the publishers, Internet entities, television/cable networks, and newspapers that deliver this content to the end consumer. Successful firms are vertically integrated, and have both. As the pace of consolidation quickens, firms are under increasing pressure to "get big, fast." Without time to grow these businesses from within, firms have instead purchased them by simply buying smaller competitors and acquiring their market share in the process. The industry has consolidated accordingly, and few independent assets remain available in the marketplace. The price to acquire reflects this scarcity, and firms now trade well in excess of book value.

One of the largest production studios in the world, Artisan Entertainment, has pursued this strategy aggressively, carefully building its franchise from within when prudent, and acquiring small but well-known brands that add value. A savvy player, Artisan has been careful to purchase only those firms it deems undervalued in transactions immediately accretive to earnings. Consequently, the firm has enjoyed steady earnings growth for years, and has therefore been rewarded by Wall Street with solid credit ratings and a premiere multiple. At this stage of the game, however, the pace of expansion has grown frantic, and the firm must rapidly broaden its distribution in a meaningful way. No longer able to build to scale or acquire cheaply, Artisan must now shift gears and acquire a large distributor able to match its scale and distribute its product. To do so, the firm will have to pay up and make an acquisition that many investors would deem unnecessarily expensive.

After scouring the market, Artisan moves to acquire Magnetic Celluloid, a large player in the videotape rental industry. Magnetic offers all that Artisan could hope for: not only does the firm own and operate an international chain of video rental stores, it also manufactures and distributes the tapes through wholesale distributors, direct marketing, and more recently the Internet. Immediately, the acquisition of Magnetic would allow Artisan to be fully integrated vertically and distribute its content throughout the world. Of grave concern to the CFO and CEO, however, is the impact the acquisition will have on Artisan's financial statements. Although a great fit strategically, Artisan would have to pay dearly for Magnetic. Because Magnetic's price-earnings ratio is greater than Artisan's, the firm would take a sharp hit to earnings should it proceed with the acquisition accounted for as a purchase. Furthermore, Artisan would pay a significant premium to book for Magnetic, creating a drag on earnings for years to come through goodwill amortization. Thus, Artisan proposes accounting for the acquisition under the pooling method. Accounting for the transaction by this method would solve all their problems, at least on paper. Aware of the forthcoming changes in accounting principals that would eliminate the pooling method, Artisan works diligently and ensures its ability to meet all relevant accounting criteria, should it proceed with the transaction in this manner. In doing so, the firm would avoid this prolonged reduction in earnings.

Although this looks much better from an earnings standpoint, several members of the audit committee voice their concern over the quality of the assets and the manner in which they are reported in the financial statements. Specifically, The Magnetic Celluloid franchise represents the best of the past and present, but not the future. Although the videocassette is ubiquitous today and fits perfectly within Artisan's strategy, technology will at some point move the industry toward a video-on-demand format, delivered through either cable, satellite, or the Internet. Someday the concept of walking into a video store to rent a movie in the form of a tape will seem arcane, as will the present state of Magnetic's business model. Today, however, Magnetic brings tremendous impact to Artisan's business, adding an entirely new distribution channel and a premier global name. Magnetic not only fits strategically, but also generates significant free cash flow. This situation puts management in an ethical quandary.

In light of this trend, how should those assets be valued today? Are historical figures based on the pooling method appropriate? Under pooling, Artisan would neither write down the hard assets of limited future value, nor would it amortize the significant premium to book in the form of goodwill. This would be both legal and beneficial to shareholders, at least in the short term; the company would avoid an immediate hit to earnings (and stock valuation). Prospective and long-term investors in the company, however, would bear the true cost of these decisions in the form of decelerating earnings, a reduced return on equity, and write-downs. These concerns may be misplaced, however, if the acquisition achieves management's strategic goals. Many analysts and investors view this as prudent financial management. What ethical issues do the CEO and the CFO face? What ethical dilemmas must be resolved before the firm can move forward with business? How would you address this situation in good conscience, knowing that you could account for (get away with) a transaction using pooling accounting? What management issues do you face if you take the unexpected hit to earnings?

Required
1. **Identify stakeholders**   List the parties involved. First list those parties directly affected by the various results of these accounting transactions and the way they are reported. List the size and scope of each party (e.g. an individual, a population). Then list those parties indirectly affected in the same manner. Next to that list, note the extent to which they stand to benefit or be harmed under the various transactions and their various interpretations.
2. **Identify ethical issues**   From an ethical context, what are the moral issues involved? Here, the student should take a step away from the accounting and focus on the argument from a greater perspective of right versus wrong. Although ideally each proposed solution could be classified as good or bad, rarely will this be the case; resolutions are usually characterized by various shades of gray. Some may have both a good and bad connotation depending upon the viewpoint of the treatment.
3. **Identify alternative solutions**   In a cost/benefit analysis, the materiality and the impact of the various treatments should be closely examined. Here, common sense and prudence should be your overriding thought process. In those seemingly all-too-frequent cases where the treatment could go either way and the impact be equal on both sides, clearly the accountant should choose the method that he or she feels will provide the clearest picture of a given transaction or organization.
4. **Make a decision: select a preferred solution**   The hardest part requires the least explanation. That's what you will be paid (and evaluated) for.

C10–55	MONOLITH FINANCIAL

Credit Analysis: The Pressure to Agree

As a traditionally trained accountant working in the risk management group for Monolith Financial, you have for years been performing credit analysis on behalf of the firm and its clients in the merchant banking and syndicated loan group. Recently promoted to a high profile senior risk management position, you now meet regularly with senior management and the new investment-banking group, conducting credit analysis on the firm's larger counterparts and clients, both old and new. In this role, you determine the creditworthiness of various firms applying for loans. If granted, these loans may either be held by the firm for its own account, be placed in trust accounts managed by Monolith Financial, sold to other banks, or securitized (packaged) and sold on the open market, usually at an attractive profit. As such, you serve as a fiduciary to clients and shareholders.

After doing extensive work on Mechanized Medical, a large client new to the firm, you have severe reservations about their financials and the quality of their balance sheet. Specifically, they compete in the highly competitive medical devices industry. Their products are extremely complex and difficult to perfect because of their interaction with the human body. In spite of tremendous regulatory scrutiny, they are continually subject to lawsuit due to flaws and imperfections, even though significant time and money is spent at the R & D stage. Furthermore, the technology in this arena is rapidly evolving and frequently renders marquee products obsolete. Although Mechanized currently enjoys a dominant position in this industry, it relies on older products for the majority of its revenues. These products have a large installed base, and therefore may be subject to liability claims. These material facts introduce volatility, and therefore risk, into the earnings stream. With the exception of two speculative technologies early in the development stage, Mechanized has few promising products in the pipeline, and therefore relies on its preexisting patents. For these reasons, you have concerns about the firm's potential to generate revenues and meet its debt service requirements. On the balance sheet side, the firm's assets consist primarily of intangible assets in the form of patents. As a credit analyst, you are concerned about the quality of those assets. As they are intangible, they tend to be illiquid. Their valuation is highly subjective and not guaranteed to generate revenues. Of greatest concern to you, however, are the technological threats to each patent: when a new and improved technology emerges with FDA approval, the market abandons older products in favor of the newer technology. This rapid erosion in earnings power can decimate the value of these assets, many of which may be backing outstanding loans. In light of these facts and concerns, you recommend in a research report that Monolith pass on Mechanized, and not extend credit to the firm.

Less than an hour after issuing the research report, the managing director storms into your new office (the one overlooking the ocean), demanding to know why you are "severing one of the firm's best (most lucrative) business relationships." Monolith, he explains, will not only be extending credit to Mechanized, but also advises the firm through the investment banking side, and plans to bring them public next spring. This one relationship will be worth tens of millions of dollars over the next year, and will continue to be lucrative thereafter. "How can we deny the firm's loan application, and then turn around and sell the firm to the public as an attractive investment opportunity?" he asks "With a smile." The investment banking side of the firm would also weigh in on your career prospects. The managing director asks you to take another look at the credit. The firm does enjoy a dominant position within the industry. With a growing installed base, doctors throughout the country are increasingly familiar with the product and are comfortable with its design and benefits to the patient. In this respect, he argues, Mechanized owns the industry standard. He cites their sharp growth in revenues and declining expenses. Furthermore, the risk to the firm will be minimal, as this loan can be placed in trust accounts, put out for the bid on Wall Street, or sold to one of the firm's mutual funds. He senses your unease, and presses you to go back to work and reconsider your stance.

As a newly promoted executive living in the real world, happy to be promoted to a senior position within the firm, you face a serious dilemma. Relying upon the education and credit analysis skills that have brought you so far, you have determined that this company presents far too great a risk of default and, therefore, have decided against lending to it. Despite the tremendous growth, its earnings are volatile and certainly not assured. Even more important to a creditor, the balance sheet offers little assurance; the assets are intangible and highly illiquid. Subject to intense competition and technologic innovation, their future value can never be certain. Your managing director, however, sees the credit differently. He sees the "bigger picture" and wants you to change your professional opinion. He cites strong revenue growth, a dominant position in a growing market, and experienced management. He also cites the other business units that are dependent on you. They want to extend the loan to Mechanized and secure more business in the process. These are coworkers and colleagues, most of whom have for years rated Mechanized very favorably in their credit work. Their business and their bonus will be affected by your work. The risk to the firm may be minimal due to the potential resale of the loans to other clients and mutual funds. In this respect, you may be able to extend credit and not leave the firm exposed. In a highly visible position, you are the only one leaning against the wind. What do you do, and how do you resolve these issues?

Required
1. **Identify stakeholders**   List the parties involved. First list those parties directly affected by the various results of these accounting transactions and the way they are reported. List the size and scope of each party (e.g., an individual, a population). Then list those parties indirectly affected in the same manner. Next to that list, note the extent to which they stand to benefit or be harmed under the various transactions and their various interpretations.
2. **Identify ethical issues**   From an ethical context, what are the moral issues involved? Here, the student should take a step away from the accounting and focus on the argument from a greater perspective of right versus wrong. Although ideally each proposed solution could be classified as good or bad, rarely will this be the case; resolutions are usually characterized by various shades of gray. Some may have both a good and bad connotation depending on the viewpoint of the treatment.
3. **Identify alternative solutions**   In a cost/benefit analysis, the materiality and the impact of the various treatments should be closely examined. Here, common sense and prudence should be your overriding thought process. In those seemingly all-too-frequent cases where the treatment could go either way and the impact equal on both sides, clearly the accountant should choose the method that he or she feels will provide the clearest picture of a given transaction or organization.
4. **Make a decision: select a preferred solution**   The hardest part requires the least explanation. That's what you will be paid (and evaluated) for.

INDEX

Black, Fischer, 109n
Black-Scholes option pricing model,
    109–110
Bleaker Fruit Company, case, 241–242
Bloom, B. S., 193n
Bloomberg.com, 78
Bloomberg reports, 80
Bloom's taxonomy of thinking skills,
    193–194
Board of directors
    control environment, 213–214
    enforcement of business ethics, 217
Bounded rationality, 152
Break-even analysis equation, 39
Bredemeier, B. J. L., 224n
Brown, L. D., 18n
Brown, P., 110n
Brunswik, E., 158n
Brunswik Lens model, 158–161
Burke, James, 210
Business combinations, cases, 285–292
Business ethics, 207, 210–218
    accountants' role in, 216–218
    cases, 292–295
    components
        board of directors, 213–214
        codes of ethics, 214
        control environment, 213
        enforcement, 215
        ethical culture, 212–213
        federal/state laws, 214
        management, 214
        ombudsmen, 215
        whistle-blowing, 215
    corporate strategies, 211
    definition, 211
Business Roundtable, 17

C

Cable modem, 74–75
Calico Fashions, Inc., case, 268–269
Caltron Computers, Inc., case, 242–243
Campbell, D., 81n, 87
Campbell, D. J., 164n
Campbell, M., 81n, 87
CAP; *see* Committee on Accounting
    Procedures
Capital asset pricing model, 105
Capital lease, 126
Capital markets research models, 98–112
    accounting history, 111–112
    dividend policy decision models, 99–100

mix and cost of capital models, 103–108
option-pricing models, 108–110
positive accounting, 111
valuation models, 100–103
Carly Mack Corporation, case, 272–273
Carnegie Mellon University, 152
Cartwright, D., 9n
CASB; *see* Cost Accounting Standards
    Board
Case, Stephen, 75n
Case analysis
    complex cases, 56–61
    models of, 50–61
    and reporting method, 56
    simple cases, 51–56
Case development research, 45–46, 46,
    47–48
Case method, 118, 122
    case development research, 46, 47–48
    compared to exercise/problem approach,
        48–50
    definition, 46–47
    for ethical training, 226–232
    nature of case studies, 46–47
    use of, 45–46
Case protocol, 47
Certified public accountants, ethical
    conduct, 205–210
Chaffee, J., 181n, 182n, 194n, 195n, 199n
Chandler Stores, Inc., case, 269
Chaney, G. A., 131
Cheatham, Carole, 141n, 146
Cheatham, Leo R., 141n, 146
*Checklist for Defined Benefit Pension Plans and
    Illustrative Financial Statements*, 65
*Checklists and Illustrative Financial Statements
    for Banks*, 65
*Checklist Supplement and Illustrative Financial
    Statements for Construction
    Contractors*, 65
Child development model, 221
Chrysler Corporation, 99n
Clarity, 129–130
Classification, 189, 191
Cleartronics,Inc., case, 269–270
Client data files, 47
Coates, J. Dennis, 141n, 147
Code of Professional Conduct; *see*
    American Institute of Certified
    Public Accountants
Coercive power, 10–11
Cognition, 193
Cognitive abilities, 166
Coherence, 129–130